ROMEACCESS®

S0-AGK-323

via della Conciliazione

(Rome's most vilified street) leads directly to **St. Peter's Basilica**. Its construction (1936-1950) demolished medieval dwellings as well as one of the greatest manmade surprises in the world: the impact of suddenly coming upon **Bernini**'s colonnaded **St. Peter's Square** after wandering through one of the 2 dark, narrow streets that led from **Castel Sant'Angelo** to St. Peter's. The modern street is not in perfect line, even though some of the Renaissance buildings that were sliced back had their old facades replaced. The fascist-era architects **Marcello Piacentini** and **Attilio Spaccarelli** (whose name translates as Attila, the Little Chopper) sought to rectify that by planting 2 rows of nontraditional street lights set on modern obelisks, which the Romans quickly dubbed white suppositories. If it were not for the whale-size tourist buses and the cars that fill this street by day, the destruction of **Borgo Vecchio** and **Borgo Nuovo**, the 2 old, narrow lanes, could be given faint praise for allowing one a better view of the remaining buildings of note. As it is, these must be viewed through the preposterous stone lampposts.

Getting Here If time is short, take a taxi to the **Vatican Museum** entrance (*ingresso dei Musei Vaticani*) and return to St. Peter's afterward, on foot, following the Vatican walls to your right as you leave the museums, or take the Vatican's bus service between the 2 points; buses depart every half-hour. The fastest approach to the Vatican area from the Stazione, Piazza Barberini, or Piazza di Spagna is by the **subway** (Metro). The actual ride to the Vatican stop, **Ottaviano**, also the end of the line, takes no more than 5 minutes. There is then a 10-minute walk down Via Ottaviano or Via Silla to **Piazza Risorgimento**, a square

with trees and skirted on one side by Vatican walls. Other than hoofing it, the most economical way is to take the **bus**—Nos. 62 and 64 are your best choices. If you take the 62, get off after it crosses the Tiber. If you take the 64, stay on until the end of the line. Make certain that the 62 and 64 are going to the Vatican, and not returning from there, as the bus-stop signs are misleading.

There are good, reasonably priced clothing stores on Via Ottaviano. **Via Cola di Rienzo,** running off Piazza Risorgimento, is an even better shopping street for almost everything. **Castroni** (Via Cola de Rienzo 196) is not only an excellent coffee, croissant, and sandwich bar, it caters to the foreign community by selling foreign food specialties (marshmallows, chutney, American packaged coffee, couscous, etc).

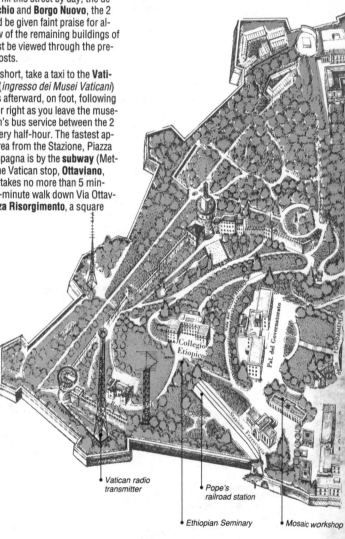

Collegio Etiopico

Pal. del Governatorato

Stazione Ferroviaria

Vatican radio transmitter

Pope's railroad station

Ethiopian Seminary

Mosaic workshop

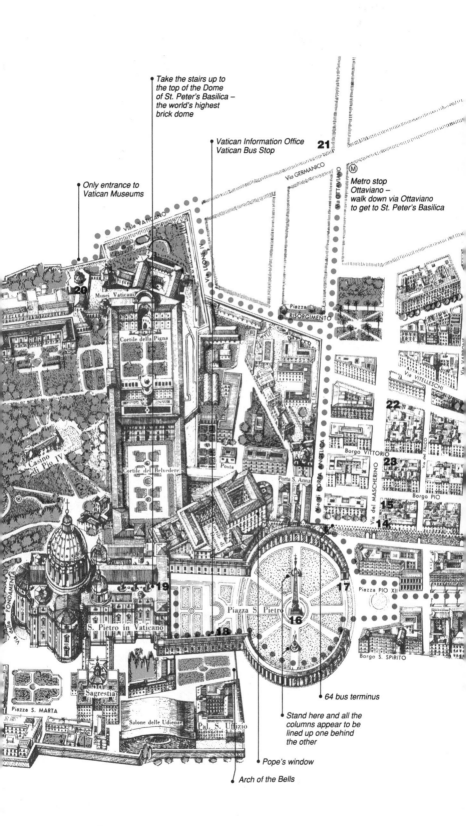

Take the stairs up to the top of the Dome of St. Peter's Basilica – the world's highest brick dome

Vatican Information Office
Vatican Bus Stop

21

Only entrance to Vatican Museums

Via GERMANICO

Metro stop Ottaviano – walk down via Ottaviano to get to St. Peter's Basilica

Viale VATICANO

20

Musei Vaticani

Cortile della Pigna

Piazza RISORGIMENTO

Via VITELLESCHI

Via delle FONDAMENTA

Casino di Pio IV

Cortile del Belvedere

Posta

Porta S. Anna

Borgo VITTORIO

22

Via del FALCO

23

Borgo PIO

15

Via del MASCHERINO

14

6

19

Cortile di

17

Piazza PIO XII

16

Piazza S. Pietro

S. Pietro in Vaticano

18

Sagrestia

Piazza S. MARTA

Salone delle Udienze

Pal. S. Uffizio

Borgo S. SPIRITO

64 bus terminus

Stand here and all the columns appear to be lined up one behind the other

Pope's window

Arch of the Bells

1 The USO Club Caters, like every place on the street, to Roman Catholic visitors (but religious affiliations are not asked, of course), and this may be the only World War II USO Club still in business. It has a friendly, mostly Italian staff ready to answer questions. One can sit down and rest, or use the Coke machine. If there is a babysitter on duty, the tots can be parked here and spared the very long

Via Della Conciliazione

walk ahead. During the Ecumenical Council (1963-1965), the American bishops used the USO's basement for what were then almost clandestine press briefings. The whole block dates from 1940. ♦ Via della Conciliazione 2. 6864272

2 Pius XII Auditorium Vatican property that has been leased to Rome's symphony orchestra, called **Santa Cecilia**, as Rome has had no proper concert hall since the 1930s, when the auditorium in Augustus' Mausoleum was dismantled (see page 107). Concerts are usually at 5 and 9PM, and when the conductor is someone of **Leonard Bernstein**'s caliber, they are sold-out. Even so, by arriving 30 minutes early, the odd ticket often can be obtained. An earnest and anxious look will help there. ♦ Seats 2000. Via della Conciliazione 4. Box office 6541044

3 Santa Maria in Traspontina (1637) The only church along the street that, until 1985, also ran the only movie theater on the street— in the church's refectory on the right. Construction began in 1566. ♦ Via della Conciliazione 14

4 Paoline Book Store A wide selection of religious and art books and maps in English. Another good bookstore—which sells the Vatican's own video cassettes as well—is the **Ancora**; it is in the last, arcaded building on the left at the end of the street. The newsstand near the Ancora (in the square) has many newspapers available in English, including the English weekly digest of *L'Osservatore Romano*, the Vatican newspaper. ♦ Libreria Paoline, Via della Conciliazione 18. 6864872, 6865021

5 Palazzo Torlonia (1504, **Andrea Bregno**)
The handsomest edifice on the street. It ought to be, because it is almost a replica of the **Cancelleria Palace**, a great Renaissance building between Piazza Navona and Campo dei Fiori (see page 112). Both are by the same architect. Its first owner was an Italian cardinal. The next was the British monarchy, whose ambassador was quartered here until **King Henry VIII** broke with Rome and set up his own Anglican Church. A banking family that made its fortune during Napoleon's occupation of Rome now owns the building, and the current **Prince Torlonia**, said to be the richest man in Rome, is one of the high-ranking laymen in the Vatican as well (see the other Palazzo Torlonia in the Trastevere walk).
♦ Via della Conciliazione 30. 6861044

6 Albergo Alicorni (Hotel Unicorn) $$
(16th century) Formerly belonging to the Dominican Order, since 1985 it has been under the management of **Patrizia Diletti**—the Diletti family has run the hotel for years. Décor of comfortable antiques and Baroque bar. 45 rooms. ♦ Via Scossacavalli 11. 6541394, 6865786; fax 6865078

• *Castel St. Angelo*
(see Tiber Walk, page 120)

Piazza ADRIANA

Castel S. Angelo

Lungotevere CASTELLO

Mausoleo di Adriano

Ponte S. Angelo

Ponte Umberto I

7 Palazzo dei Penitenzieri (1450-1492, **Baccio Pontelli**) Built as an Italian cardinal's private residence by the Florentine architect. Facade similar in style to the Palazzo Venezia.
♦ Via della Conciliazione 33

Within the Palazzo dei Penitenzieri:

Hotel Columbus $$ Occupying most of the Penitenzieri palace today. Its lobby and frescoed public rooms on the floor above, and the courtyard with a well, retain a certain cardinalate air. Today, many foreign cardinals prefer staying here rather than in their religious institutes, which are gratis. Some rooms are a bit spartan and the prices likewise. Incoming/outgoing telephone calls are a nightmare, but the staff is pleasant. ♦ 6865245, 6865435; fax 6865245

Within the Hotel Columbus:

Pierdonati Restaurant $$ Within the hotel, but it has a separate entrance. The fare is not worthy of a Renaissance cardinal; however the pseudoantique ambiance is pleasing.
♦ Closed Thursday. Via della Conciliazione 39. 6543557

8 Palazzo dei Convertendi (c.1510, **Bramante**) Formerly at the end of Via Scossacavalli, dismantled in the late 1930s and reassembled here. This is also the building where **Raphael** died, having been forcibly separated from his lady love, **La Fornarina** (see **Romolo Restaurant** on page 90). ♦ Via della Conciliazione 34

9 Caffè San Pietro $ An espresso bar that has been expanded into a luncheon cafeteria. **Ali Agca** had a last cup of coffee here before entering St. Peter's Square the day he tried to kill **Pope John Paul II**. ♦ Closed Friday. Via della Conciliazione 40. 6864927

10 Alfredo a San Pietro ★★$$ Fettucine *rosa*, scaloppine *alla crema*. Proprietor is addressed as *contessa* (countess). ♦ Closed Friday. Via dei Corridori 60. 6869554

Restaurants/Clubs: Red	Hotels: Blue
Shops/Parks: Green	**Sights/Culture: Black**

5

11 Leonine Wall (c. 850) After the Saracen raid on the Vatican treasury in 849, **Pope Leo IV** built a defensive wall from Castel Sant'Angelo to encircle the hill behind St. Peter's and out to the Tiber. An enclosed passage along the top of wall is also an escape route for popes needing the security of Castel Sant'Angelo. In 1527 **Pope Clement VII** picked up his skirts and dashed from his Vatican Palace to the castle (see the **Sacks of Rome** on page 57).

12 Hostaria Orfeo da Cesaretto ★★$$ This pink-tableclothed eatery is not for the mass market. First-pressing olive oil, crunchy fresh bread, fresh fish cooked as you wish. Spaghetti *tartufo di mare* (type of large clam), risotto *verde*, and *tagliolini tonno afumicato* (smoked tuna) are good starters. Traditional *piccate al limone* or *filetto al barolo* (steak in red-wine sauce). Only at night—pizza, as well as crème brûlée for dessert. ♦ Closed Monday. Vicolo d'Orfeo 20. 6879269

13 Hostaria Roberto ★★$$ Fairly diversified menu: rigatoni *alla Norcina*, cannelloni, polenta *Abruzzese*, saltimbocca *alla Romana*, omelete. Our favorite for Christmas Eve dinner before going into St. Peter's for the pope's great moment. ♦ Closed Tuesday. Borgo Pio 60 (Vicolo delle Palline) 6543957

14 LMP Ostentatious jewels to embellish the rites of your parish church. Sometimes beautiful, mostly modern and spikey. Chalices, reliquaries, priests' gear, but also lay gifts in silver and glass. ♦ Via del Mascherino 8. 6864316

15 CocaColor Photo Augusto does fast printing of your vacation snaps, with a smile, in as little as one hour. ♦ Via del Mascherino 16. 6879498

Vatican City

The youngest European state and the smallest, covering only 107.8 acres, or about the size of an average golf course. It was created on 11 February 1929 by the strokes of 2 pens, one held by the pope's secretary of state, the other by the Italian dictator, **Benito Mussolini**. It is one of the 2 sovereign states existing as enclaves on the Italian peninsula, the other being the world's oldest republic, San Marino. Vatican City is not a republic. It is ruled by one man, the **Bishop of Rome**, the rank that also gives him the title of pope. He is Europe's only absolute sovereign ruler.

You enter Vatican City when you cross the line of white travertine stones that runs across St. Peter's Square between the open extremes of **Bernini's** colonnade. **Arco delle Campane** (Arch of the Bells), to the left of **St. Peter's**, is a second visible entrance to the Papal State. If you walk from the square around the right-hand perimeter to the Vatican museums, you will pass a third entrance (with a traffic light) called the **Porta Sant'Anna**, the gate leading to the Vatican City drugstore, supermarket, bank, main post office, etc. (See entry no. **17** for the branch post office open to everyone.) St. Peter's church and the Vatican museums are the 2 places inside Vatican City open to the general public; otherwise entrance is by permission, only.

Neither St. Peter's nor St. Paul's were included within the 3rd-century Aurelian walls and thus were repeatedly sacked by invaders. In 850 **Pope Leo IV** put up his own defensive Vatican walls, called the *Leonine*, with 46 fortified turrets. The pope ruled Rome and most of central Italy until the 19th century. Papal Rome fell in 1870 to Italian troops, who were heartily welcomed by the Romans—who thought they were being over-taxed by the pope—thus consolidating Italy as one country for the first time since the Caesars. At the time, the pope left his summer residence in the **Quirinale Palace** in something more than a huff and declared himself a prisoner in Vatican City. His successors carried on his feud with the Italian usurpers until Mussolini drew up a pact that gave back to the pope some of the palaces that had been seized in 1870, provided some cash for what the Italian king had retained, and created Vatican City as the papal domain.

There are about 1000 men, women, and children living in Vatican City as citizens or staff. Most of the Rome-based cardinals and bishops do not live here but are entitled to Vatican passports, and about half of the lay employees live elsewhere but retain their original nationalities. The Vatican City income is generated mostly from postage stamp, museum ticket, postcard, and religious object sales as well as through profits from the drugstore and supermarket. The Vatican publishes its own daily newspaper, *L'Osservatore Romano* (written mostly in Italian—but there are weekly digests in various languages, including Polish and English), and has its own radio station broadcasting in 26 languages around the world. The Italian government mints the Vatican coins and makes the **SCV** (Stato Citta Vaticano) license plates for its cars. Even though the speed limit is 20 miles per hour, there are many crushed fenders because of the narrow roads inside the walls.

The beautiful **Vatican gardens** may be visited by bus tour or on foot (inquiries at the Information Office in the square), but remember that a classic Italian formal garden is short on flowers and long on architectural landscaping. The **Swiss Guards** come from that country's Catholic cantons, and their main job is sentry duty. Their bright-colored uniforms, designed by **Michelangelo**, bloom perennially at the **Arch of the Bells** and the **Porta Sant'Anna**. There is a Vatican prison, but by agreement anyone meriting imprisonment is turned over to the Italian police. There is also a small railway station, used exclusively to bring duty-free goods in from Italy on its 160 yards of track. **Pope John XXIII** (1957-1963) was the first and probably the last passenger to use the pink, yellow, and green marble station, when he left Rome for a visit to the shrines of Loreto and Assisi.

16 Piazza San Pietro (Saint Peter's Square) (1656-1667) Designed and built by **Bernini** 100 years after construction of St. Peter's Basilica had begun. The square is actually an ellipsis, 262 yards wide. Bernini's greatest colonnade, like 2 arms embracing the visitor (or 2 hands facing each other in prayer), is made up of 284 doric columns, 64 feet high in 4 rows. It is topped with 140 statues of saints. The name of the pope who commissioned Bernini, **Alexander VII** (of the **Chigi** banking family from Siena), is inscribed along the colonnade, but is virtually invisible from the street level. Children of all ages delight in finding the stone markers between the fountains and the colonnade from where all the columns on that side of the square appear to line up, one behind the other, in groups of 4.

The 135-foot-high obelisk in the square's center was brought to Rome from Heliopolis, Egypt, in AD 37 by the **Emperor Caligula** to decorate a chariot racing circus he was building.

This racetrack was completed by **Nero**, who named it for himself and used it for orgies as well as sports. There are no visible remains of the **Circus Neronis**, which resembled the **Circus Maximus** (see page 137); about the length of 2 football fields, it encompassed all of the left half of Bernini's square and ran due west almost to the present railway station behind St. Peter's. The hieroglyph-less obelisk was made by the Egyptians to Roman specifications. It stood where Caligula placed it, just inside the present Arch of the Bells to the left

Via Della Conciliazione

of St. Peter's, until 1586, when **Pope Sixtus V** ordered it moved to its current location. Because the obelisk weighed 312 tons and was all in one piece, it had to be lowered to the ground by winches and rolled into the square on logs. Mounting it on its new pedestal was not easy, and required 44 winches, 900 men, and 140 horses. The Pope decreed that anyone present who spoke, and thus perhaps distracted the workers, would be punished by death. As the men and horses were tugging away, a sailor from San Remo passed by. His nautically trained eye saw that the ropes were so taut they were in danger of snapping. *Put some water on the ropes*, he shouted in his Genovese dialect. His wisdom was taken; he saved the day and probably the obelisk as well—and was not punished. The Pope ordered a golden ball that adorned the obelisk's point to be removed. The ancients, who invented legends as easily as we invent new pop groups, had claimed that the ball contained **Julius Caesar**'s ashes, but it turned out to be empty. It was replaced with the present iron cross. The Church, not to be outdone by the ancients, claimed that the piece of wood placed inside this iron cross, was a splinter of the **True Cross** (the one on which **Jesus** was crucified). One of the Latin inscriptions around the pedestal reads: *Behold the Cross of the Lord; fly ye enemies; the Lion of Judah has conquered.*

The 46-foot-high twin granite fountains were erected about 50 years apart by different architects; the one on the right is older (1613). Above the right colonnade the tallest and broadest building is the **Apostolic Palace**, where the pope lives and works with his closest aides. At noon on Sunday the pope—if he happens to be in Rome between foreign visits—appears at his library window to give a homily and his blessing to the crowds in the square. The ceremonial entrance to his palace is at the end of the right colonnade, called the **Great Bronze Door**, guarded by Swiss Guards in their finery and plainclothesmen in mufti.

17 Vatican Post Office Reputed to be faster than the Italian mails—but that's not saying much. Prominently located at the far right of the square, next to **Bernini**'s colonnade, is a permanently parked blue trailer (next to a first-aid trailer), where you can buy distinctive Vatican stamps, some of them philatelic, and mail your love letters and postcards. (Don't get this trailer confused with the Italian Post Office trailer outside the colonnade at the other end of the square.) Vatican City post-marks can be had if you drop mail in the blue mailboxes, provided they bear Vatican stamps. Italian mailboxes are red. (The Italian competition has the advantage of being open on Sunday, but their stamps, though marginally less expensive, are unholy.) ♦ M-F 8:30AM-7PM; Sa 8:30AM-6PM. Piazza San Pietro. 6982

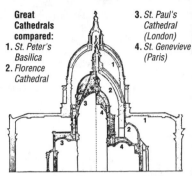

Great Cathedrals compared:
1. St. Peter's Basilica
2. Florence Cathedral
3. St. Paul's Cathedral (London)
4. St. Genevieve (Paris)

Via Della Conciliazione

18 Vatican Information Office To the left of the basilica's steps are orange signs indicating useful services: an information center and souvenir shop, a first-aid station, a bookstore, and a place selling special Vatican stamps for collectors. One orange sign indicates where the special bus departs (every half-hour 9AM-12:30PM) for the Vatican museums, if you do not want to walk. There is also a restroom; there is another on the other side of the square, through the colonnade near the Vatican post office. The old canard that VAT 69 whiskey was named after the Vatican phone number is not far off: the Vatican switchboard number is 6982.

19 St. Peter's Basilica Construction on the first St. Peter's church began in 315 on orders from **Constantine**, the first emperor who con-

verted to Christianity—at the end of his life, they say. It was to be built over the spot where **Peter the Fisherman** was believed to have been buried in the year 64, after his execution in the nearby **Circus of Nero**. The first church was completed in 349 and was almost as large as today's building. It was **Pope Julius II** who wanted a more appropriate and up-to-date setting for the tomb Michelangelo was then making for him. (See the *Moses* in San Pietro in Vincoli on page 41.) **Bramante** was given the job of slowly demolishing the older church (services were to continue throughout), earning the architect the nickname of *Mr. Destroyer*. Building on the new church began in 1506. It was to be in the form of the Greek cross but the Pope and Bramante died before 10 years had passed. Over the next 30 years, 6 other artists were brought in, including first **Raphael** and then Michelangelo, each one changing the design. After Michelangelo's death (1564), 4 more tried their hands during different periods. The facade by **Carlo Maderno** was finished in 1614. The clocks were added by **Giuseppe Valadier** in 1822. It is from the church's central balcony that the pope gives his Christmas and Easter blessings to the city and the world, and where the name of a new pope is announced.

The interior, not counting the 26-foot-thick walls, is 610 feet in length, or about 2 yards longer than London's St. Paul's. The diameter of Michelangelo's dome (cupola) is nearly 2 yards less than the Pantheon's dome. However, St. Peter's dome is many times taller, rising to a height of 448 feet (counting the cross on top). Before his death in 1564, Michelangelo saw the dome rise as far as the top of the *drum* (230 feet).

Once inside St. Peter's 5-gated porch (portico), note the last door on the right is open only on Holy Years (usually every 25 years). Most of the other doors are ancient, but one bronze door (first on left), dating from 1963, is the work of **Giacomo Manzu**; the inside panel features a portrait of **Pope John XXIII** welcoming some of the bishops to the Ecumenical Council in 1962, including the church's first black African cardinal.

Inside the church, many react with *it doesn't look all that big*, because the scale is so large and so uniform. Note that the visual line is broken by pillars almost the size of houses. It

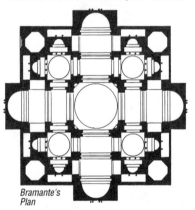

Bramante's Plan

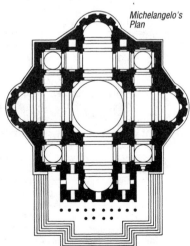

Michelangelo's Plan

also does not seem to some people to be a place for meditation.

The markers in the central aisle measuring the length of other famous great churches can be considered a bit of blarney since they are not all accurate. The Milanese, for example, see it as yet more proof of Rome's envy of Italy's most important city. Milan's great Gothic cathedral is inscribed here as being 134.94 meters (443 feet) long, whereas it is actually 154 meters (slightly more than 505 feet).

The gilded, glittering bronze roof tiles from the ancient Roman Temple of Venus and Rome were dismantled by **Pope Honorius** in AD 400 and put on the roof of St. Peter's. In AD 846 the Saracens stole them, and nobody ever found out where they were taken, or which mosque they eventually adorned.

Ralph Waldo Emerson called St. Peter's *an ornament of the earth...the sublime of the beautiful,* and asked *have the men of America never entered these European churches that they build such mean edifices at home?*

A Red porphyry disk Set in the pavement near St. Peter's central door, at the beginning of the middle nave, this was taken from a pagan basilica. It marks the spot where more than 20 emperors, from **Charlemagne** to **Frederick II**, knelt to be crowned by the pope.

B Pietà (1500) The marble statue of the Virgin holding the dead body of Jesus in her lap was done by Michelangelo when he was 25 years old and is the only piece he signed—his name is carved in the hem of the cloth that crosses the Virgin's breast. Until 1972, this work was visible from a distance of a few feet, protected only by the chapel's altar rail. That year a mad Hungarian (subsequently naturalized as an Australian) climbed the rail and gave the marble several hammer blows before someone stopped him. (The tip of the Virgin's nose was knocked off, for example.) The pieces were collected where possible and the restoration is perfect, but the visibility—due to the distance and the bullet-proof glass encasement—is severely reduced.

C Monument to Sweden's Queen Christina Queen Christina abdicated her throne upon becoming a Roman Catholic and was eventually invited to liven up Rome's papal court. She died in Rome in 1689. (See Palazzo Corsini on page 89.) The scene of her second baptism in Innsbruck is depicted in the bas-relief. Above is a profile of her, said to be flattering compared to a contemporary report that described her as being dumpy and moustached. In the next chapel are monuments to **Pius XI** (1922-1932) and **Pius XII** (1939-1958). The latter statue is by **Francesco Messina** and shows the World War II pope with incredible spidery hands.

D Bronze statue of a seated St. Peter Millions of kisses have been wearing away the right foot since 1857, when **Pope Pius IX** granted an indulgence of 50 days to anyone who kissed it after going to confession. The bronze is thought to be a 13th-century Florentine work. Every year on 29 June, the feast day of St. Peter and St. Paul, it is dressed in royal robes.

E Bernini's Baldacchino (1633, canopy) Located over the high altar, built more or less over the **Tomb of the Fisherman**. The altar is reserved for the pope to celebrate Mass on special occasions. The canopy was commissioned by **Pope Urban VIII**. The bees that are found in Urban's (Barberini was his family name) coat of arms are seen everywhere, even hiding among the bay leaves of the swirling 95-foot-tall bronze columns. The bronze came from the crossbeams of the Pantheon's portico, which the Pope did not hesitate to melt down for his own use. This led to one of the most famous of Rome's many antipapal pasquinades—*quod non fecerunt barbari, fecerunt Barberini* (what the barbarians didn't do, the Barberini did).

F St. Peter's Throne (1665) Bernini's magnificent bronze altar, topped off with scores of putti frolicking in a sunburst, encases an ancient wooden chair that legend said St. Peter had sat in while delivering his first sermons to the Romans. When removed in the 1970s, the wooden chair was found to be made from parts of 2 chairs—one from the end of the 3rd century, the other from the 9th—cobbled together. The older section is decorated with carved ivory panels depicting the 12 labors of **Hercules**. A replica is on view in the Treasury.

Though there are dozens of eating places in the Vatican area, in general both price and quality are modest. **Borgo Pio** is the street with the greatest cluster of restaurants.

G Tomb of Urban VIII (1647) Though he did not die until 1644, this pope took no chances and ordered Bernini to design this tomb in 1628. When unveiled, its fame soon spread across Europe and it became the inspiration for all Baroque tombs or funeral monuments, not all of them as outstanding as this.

H St. Peter's Treasury The Treasury is reached by the corridor built in the 18th century to connect the new Sacristy with the church itself. The Treasury contains gifts given to St. Peter's by popes, emperors, and kings. They are mostly religious objects in silver or gold, beautifully worked and encrusted with jewels. Worth the small admission fee alone is the *Tomb of Pope Sixtus IV* (1493), a gigantic bronze work of the early Renaissance by **Antonio del Pollaiuolo**, to be viewed from an elevated platform. It was made for the first St. Peter's—the Treasury museum has some interesting drawings of the earlier church also on view. The creation of this Treasury may not have been such a good idea as it was on every invading army's hit list and was systematically raided by the Vandals in 455, the Saracens in 846, the Normans in 1084, the Spanish in 1527, and finally by Napoleon's looting troops. There are still some dazzling items in its 9 small rooms. The more recent additions to the Treasury include gifts made to popes by visiting heads of state. However, **Lyndon B. Johnson**'s bust of himself, presented to a somewhat surprised **Pope Paul VI**, has somehow not yet found its niche in the Treasury.

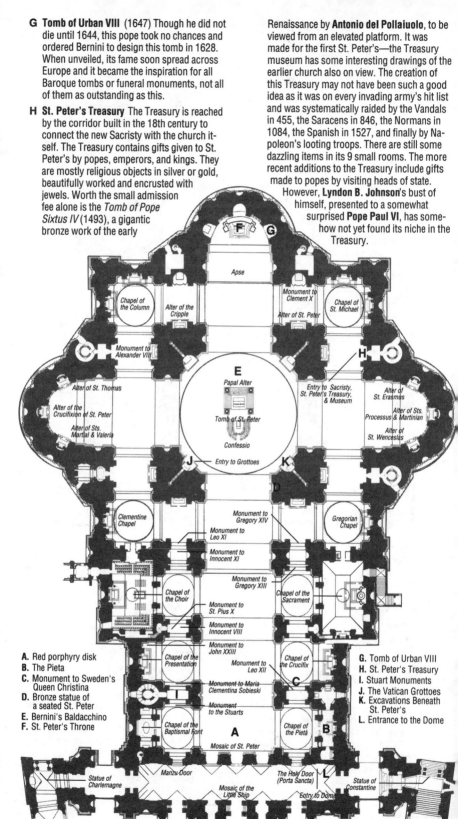

A. Red porphyry disk
B. The Pieta
C. Monument to Sweden's Queen Christina
D. Bronze statue of a seated St. Peter
E. Bernini's Baldacchino
F. St. Peter's Throne

G. Tomb of Urban VIII
H. St. Peter's Treasury
I. Stuart Monuments
J. The Vatican Grottoes
K. Excavations Beneath St. Peter's
L. Entrance to the Dome

I Stuart Monuments In 1820 **Antonio Canova**, one-time honorary president of Philadelphia's Academy of Fine Arts, designed this highly original monument to the last of the Stuarts: **James III** (who died in 1766) and his sons, **Bonnie Prince Charlie** and **Cardinal Henry Stuart**, the Duke of York. The Stuarts settled in Rome after fleeing England with the English Royal Seal. When Cardinal Henry Stuart returned it to **King George IV** in the 1820s, the British monarch graciously paid for the actual Stuart tomb, in the Vatican grottoes. Facing it is the monument to James' wife, **Mary Clementine Sobieski**, where the inscription is written—and history rewritten—*Queen of England, France and Ireland* (obvious confusion with her predecessor Mary Queen of Scots).

J The Vatican Grottoes This crypt lies between St. Peter's present floor and the mostly demolished ruins of the first church built by **Constantine**. Some pillars of the older church are visible in the grottoes, which contain the tombs of many popes, including the only English pope, **Nicholas Breakspear**, who in 1154 took the name of **Hadrian IV**. **Popes Pius II, Pius XII, John XXIII, Paul VI** and **John Paul I** have their tombs here as well. The entry to the grottoes is reached by a narrow staircase behind either the giant statues by Bernini of **St. Andrew** or that opposite of **St. Longinus**, the latter being a Roman centurion who pierced Christ's side with his lance and who was later converted. The obligatory exit is near the **Holy Year Door** in the church's portico.

K Excavations Beneath St. Peter's (gli Scavi) In 1939, when workers were preparing a tomb for **Pius XI** in the grottoes, they accidently came upon parts of the first St. Peter's church and beneath that a pagan and a Christian graveyard. The pagan tombs date from the 2nd and 3rd centuries AD and are more numerous and brightly decorated. It is a miniature necropolis. The Christian tombs are more impoverished and date from the 2nd century. One niche, containing human and animal bones, has scratched on it a grafitto that has convinced one Vatican cryptographer that it says *Peter is here*. One problem is that St. Peter's skull has been venerated for at least 1000 years in Rome's cathedral of St. John Lateran and this niche contained most of a human cranium.

The legend that Peter was crucified and quickly buried by his followers just outside the walls of Nero's Circus is, however, very strong. The excavations are not open to the general public, but anyone with some qualifications can write well in advance for permission to go on one of the small, infrequent guided tours. The expert serving as guide may not always speak English. The visit takes about one hour.

To join a tour of these ruins, write ahead to the Office of Excavations, Vatican City, giving several possible dates. No children under 14 admitted. If it is low season, a telephone call

(6985314) might produce the good news that one of the tours has an opening the next day.

L Entrance to the Dome Take the elevator or stairs to the inside of the dome, where your first thrill may be looking down on the people 160 feet below, encircling the papal altar and looking smaller than the Barberini bees had just looked. From there, another staircase goes up to a gallery 238 feet above the

Via Della Conciliazione

church's floor. If this is not enough, there are more stairs, still within the shell of the dome, taking you 322 feet above ground level. The intrepid climber can then take a narrow spiral staircase to the exterior gallery (where you'll be 352 feet above the altar that runs around the lantern of the world's highest brick dome). If you do not make the entire climb, you can wait for your companions on the wind-swept rooftop, where there is a coffee bar and a miniature Vatican post office.

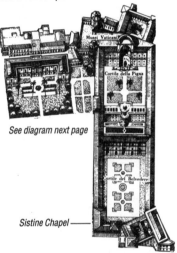

See diagram next page

Sistine Chapel

20 Vatican Museums (Musei Vaticani) The single entrance for all the museums is on Viale del Vaticano, a brisk 15-minute walk from St. Peter's Square down the Via di Porta Angelica (also the terminus of the 64 bus line). Though there is no risk of losing one's way since you just follow the walls, it can become unpleasant if you collide with groups of tourists going the other way on the narrow stretch of the sidewalk. A bus that departs from (and returns to) a spot near the orange sign in St. Peter's Square, and also takes you across the Vatican gardens en route, may be a better bet if there are not too many people waiting for it. Do visit the museums in the early hours because they are far less crowded, and the ticket window shuts at 1PM in winter and 4PM during the peak tourist season. St. Peter's is one of the few churches in Rome that does not shut at noon for the lunch break and is open until 6PM in winter and 7PM in summer, so it makes sense to go there after you have seen the museums. As soon as you find the museums' entrance, and get inside, take the elevator up. (At the end of your visit you can descend to the exit down the grand helicoidal staircase with its twin circular ramps that permit 2 streams of visitors to move simultaneously up and down without passing each other.) Allow at least 2 hours for the museums, but they are worth a long morning of your time. For those who want to walk all

Via Della Conciliazione

4-1/2 miles of galleries, leave 2 good days! The short trip suggested below permits you to see the most famous masterpieces without becoming totally exhausted. Come by subway; the museums' entrance is not far from the Ottaviano stop.

Cassette guides can be rented in English, French, German, Spanish, Japanese, and Italian. The museums' hours are complicated and change from year to year in accordance with the Church calendar, so check with your concierge. The schedule is arranged so that the museums are never closed more than 2 days in a row; even if you are in Rome for as little as 3 days, you can still see the museums' masterpieces. Though the ticket windows close an hour earlier, the museums are open

until 2PM most of the year. There is a special itinerary for disabled visitors. Nourishment can be found in the snack bar. ♦ Admission; reductions for those under 27 with student cards. M-Sa 8:45AM-4PM, the week before and the week after Easter, July, Aug, Sep; M-Sa, last Su of the month 8:45AM-2PM, 1 Oct-June. Closed 1 Jan, 6 Jan, 11 Feb, 19 Mar, Easter Su and M, Ascension Th, Corpus Christi Th, 1 May, 29 June, 15 Aug, and the day before or after 1 Nov, 8 Dec, 25 Dec, and the day before or after. Viale Vaticano. 6983333

A **Egyptian Museum** (Museo Gregoriano Egizio) Stunningly remodeled in 1989 for the 150th anniversary of its creation by **Pope Gregory XVI**. Several of the museum's pieces date from the times when **Julius Caesar** annexed **Cleopatra** and their 2 great civilizations influenced each other's art and culture. Pope Gregory took many of these sculptures from **Hadrian**'s Villa at Tivoli (see page 148). In the 3rd room is a statue of the god **Osiris**, done in the image of Emperor Hadrian's young male lover, **Antinous**, who died in Egypt and whom the grieving ruler elevated to divinity—Juan Peron tried to do something similar with his Evita. There are also statues of Egyptian queens, pharaohs, gods and goddesses, and a black-granite throne belonging to **Rameses II**

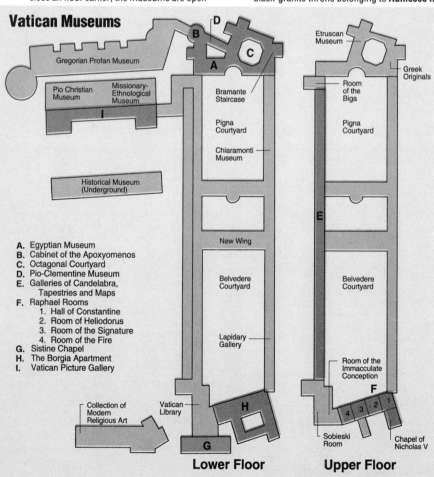

Vatican Museums

Gregorian Profan Museum

Pio Christian Museum

Missionary-Ethnological Museum

Historical Museum (Underground)

Etruscan Museum

Greek Originals

Bramante Staircase

Pigna Courtyard

Chiaramonti Museum

Room of the Biga

Pigna Courtyard

New Wing

Belvedere Courtyard

Lapidary Gallery

Belvedere Courtyard

Room of the Immaculate Conception

A. Egyptian Museum
B. Cabinet of the Apoxyomenos
C. Octagonal Courtyard
D. Pio-Clementine Museum
E. Galleries of Candelabra, Tapestries and Maps
F. Raphael Rooms
　1. Hall of Constantine
　2. Room of Heliodorus
　3. Room of the Signature
　4. Room of the Fire
G. Sistine Chapel
H. The Borgia Apartment
I. Vatican Picture Gallery

Collection of Modern Religious Art

Vatican Library

Sobieski Room

Chapel of Nicholas V

Lower Floor

Upper Floor

(13th century BC). That pharaoh's mother, **Queen Tuia**, is the subject of an enormous statue in the 5th room. One of the rare museums where you can see mummies.

B **Cabinet of the Apoxyomenos** Immediately to your left when you return from Egypt, you pass through a square vestibule and a round vestibule into a small apartment, part of the **Pio-Clementine Museum**. Pope Leo X lent this pair of rooms for 3 years to **Leonardo da Vinci** to carry out experiments in alchemy (turning base metals into gold). The great Renaissance painter and savant knew better than to waste his time on such dreams, so he used it instead to study anatomy for his drawings. The pope finally evicted Leonardo when he heard rumors that he had received ladies of easy virtue here in order to examine them for his gynecological sketches. In the center of the 1st room stands a Roman copy of an original bronze of Apoxyomenos (*The Cleanser*) by **Lysippus**, famous in the 4th century BC. The difficult name (from the Greek word meaning *to wipe off*) identifies a victorious athlete who is seen wiping oil from his skin with a scraper, or *strigil* (now lost), after a wrestling match. One of the first statues to be made for 3-dimensional viewing, it was found in 1849 in Vicolo dell' Atleta (Athlete's Alley) in nearby Trastevere. From the 2nd room you can see what wags call the *pope's elevator*, a circular staircase designed by **Bramante** in the form of a smooth ramp so that the pontiff could be carried to the upper floors of the Vatican on muleback.

C **Octagonal Courtyard** (Cortile Ottagono) Like the cabinet you just visited, this patio is also part of the **Pio-Clementine Museum**. It houses some of the major sculptural works in the Vatican, including the *Laocoön* and the *Apollo Belvedere*. Laocoön, one of Apollo's priests, is shown here in one of the 2nd century BC's most awkward moments. It was nevertheless a scene that **Agesandrus of Rhodes** and 2 colleagues turned into a moving sculptural composition. Two serpents surprised the priest and his 2 sons and they are shown here fighting for their lives. The dismembered group was found in Rome and reassembled in 1532. In 1905 an archaeologist named **Ludwig Pollak** saw a marble arm in a shop near the Colosseum and realized that it was the missing arm of *Laocoön*. Restoration was done in 1957. A photo of the 16th-century botched-up restoration stands near today's presumably correct version. The *Apollo Belvedere*, a Roman copy of a Greek bronze of the 4th century BC, was considered the most perfect example of Greek art handed down to us (thanks to the Roman copyist)—at least until the 1970s, when a scuba diver found the 2 original Greek statues known as the *Riace Bronzes*. The originals are now in a museum in Reggio Calabria. When **Napoleon** carted off classical statues that stood in the arches of the Belvedere courtyard, the pope purchased as replacements 3 statues that **Antonio Canova** had sculpted around 1800; they are his

Perseus, holding the severed head of the *Medusa* (itself inspired by the *Apollo Belvedere*), and 2 statues of boxers mentioned in the sports pages of antiquity.

D **Pio-Clementine Museum (of Greco-Roman sculpture)** In the first room you enter from the **Octagonal Court**, you see ancient statues of animals, including the Roman marble copy of a 4th-century BC Greek bronze showing

Via Della Conciliazione

Meleager with a wild boar's head and a dog. The fine mosaics on the wall were made from tiny chips of marble in the early centuries of the Christian era, and the larger ones on the floor are from a later and possibly more decadent period of the empire. To your right is the **Galleria delle Statue**, where the *Sleeping Ariadne* (11) and the *Satyr at Rest* (22) are to be noted. The adjacent galleria contains a seated **Jove** (77) and busts of **Julius Caesar** (122); a young man thought to be **Augustus** (124); **Hadrian** (133); and **Antinous** (51) and his rival for Emperor Hadrian's attention, **Sabina** (49), the official empress. Next, retrace your steps through the busts and the animals into the **Room of the Muses**; in the center, with its back to you, is the truncated but sublime *Belvedere Torso*, which bears the inscription *made by Apollonius, Athenian, son of Nestor*, identifying it as a 1st-century BC Greek original. You can see that this powerfully articulated sculpture must have profoundly influenced **Michelangelo**, particularly in his Sistine ceiling paintings. Beyond, in the **Round Room**, is a great porphyry basin found near the Senate building in the Roman Forum; a large statue of the **Goddess Ceres**, one of **Juno**, and a famous Roman copy of a Greek statue of **Jupiter**. The gilded Hercules probably dates from the 1st century BC, and was found in **Pompey's Theater** (where Caesar was stabbed; see page 111). No. 4 is another statue commissioned by Hadrian, showing Antinous in the guise of **Dionysius**; nearby is a bust of Antinous and between the 2 is a large head of the emperor himself, as if he were keeping an eye on his friend. In the room shaped like a Greek cross, statue No. 21 is thought by some to be the likeness of **Cleopatra**, Caesar's mistress and mother (by *caesarean section*) of his son **Caesarion**. The 2 gigantic sarcophagi are made of porphyry. The one decorated with a ram (representing Christ) was the tomb of **Constance**, the daughter of **Emperor Constantine**, who killed her husband. The other was originally made for the Emperor himself, but since Constantine died and was buried in Constantinople it was used as the tomb of his beatified mother, **St. Helen.**

In 1309 the French captured the papacy and moved it to Avignon, where it stayed for almost 70 years.

Restaurants/Clubs: Red	**Hotels:** Blue
Shops/Parks: Green	**Sights/Culture:** Black

E Galleries of the Candelabra, Tapestries, and Maps Climb the **Simonetti Stairs** as you leave the Greek Cross Room, and you will find this long corridor with windows on both sides, which was originally an open-sided walkway between 2 papal palaces. The first section is named after the monumental marble candlesticks beautifully sculpted almost 2000 years ago. From the windows on the

right you have a good view of the **Vatican Gardens** with their rolling lawns and spreading trees; nestled in the center is the loveliest of several pavilions, the **Casina of Pius IV** with its exquisite courtyard and shell shapes. On the left you look down on the **Courtyard of the Pine Cone**; **Bramante** designed the palazzo facade (behind the pine cone) based on the early Roman architect **Vitruvius'** description of contemporary ancient Roman villas. In this long gallery you will notice that old Roman statues of healthy-looking lads had fig leaves plastered on or ripped off, depending on whether the current pope was a man of the world or a prude. In the process many fine sculptures were disfigured, and certain restorers were allegedly nicknamed *Mr. Fig*. Heads, too, would roll, or simply fall off; as often as not another statue's head would be stuck onto a headless body, whether the marbles matched or not. Second-century AD mosaics in the very precise *vermicelli* style show some of the delicious fresh food used in a typical Roman banquet: chicken, fish, dates, squid, and asparagus. The fine tapestries in the central gallery of this corridor, representing the life of Christ, were made in 1524-1531 in the Brussels workshop of **Pieter van Aeist** from designs by **Raphael's** students. The second on the left includes camels and an elephant, which are realistic since the popes at this time had a private zoo, whereas earlier "likenesses" of exotic animals had been invented by the artists. Further down on the same side is *Supper at Emmaus*, showing Christ appearing to his disciples; the perspective is so perfect that the table, like Christ's eyes, seems to follow you around as you pass by. (Don't miss the carefully painted bottle and glasses in the wine cooler below the table on the right.) On the right wall are 17th-century tapestries from the Rome workshop set up in 1627 by **Cardinal Francesco Barberini** illustrating the life of his uncle **Pope Urban VIII**, in which you see the giant bees that are their family emblem. The final section of this triple gallery is 315 feet long, the height of St. Peter's basilica. Its walls are covered with frescoed maps designed by the great cosmographer **Ignazio Danti** and painted here 1580-83. They show papal lands and other regions of Italy, notably 16th-century Venice, as well as boisterous sea battles.

F Raphael Rooms (Stanze di Raffaello) The rooms originally had frescoes by earlier masters, including the extraordinary **Piero della**

Francesca. **Pope Julius II**, not wanting to live in the Borgia apartment downstairs that his detested predecessor **Alexander VI** had created, commissioned Raphael to redecorate these walls, bringing the brilliant young painter (then 25) from central Italy for the job.

Room 1, Hall of Constantine (1517-24)

Painted by Raphael's assistants from his sketches after his death. The frescoes depict the life of the 4th-century Roman emperor **Constantine**, including his victory over **Maxentius** at Rome's Ponte Milvio (which is still standing; see page 138) and his conversion to Christianity. From the corner of the adjoining **Room of the Chiaroscuri** a door leads to the **Chapel of Nicholas V**, with frescoes (1447-51) depicting scenes from the lives of saints **Stephen** and **Lawrence** by Fra Angelico; he had been the first of a stream of great Renaissance masters lured down to Rome by popes who had seen or heard of the miraculous artistry they were practicing up in Florence. Look at the painted trompe l'oeil brocade on the lower walls. This tiny chapel is exactly as Pope Nicholas left it 5 centuries ago.

Room 2, Room of Heliodorus (1512-14)

Of the 2 important frescoes here, one shows the *Miracle of Lake Bolsena*. (A previously skeptical priest on his way to Rome saw consecrated bread dripping blood on the altar cloth.) In the other, **Pope Leo I** drives **Attila the Hun** away from Rome in 452. (Attila, on the black horse, is understandably alarmed by the armed saints Peter and Paul conjured up by the Pope.) Pope Leo originally looked like the man who commissioned the fresco, **Pope Julius II**, but when he died in 1513 his image was painted over with the likeness of **Giovanni de' Medici**, the new pope. As it happened, Raphael seems to have spotted a rising star in the Medici cardinal since he had already painted him standing behind the pope (the one with the red hat in the left foreground). This may be the only great painting where the same figure appears twice. On the opposite wall, in the *Expulsion of Heliodorus*, Raphael's impressive portrait of Pope Julius was allowed to remain intact. He is sitting on the portable throne (Raphael painted himself as one of the chair-carriers), and the theme praises Julius for driving foreigners from Italy. The fourth major fresco in this room, the *Deliverance of St. Peter from Prison*, is significant for the ethereal light emanating from the angel in the center.

Room 3, Room of the Signature (1508-11)

Where the popes signed papal bills, and the site of Raphael's first major fresco, *The Dispute Over the Sacrament*, which shows that he was still under the influence of his teacher **Perugino**, but was starting to crystalize his own style. Opposite is the *School of Athens*, a masterpiece in balanced composition, in which Raphael painted the then newly discovered (ancient Greek) philosopher-heroes of the Renaissance, along with some contemporary heroes of his own. In the center, at the top of the steps is **Plato** (really a portrait of Leonardo da Vinci) discoursing with **Aristotle**; note the symbolism of Plato pointing up to the Spiritual World while Aristotle points down to Earth. **Epicurus** is suitably crowned with laurel leaves. The seated solitary figure with drooping stockings and his head resting on his hand is officially the philosopher **Heraclitus** (*all knowledge is self-knowledge and all reality is flickering like fire*, to paraphrase his philosophy) but the head is that of the man Raphael most admired, Michelangelo. The bent-over bald man on the right holding a compass is **Euclid**, but is also a portrait of Raphael's protector, the architect **Bramante**. In the foreground on the far right, their heads level with the blue-and-white columns, are the more established painter **Sodoma** (that was his nickname) and, peeking timidly behind him, the face of Raphael himself. On the window wall is **Parnassus**, with **Apollo** playing a lyre and encircled by his muses. Later additions to this room are early graffiti, including praise of **Martin Luther** dating from the 1527 Sack of Rome, and more visible and recent century scratches such as *Dubois 1829*. (These later graffiti are in the window embrasure behind the beautiful round marble tables used for seats in the Renaissance.)

Room 4, Room of the Fire (1514-17)

Except for his masterly *Fire in the Borgo*, with its exciting spiral composition, these frescoes were executed by Raphael's helpers based on his drawings. The ceiling is by Perugino, and the subject of the room's decorations is a great fire in 847 around St. Peter's that **Pope Leo IV** extinguished by making the Sign of the Cross. The old St. Peter's is in the background. Over the window: *Coronation of Charlemagne* by **Leo III**.

Fresco literally means fresh, referring to the fact that frescoes were painted while the plaster was still wet, as opposed to a secco, which was painted when the plaster dried. The procedure for actually painting a fresco involved a combination of artistic skill, timing, and patience. Usually a pencil drawing of the design was made on the crude plaster surface of the ceiling. (A notable exception is the Sistine Chapel: recent renovations have revealed that Michelangelo painted directly onto the wet plaster without making a drawing first.) Next, wet plaster mix was placed onto the area to be painted on a section-by-section basis. The painter needed to wait until the mixture reached its optimum consistency, part humid-part dry, to prevent the paint from disappearing into the absorbent mix. When the mixture reached this desired state, the painter worked swiftly to create the full effect of the flow of paint and plaster together. If the mixture, called the *sinopia*, dried and hardened before the painter could get the design painted, the unique effect vanished. The painter also needed to account for seasonal changes; in the winter the plaster dried more slowly but the daylight was shorter, while during the summer the reverse occurred.

G The Sistine Chapel

Built toward the end of the 15th century by **Pope Sixtus IV**. He had the best artists available decorate it, including **Botticelli, Perugino, Ghirlandaio, Pinturicchio**, and **Signorelli**, who painted frescoes along the 2 side walls. Since medieval times, the church has divided history into 3 periods: the first, before Moses received the Law from God; the sec-

ond, the period that followed the Law; the third, the period after the birth of Christ. Whereas Michelangelo's ceiling deals with the first period, the frescoes on the side walls deal with biblical events of the last 2 periods. Note that in Perugino's *Handing Over of the Keys* the artist included in the background Rome's Arch of Constantine, which was to be built 300 years after the event portrayed in his fresco presumably took place. The side walls also have imaginary portraits of the first 28 popes done by lesser artists. The lower parts of the side walls (with painted curtains) were once covered with tapestries designed by Raphael, including the one of *The Miracle of the Fishes*. These are now kept in the Pinacoteca, but in 1983 they were hung here on the original hooks, thus making the world's most valuable walls and ceiling that much more priceless.

Though the frescoes on the side walls merit attention, they are dwarfed by the later frescoed ceiling that the young Michelangelo, working mostly alone and frequently lying on his back, painted in the 4 years 1508-1512. The ceiling was originally painted blue with gold and silver stars. The 33-year-old Florentine had first tried to refuse the papal commission since he considered painting to be a simple pastime, not worthy of a sculptor/architect. He acquiesced after the Pope threatened war against Florence. His frescoes cover almost 15,000 square feet with over 300 figures. The central panels in the ceiling (which should be read in the direction in which you procede through the chapel) depict the 5 major events from the Book of Genesis, followed by The Fall of Man, Noah's Sacrifice, The Flood, and Noah's Drunkenness. Many experts consider Michelangelo's Sistine ceiling to be man's greatest artistic achievement. *The Creation of Adam*, the young man languidly reaching out toward God, with the dramatic tension in the space between their fingers, is perhaps the most thrilling painting on earth.

Restoration of the ceiling, the removal of centuries of grime caused in part by the candles and torches used for illumination before electricity, began in 1985 and lasted 5 years. Among the discoveries made during the cleaning is the fact that Michelangelo could paint his fresco directly onto the wet plaster—that is, without first having to sketch his design on the wall. The total absence of black, combined with the prevalence of deep shadows to make the figures jump out at you, and the shock of the vivid, almost garish colors he used, particularly electric orange and Nile green, mean that some pages of art history are now being rewritten.

The Last Judgment (behind the altar)

A couple of decades after painting the ceiling, Michelangelo was asked by **Clement VII**, one of the Medici popes, to paint a fresco of *The*

Via Della Conciliazione

Last Judgment on the wall behind the chapel's altar. By then in his 60s, Michelangelo spent almost 7 years on this masterpiece. It caused a scandal at its unveiling because Christ was

shown without a beard and because of the nudity. Twenty-three years later, another pope, **Pius IV**, gave another painter, **Daniel da Voltera**, the shameful task of putting loin-clothes on the nudes. Candle smut from the altar has made this fresco almost invisible. When the restorers begin on *The Last Judgment*, they will not remove the loincloths, because recent examinations reveal that before painting on the loincloths, the artist/censor had effaced the private parts below. Other later restorations, including some covering of nudity, will be removed, however.

The entire Sistine Chapel restoration is being financed by the **Nippon Television Network** of Tokyo. It has given the Vatican $3 million, and in return has exclusive rights to all forms of

The Sistine Chapel
Walls
A Baptism of Christ
Perugino, Ghirlandaio, Fra Diamante
B Temptations of Christ
Botticelli, Fra Diamante
C Calling of the First Apostles
Ghirlandaio
D Sermon on the Mount
Rosselli, Unknown
E Handing Over of the Keys
Perugino, Unknown, Botticelli
F Last Supper
Rosselli, Botticelli, Ghirlandaio
G Resurrection
Paludano (replaces Ghirlandaio), Botticelli, Ghirlandaio
H Disputation Over the Body of Moses
da Lecce (replaces lost Signorelli), Ghirlandaio, Unknown
I Testament of Moses
Signorelli, Botticelli, Rosselli
J Punishment of Korah, Datan & Abiron
Botticelli, Fra Diamante
K Moses Receives the Tablets of the Law
Rosselli, Fra Diamante

L Crossing of the Red Sea
Rosselli, Fra Diamante
M Events from the Life of Moses
Botticelli, Unknown, Ghirlandaio
N Journey of Moses
Perugino, Ghirlandaio, Botticelli
O The Last Judgement
Michelangelo

Michelangelo's Ceiling
1 Division of Day From Night
2 Creation of the Heavens
3 Division of the Land from the Waters
4 Creation of Adam
5 Creation of Eve
6 The Fall
7 Noah's Sacrifice
8 The Flood
9 Drunkenness of Noah
10 Zachariah
11 Judith & Holofernes
12 David & Goliath
13 Punishment of Haman
14 Jonah
15 Brazen Serpent

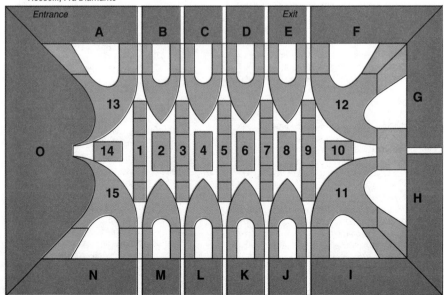

photography of the restoration work and the restored frescoes, and publications ensuing, for many years to come. The restoration was the subject of an intense dispute when a group of artists, mostly American abstract painters who had not even seen the work in progress, declared that the restorers were endangering Man's cultural heritage; they demanded that the work be stopped until an international inquiry could be carried out. The Vatican, as it has throughout its long history, faced down the criticism and went blithely on with its chosen task. In this case at least, it was right.

Today, the Sistine Chapel is infrequently used for religious services, so as not to deprive the public of access. This is where the cardinals meet in conclave (sleeping in improvised quarters nearby) when they are summoned to elect a new pope. During the high-tourism season, the Vatican regulates the flow of visitors (the humidity from human breath is also damaging) to the chapel by switching the directional arrows. On calm days it can be reached in a brisk 8-minute walk from the elevators by following the signs. Since every guidebook in every language urges its readers to proceed at once to the Sistine Chapel when the museum doors open at 8:45AM, and before the organized tours get themselves organized, a better plan is to start your sprint at 9:15AM. Binoculars (not opera glasses) may be useful.

H **The Borgia Apartment** Built by the second (and final) Borgia pope, **Alexander VI**, in 1492, the year Columbus set out to find a shortcut to India, and where most of the succeeding popes lived for the next 100 years until the present papal apartment was built. Alexander had **Pinturicchio** do the frescoes. Living quarters of Renaissance rulers in Rome, Florence, Mantua, and Venice were cramped by today's standards. Note the scratches on the window seats for a board game popular at the time. The 4th room has the best frescoes: the Borgia bull (the family symbol) on the ceiling; the Pope's favorite daughter, **Lucrezia**, posed for the portrait of **St. Catherine the Blonde**. In the 5th room, in the fresco of the Resurrection, Pope Alexander is kneeling and the young soldier standing nearby is thought to be his son **Cesare**; the young Roman (not in uniform) is thought to be Cesare's brother, whom he murdered. In the Borgia Apartment and nearby rooms is the **Collection of Modern Religious Art** opened in 1973 by **Pope Paul VI**. It includes paintings and sculpture by contemporary masters from **August Rodin** to **Ben Shahn**.

I **Vatican Picture Gallery** (Pinacoteca) Eighteen rooms with some of the world's most famous masterpieces. Pictures are numbered in chronological order starting with the 11th century. In Room II is **Bernardo Daddi**'s *Madonna del Magnificat* (174), a favorite with art connoisseurs. In Room VIII, all works are by Raphael, including 8 of the tapestries he designed for the Sistine Chapel. His recently re-

stored *Transfiguration* (333) is a universal favorite. In Room IX is a rare painting by Leonardo da Vinci; its subject is **St. Jerome**, in monochrome and unfinished. In Room XII is Baroque art, the favorite of the rich late 16th- and early 17th-century popes, including a fine **Caravaggio**. In the Room XVIII is a rich collection of 115 Byzantine icons formerly in the Apostolic Library.

Via Della Conciliazione

Bests

Professor Carlo Pietrangeli
*Director General of the
Pontifical Museums and Galleries*

My preferences in our museums are the following:

Tapestry of the *Miracles of the Fishes* made from a design by Raphael.

The Aldobrandini Wedding Scene, *Nozze Aldobrandini*, a fresco found in 1608 on property of the Aldobrandini family, probably a copy of a painting of Alexander the Great's wedding to Roxanne.

The Apollo Belvedere.

Madonna del Magnificat by Bernardo Daddi.

Madonna of Foligno by Raphael.

Mosaics, as an art form using colored pebbles, started in Greece around the 8th century BC. By the time they reached Rome they had been refined and had become decorative patterns of cut marble. Primarily black-and-white at first, colored stones were eventually included. Later, pieces of glass paste were mixed with the stones, or used alone in harmonious pictorial compositions. After the fall of Rome, the Church kept the tradition alive, and even inspired a new flowering of the Byzantine style, notably in Ravenna where the emperors fled. The **Vatican Studio of Mosaics** is the best known surviving center for this art form; the studio repairs existing old mosaics and creates new ones with religious or lay subjects. Since 1935 until his death in 1985, the late **Professor Odorado Anselmi** was the finest artist the Vatican had. Due to subtlety of color gradation and fine rendering, his original artworks have now become collector's items, and the mosaics still being made by his foreign following are much sought after.

Like waves, history has crests alternating with troughs. Periods of great libertarianism are followed by times of moral and political repression. Thus, the era of *dolce vita* (good living) in the pontifical court, incited by the Renaissance, was traumatized by the teaching of Martin Luther's Protestant Reformation and the Sack of Rome. The Church authorities responded with the repressive measures of the Counter Reformation, including the Inquisition. The establishment of new, more self-denying religious orders was intended to prevent people throughout the Christian world from converting to Protestantism.

21 Girarosto Dal Toscano ★★★$$ Even if your feet can't move another inch, force them to totter 3 short blocks almost straight down from the Vatican Museums to **Pietro Bruni**'s pleasant rotisserie. Pasta dishes include *bombolotti* Giulio Cesare (elbow maccaroni with sausage meat), fettucine *ai funghi porcini,* and spaghetti *alla chitarra* (sauce of pigs' cheeks and tomato, and delicious). Being Tuscan,

Via Della Conciliazione

Pietro serves *fagioli* (white beans in oil and garlic) and great T-bone steaks done on the spit, but unlike most of his compatriot restaurateurs he generally charges by the portion of beef rather than by the *etto* (10th of a kilo). Fresh sardines, served Tuesday and Friday, are good for cholesterol watchers. House wine comes in straw flasks, and the house dessert is cream cake with hot-chocolate sauce poured on at the last moment. But our delight is the very dark-chocolate mousse, enjoyed while sitting under the double canopy on the sidewalk. ♦ Closed Tuesday. Via Germanico 56. Reservations recommended. 314719

22 San Paolo Multimedia You will be waited on by nuns in this pious place positively reeking of sanctity. Books, tapes, and films for sale in 4 languages, including English, mostly on Christianity. One video casette with **Professor Arnold Toynbee** presents *The Four Great Religions: Hinduism, Buddhism, Islam and Christianity.* While no one would dispute the greatness of these 4, there are other religions that could be mentioned—Animism for instance. ♦ Via del Mascherino 94. 6872354; fax 6548093

23 Sapal Sport If you yearn for vice in the shadow of St. Peter's, this is where you can buy slot machines and a roulette wheel. If you want to exercise, there are sports clothes and equipment. Jigsaw puzzles and sneakers, too. ♦ Via del Mascherino 50 (Borgo Vittorio) 6869381

24 HANI ★★$$ Rome's only Korean restaurant is patronized also by Koreans. The national favorite seems to be thin slices of beef, marinated, like everything else here. You can have it raw. Or as *bolghogi,* simmering in hot sauce over a bunsen burner at your table. But it is hard to keep the waiter from over-cooking it,

so tell him to stop as soon as it goes from red to pink. No. 26 is a full-course dinner, reasonably priced, with spicy soup, pickled vegetable, and hot salad. The only dessert other than fresh fruit is ginseng tea, a noted aphrodisiac. ♦ Closed Tuesday. Borgo Angelico 26. No credit cards. 6547551

25 Primo (Number One) ★$ The smiley **Angelo** and his trendy-looking wife are Chinese, as is their reasonably priced fare. Ravioli *al vapore* is not a vapid Italian pasta dish, but a steamed dim sum dumpling. Vermicelli *con verdura* are not jeweled worms but Chinese rice noodles with vegetables. Also recommended are chicken with cashews and shrimps with hot sauce. Don't forget Marco Polo brought pasta back from Cathay to Venice. ♦ Closed Tuesday. Via degli Ombrellari 18. 6864225

26 Hostaria Tre Pupazzi ★$ Plain Roman cooking under the watchful eye of the cordial manager. ♦ Closed Sunday. Borgo Pio 183 (corner of the Street of 3 Puppets—so named for a fragment of medieval sculpture of 3 figures set in wall near restaurant's side door) 6868371

27 Hotel Atlante Star $$$ Guests with reservations are whisked by limousine from Rome airport to this trendy 60-room hotel. **Benito Mencucci** also has the **Atlante Garden**, a short distance away. He recently beautified the Star, installing a Royal Suite complete with giant circular Jacuzzi, and a business/conference center with (says the brochure) closed circuit TV and hostesses on request. ♦ Via Vitelleschi 34. 6879558; fax 6872300

Within the Hotel Atlante Star:

Les Etoiles ★★$$$ Apparently Benito felt he had to encase this panoramic terrace in glass to satisfy our national need for air conditioning, but he does like to leave the windows open in summer so that you get both AC and the feeling of being on a Roman roof garden within spitting distance of St. Peter's—which you are. Peep between the flower pots at the nunnery nearby; you might spot a resident hanging out her bloomers. The *nuova cucina* creations are by **Lino Pisu**, who left his native Sardinia and traveled widely before settling in this elegant restaurant. The result is imagination and exoticism. ♦ 6879558

28 Tiroler Keller ★$ One of Rome's better beer halls with both German and Italian cuisines. Spaten beer on tap. ♦ Closed Monday. Via Vitelleschi 23 (near Castel Sant'Angelo) 6869994

Restaurant Tips
The quality of food is probably good if the prosciutto is cut by hand, whitebait marinated with lemon juice (*alici marinati*) is on the menu, and the pasta is cooked to order—it will take a little more time but will never be soggy.

Restaurants/Clubs: Red	Hotels: Blue
Shops/Parks: Green	**Sights/Culture:** Black

Renaissance Artists and Architects

Stop and consider for a moment the number of fine artists and sculptors living at one time. What propelled this flowering of the arts? Was it the social climate (an enlightened society and rich patrons)? Was it simply the need to decorate new buildings? Or was it a natural blossoming of talent? Note that half of those listed below were alive when Columbus sailed the ocean blue, in 1492!

1267-1337	Giotto
1284-1344	Simone Martini
1290-1348	Bernardo Daddi
1383-1447	Masolino (Tommasso di Cristoforo Fini)
1386-1466	Donatello (Donato di Betto)
1387-1445	Fra Angelico (Giovanni da Fiesole)
1406-1469	Filippo Lippi
1415-1492	Piero della Francesco
1420-1497	Benozzo Gozzoli
1431-1498	Antonio del Pollaiuolo
1431-1506	Andrea Mantegna
1444-1514	Donato Bramante
1445-1510	Sandro Botticelli
1445-1523	Perugino (Pietro Vannucci)
1449-1494	Domenico Ghirlandaio
1452-1519	Leonardo da Vinci
1475-1564	Michelangelo Buonarrati
1475-1550	Luca Della Robbia, the younger
1477-1549	Sodoma (Giovan Antonio Bazzi)
1481-1536	Baldassarre Perruzzi
1483-1520	Raphael Sanzio
1483-1546	Sangallo the Younger
1486-1570	Sansovino (Jacopo Tatti)
1490-1576	Titian (Tiziano Vecellio)
1499-1546	Giulio Romano (Giulio Pippi)
1500-1571	Benevenuto Cellini
1507-1573	Vignola (Jacopo Barozzi)
1511-1574	Giorgio Vasari
1528-1588	Veronese (Paolo Caliari)
1540-1602	Giacomo della Porta
1562-1629	Pietro Bernìni (Father of Gian Lorenzo)
1573-1610	Caravaggio (Michelangelo Amerighi)
1598-1680	Gian Lorenzo Bernìni (The Great)
1599-1667	Francesco Borromini

In Italy they weigh food by the *etto*, which is 100 grams (one tenth of a kilo). So 500 *etti* equal approximately one pound.

Unusual Shops

Dal Co' Those czarinas of fashion who have their shoes made to measure call this the top. ♦ Via Vittoria 65. 6786538

Alinari Since the nonagenarian proprietor of the Old Photograph and Book Shop on Lungotevere died, this is the place to look for old photos. ♦ Via Alibert 16A. 6792923

Avignose Superb collection of terra cotta and marble, including obelisks, boxes in the shape of **Palladio**'s *La Malcontenta*, large stands for coffee tables that look like marble (but are really terra cotta), and bookends painted to look like marble. ♦ Via Margutta 15/16 and Via dell'Orso 73. 3614004

Mosaic Studio inside the Vatican Special permission required for entry can be obtained by applying to the **Vatican Information Office** on the left of the Colonnade near the first-aid room. Here you will see the mosaics being cut and assembled in a variety of amazing pictures, including images by **Van Gogh, Goya, Picasso**, and traditional religious objects.

G. Guiliani A confectionery shop for the connoisseur. Specialties include marrons glacés (everyday, not just in December) and sugar-coated violet petals—the most delicate after-dinner sweet one can imagine. ♦ Via Paola Emilio 67. 312241

Confetteri Moriondo and Gariglio The lurid red paint that delineates the rough arc where this little shop hides must not put you off—this is the only fresh chocolate-maker in town; you can eat the fondants that were made last night. The difference in taste is amazing. **Marcello Proietti** learned under his maestro the secrets of sophisticated chocolate-making. The shop opened in 1886. **Prince Colonna** used to come to the shop as a child, so when he heard that the lease expired on the old shop, he offered a "hole in the wall" in his palazzo as long as there was no name outside to mar the building. Nothing could stop the cognescenti from piling inside the tiny shop to wait their turn. By appointment to the President of Italy (who gave a box to **Queen Elizabeth II**, who absolutely adored them). ♦ Via della Pilotta 2. No credit cards. 6786662

La Corte (a "don't tell" secret) Succulent smoked salmon, *spigola* (sea bass), turkey, swordfish, and trout. Made in Italy by a retired English diplomat. One pound of presliced salmon: 35,000 lire. ♦ Via della Gata (in the Palazzo Doria Pamphili)

Religious shops down Via dei Cestari Window shopping for silver chalices and religious vestments (with gold embroidery) for Easter or Christmas is fascinating, and certain things are actually slightly cheaper in these stores than in lay shops, especially shoes and simple cardigans. One of the nicest items is a pair of pure lisle cardinal's socks in fiery crimson.

Books on Italy

Louise Mc Dermott keeps a stock of the most important out-of-print and rare books in English about Rome and the rest of the country. Ask for her latest catalog. ♦ Via Giubbonari 30/9. 6545285

Via Veneto

(stress on the first *e*, and properly, Via Vittorio Veneto) has been a fun-loving area since it belonged to **Julius Caesar**. Its wildest moments were in the 1950s and '60s, the period known as the **Dolce Vita**. At that time, sexy movie stars from **Sophia Loren** and **Ingrid Bergman** to **Errol Flynn** and **Anthony Quinn** sat in the sidewalk cafés surrounded by flash-popping paparazzi photographers. This era of nightlife and exhibitionism was recorded for posterity by Rome's leading moviemaker, **Federico Fellini**, in *La Dolce Vita* (1959), with **Marcello Mastroianni**—and with **Anita Ekberg** dunking in the nearby Trevi Fountain. Recently, **Liv Ullman** was spotted at the **Café de Paris**; Gina Lollobrigida, Ursula Andress, and **Audrey Hepburn** may pass by at any time. The cafés that get the morning sun, especially the famous **Doney's**, are described locally as being on the *foreigners' side*; so if you want to be on the *Italian side* you will have to sit in the shade—where there were a couple of shootouts in the 1970s and '80s. No problem. Here the authentic Romans make business-with-pleasure appointments to talk, sip coffee, nostalgically watch the elegant world go by, or try to pick up a passing tourist or streetwalker. Via Veneto is a relatively new street (1887) in a very ancient Roman quarter that was all vineyards and gardens until a hundred years ago. The politician and writer **Sallust** (86-34 BC) obtained such a magnificent rural estate from his patron Julius Caesar that he devoted the rest of his life here to writing the history books that made his name famous and that whitewashed his benefactor's spotty reputation—an early example of government leaders manipulating the media. Sallust's neighbor **Lucullus** (110-56 BC), general and epicure, organized orgies and sumptuous banquets in the adjacent estate and is immortalized by our word *Lucullian*, used to describe lavish or luxurious feasts. This tradition is continued on Via Veneto by an array of restaurants, cafés, and hotels too numerous to list completely.

Luxury is the keynote, exactly as intended by **Rodolfo Boncompagni-Ludovisi**, Prince of Piombino, when he created this whole area out of his family's country playground in a late 19th-century real-estate scheme. In the vast gardens of the **Villa Ludovisi**, inherited via his 17th-century ancestor **Pope Gregory XV**, Rodolfo laid out broad avenues for an upscale residential quarter and speculated in palazzos, which he hoped would help recuperate the family fortunes. Via Veneto was the central thoroughfare and, to attract the elegant carriage trade, Prince Ludovisi (whose descendants still inhabit the area) abandoned the originally planned straight line from **Piazza Barberini** up to **Porta Pinciana** in favor of the broad S-curve we see today, so that even the oldest cart horses could make it up the hill. For himself, he reserved the area that is now the **American Embassy** complex, but he and his family lived there only from 1890 to 1892, when the Bank of Italy foreclosed! The prince had created an area so elegant and expensive that he could not afford to live there himself.

Restaurants/Clubs: Red
Shops/Parks: Green
Hotels: Blue
Sights/Culture: Black

1 Piazza Barberini Until about 1800, this was an open field marking the lower edge of 2 great private estates. On what is now the Via Veneto side was the immense **Villa Ludovisi**, with its kitchen-gardens and vineyards, and on the other side was the **Barberini Quarter**, with its main gates standing at the entrance to what is now **Via Barberini**. Only **Via San Nicola da Tolentino** passed between the 2 estates. This small street became a bustling thoroughfare in the middle of the 19th century, when **Pope Pius IX**—before he lost his temporal power as ruler of Central Italy—had the main Rome railroad station built in the nearby **Termini** area (named after the Baths, or *Terme*, of Diocletian). Via San Nicola da Tolentino was then the only road leading from downtown Rome to the new station, and from then on Piazza Barberini became the hub of hotels and shops that we see today.

1 Bernini's Fountains The 2 gorgeous fountains in this piazza by **Gian Lorenzo Bernini** demonstrate the importance of the shell motif in Baroque sculpture. The most famous is the centrally placed *Triton Fountain* (*Fontana del Tritone*, 1637) with a semi-god merman blowing a high stream of water out of a conch shell while kneeling on 2 scallop shells held aloft by 4 dolphins. This is Bernini's earliest and most easily appreciated fountain. At the corner of Via Veneto his *Fountain of the Bees* (*Fontana delle Api*, 1644) has 3 giant bees crawling along a scallop shell to drink in the vast basin. It is inscribed to the glory of **Pope Urban VIII**, patriarch of the Barberini family—whose family emblem is the busy bee that was repeated frequently in this square and their adjacent palazzo. Some see the origin of this ubiquitous family symbol in the fact that in the early 17th century Rome was invaded by swarms of bees, at about the time the Barberini name, of Florentine origin, became important in Rome.

2 Hotel Bernini Bristol $$$ Listed as one of Rome's 9 luxury-class hotels, but lacks the excitement and prestige of the others. This location is noisy and the architecture—for which it tries to compensate with lavish use of marble—is uninspired. The bar, just beyond the front hall, is a good place to meet and start your day's walking tour. The elegant restaurant on the mezzanine also serves breakfast 7-10AM. One hundred twenty-four rooms
♦ Piazza Barberini 23. 463051; fax 4824266

3 La Baita ★★$$$ Arguably the best (but not cheapest) sandwiches in town are available until midnight in this tiny café on the lowest corner of the Via Veneto. Smoked salmon on dark bread melts in your mouth. In the back room, decked out like a Swiss chalet, is an

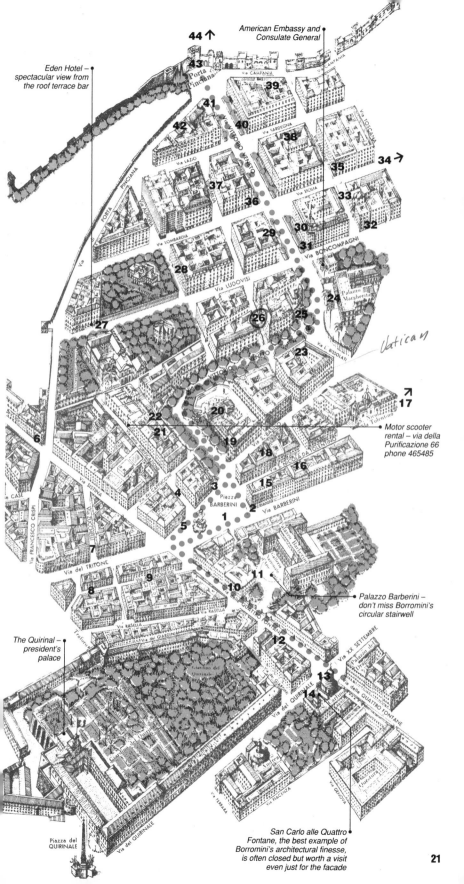

Eden Hotel –
spectacular view from
the roof terrace bar

American Embassy and
Consulate General

44 ↑

43

Porta
Pinciana

via CAMPANIA

39

41

42

40

via SARDEGNA

38

via LAZIO

35

34 →

37

via SICILIA

33

36

32

via LOMBARDIA

30

29

31

via BONCOMPAGNI

28

24

Palazzo
Margherita

27

Vatican

26

25

23

via L. BISSOLATI

17 ↗

20

22

21

Motor scooter
rental – via della
Purificazione 66
phone 465485

19

via S. BASILIO

18

via SISTINA

via del TRITONE

16

via NICOLA DA TOLENTINO

6

via del TRITONE

4

3

15

Piazza
BARBERINI

via BARBERINI

Via CASE

2

5

1

via FRANCESCO CRISPI

7

9

8

10

11

Palazzo Barberini –
don't miss Borromini's
circular stairwell

The Quirinal –
president's
palace

Giardino del
Quirinale

12

via XX SETTEMBRE

13

14

via delle QUATTRO FONTANE

via del QUIRINALE

via GENOVA

via PIACENZA

Piazza del
QUIRINALE

via FERRARA

San Carlo alle Quattro
Fontane, the best example of
Borromini's architectural finesse,
is often closed but worth a visit
even just for the facade

indifferent restaurant, heavy on meat dishes. ♦ Closed Sunday. Via Veneto 2 or Piazza Barberini 16. 462212

4 Opera According to discogoers, this acid-house disco has the best sound system and acoustics in Rome. Wednesday nights seem to gather the "hippest" crowd. ♦ Cover. Daily 11PM-3:30AM. Via della Purificazione 9. No credit cards. 4745578

5 Magia Under the staircase in the entrance to this building, 2 enterprising Roman women present their collection of inexpensive jewelry. ♦ Piazza Barberini 5. 486858

5 Il Transistor Tiny gift shop for tiny toys. It sometimes carries new transistorized gadgets not yet available in the US. ♦ Piazza Barberini 6. 4740612

5 Moriconi Knickknacks of silver and Venetian glass to take back as presents. Handsome frames for your photo-portrait. ♦ Piazza Barberini 7. 461949

5 Cir Hand-embroidered linens and baby clothes. Bring them back something special to remember you by. ♦ Piazza Barberini 11. 465470

5 Araldica Fine printing and engraving for your personal cards and announcements. In 24 hours Araldica will turn out an elegant printing job, but engraving or embossing takes a couple of weeks. By the time you get permission to marry in St. Peter's, your invitations will be ready for mailing. ♦ Piazza Barberini 14. 461395

♯♭ **TAITÙ**

6 Taitù Designer **Emilio Bergamin** had the excellent idea of color coordinating his beautiful china so that you can mix and match. His latest design idea is wood or marble trompe l'oeil for plates. ♦ Via Sistina 94. 6781108

In 1920, **D.H. Lawrence** observed that the modern Italian is much closer in temperament and social habits to the pleasure-loving Etruscans than to the orderly and righteous ancient Romans.

7 Il Giardino ★★★$$ Charming restaurant. Where there was once an outdoor courtyard (the *giardino*), there is now an additional room. Healthy house wine in liter carafes. Glorious antipasto trays heaped with delicacies. Spaghetti *alle vongole*, or any other way your heart fancies. Luscious puddings, crème caramel, and *chockie* (chocolate) cakes. Smiling service and reasonable prices make this the garden of paradise. ♦ Closed Monday. Via Zucchelli 29. 465202

8 Colline Emiliane ★★$ The appearance of this pasta shop is so unprepossessing that you might be tempted to pass it by. Don't—even though it only has white tableclothes. Between those plain board walls and on those kitchen-furniture tables you will be served unforgettable, mouth-watering specialties from the region around Bologna and Emilia-Romagna. Take any of the various openers with Parma ham; those with the homemade pasta are particularly memorable. Then try the veal cutlet Bologna-style and the chocolate dessert. Truffles are a specialty in season—but watch the cost. Take the wine suggestion or the house white (Sangiovese). The place is always full, so the turnover of food is sufficient to guarantee day-to-day freshness. But do reserve. ♦ Closed Friday and August. Via degli Avignonesi 22. 4817538

9 Gioia Mia (My Joy) ★$$ A joy for you as well as for the kids, who will love the chow and learn to say *ciao* to the waiters. One cannot take oneself too seriously sitting in a restaurant surrounded by pictures and sculptures of naked babies filling wine glasses in their own natural manner. You will want to take the house wine label home. And drink another bottle because it *slips down a treat*. The pasta and meat dishes, however, are not to be laughed at. No fish. ♦ Closed Sunday and 15 July-15 August. Via degli Avignonesi 34. No credit cards. 462784

10 Anglo-Americano Hotel $$ This little jewel is next to the Palazzo Barberini. Everything has been remodeled; each of the 110 rooms has a color TV and minibar. No restaurant (except for breakfast), but you won't go hungry on the adjoining Via degli Avignonesi. ♦ Via delle Quattro Fontane 12. 472941; fax 4746428

11 Palazzo Barberini (1633, Bernini) This bulky pile shows how seriously 17th-century popes took themselves. The Barberini family's pontiff, **Urban VIII**—who immediately followed his Ludovisi neighbor, Gregory XV, to the throne of St. Peter in 1623—had Rome's top Baroque architects, **Carlo Maderno, Gian-Lorenzo Bernini**, and **Francesco Borromini**, working on this palace from 1625 to 1633. From the outside, it is imposing, harmonious, and designed to impress, but it lacks lightness of touch or change of pace. As exceptions to this comment, see the last windows on either end of the top floor of the main (west) facade—designed by the fanciful young Borromini while he was apprentice, first to Maderno, whom he worshipped, and then to Bernini, whom he hated. These 2 windows show the ability to redesign flat classic forms into new and spectacular sculptural motifs, which later made Borromini the most exciting architect of Baroque Rome. Go inside, turn right to enjoy Borromini's oval circular staircase with its gently rising steps, and then left to compare it with Bernini's heavy square stairwell. Borromini committed suicide in 1667 at the age of 68, having complained that Bernini was shamelessly stealing all his ideas and designs. ♦ Via delle Quattro Fontane 13

Within the Palazzo Barberini:

National Gallery of Ancient Art One flight up Bernini's square staircase in Palazzo Barberini is the city's collection of 13th- to 16th-century paintings. These hang in the most gorgeous reception rooms of the Barberini Palace—the first floor above ground level being, in an Italian palazzo, the most important floor, or *piano nobile*. Most famous here is **Raphael**'s early 16th-century portrait (Room 8) of his mistress and favorite model, **La Fornarina** (see Romolo Restaurant on page 90); she displays very real breasts and a very convincing smile, but many art experts insist it's a fake and was actually painted by Raphael's follower **Giulio Romano**. The other great portraits here are of the philosopher **Erasmus of Rotterdam** (1517) by **Quentin Massys** (Room 12) and of **Henry VIII** (1540) by **Hans Holbein the Younger** (Room 13). Don't miss the ballroom (1633-39, **Salone**), where **Pietro da Cortona**'s fool-the-eye fresco shows the Barberini family symbols fairly bursting through the Baroque ceiling. ♦ Admission. Tu-Sa 9AM-2PM; Su and holidays 9AM-1PM. Via delle Quattro Fontane 13. 4754591

12 Quattro Fontane Hotel $ Not all rooms have a bath, but they are all cozy and the price is right. Some businesspeople from Milan like to stay here because it is *centralissimo* and has that traditional small-hotel look, which is rapidly disappearing from this busy city. Forty rooms. ♦ Via delle Quattro Fontane 149 A. 4814936

The classic Italian meal unfolds thusly:
Antipasti—usually a selection of cold cuts, vegetables, olives, shellfish . . .
Primo Piatto—often *pasta*, although it could include *risotto*, *polenta* or soup.
Secondo Piatto—meat or fish.
Insalata—salad and/or vegetables.
Dolce—dessert, often fruit and a ricotta or mascarpone cheese dish.
Espresso

Restaurants/Clubs: Red	**Hotels:** Blue
Shops/Parks: Green	**Sights/Culture:** Black

13 Quattro Fontane (The Four Fountains) (1589) **Pope Sixtus V**, Rome's great Baroque city planner, ordered these fountains placed at

the 4 corners of this crossroads—at private individuals' expense. It was a Baroque concept to carve straight streets through the medieval jumble of hovels and alleyways to connect major places of pilgrimage, and to position works of art such as fountains or obelisks so as to emphasize the esthetic (or spiritual) importance of the vista. Here we stand at the junction of 2 religiously key streets: **Via Quirinale**, leading from the former papal Summer Palace to the city gate known as **Porta Pia** (door of the faithful), and **Via Quattro Fontane** (the extension of Via Sistina), stretching from the **Church of Trinita dei Monti** at the top of the Spanish Steps to the important **Basilica of Santa Maria Maggiore**. At each end of this symbolic cross—except in front of the Porta Pia—is a monumental obelisk like an exclamation point emphasizing the importance of this nexus. The 4 newly restored fountains have reclining statues representing the **Tiber River**, the goddesses **Juno** and **Diana**, and the **Nile River** (reading clockwise starting at the Church of San Carlo). The lovely *Diana Fountain* is by **Pietro da Cortona**; the others are attractive but not remarkable. If you have enough courage to stand at this busy corner, you can look down these exciting vistas. You might take a half-hour detour down Via Quirinale, past the **Church of San Carlo alle Quattro Fontane**, by the great architect **Borromini**, down to the **Church of San Andrea al Quirinale**, one of the masterpieces of **Bernini**, his rival in Baroque building. Filling the entire block opposite this is the Baroque, late 16th century **Quirinale**

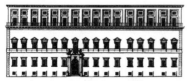

Palace, which was the summer residence of the popes (who now journey an extra hour to their rural villa in Castelgandolfo) from 1592 until 1870, when it became the official residence of the kings of United Italy. Since 1947 it has been the palace of the presidents of the young republic. Of course, in Italian any urban building worth mentioning is referred to as a

palazzo—a word derived from the name of the neighboring Palatine hill (see page 38)—but the Quirinale is one building in Rome that has always housed the chiefs of state, and is palatial from every viewpoint. ♦ Via Quattro Fontane at Via Quirinale

14 San Carlo alle Quattro Fontane (1634-8; facade, 1667 Borromini) The first and the last architectural work of this great genius of Roman Baroque. It is a monastery church built for the Spanish Discalced Trinitarians, an obscure and poor religious order with only a tiny irregularly shaped piece of hilly land on which they needed living quarters and a garden (neither of which can be visited), and the present church and cloister. The facade—which is usually referred to by the diminutive *San Carlino*—is a heavily ornamented double S-curve on 2 floors, wedged in between one of the Four Fountains (which cuts off the corner of the site) and the plainer entrance to the adjoining cloister. The site is so compressed that there is no point from where you can see the elaborate exterior, particularly the dome, which prefigures that of Borromini's Sant'Ivo alla Sapienza (see page 105). The interior of the church picks up and intensifies the alternating concave and convex wall treatment, with such a profusion of columns and niches that it is hard to discern the complicated geometric floor plan—like a football pinched in at 4 places. Nor do you get any help in grasping the true shape of the church from looking up at the dome, which is oval-shaped and does not seem to be an extension of the highly confined area for the human beings below—but rather a soaring intrusion into Heaven above, bathed in light from semihidden windows. Symbols are central to Borromini's approach to building. Many of the shapes were taken from ancient Roman buildings and other architectural models, but their use by Borromini was revolutionary, for he was trying to make buildings that were not so much walls and floors and ceilings as undefinable magical dimensions that force the beholder into spiritual contemplation. Don't miss the adjoining cloister, a simple rectangle that Borromini has treated in the architectural style Michelangelo pioneered, called Mannerism, which is a complex perspectival system. Specifically, notice that the upper floor, with its masonry colonnade, would normally be held up by columns placed at the 4 corners, whereas Borromini has perversely chopped off the angles and omitted corner columns. But the overall effect of this cloister is in keeping with the Baroque mode: relentless movement. The alternating shapes of the bays prevent the eye from coming to rest, as do the balusters along the upper tier, with alternating inverted shapes that dance magically around the cloister. ♦ M-F 8:30AM-12:30PM, 4-6PM. Via del Quirinale

15 Da Tulio ★★★$$ An honest Tuscan trattoria. Tulio is retired now, but his cousin **Dulio**, or young **Gianni**—unless they spot you as the one-shot tourist you are—will place a half-gallon straw-wrapped *fiasco* (flask) of Chianti on your table and order you the best T-bone (*fiorentino*) in town. Take both. You'll only pay for what you drink of the wine. The steak is charged by the kilo or fraction thereof, and one is enough for 2 people—especially if you start with *pappardelle alla lepre* (pasta with a hare sauce) or 2 artichokes *alla Romana* (you eat it all, cooked and stuffed with mint leaves). ♦ Closed Sunday and August. Via San Nicola da Tolentino 26. Reservations recommended. 4818564

15 I Tre Moschettiere ★$$ Unpretentious, no-nonsense place for good Roman food. ♦ Closed Saturday. Via San Nicola da Tolentino 23. 4814845

16 Morelli Electric Razors Everything electronic can be dependably repaired here, in electric-razor heaven. The simpatico Morelli family even has a small museum of vintage Sunbeams, Remingtons, and Brauns. In addition to bailing you out when your shaver breaks down, they will show you the latest selection of electronic gadgets so you can bring something amazing to the folks back home. ♦ Via San Nicola da Tolentino 58. 4744918

17 Edoardo ★★★$$$ In our first edition we rated Edoardo as a 4-star "don't tell" hole in the wall. It was so successful it has moved, expanded, and gone up-market. That 4th star was because of the surprise element, but luckily the *cucina* is still marvelous. The emphasis has shifted from antipasti and pastas fo fine fish and meat courses. The piano music is lovely with dinner. And Edoardo himself is just as great. ♦ Closed Sunday. Via Lucullo 1. 486428

18 Sandy The first place in town (and the best) to make your photocopies. **Sylvia** will reproduce color on glossy or matte paper (Ciba), on ordinary paper from slides (Laser)—or do just simple old black on white (if you're writing

your memoirs). Stays open during lunch. ♦ Closed Saturday. Via San Basilio 58. 4818533

19 Banca Nazionale del Lavoro Foreign exchange office open from 8:30AM to 6PM Monday through Saturday! At other times you'll have to go to the railroad station or your hotel. ♦ Via Veneto 11

20 Church of the Immaculate Conception (Santa Maria della Concezione) (1625) At the right of the front steps of this otherwise unimpressive church you enter Rome's most ghoulish chamber of horrors, called the

coemeterium (Latin for cemetery). The bones and skulls of thousands of Capuchin monks have been crafted into decorative tableaux capable of chilling the most resolute libertarian or fun-lover. Some bones actually look like acanthus leaves, and others lend themselves to Baroque tracery. According to one sign, **Pope Paul VI** (1963-78) granted plenary indulgence to those who visit on the first Sunday in October. Appropriately placed in the chancel above is the famous inscription on the tomb of church founder, **Cardinal Antonio Barberini** (brother of **Pope Urban VIII**): *Hic jacet pulvis, cinis et nihil.* (Here lies dust, cinders and nothingness.) Each visitor to the cellar-cemetery is expected to give about a dollar (in any currency) to the friar in attendance; give or not, you cannot photograph. ♦ Free. Daily 9AM-noon, 3-7PM, 1 June-15 Sep; daily 9:30AM-noon, 3-6PM, 16 Sep-31 May. Via Veneto 27

21 Hotel Alexandra $$ Experience the old-world turn-of-the-century ambiance of high ceilings and creaking polished wood in the 50 large rooms at upper-middle prices near the bottom of the city's best-address street. ♦ Via Veneto 18. 461943

21 Hotel Imperiale $$ Similar in style and price to its neighbor, Hotel Alexandra. One of these 2 was a former bordello—the game is to figure out which one. Eighty-four rooms. ♦ Via Veneto 24. 4756351

22 Beauty-3 Aldo, Alvaro, Franco and their team can dress your hair, paint your nails, and wax your legs to ivory smoothness. A fast and fairly inexpensive emporium where you don't normally need an appointment. (Some hotels have hairdressers; that can be an advantage when they are open on Monday.) If you want a quick shampoo and set, drop in here and they'll take care of you immediately. There's even someone who speaks pidgin English! Beauty products and perfumes are on sale at the entrance. ♦ Tu-Sa 9:30AM-7PM. Via Veneto 34A (Via San Isidoro 3, one flight over the bar) 4743650

23 Caffè delle Nazioni $ For a real cheapy, stop here for pizza (even at lunch), pasta, and beer on tap. Also a tourist menu of sandwiches, ice cream, and coffee. Sit outdoors with the tourists when it's warm, or inside with the employees from the adjacent headquarters of Italy's richest bank, BNL, and biggest industrial group, IRI. ♦ Via Veneto 97. No credit cards

24 American Embassy and Consulate General (1886, **Gaetano Koch**) The embassy itself has become a fortress, but you can line up to enter the Consulate General in the separate pavilion further up the Via Veneto just before the intersection of Via Boncompagni. Between the 2 is the **USIS** library. The library has recent US magazines and newspapers as

Via Veneto

well as reference books—all intended for serious research. The Consulate General is where you hope to replace your stolen or strayed passport, but don't bother to go without a couple of suitably sized photographs obtainable just up the street at **Daisy's** in the courtyard of Via Veneto 183. (To support your insurance claim you should also get from the Rome police, with the help of your hotel concierge, a certificate in which you declare your loss.) For passport or any notarial service you will need identity documents to show who you are, as well as dollars or lire to cover these fairly expensive transactions. The Consulate General's office of American Services will cheerfully help US citizens in cases of emergency, but don't bother to ask for a handout, the baseball scores, or travel advice. Try American Express or phone home collect.

The main embassy building is called **Palazzo Margherita** in honor of **Queen Margaret of Savoy**, who moved here from the royal Quirinale Palace in 1900 right after the assassination of her husband, **King Umberto I**—the son of United Italy's first monarch and a contemporary of **Prince Ludovisi**, who had the palace built a dozen years earlier. The merry widow animated Rome for 26 more years, making Palazzo Margherita a center of pomp and national glory. (She revered and befriended **Mussolini**.) After the Queen's death, the palazzo became an office building, and at the end of World War II it became the US Embassy to Italy. There is a separate US Embassy to the Holy See near the Vatican. ♦ Via Veneto 119A (Consulate, Via Veneto 123) 46741

25 Hotel Ambasciatori Palace $$$ Among the 9 luxury-class hotels. A real palace (145 rooms), but somehow maintains a personal atmosphere because of the easy accessibility of the front desk. The 1920s elegance is at its zenith in the series of frescoes by **Guido Cadorin** showing the smart set of those times at play. To emulate them, join the in-group at the small but animated bar, or eat at the **Grill Bar ABC**. ♦ Deluxe ♦ Via Veneto 70. 473831; fax (same as phone)

Within the Hotel Ambasciatori Palace:
Grill Bar ABC ★★$$$ Go in either right opposite the American Embassy gate or through the Ambasciatori Hotel, of which this is the appropriately luxurious restaurant. Modern Italian design provides a distinctive background for an important banquet—business or pleasure. It's best in summer when the restaurant moves upstairs to a quiet terrace suspended over the graceful Via Veneto. Refined menu and service. Lavish choice of fine wines, including a *Brunello di Montalcino* that can stand up to the best Bordeaux—but it's not given away. ♦ Via Veneto 66. 4740950

26 La Residenza $ In a quiet street one block from the Via Veneto, this small attractive villa/hotel is a favorite spot for US diplomatic families newly assigned to the nearby embassy. You can get a good-size room with a TV and minibar, and perhaps even a balcony on which to replenish your tan. No restaurant, but that is a good inducement to scour Pasta City. Continental breakfast is included in the modest price, and the breakfast buffet table is famous. No pets. ♦ Via Emilia 22. No credit cards. 4744480

27 Eden Hotel $$$ This upscale hotel, part of the very British **Trust House Forte** chain, offers all the amenities expected at a deluxe establishment. Ideally located halfway between Via Veneto and the Spanish steps, it has a breathtaking view from the roof terrace. Go up there for drinks at the charming and well-managed bar, where you can sit outside when it's warm, and stay for dinner at the adjoining dining room. One hundred ten rooms. No pets. ♦ Deluxe ♦ Via Ludovisi 49. 4742401; fax 4821584

Within the Eden Hotel:
Roof Garden ★★$$$ This used to be called **The Penthouse** but was renamed since too many lonely men came here expecting to find a bunny club. They must have been comforted to find the good food and the enjoyable view. Excellent pasta and fresh vegetables and fish. Just think of yourself as being in the Garden of Eden. ♦ Closed Saturday, Sunday. No credit cards. 4743351

MARCELLO

28 Marcello ★★★$$ The best quality-to-price ratio within 2 blocks of Via Veneto, and perhaps the Roman restaurant that is most imaginative in appealing in appealing to the eye as well as the palate. Gnocchi on Thursday—the specialty of the day all over Rome—comes on a large oval dish with a mouth-watering veal roast and fresh vegetables; we dare you to get through it all. The lowly *baccalá*, a Roman specialty of salted codfish, is transformed into a sophisticated antipasto by the addition of miniature raisins, pine nuts, tomatoes, and chickpeas. Try steak *à l'orange* or risotto with red wine. The crystal is handsome, the house white wine is frequently sparkling and dry, the summer desserts include Marcello's improvement

---

Restaurants/Clubs: Red   **Hotels:** Blue
Shops/Parks: Green   **Sights/Culture:** Black

on the ice-cream sundae, served in an enormous snifter with fresh fruit and no artificial flavoring. This is one of the rare restaurants where you should put yourself entirely in the hands of the host; Marcello will not try to run up your bill. He is also learned about the history and archeological wonders of his city. He calls this establishment an *osteria* (hostelry), implying that it is an unpretentious eatery for the locals. Don't you believe it. Since there are only a dozen tables inside, plus a half-dozen outside in good weather, do reserve. ♦ Closed Sunday. Via Aurora 37. Reservations recommended. 4759467

29 Café de Paris ★$$$ Closer to the newspaper and magazine stands than Doney's, and the waiters are more attentive. Inside you can sit in an elegant snack bar and have tea or lunch for only twice the going rate. Try the excellent *frullato di frutta* (fresh-fruit shake). ♦ M-Tu, Th-Su 8:30AM-1AM. Via Veneto 90. 465284

29 Regina Carlton $$ Yes, there is a plush palace shining in the middle of the Via Veneto for those who prefer intimate hotels. It is small enough so that the concierge will remember who you are, yet large enough (134 rooms) so that he will not watch to see if you are sneaking nonregistered guests into your room. This is one of the few hotels that will accommodate a passerby who drops in just to make a phone call; elsewhere the reply is always that there is a coin booth on the street (although it is either inoperative or there is a queue). ♦ Via Veneto 72. 476851; fax 485483

30 Doney's ★$$ After its recent refurbishing Doney's looks more like Doney's than ever. **Hemingway** is gone but there is room for a few more Americans among the North African businessmen who make this sunny street café their Rome headquarters. Or go indoors and choose among a tearoom, a restaurant, and a coffee bar. Use of the glistening restroom is absolutely free. ♦ Tu-Su 8AM-2AM. Via Veneto 145. 493405

31 Hotel Excelsior $$$ (1911, **Otto Mariani**) Architecturally the most imaginative of Rome's great hotels. With its minaret towering over the central point of the Via Veneto, it naturally became the mecca for Hollywood stars in the 1950s. The marble-and-gold-festooned upper lobby, leading to an attractive bar, is a little more commercial then that of the impeccable Grand Hotel 5 blocks away, which is the other Rome showplace of the leading Italian chain, **CIGA**. Since the **Aga Khan** bought CIGA in the mid '80s, the Excelsior has been embellished room-by-glorious room. So take a modernized suite or an old-fashioned single and you won't be disappointed. Barber, coiffeuse, and photographer on the premises. Pets accepted. ♦ Via Veneto 125. 4708; fax 4756205

Within the Hotel Excelsior:

La Cupola ★★$$$$ Nouvelle cuisine in a late 19th-century aspidistra setting. Your spaghetti will come with tomato, sweet olive, and caper sauce, your noodles with lamb and sweet peppers, your macaroni with sausage, mushrooms, and black truffles. What more do you want? Whatever it is, they probably have it. ♦ Via Veneto 125. Reservations required. 4708

32 Jackie O' Just for nostalgic reasons, go to this nightclub left over from the days when there was still something elegant about nightclubs. ♦ Cover. Daily 11PM-3:30AM. Via Boncompagni 11. 461401

33 George's ★★$$$$ If you go for snobbism, come here. We would give high marks to the

Via Veneto

piano bar for an after-dinner treat. This is one of the famous hot spots that opened after World War II. It catered to the swanky and titled international set that elbowed its way through the Dolce Vita and the riffraff on Via Veneto. Dining here helped them avoid the photographers, at least until they finished eating. Miraculously, they still exist, sitting around candlelit tables on the garden terrace sipping Dom Perignon and being served flaming dishes by impeccable *camerieri* in white-tie and tails. The specialties are a delicious sliced raw steak called *carpaccio*, salad *alla Morra*, and crème brûlée for dessert. ♦ Closed Sunday and August. Via Marche 7. Reservations required. 484575, 4745204

34 Girarrosto Fiorentina ★★$$$ Another star of the restaurant street open late for the theater crowd. The T-bone steaks are the same as at the nearby **Girarrosto Toscana**, but here the atmosphere is more elegant and demure. ♦ Closed Friday. Via Sicilia 44. Reservations recommended. 460660

34 Zi Umberto ★★★$ This is another unpretentious mom-and-pop pasta shop where you won't go wrong. **Elena** and **France Paoletti** pride themselves on the game they serve during the hunting season, and on generally sticking to seasonal food in all other domains as well. Follow their advice, particularly for pasta with meat or game sauce. The house white wine is Verdicchio, which is very spiffy-o! ♦ Closed Sunday. Via Sicilia 150. No credit cards. 464519

Roman law requires menus to indicate whether fish is fresh or frozen.

34 Piccolo Abruzzo ★★$$ Still the same attractive place but no more pasta-mania. Elegant cooking, delicious pasta, and a serene atmosphere. If you're in need of a hotel, give the **Spring House Hotel** a call (Via Mocenigo 7-00192 Roma, 3020948)—it is owned by the

Via Veneto

proprietor of **Piccolo Abruzzo**. ♦ Closed Sunday. Via Sicilia 237. Reservations recommended. 4820176

35 Giovanni ★★★$$$ The glorious cuisine of the Marche region, on the Via Marche. Despite its elegant formality and distinguished cuisine, this is just a family affair. **Giovanni Sbrega** still takes care of the swarms of serious eaters with the help of his wife, son, daughter, and nephew. They give you the best of family cooking. The great specialties are lentil soup Castellucio and tiny grilled Adriatic squid (*calamaretti*). Book well in advance for Friday's fish, and don't ask if it's fresh because you just might hurt their feelings. *Of Course It's Fresh!* You can also trust their wine suggestions. ♦ Closed Friday night, Saturday. Via Marche 64. 493576

raphael salato

36 Raphael Salato Real pros claim that shoes are the only thing to buy on Via Veneto. Certainly Raphael is high on quantity since there are 3 shops within a block of each other (and another at Piazza di Spagna 34), and the quality of the shoes, bags, and leather goods is high. **Raphael Junior** for spoiled kids (Via Veneto 98,465692). ♦ Via Veneto 104 and 149. 493507, 484677

37 Mandarin ★★$$ Taiwanese food in a stylish setting. The rare Chinese restaurant where you can always get steamed dim sum dumplings as well as the fried variety. Rice noodles for the pasta-starved Italians you may wish to invite here for a different but tony dinner. Don't get into an argument about whether Marco Polo brought the ravioli and spaghetti back from, or out to, China. Just concentrate on the superb tofu *ma po* and chicken *cartoccio* (in a bag). Quality is high, but they skimp a bit on portions and courtesy. Half-

hearted muzak goes *diddly-diddly*. ♦ Closed Monday. Via Emilia 85. 4755577

38 Andrea ★★$$ A standard smart restaurant—short on charm and long on lire. The food is good, and if you want modern elegance and are in the neighborhood, you won't go wrong. Andrea also runs the trattoria across the street. ♦ Closed Sunday. Via Sardegna 28. 493707

38 La Cupella ★$$ Don't believe those guidebooks that describe this spotless trattoria/pizzeria as a later addition to the **Andrea Restaurant** across the street. In fact, La Cupella is the original restaurant founded by the grandfather of the present Andrea who runs it along with his brother. Their parents, **Aldo** and **Francesca**, run the more elegant Andrea, but it was a later addition to the family holdings. The cuisine is typical of the Abruzzi region: down to earth, hearty food. From the grill, try Abruzzo sausages or little tender lamb chops that seem more like goat ribs. Grilled Abruzzo cheese can fill you up as can that delicious spiced, unleavened bread they put on the table hot from the grill. ♦ Closed Monday. Via Sardegna 39. 493805

39 Girarrosto Toscano ★★$$$ At the end of an exhausting day studying Roman folkways, treat yourselves to dinner in this bustling cellar. The price is high because you are here to eat a gigantic T-bone steak from the roaring grill, laced with Chianti and topped off with assorted ice creams (*gelati misti*). It's good solid fare and you will enjoy looking at the others looking at you. But what you don't realize when they pass out those little hors d'oeuvres (antipasti) you didn't order is that they are not on the house. And even now that you know you won't be able to resist the delicious little mozzarella eggs, the Tuscan salami, the prosciutto with melon, the omelets, and meatballs. Dinner served until 1AM. ♦ Closed Wednesday. Via Campania 29. 493759

40 Flora $$$ (1900) Technically, it does not rate deluxe, but for our money it is better than some that do. Best location, at the very top of the Via Veneto, just through the Aurelian wall from the Villa Borghese park. Built on generous lines, it offers big old-fashioned rooms for big new-fashioned prices. Both public and private rooms are elegant and inviting. Ideal for a love affair, except for the dining room, which is functional rather than romantic. There is even a somewhat old-fashioned hairdressing salon for madame, mademoiselle, or even monsieur. One hundred seventy-six rooms. No pets. ♦ Via Veneto 191. 497821; fax 4820359

41 Fotouno One-hour photo developing and printing, under American management. Located in the long passage to the Metro station that you enter on the corner of Via Veneto and Via di Porta Pinciana.

The design of **Villa Borghese** was based on the design of classical Roman villas.

41 Harry's Bar ★★$$$ No relation to Venice's best, except you can start with a delicious glass of champagne laced with fruit juice. It is one of those deep-mahogany-colored wood places with tables a couple of yards apart, which is supposed to make you think of a London club. It does make for easier conversing than most Roman trattorias, which could use some soundproofing on their high masonry walls and ceilings. **Desideri** is the name of the maître d'hôtel, and he will tend to your desires. The fresh scampi curry on white rice and the osso buco on saffron rice are 2 outstanding choices. Fine wines, even the house white. *People Magazine*'s Rome correspondent **Logan Bentley** comes for the only great iced tea in Rome. ◆ Closed Monday and May. Via Veneto 150. Reservations required for dinner. 4745832

42 Eliseo Hotel $$ Member of the **Best Western** chain. Ask for a room overlooking the gardens of the French Academy—or at least go up to the rooftop restaurant for one of the most unforgettably romantic views of Rome since **Hubert Robert** painted these same towers of the Villa Medici seen through the soaring trees. Fifty rooms. ◆ Via di Porta Pinciana 30. 460556; fax 4819629

43 Porta Pinciana (AD 403) This monumental travertine gate dates from the time of **Emperor Honorius** at the beginning of the 5th century. It breaches the famous Aurelian walls that have surrounded Rome for 17 centuries, having been started by the **Emperor Aurelian** in AD 271 and finished within a decade by one of his successors, **Emperor Probus**. At the height of the Empire in the 2nd century AD, the Romans boasted that the Walls of Rome were in Syria, England, and Spain. Soon, however, pressures from the Barbarians (north), vandals (south), and many others forced Rome to finally build a mighty wall around the nucleus of the civilized world, at the very heart of it—the white-marble city of Rome. When Rome became the capital of United Italy (1870) the progressive elements wanted to make the city modern and the first thing their eyes lit upon was that crumbling old wall. Let's give Rome a spanking new image, no more ruins, was their attitude. In this vein, they cut down the 100-year-old trees in the great gardens of the palaces that became municipal property (see page 88), pushed through the embankments on either side of the river, and nearly tore down the Aurelian Walls. They were stopped by an Italian painter/ceramicist and his French wife. These 2, with their family, squatted in this part of the wall and garnered so much public support that the municipality finally gave in. The couple's descendants still live in cramped quarters in the wall 2 blocks from here and continue the tradition started by their famous ancestor, who discovered the secret of making the black paper-thin pottery that the ancient Etruscans perfected; an art form that was lost for over 1500 years.

44 Borghese Gardens In Italian always called *Villa Borghese*—the word *villa*, meaning a park or country estate to which the princely owner would escape for a few hours of relaxation. The main building on the estate is called the casino, which literally means little house, and only later took on the connotation of gambling pavilion since that was one of the favorite means of relaxation for the gents. This vast park (6 kilometers, or almost 4 miles in perimeter) was originally acquired and laid out at the beginning of the 17th century by **Cardinal Scipione Borghese** when his uncle became **Pope Paul V**. (The word *nepotism* means

nephewism and originated in Rome, where the popes, usually lacking legitimate offspring, took good care of their nephews who, at literally any age, could be elevated to cardinal and endowed with palaces and works of art for the eternal glory of the family.) While you are jogging around Rome's major public park, you can complete this language lesson by considering how inappropriate even the name Borghese is, since in Italian it means middle class, and there was never anything bourgeois about that family. Don't miss the bird-cage house near the casino, and the **Piazza di Siena** (named after the Borghese hometown), where international horse shows are held in the spring.

Within the Borghese Gardens:

Borghese Museum and Gallery. (1614, **Giovanni Vasanzio**) Cardinal Scipione Borghese had this built (on the eastern side of the gardens) to show off his magnificent ancient statues. That collection was shipped off to the Louvre by **Napoleon** when his sister **Pauline** married **Prince Camillo Borghese**, who in return received an estate in Northern Italy where he could contemplate the racy life his wife was leading back in Rome. The current sculpture collection was started by **Francesco Borghese** soon after Camillo's death and occupies the ground-floor "museum." The upper floor is called the Gallery because it contains the paintings Cardinal Scipione Borghese collected, which hung in the gallery of the family palazzo (see page 79). The Cardinal, whose exquisite taste in art places him high among the world's greatest collectors, is well represented as a bon vivant in 2 portrait sculptures in the central room upstairs—by Rome's most ubiquitous genius, **Gian Lorenzo Bernini**, whom Scipione seems to have discovered. Two centuries later the great sculptor was **Antonio Canova** (1757-1821), and he produced the most exciting marble downstairs representing the other leading member of the Borghese clan, **Pauline Bonaparte**, in a characteristically dissolute pose—as the nude Venus, goddess of love. When you can finally pull yourself away from Pauline, admire the sculptures Bernini did while still in his 20s. In successive rooms are his *David* (compare the Baroque excitement here with the Renaissance calm of **Michelangelo**'s more famous work in Florence), *Apollo and Daphne*, and the *Rape of Persephone*. Upstairs in the picture gallery you will immediately come upon 2 gorgeous **Raphaels**, his *Deposition* (1507) and *Lady with Unicorn*. The central room contains 4 of **Caravaggio**'s finest paintings, including the *Madonna of the Serpent* (1605) as well as a sexy *Diana* (1618) by **Domenichino**. In the last room is **Titian**'s world-famous *Sacred and Profane Love* (1512) as well as a fine Venetian painting, *Virgin and Child*, by **Giovanni Bellini**, and the Sicilian **Antonello da Messina**'s *Portrait of a Man*—whose self-

Via Veneto

assured, enlightened look seems to sum up the transition from the 16th to the 17th centuries, which is what Scipione Borghese's museum is all about. Only 25 people are allowed in every half-hour, but in the afternoon there's never a wait. The upper floor is temporarily closed for remodeling—date of reopening unknown. To inquire, phone 858577. ♦ Admission. M, Su 9AM-1PM; Tu-Sa 9AM-7PM

Villa Giulia National Museum (1553, Vignola) Also known as either the **Villa di Papa Giulio**, since **Pope Julius III** had it built, or the **Etruscan Museum**, since it now houses the world's greatest collection of art and artifacts from that enigmatic pre-Roman civilization. This pleasure dome, built by a fun-loving pontiff who enjoyed classical sculpture, has been turned into one of the greatest exhibitions of Etruscan masterpieces in the world. Pope Julius was in every sense a Renaissance man and he consulted the greatest artists of the time, including **Michelangelo**, about how to convert his small house on this site into a magnificent villa in the contemporary Renaissance style. Its highpoint is the inner courtyard, where the garden intersects with the building and culminates in a nymphaeum, or outdoor living/dining area, inspired by ancient Roman architecture. Pope Giulio spent a mint on this place so he could bring boatloads of friends upriver from the Vatican to spend the day idly enjoying all the beauty nature and man could offer. It serves this purpose well.

Although some mysteries about the Etruscans still exist today, their way of life is extensively illustrated in the wall paintings and artifacts found in thousands of their tombs. From the 9th to the 4th century BC the Etruscans built their centers of civilization in the area roughly between present-day Florence and Rome. They were, in fact, the first inhabitants of Rome and drained the swamp that became the Roman Forum. Early kings of Rome were Etruscan and the artistic heights reached by these superb people can be seen from even a brief visit to Papa Giulio's.

In the first rooms of the museum's ground floor you will see bronze replicas of the round and oval huts of the Early Etruscan period. These were used as urns to contain the ashes of the dead, who were buried, like the Egyptian pharaohs, surrounded by their most prized possessions. In the 9th room are the stars of the show, the lifelike *Bride and Bridegroom* in terra cotta. Lying happily atop their own burial casket, they are apparently enjoying themselves at their own funeral banquet. There is something so tender and loving about this handsome young couple that one almost forgets that—as with much of Etruscan art—death, or perhaps life after death, is the major theme. On your way to the slightly morbid banquet, don't miss the sculptures of Hercules and Apollo, also in earthenware, which originally adorned a temple roof. All of these are from the 6th century BC and are surprisingly realistic and lively.

As you wander and wonder through the superb ground floor and somewhat less interesting upper floor you will get an impression of the intensely domestic life of the Etruscans as shown in their cooking instruments, mirrors, and eating utensils. Many of the vases, black and shiny with beautiful modern-looking paintings running around them, were imported by the Etruscans from Greece. Some are Etruscan copies with pornographic subjects. Still others have covers with handles representing animals or humans. These are exquisite male and female forms, some of them of athletes obviously participating in sports—which Etruscan men and women did together. In fact, women must have had an enviable place in Etruscan society, almost on a par with their men. The *Bride and Bridegroom* sculpture was considered shocking in later times because the Romans would never have shared their banquet couch with their wives. An Etruscan temple, reconstructed outdoors, shows how richly painted their buildings apparently were. Highly recommended. Snack bar. ♦ Admission. Tu, Th-Sa 9AM-2PM; W 9AM-2PM, 3-7:30PM; Su, holidays 9AM-1PM. Piazza Villa Giulia 9. 3601961

Architectural Terms

Atrium The central hall of a Roman house—usually open-air.

Architrave In classical architecture, the part resting on the capitals of the columns. Also the molding around a door.

Column types: (see page 49)

    Doric The most simple, unadorned—and the earliest.

    Ionic With 2 swirls on either side like a ram's horns

    Corinthian Rather busy, with acanthus leaves.

Capitals Tops of columns.

Convex A form that is curved or rounded outward, like a segment of the exterior of a sphere.

Concave A form that is curved or rounded inward, like a segment of the interior of a hollow sphere.

Ogee A pointed arch having on each side near the apex a reversed curve. Also a molding with an S-shaped profile.

Pediment A triangular space forming the gable of a 2-pitched roof.

Putti Two or more cherubs.

Conservation

The Conservation of Rome's Ancient Monuments, or Why Are All Those Monuments Covered?

Adriano La Regina
Archaeological Superintendent of Rome

The great marble monuments of Rome are decaying at a rapid pace as the result of a chemical change that takes place (transforms and finally destroys their surface) when they come in contact with the polluted city air.

The irreversible process of chemical transformation takes different forms, depending on how the various components combine and interact, but in any case, the final result is that the marble surfaces turn to plaster. Each layer of plaster disintegrates as soon as it becomes exposed, due to the disappearance of the preceding surface.

The current state of scientific knowledge does not provide the possibility of permanently restoring the marble monuments in the sense of preventing any future recurrence of this decay. There is no definitive cure, only the possibility of curbing the process within certain limits through operations that are as meticulous as those performed on paintings.

Experimental operations have already been carried out on several monuments, such as the architrave of the Temple of Romulus in the Roman Forum and the Trajan frieze of the Arch of Constantine. The columns of Trajan and of Marcus Aurelius, the arches of Septimius Severus and of Constantine, and the Temple of Saturn are partially or completely covered with scaffolding, which is needed to carry out the work. It also serves the important function of protecting them from rain, heat, and wind. This scaffolding has changed the appearance of Rome, but it is unavoidable and will be present for some years. In partial compensation, these scaffolds enable scholars to climb up to study the sculptural elements on the surface of the monuments.

The first step in cleaning is the careful, manual removal of layers of detritus, powder, smog, and in some cases, material previously applied in misguided attempts at restoration. This meticulous work is necessary before the experts can even start consolidating the surfaces and protecting them with water-repellent products. In the future, this must be followed by regular maintenance work, including inspection, cleaning, and other processes to impede further formation of dirt, as well as the constant application of protective substances and the mounting of temporary or seasonal structures to afford protection against the elements.

All these forms of direct protection are, of course, insufficient without a program to reduce the sources of pollution. Regulations must be adopted to modify the city's heating installations and auto exhausts. Rome does not have a serious industrial pollution problem, but a more rational urban traffic plan must be adopted to reduce the devastating effect of public and private transportation. Traffic in the center of Rome must be largely eliminated, a process that requires assigning different functions to various urban sectors—part of an overall, organic vision and a radical shift in how we look at and use the Eternal City.

Giorgio Pavone

Rome is over 2000 years old, and you feel its history when:

Walking in the **Roman Forum**.

Seeing the **Circo Massimo**, where 250,000 people jammed to watch the chariots race.

Admiring the remains of **Claudius' Aqueduct**, which brought water to Rome, not only for drinking but also to fill the swimming pools and the Roman baths of the Imperial City.

Visiting **Ostia Antica** and realizing that the method for heating the Roman villas was by far superior to that of today's—instead of our radiators, they had double walls through which steam passed giving a uniform heat to the 4 walls.

Thinking of the turning doors that closed their public baths in order not to be seen from outside and in the meantime not to let the cold get in.

Thinking of the peak of civilization Rome had reached 20 centuries ago. I really feel proud of being Roman-born, and you can appreciate the famous phrase that Roman citizens used to utter when in need: *Noli me tangere, cives Romanus sum* (do not touch me, I am a Roman citizen).

Rome's nightlife has an intimate style. Here are a few restaurants, discos, and nightclubs that are not touristy:

La Graticola, located at Via Boncompagni 11, just around the corner from the Via Veneto, is an excellent restaurant with particularly good Italian food. Maître d' Reider (pronounced *Rider*) will meet all your requests.

L'Augustea, Via della Frezza 5—it looks like a garage but you meet lots of people on Sunday night.

Dal Bolognese, Piazza del Popolo 1.

Il Matrociano, Via dei Gracchi 55, also crowded on Sunday night.

At the same address (they all belong to the same owner, Beatrice Iannozzi) are the world-famous **Jackie O'** disco and **Prive**, a piano bar. The first has been a must of Roman nightlife for many years, while the second is for more relaxed people who want to enjoy drinks and food without being deafened by noisy music.

For younger people I suggest **Histeria**, Via Giovanelli 3, managing director Carmelo di Ianni. The crowd starts to arrive after midnight. This is a disco where the music reaches the highest peaks.

Also in this group but much bigger, the **Acropolis** (Via G. Schiaparelli 29).

In imitation of Dante—the **Inferno** disco and the **Olympus** restaurant.

Olympo, Piazza Rondanini 16, is a bar owned by Andrea Pugliese. It has become a must for people who want to have a drink and a chat in a pleasant atmosphere before going to bed.

via dei Fori Imperiali

(Street of the Imperial Forums) is one of the only streets in the dead-center of Rome to have been built in the age of the automobile. However, this is not the only reason for its exceptional width. In 1932, the Italian dictator **Benito Mussolini** wanted to be able to see the **Colosseum** from his office balcony in the Palazzo Venezia, and he wanted a place to stage his pompous military parades. He ordered the demolition of all medieval and Renaissance churches and palaces standing in the direct line from **Piazza Venezia** to the Colosseum. When Hitler came to Rome, he and Mussolini could review the Italian troops from temporary grandstands on this street. Mussolini named the boulevard *Via del Impero* in honor of his fascist empire.

Fortunately, many monuments that celebrate the earliest achievements of Roman civilization have survived—some wholly intact, others with only vestiges of their grandeur. Systematic excavations of the **Palatine**, one of Rome's Seven Hills, were initiated in 1724 by **Francis I of Parma**, who inherited the **Villa Farnese**. Through his efforts, the **Domus Flavia** was uncovered. Other buildings were excavated under **Napoleon III** in 1860, including **Tiberius' Palace**, **Livia's House**, and the **Temple of Apollo**. The Palatine was home to the early emperors as they all built imperial palaces here.

Although in 1985 permission was granted to begin excavation under the part of the gardens that line the street, two-thirds of **Julius Caesar's Forum** and all of the **Emperor Nerva's Forum** still lie buried beneath.

On a wall along the street, on the right-hand side near the Colosseum, are 4 maps that show the extent of the Roman Empire at different periods in history.

1 San Clemente Perhaps the only church guaranteed to interest everyone. Several early Roman churches were built on temples of earlier religions or superimposed on earlier churches, but San Clemente takes the layer-cake. Under one roof, it offers 3 successive places of Christian worship built between the 1st and 12th centuries with a rather special pagan temple beneath the 3. Capsulized in one place, layer by layer, is the architecture and art of almost the entire Christian era, as well as a place where the Romans worshipped the Persian god Mithras—another imported religion.

(The Romans built temples to all sorts of different gods—to hedge their bets.)

Enter the 11th-century church from the side door on **Via San Giovanni in Laterano**, where the 18th-century Baroque additions are the first thing you see. In the center of the nave, looking like a low-sided roofless box, is a dainty marble choir enclosure, some of whose columns came from **Trajan's Forum**; this lovely white frame, dating from the 6th century, was moved up here a thousand years ago from its previous location in the original 4th-century church below. The canopy over the high altar was also brought upstairs from the older church. Its anchor design is connected to the martyrdom of **St. Clement**, the fourth pope, and probably a converted Jew. He was held responsible for making too many other converts, so Trajan banished him to the Crimea early in the 2nd century. He continued his subversive religious activities there and was thrown into the Black Sea with an anchor tied to him. When the water miraculously receded, his body was recovered by his converts and eventually brought to Rome for burial. Most magical of all is the hemispherical dome above, which glistens with a green, blue, red, and gold mosaic. This is late Byzantine, like the one on the facade of Santa Maria in Trastevere (see page 92), and those in Istanbul, Venice, and Ravenna. Notice the elaborate palaces and temples depicted at the opposite ends of this semidome, presumably representing the artist's dream of the Heavenly City (the realization of which he was unconsciously contributing to, right here in the eternal city).

Enter the lower church by purchasing a ticket in the sacristy (opposite the church's entrance) from the Irish Dominican priest on duty; his order was given custody of this church in 1677. Proceed down a flight of steps built in 1857, when **Father Mullooly** began excavating the older church. Some of the walls in the lower 4th-century church were built to support the newer church when it was under construction 700 years later; the older church was also filled in with rubble for additional support. However, glimpses of the older church's frescoes can be seen at every turn. These have faded badly since the 19th-century excavations, but 3 copies were made at the time and can be seen at the entrance to the stairs. The picture of a woman set in a niche is a 5th-century portrait of either the **Virgin Mary** or the prostitute **Theodora**, who became the empress when she married **Justinian**. The 12th-century fresco on the left wall that recounts an incident in **St. Clement**'s life has the first inscription to be written in Italian rather than Latin.

Near the bust of **Cardinal O'Connell** of Boston, who in 1912 collected funds to drain the flooded lower level, is the entrance for de-

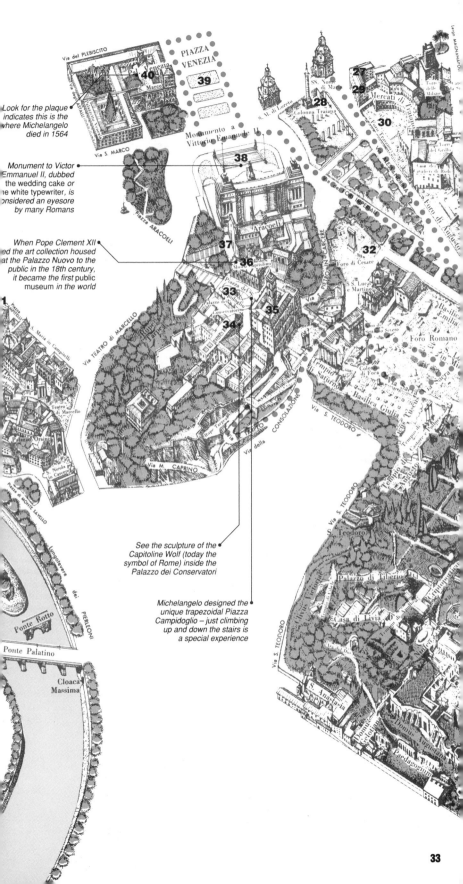

Look for the plaque indicates this is the where Michelangelo died in 1564

Monument to Victor Emmanuel II, dubbed the wedding cake or the white typewriter, *is considered an eyesore by many Romans*

When Pope Clement XII ed the art collection housed at the Palazzo Nuovo to the public in the 18th century, it became the first public museum *in the world*

See the sculpture of the Capitoline Wolf (today the symbol of Rome) inside the Palazzo dei Conservatori

Michelangelo designed the unique trapezoidal Piazza Campidoglio – just climbing up and down the stairs is a special experience

PIAZZA VENEZIA

Via del PLEBISCITO

Via S. MARCO

Piazza ARACOELI

Monumento a Vittorio Emanuele II

Aracoeli

SS. Nome di Maria

S. M. di Loreto

Colonna Traiana

Mercati di

Foro di Traiano

Casa dei cavalieri di Rodi

Foro di Cesare

S. Luca e Martino

Foro Romano

Basilica Emilia

Tempio di Saturno

Colonne di Foca

Basilica Giulia

Via TEATRO di MARCELLO

Teatro di Marcello

Palazzo Orsini

S. Maria in Campitelli

S. Nicola in Carcere

Via della CONSOLAZIONE

Via S. TEODORO

Via M. CAPRINO

Lungotevere dei PIERLEONI

Piazza di MONTE SAVELLO

Ponte Rotto

Ponte Palatino

Cloaca Massima

S. Teodoro

Palazzo di Tiberio

Casa di Livia

S. Anastasia

Domus Augustana

Paedagogium

21 40 39 38 37 36 33 35 34 32 30 29 27 28 1

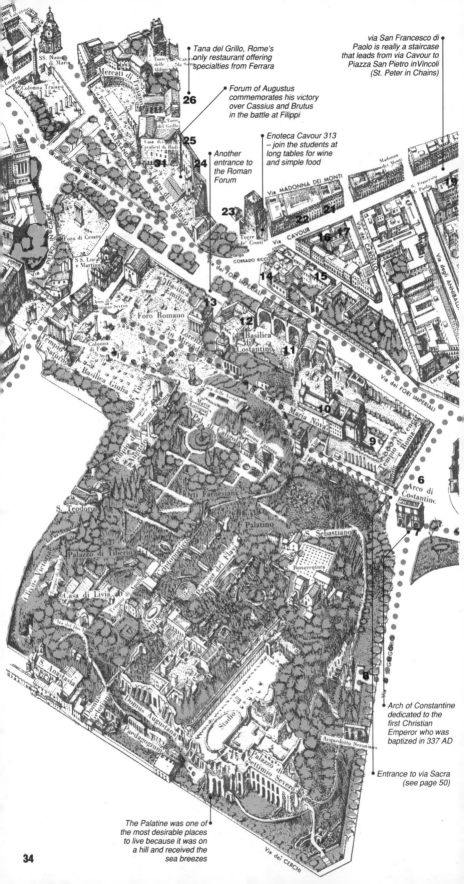

Tana del Grillo, Rome's only restaurant offering specialties from Ferrara

Forum of Augustus commemorates his victory over Cassius and Brutus in the battle at Filippi

Enoteca Cavour 313 – join the students at long tables for wine and simple food

via San Francesco di Paolo is really a staircase that leads from via Cavour to Piazza San Pietro inVincoli (St. Peter in Chains)

26

25

31

24

Another entrance to the Roman Forum

23

22

21

16 17

19

14

15

13

12

11

10

9

6

Arco di Costantino

7

6

8

The Arch of Constantine dedicated to the first Christian Emperor who was baptized in 337 AD

Entrance to via Sacra (see page 50)

The Palatine was one of the most desirable places to live because it was on a hill and received the sea breezes

34

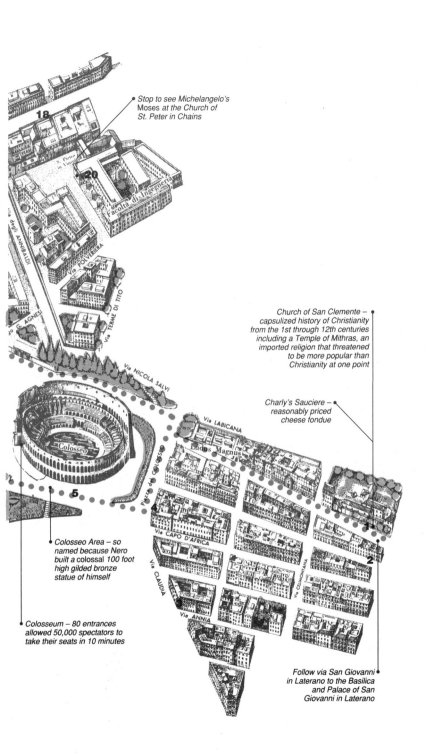

Stop to see Michelangelo's
Moses *at the* Church of
St. Peter in Chains

Church of San Clemente –
capsulized history of Christianity
from the 1st through 12th centuries
including a Temple of Mithras, an
imported religion that threatened
to be more popular than
Christianity at one point

Charly's Sauciere –
reasonably priced
cheese fondue

Colosseo Area – so
named because Nero
built a colossal 100 foot
high gilded bronze
statue of himself

Colosseum – 80 entrances
allowed 50,000 spectators to
take their seats in 10 minutes

Follow via San Giovanni
in Laterano to the Basilica
and Palace of San
Giovanni in Laterano

scending to the **Temple of Mithras**, a religion that the Roman soldiers brought here from the Middle East and that, until it was outlawed in AD 395, threatened to be more popular than Christianity. (Roman legionnaires even built a Mithraic temple in London.) Mithras was a god who sprang from rock. He was ordered by Apollo to kill the bull that symbolized fertility, on the condition that none of the bull's blood be spilled. A scorpion attacked the slain bull and the blood that spilled from the bite brought evil into Apollo's then-perfect world—similar to the snake disturbing the Garden of Eden's bliss. Converts to this religion were sprinkled with blood from a freshly slain bull, and as in the rival religion, Christianity, were promised a better life after death. This temple was later converted into the pri-

Via Dei Fori Imperiali

vate house of **Titus Flavius Clemens**, a cousin of the **Emperor Domitian**.

Stop Press: New Discovery! The other fascination of this church is that it is a perpetual archaeological dig. In 1989, in a spurt of energy, chief digger **Professor Federico Guidobaldi** and his students uncovered more layers of history in the bowels of the basilica. A dozen feet below the present sacristy they found the floor of a 6th-century sacristy where **Pope Gregory I** used to prepare himself for Mass until his death in 604. The floor is a handsome mosaic of colored marble paving blocks intersected by rows of marble hexagons—and next to it is a 6th-century bathroom for His Holiness' use. Even more exciting is a terracotta sarcophagus in a wall niche that dates from the 1st century and contains...human bones. Whose? Watch this space. ♦ Via San Giovanni in Laterano

1 Charly's Sauciere $ Specialty: cheese fondue. Small and pleasant. ♦ Closed Sunday and August. Via San Giovanni in Laterano 268. 736666

2 Tre Scalini ★★$$$ (Not to be confused with the famous ice-cream parlor-cum-restaurant in Piazza Navona.) A contrast exists between the exquisitely restrained nouvelle cuisine portions and the size of the bill. Not exactly traditional Roman fare; however, if your pockets are deep and you have lots of time to kill it may be worth an evening. The restaurant is owned and run by the wife-and-husband team of **Rosanna** and **Matteo**. Fixed-price menu and à la carte. ♦ Closed Monday. Via dei Santi Quattro 30. Reservations required. 732695

3 La Taverna dei 40 ★$ A cooperative operation by young people for young clients. Sometimes slightly chaotic in service. On Tuesday and Friday the pride of the place is fresh fish. ♦ Closed Sunday in winter. Via Claudia 24. 7000550

4 Al Gladiatore ★$$$ Attractive restaurant with indifferent service. So many tomato-based sauces make one wonder what they ate before this discovery came over from the New World. Bottled house wine from Lanuvio. *Bruschetta* (toasted peasant bread with tomatoes, olives, or pâté). *Frutta di mare* (unsalted seafood salad). Outstanding *canolichie alle erbe* (small macaroni in tomato sauce) with 14 herbs that *La Mamma* brews (and keeps secret). The tiramisù is adequate for dessert but the chocolate mousse is too pale to pass the *Marie-France* test that only black is beautiful. In summer you sit on the sidewalk with that superb view of the Colosseum only partially obscured by the rush of Fiats. ♦ Closed Tuesday. Piazza Colosseo 5. 7000533

5 Colosseum The correct and almost forgotten name is the **Flavian Amphitheater**. Construction began in AD 72 by **Vespasian** on the site of **Nero**'s artificial lake, which adjoined his **Golden House**. It was completed in AD 80 under Vespasian's son **Titus**, whose family name was **Flavia**. Titus used Jewish captives from Jerusalem as masons. The Colosseum has 4 stories, the 1st Doric, the 2nd Ionic, the 3rd and 4th Corinthian. This oval covers an area of over 7.5 acres with an exterior circumference of nearly 2000 feet. The height is 150 feet. Most of the huge pockmarks in the facade were caused by removal of iron clamps intended to hold the stones together and as hooks for torches and banners.

The Colosseum had 80 entrances that allowed 50,000 spectators to take their seats in 10 minutes before the starting whistle or trumpet. There were also special gates: one for the emperor's family, one called the Gate of Life for victorious gladiators, one called the Gate of Death for vanquished gladiators. The gladiators' locker room, from which they reached the arena by an underground passage, can be seen in the ruins at the beginning of the nearby Via San Giovanni in Laterano. The wild animals they fought were kept in cages beneath the arena's wooden floor, which was covered with sand (the Latin word for sand is *arena*). The Colosseum's inauguration was comparable to a world's fair and lasted 100 days during which 5000 beasts, mostly imported from Africa, were slain along with many gladiators. The 1000th birthday of Rome's founding was celebrated in AD 249 by 2000 gladiators (many also imported), during which 32 elephants, 10 tigers, 60 tamed lions, 10 giraffes, 40 wild horses, and 6 hippopotamuses were slain. The last gladiatorial combat here was in AD 405. The animals were brought up to the arena level on dozens of rope-pulled elevators so that 100 wild beasts could simultaneously appear in the ring. You can still see the grooves in the elevator shafts. There is no historic proof that early Christians were martyred here as such, but anyone sentenced to death by law could, during intermittent periods, be given the cruel and unusual sentence of being fed to the lions, unless he outsmarted the beasts.

Restaurants/Clubs: Red
Shops/Parks: Green
Hotels: Blue
Sights/Culture: Black

Public executions in Rome were a common spectacle until the 19th century. During the Renaissance, the Colosseum was used as a marble quarry by nouveaux riches families who were putting up their townhouses in Rome. Until the late 18th century, shops, stables, and bricked-in human dwellings filled most of the 80 entrances. The large wooden cross was erected for the 1950 Holy Year.

In the 8th century, for reasons never explained, an English historian called the **Venerable Bede** prophesied *as long as the Colosseum stands, Rome shall stand; when the Colosseum falls, Rome shall fall; when Rome falls, the world shall end.* Subsequent governors of Rome have been busily shoring up the building ever since. For example, many exotic wild plants grew in the crevices of the monument until recently, when they were uprooted

because they were dangerous to the stability of the building. Their seeds were probably brought here in animal feed from the Middle East and Africa, along with the beasts meant for public entertainment and slaughter.

(Until recently, guidebooks recommended visiting the Colosseum by moonlight but modern muggers have put an end to that.) ♦ Tu-Su 9AM-7PM, May-Sep; Tu-Su 9AM-3:30PM, Oct-Apr

6 Colosseum Area Excavations As a result of recent excavations you can see a series of concentric circles made of antique Roman conglomerate on the Roman Forum side of the Colosseum. This is the site of **Meta Sudans**, an ancient fountain that stood here until 1936. Nearby, the hated **Emperor Nero** had a 150-foot-high gilded bronze statue of himself erected. He had it set upright by 12 pairs of elephants. The statue was so large it was called colossal, which gave its name to the Colosseum.

7 Arch of Constantine (315) Rome's largest and best-preserved arch. The Senate dedicated it to **Constantine** when he was emperor for his victory over **Maxentius** at Rome's still extant **Ponte Milvio**. Preservation of the arch was due to the fact that centuries later members of a noble family incorporated it into their fortress. That medieval structure was stripped away in 1804. Constantine's arch is like a museum. Its carvings were stolen from other edifices to give Constantine a worthy and majestic arch. Some of those at the top level are probably from **Trajan**'s arch, and one depicts **Marcus Aurelius**' triumphant return to Rome. Not until you reach the crossbeam stone over one of the 2 smaller lateral arches is there a frieze depicting Constantine addressing the joyful crowd. The artistic quality was so low in the 4th century AD that the arch to the first Christian emperor had to be decorated with figures of Hercules and Apollo plundered from pagan temples. Some of the scenes were originally carved in honor of the **Emperor Hadrian**, and the profile of Constantine's great and good friend **Antinous** can be recognized with binoculars. Constantine was not yet a Christian himself (he was baptized at the end of his life, in 337); however, when the arch was built he declared that the new belief in Christ could coexist with his own belief in Jupiter. The inscription on the arch says the emperor was divinely inspired without saying which god or goddess was then at work.

8 The Palatine One of the **Seven Hills**. This is a real hill rising to 164 feet above sea level and 131 feet above the Forum. (The latter being a marsh that had to be drained.) It was the first of Rome's Seven Hills to be inhabited. The Palatine's height gave it strategic protection from invaders, but perhaps more importantly, it received the sea breezes, making it desirable real estate for more than 1000 years. In Republican times, the nouveaux riches waited for a property owner to die or fall from grace in order to move onto the Palatine. **Augustus** was born here in a simple house, and when he became Rome's first emperor, he wanted to remain in his family home. Pressure, perhaps from his wife, **Livia**, eventually forced him to build the first imperial palace here on the Palatine. (The word *palatine* probably derives from the minor god of shepherds, Pales, and the word and the hill Palatine have given us the word *palace*.) Every emperor after Augustus lived here and most of them, if they lived long enough, added their own new royal palaces; sometimes they demolished the upper parts of older palaces to do so. Even the early kings of Rome chose to live on the Palatine, and when the popes began to acquire more temporal power they lived in the remodeled imperial palaces. In medieval times, the hill and its ruins were partly taken over by monasteries. During the Renaissance, 2 wealthy families, the **Barberini** and the **Farnese**, built summer houses on the hill. In the 16th century, the Farnese went so far as to fill **Tiberius**' palace with rubble and then planted the world's first botanical garden. In the early 19th century the Barberini family refused to let **Pope Pius VII** have **Giuseppe Valadier**, his court architect, restore the **Arch of Titus**, then in danger of collapsing, because it was on their property and they would not tolerate trespassers. In 1860 **Napoleon III** acquired the **Farnese Gardens** and allowed the first excavations.

Aside from offering stupendous views of Rome, the Palatine does not ring as many memory bells for most people as does the Forum, and little is left of its once great palaces. Only the so-called **House of Livia** can be thought to be at least partially intact. With everyone scrambling to build a house on this hill, and then a temple to a deserving god, the ruins stand cheek by jowl sometimes one century on top of another, and the name plates and directional signs are almost nonexistent. Also, because of the layers of building and the many ancient terraces, maps of the Palatine are at best confusing. However, thanks to the lush vegetation, the pine trees, the open spaces, and above all, the views, it is a delightful place for a stroll to try to puzzle it all out. Just a walk through the labyrinths of the Palatine can provide immense pleasure.

Worth trying to find on the Palatine:

Livia's House (Casa di Livia) Below ground level, covered with asbestos-type roofing, 3 smallish rooms with faded wall paintings off a courtyard where the cooking was done. Lead drain pipes bear the stamp of **Julia Aug**(usta); this could have been the **Emperor Augustus'** old family home, not his wife, Livia's.

Cryptoportico A 425-foot-long subterranean tunnel built by **Nero** (near Livia's house) burrowed under **Tiberius'** Palace as a link to all the other imperial palaces. Legend had it that **Caligula** was stabbed in the tunnel.

Temple of Apollo Aziaco Built in 28 BC to celebrate the Roman victory at Anzio in the year 31. Recent excavations have found **Augustus'** imperial palace (36 BC) ruins nearby.

House of Griffins As the oldest house dating from pre-Empire days on the Palatine, it offers some idea of the splendor of Republican Times.

Domus Augustana Not **Augustus'** palace, but one built in **Diocletian's** time for use by any emperor; the name translates as the *House of the August One* and it is located near the Palatine's own museum, the **Antiquarium** (formerly a convent). The part best preserved today is due to its being incorporated in the 16th century into the villa for the **Mattei** family and in the late 19th century into a curious dwelling for an eccentric Scotsman, **Charles Mills**, the last plebian to build a Palatine house.

The Augustana Stadium Located below the Antiquarium, this expanse was built for private family games such as croquet and footraces. The Gothic king, **Theodoric**, used it for horse shows in the 5th century AD.

Temple of Magna Mater Translated as *Temple of the Big Mama*, it was built to honor **Cybele**, who consulted her scrolls of prophecies in 204 BC, enabling the Romans to win a decisive battle in the Punic wars.

The Belvedere A modern term for what may be the best moment of your Palatine walk, as it is the south parapet overlooking the **Circus Maximus**, the biggest horse- and chariot-racing course throughout the Roman Empire. The **Appian Way** began to the left of the Circus, where today the **United Nations' Food and Agriculture Organization** has its headquarters. (It was originally built by **Benito Mussolini** to be his **Ministry for the African Colonies**.) The Circus bleachers are no longer here and the last horse or chariot race was run in the 5th century AD. On the Belvedere you will be standing on what are called the **Severian Arches**, though they were actually first built at the beginning of the 2nd century AD by **Domitian**, who had to artificially expand the Palatine to make room for his palace. Then **Septimius Severus** built the arches higher for

the foundations of his palace. It had a 295-foot-long facade facing the Circus Maximus. The **Imperial Box** was part of the facade, allowing the royal family to watch races or other shows without mingling with the mob. These arches can be seen from the Circus.

The more valuable wall paintings and statues excavated in the last century on the Palatine are housed in the ruins of the **Baths of Diocletian** (see page 144), known today as the **National Museum of Rome**, or **The Terme Museum**. However, it is world-famous for never being open. The lesser but no less endearing objects removed from their Palatine sites (such as the **Paedagogium**, a school for imperial page boys, which has a graffito showing a donkey being crucified with the caption—*Alexamenos worships his god*—

Via Dei Fori Imperiali

poking fun at a new Greek boy who came from a Christian family) have been housed in the Antiquarium, also known to never be open. Entrance for both the Palatine and the Roman Forum is on Via San Gregorio between the Arch of Constantine and the Circus Maximus.
♦ M, W-Sa 9AM-1 hr before sunset; Su 10AM-1 hr before sunset

9 Temple of Venus and Roma Built by **Antoninus Pius** on the **Velia Ridge**—partly bulldozed by Mussolini in 1932 to create his military boulevard—this was the largest temple in Rome, measuring 361 by 174 feet, excluding the terrace facing the Colosseum, which was 426 by 328 feet. It was unique in having 2 facades: one of Venus that faced the Colosseum and one of the goddess Roma that faced the Forum. Some of the 50 columns of the portico were set upright again in 1935. The temple was designed by the **Emperor Hadrian** and ridiculed by the professional architect **Apollodorus of Damascus**, who said that if the 2 giant statues of the goddesses tried to stand up they would crack their skulls on the roof. The temple was built over the site of the vestibule to **Nero's Golden House**, where he put a colossal statue of himself. The Golden House was so large that it stretched up the adjoining Oppio Hill, beyond the Colosseum. Nero was nothing if not Neronic.

10 Santa Francesca Romana or Santa Maria Nova Built in the 10th century to replace **Santa Maria Antiqua**—the new, as always, replacing the old—this structure incorporated an 8th-century oratorio that had been built using part of the temple dedicated to the goddesses Venus and Roma. The bell tower is 12th century and the facade (1615) is the most modern addition to the exterior of this Benedictine church. **Saint Frances**, a Roman woman who founded the Oblate religious order in 1421, has been declared patron saint of automobile drivers, which brings Rome's cab drivers to her church by the thousands for an annual blessing. Her preserved body is exhibited on the 9th of each month.

The interior is mostly Baroque, but there is a bit of almost every century. The painting over the main altar was discovered when a 19th-century painting was being restored and the 12th-century work beneath it emerged. Almost miraculously, beneath that fresco was yet another painting, probably of the 5th century. *Waste not want not* was an early Christian virtue.

For magic fanciers, this church also contains paving stones that bear the imprints of **St. Peter**'s and **St. Paul**'s kneecaps. They were challenged by **Simon Magus**, a leading magician, to a test of levitation. He won the contest, but crashed to earth and was killed. The 2 saints were praying so hard for their own levitation that they dented the stone, a less hazardous trick.

Via Dei Fori Imperiali

11 Basilica of Maxentius After **Constantine** defeated Maxentius, he changed the building to move the main entrance to the Via Sacra in order to put his own colossal statue here for adoration, thus it is also known as the **Basilica of Constantine**. Construction started in AD 306 on what was to be one of the largest covered buildings in the world. The still standing arches, which subsequently inspired Renaissance architects, measure 80 feet by 67 feet by 57 feet. Earthquakes have caused some of the building stones to fall, and in the 7th century a pope removed the gilded bronze roof to decorate the first St. Peter's Basilica (now demolished). Until 1979, summer concerts and movie festivals were held beneath the remaining vaults, now declared unsafe because motor vehicle vibrations have weakened these soaring spheres.

12 Church of Saints Cosmas and Damian Built by **Pope Felix IV** early in the 6th century in the main hall of the **Temple of Peace** (AD 71). Some polychrome-marble pavement of the original temple can be seen behind the church. The vestibule facing the Roman Forum made use of another pagan temple. Today's Franciscan church has some 6th-century mosaics and frescoes as well as a manger scene from the 17th century.

13 Church of San Lorenzo in Miranda This is the closest church to the Roman Forum and was built by incorporating a pagan temple. It is almost always closed.

14 Angelino ai Fori $$$ **Bobby Kennedy** gave a birthday party here for **Ethel** in 1962, and presented her with a Vespa, on which she scooted around the tables. Writer **Curtis Bill Pepper** once considered it the top, but alas and alack it is no longer a culinary Colosseum—except for its location. Being situated at a tourists' transitpoint is a disincentive to quality control. A former US secretary of HEW who was visiting Angelino ai Fori during a recent trip quipped that the angels must have deserted the Forum. Seafood, especially scampi, is the specialty, but never on Monday. Tables outside in summer. ♦ Closed Tuesday. Largo Corrado Ricci 40. 683359, 6791121

15 Convento Occupato (Occupied convent) Built in the 16th century as **Palazzo Rivaldi**, this medieval construction around 2 courtyards is where the holy sisters lived rather well, as there were also orchards and gardens that reached to the Colosseum and the Basilica Maxentius. In the courtyards are vestiges of elaborate grotto fountains and a school for orphans and beggar children. In the 1970s, the convent was occupied by young Communist squatters who were fed up with the city fathers for not giving them space for recreation. The edge of the convent is where the Forum of Peace abutted. ♦ Via del Colosseo 61

16 Su Recreu ★$$ Tucked behind Via Cavour, this restaurant recently changed hands and now has few Sardinian specialties. Antipasto plates delight the eye and whet the appetite. Green vegetables and seafood salads, strangely shaped shellfish, and *carta da musica* (music sheets—hot, crunchy Sardinian-type bread). A welcome pause between exhaustive sightseeing. ♦ Closed Monday. Via del Buon Consiglio 17. 6841507

17 Gamela ★★★$$ *Spaghetti with beaten eggs and browned bacon, fisher style rice, two eggs to be cooked at will, grilled filet of beet, buttered spinach or oil and lemon, house's cakes* (from the English translation on the menu). Our stars should tell you the rest. Come when there is an Italian wedding party, and just follow their choices slavishly. ♦ Closed Monday. Via Frangipane 36. 6786038

18 Palatino $$ This hotel and the Hotel Forum are the only 4-star hotels near this walk. Palatino is a modern utilitarian establishment that opened in 1968. Two hundred ten rooms with all conveniences, including direct-dial phones and other goodies. A bar and restaurant, a souvenir shop, and telex services are available for guests—most of whom are Japanese. ♦ Via Cavour 213. 4814927, 4814711; fax 6799320

19 Via San Francesco di Paolo Also known as the **Salita dei Borgia**, for it is not a street but a staircase leading through a tunnel between **Via Cavour** and **Piazza San Pietro in Vincoli**. The tower in the piazza belonged to the dreaded **Borgia** family, as did the palazzo under which this tunnel passes. It was in the garden of this palace that the beautiful and notorious **Vanozza Cattanei**, mistress of **Pope Alexander VI**—and mother of his illegitimate children, **Lucrezia** and **Cesare Borgia**—gave a dinner on 14 June 1497, which ended in the murder of her only legitimate offspring, the **Duke of Gandia**. Walk briskly and carefully.

Michelangelo tucked away in Moses' flowing beard (seen beneath the lip) and also a vaguer one of his papal patron.

Near the tomb of the **Pollaiuolo** brothers, to the left of the entrance, is a fresco by **Antonio Pollaiuolo** depicting Rome during the 1476 plague. The present church was rebuilt soon after that plague. From the church's porch one can see the tower that was part of a building where the sinister **Borgia** family brewed their poison. The edifice is now the **Central Institute for Art Restoration**. This church is located along one of Rome's Seven Hills, the **Esquiline**, which is topped by the **Church of Santa Maria Maggiore** (St. Mary Major).
♦ Piazza di San Pietro in Vincoli

21 Valentino ★★$ *é un amore!* Simple but very good Roman food with the most unbeat-

Via Dei Fori Imperiali

able price/quality ratio in town. Open house wines, red and white, are good and grapey. No reservations, just wait your turn in the street until **Luciano** comes to seat you and to recommend the surprises **Vicenzo** has for you in the kitchen. Fettucine *alla burina* (literally, peasant pasta), rigatoni *alla norcina* (ridged macaroni with sausage bits and light cream), and *penne maestosa* (peas, mushrooms, and prosciutto) are the delicious specialties here. Also good are sliver of liver on the grill or a *picatina* of veal with lemon. Tripe on Saturday and gnocchi on Thursday make this a basic Roman experience. Mimosa cake or fat millefeuille wind up a memorable feast that may be enjoyed on the sidewalk in summer. ♦ Closed Friday. Via Cavour 293. 461303

22 Enoteca Cavour 313 ★$$ This is a fun place where you join the other students at long tables. Basically for wine but you get food, too. ♦ Closed Saturday lunch and Sunday. Via Cavour 313. 6785496

23 Hotel Forum $$$ A small hotel, elegant and often full. Off the beaten path unless you want to spend your time at the nearby UN Food and Agricultural Organization or playing archaeologist in the Roman Forum across the street. ♦ Via Tor de' Conti 25. 6792446; fax 6799337

Within the Hotel Forum:

Roof restaurant ★★$$$ In the summer, this restaurant is tasty as well as tasteful, with an unforgettable view directly over the imperial forums. Classic Roman food and all the pasta is good. ♦ Reservations recommended. 6792446

24 Marble Works Giulio Benassati cuts, polishes, sculpts, and sells marble, from big tombstones to little earrings. His best are the *intarsia* tables—large and small, multicolored and black-and-white—table tops with geometric designs made by the juxtaposition of different marbles, like a mosaic. Call him *Maestro.* ♦ Via Tor de' Conti 4/A. 6789740

20 St. Peter in Chains (St. Pietro in Vincoli) Best known as the church that contains **Michelangelo**'s statue of **Moses**. According to legend, this is also the site of the Roman law court where **Peter the Fisherman** was condemned to death under **Nero**. Nearly 400 years later the **Empress Eudoxia** came into possession of the prison chains Peter had worn in Rome, and her mother later gave her another set of chains that allegedly had enshackled him in Jerusalem. There was nothing to do but build a shrine worthy of these Christian relics, which are now kept under the main altar. The 20 fluted-marble columns used in the spacious church came from the law court where Peter was sentenced. In 560, the bones of the 7 **Macabees** were brought to Rome from Constantinople and are in a sarcophagus in the church's confession. The spaciousness of this early church probably is due to it being built along the proportions of the pagan law court.

Michelangelo was commissioned by **Pope Julian II** to carve a monumental tomb for him, to be placed in St. Peter's. The *Moses* is the only part of the monument, which was to have 40 statues, that the Florentine sculptor completed before Pope Julian died and the funds were frozen. Julian was still buried in St. Peter's but his grave has a simple stone marker. The *Moses* was meant to be the pinnacle of the tall monument and today is seen out of perspective on its present pedestal. The sculptures of **Rachel** and **Leah**, also by Michelangelo, represent the active and the contemplative life. Moses has been given horns as the artist's way of indicating the rays of light that shone from his head. To modern eyes, the horns may diminish the great majesty of the figure. There is a profile of

Restaurants/Clubs: Red   Hotels: Blue
Shops/Parks: Green   **Sights/Culture:** Black

25 Mario's ★★★$$ Famous for soups (where else do you find cold consommé?) and seafood. In the summer, an attractive young staff brings the open house wine to your outdoor table. The *alici* (whitebait marinated in lemon juice) are so sweet we would have been tempted to give a third star just for this exceptional first course. The spaghetti with seafood cooked in a paper bag confirmed our bias. And the dessert cart with *pinion*-nut cream cake (*torta della nonna*) clinched it. So, even though the mixed salads tend to be too salty, there it is. ◆ Closed Sunday. Piazza del Grillo 9. 6793725.

26 Tana del Grillo $$ Rome's only place offering specialties from Ferrara, even the bread. Near the Trajan market. ◆ Closed Sunday. Salita del Grillo 6B. 6798705

Via Dei Fori Imperiali

27 D.E.S. D'Antimi Photocopying All your office-type needs can be satisfied here, particularly photocopying—color or black-and-white. ◆ Via Foro Traiano 1. 6789059, 6789204

28 Trajan Column Recently restored and cleaned to pristine white, the carvings on this column are among the greatest masterpieces of ancient Rome. Erected in AD 112 to commemorate Emperor Trajan's military victories in Dacia, part of Romania, and Transylvania. Originally a bronze statue of Trajan stood on top but was replaced by one of St. Peter in 1587. The Emperor's ashes were placed in an urn at the foot of the column's 185-step interior spiral staircase. The column stands 131 feet tall and consists of 18 blocks of marble 4 feet high and 11.5 feet in diameter. The sculptor/architect **Apollodorus of Damascus** designed and decorated the column in a series of spiral panels beginning at the bottom as a chronicle of Trajan's military exploits. Some 26,000 figures are carved in the marble and are considered the finest example of Roman sculpture. It has been called the world's first comic strip in marble; the figures were originally painted bright hues like many Roman monuments. Trajan's Greek and Latin libraries stood so close to the column that the artwork at the upper part of the column could also be viewed from their roof gardens. This, and the artistically lesser Marcus Aurelius column, are the only ones still standing where they were built.

29 Ulpia $$$ Mediocre food in a great setting. The young waiters and waitresses—a rarity for Rome!—represent an improvement. Good Aprilia white wine is served out of a barrel in one of the attractive inner rooms painted with Latin inscriptions and Roman centurions' staffs. The fixed-price tourist menu is dependable nursery food. Your fellow diners are either foreigners or out-of-town Italian day-trippers. No Romans come here, so they don't know that the *torta di mandorle* is an almond cake so delicious that it makes up for all the rest. As does the view from the terrace in summer, when you sit overlooking the Basilica Ulpia and Trajan's Forum and Market. ◆ Closed Sunday. Via Foro Traiano 2. 6789980

30 Forum of Trajan This vast rectangle, larger than 4 football fields, had columns running the whole length and breadth. At the center was a gilded statue of the emperor Trajan on horseback. This forum was the latest and the most splendid of the fora. It was designed for Trajan by the imperial architect **Apollodorus of Damascus** in the 2nd century AD. A forum was a meeting place as well as a community center where business was transacted, athletics played, and people strolled under the porticos. Forums were also erected to embellish the city.

The **Basilica** was built to house the judiciary. More magnificent than Trajan's forum, it was covered with costly marble pillars and bas-reliefs. Next came the twin libraries, one for Greek manuscripts, the other for Latin. In a narrow quadrangle between these 2 rose the **Column**—still almost intact today.

In AD 312, when **Constantine**, who was already emperor in the Eastern Mediterranean, entered Rome as conqueror of this half of the Empire and saw the Forum of Trajan for the first time he could not contain his amazement. With uncharacteristic modesty he declared, *I will never be able to construct anything like it.*

Nothing disturbs the nobility of **Trajan's Forum** and **Market**: spacious, supple complexity, a daring sense of line. There were 6 floors in the hemicycle of the marketplace with 150 booths and wine houses, and probably fruit and flowers on the ground floor. The vaulted halls and arcades of the next floor housed oil and wine. Exotic goods such as pepper and spices were on the 3rd and 4th floors. The 5th floor had the offices of public assistance (similar to social security). On the 6th floor were the fish ponds—one set linked to the aqueduct to supply fresh water and another to receive salt water brought from Ostia.

The **Ulpia Basilica**, partially excavated in the 19th century around the floor of the Trajan Column, was the last imperial forum to be built and the biggest, measuring 387 by 292 feet.

31 Forum of Augustus (42 BC) Augustus the emperor built this forum to celebrate his military victory at Filippi, where among others, **Cassius** and **Brutus, Caesar**'s assassins, were slain. The wide flight of steps once led to a temple dedicated to Mars, god of war, in this case called Mars the Avenger. Augustus' complex included a hall containing his statue 7 times life-size, the base of which still carries imprints of where the colossal statue's feet had stood.

32 Julius Caesar's Forum (46 BC) This forum was partially brought to light in 1932 along with the ruins of **Caesar's Temple of Venus Genitrix**, which was originally built to house Caesar's art collection and to emphasize his claim to be a descendant of Venus. The bronze statue of Julius Caesar is a modern copy dating from Mussolini's days and the pedestal bears the inscription *dictator perpetus*.

33 Piazza del Campidoglio The modern name for the top of the smallest but most important of Rome's Seven Hills, the **Capitoline**, the site of the capital of the Western world during the Roman Empire. Here **Brutus** spoke of the death of **Julius Caesar**, here **Petrarch** was crowned with his much wanted laurel leaves. Here in 1799, **Nelson**'s troops hoisted the British flag just in time to keep **Napoleon** from taking all.

Piazza del Campidoglio as we see it today was designed by **Michelangelo** in 1538 but not fully completed until 110 years later for the triumphant entry into Rome of **Charles V**, the holy Roman emperor who had driven the infidels out of Spain and back to North Africa. This is the first modern square in Rome and to many its trapezoidal plan also makes it the city's most beautiful. The climb up Michelangelo's ramp is to be done with eyes up in order to see the *Marcus Aurelius* statue emerging against the background of the Renaissance facades. Michelangelo's plan was to turn the Capitoline Hill, once the *capitol* of the Western world, around by 180 degrees,

with all its buildings facing the Forum. He rearranged the 2 preexisting buildings, added the third, the one on the left, and designed the ramp so that the Capitoline Hill would turn its back on pagan Rome and face the Christian city. The facades on the 3 buildings are his, as is the handsome base for the *Marcus Aurelius* and the pattern in the square's pavement. This 2nd-century statue, the oldest equestrian bronze work to survive intact from antiquity, managed to avoid rapacious vandals and popes only because it had been mistakenly identified as representing Constantine, the emperor who made the world safe for Christianity. The statue was removed for urgent restoration from 1980 to 1990. It is now visible behind pollution-proof glass in a side courtyard of the adjacent Palazzo dei Conservatori.

The 2 large statues at the top of the steps are of Castor and Pollux, the twin sons Leda had after she had carnal congress with a swan who was none other than Jupiter in disguise.

Restaurants/Clubs: Red   **Hotels:** Blue
Shops/Parks: Green   **Sights/Culture:** Black

34 Palazzo dei Conservatori This building on the river side of the square was rebuilt in 1820 when the French returned some of the works

Via Dei Fori Imperiali

Napoleon had stolen and shipped to Paris. Napoleon wanted to demolish all buildings in the square to build his own Imperial Palace here. Three centuries earlier, when **Michelangelo** took over the redesigning of the building, where the Roman nobles (the conservatives of their day) once gathered to rubber stamp the latest papal edicts, he also had to find room for pieces of a colossal statue of **Constantine** that once towered 40 feet over the **Basilica of Maxentius** nearby. Sensibly, he left them outdoors in the courtyard of this building where they await you today. These colossal statues, never meant to be viewed this closely, had only the figure's naked parts in marble. The clothed parts were wooden but covered with burnished or painted bronze. At least one of the huge hands with its index finger pointing upward belongs to this statue. The other colossal head and probably the other hand are that of the Emperor's third son, **Constantius II**, who became emperor in AD 324. The courtyard also has carved reliefs representing the foreign provinces under **Hadrian**'s rule. They were taken from **Hadrian's Temple** (today Rome's stock exchange in the Piazza di Pietra). In a small room to the side, **Marcus Aurelius** awaits you; the 2nd-century philosopher-emperor is on his horse, ready to return to the square outside, where he belongs. This contemporary-looking statue, the oldest bronze equestrian sculpture that has survived since antiquity, shows him in civilian dress, extending his hand in a gesture of peace.

Continue up one flight to see the main collection. The most famous pagan statues in this museum are the *Messenger Boy Removing a Thorn from his Foot* (3rd century BC) and the

Capitoline Wolf (perhaps 5th century BC), today the symbol of Rome itself. This bronze work may be even older than the legend about a she-wolf and a woodpecker rescuing the infant twins Romulus and Remus and launching their careers as cofounders of Rome. Romulus killed Remus over a property line dispute, thus Rome is the only great city to claim a murderer, and worse, a fratricidal murderer, as its glorious forefather. The 2 sucking infants were added to the ancient wolf statue in the 15th century. Modern works of great merit are **Bernini**'s marble statue of **Pope Urban VII** on his throne (1639) and **Alessandro Algardi**'s bronze of **Pope Innocent X** (1650) in the same pose.

The stairs leading to the top floor take you to the **Picture Gallery**, where works by **Titian, Tintoretto, Rubens,** and **Velázquez** can be seen. **Veronese**'s *Rape of Europa* is a copy but it was made by Veronese himself. The biggest painting is **Guercino**'s *Burial and Glory of St. Petronilla* (1621), a somewhat obscure saint once thought to have been St. Peter's daughter, and perhaps for that reason Guercino painted this for St. Peter's Basilica. The name **Petronilla** had a revival in the first half of the 20th century when the comic strip *Maggie and Jiggs* became known in Italy as *Archibaldo e Petronilla*. This gallery's 2 **Caravaggio** pictures, one a pubescent *St. John the Baptist,* the other *The Palm Reader,* are not to be missed, nor is the large statue of **Hercules**, probably 1st century BC, designed to stand in a circular temple—almost all of its original gold-leaf covering is still intact. This floor also has a major collection of Meissen porcelain.
♦ Tu, Sa 9AM-2PM, 5-8PM (Sa 9AM-2PM, 5-11PM, 11 Apr-30 Sep); W-F, Su 9AM-1:30PM, 5-8PM. Piazza del Campidoglio. 67103695, 67102071

As **Hadrian** lay dying of dropsy above the bay of Naples, and neither his friends nor his servants would or could finish him off, although he asked them to, the beloved Emperor composed his famous poem, *Address to my Soul.*

Genial, little vagrant sprite (soul),
Long my body's friend and guest,
To what place is now they flight?
Pallid, stark, and naked quite,
Stripped henceforth of joke and just.

Thomas Spencer Jerome's translation from **H.V. Morton**'s *Traveller in Rome.*

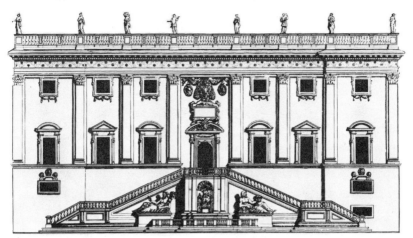

35 The Senator's Palace (1805) The facade conceals an earlier medieval structure built on walls of the 1st-century BC registry office, visible from the rear. Attempts by Romans to have their own civic government over the centuries were always thwarted by the popes, and their one-time scheme to elect 11 municipal senators was watered down by the pope to one senator—of the pope's choosing. Hence the central building is called the **Senator's**. Today, above the statue of the goddess Roma, are some of the offices of Rome's city hall. Behind this palace is a famous view of the Forum. In February 1986, the building was declared unsafe since the bell tower leans 20 inches to one side. In fact, a new Christian Democrat mayor has finally succeeded a series of Communist mayors so the lean is assumed to be to the right.

36 Palazzo Nuovo (1655) This is the museum building on the left as you face the Senator's Palace. The **Capitoline Museums** is the overall name for the 2 lateral buildings and one admission ticket is valid for both. The newer building contains master works of Greco-Roman sculpture. The best sculptures were donated by **Pope Sixtus IV** in 1471 because they were overcrowding his residence at the Lateran palace. The 15th-century dust on the marble statues has remained undisturbed. If time allows you to see only one of the buildings, choose this one. In the 18th century, **Pope Clement XII** opened this collection to the general public, making it the first public museum in the world. The best works, described below, are all one flight up.

The Dying Gaul, with its back seen as you climb the stairs, is the most famous object in this museum.

The 2 **centaurs** found in **Hadrian's Villa** (Villa Adriana).

The inevitable bust of that emperor's favorite, **Antinous**, this time crowned with laurels.

The obese infant seen strangling a serpent is called *Young Hercules* and is a portrait of the **Emperor Caracalla** at 5.

The *Capitoline Venus* (2nd century AD) has a room all to herself. Amid so many beauties, a

realistic statue of a drunken old woman begging for more wine is a startler and probably a 3rd century BC work by **Myron**.

The **Hall of the Emperors** contains 65 busts of important Romans, but not all of them were actually emperors, and too few of them are labeled.

The **Hall of the Philosophers** has more official busts of **Homer, Socrates, Cicero, Sophocles**, and **Euripides**—though not all of them are philosophers, either. The striking head said to be that of **Emperor Julian the Apostate** is actually a splendid portrait of the Roman playwright **Pindar**.

The statue of **Hadrian** depicts him as a Greek god, a familiar pose of that day.

♦ Tu, Th 9AM-1:30PM, 5-8PM; W, F 9AM-1:30PM; Sa 9AM-1:30PM, 8-11PM (Sa 9AM-1:30PM, 5-8PM, 11 Apr-30 Sep); Su 9AM-1PM. Piazza del Campiodoglio. 67103695, 67102071

37 Church of Santa Maria in Ara Coeli (Consecrated in 591) In the Middle Ages, it was the center of Rome's commercial, social, and spiritual life. First named **Santa Maria in Capitolio** when it belonged to Benedictines, it was taken over in 1250 by the Franciscans. Legend has it that here **Sybil** told the **Emperor Augustus** of the advent of the Son of God. (*Ara Coeli* is Latin for Altar of Heaven). The style is mostly Romanesque. It can be reached from the street by a steep flight of 122 steps or from the top of the Capitoline Hill. The excellent view from the steps includes the **Theatre of Marcellus** at the end of the street. In the second chapel of the left nave is a famous manger scene, at which young children are encouraged to deliver suitable sermons during the Christmas season.

38 Monument to Victor Emanuel II Dubbed by foreigners the *wedding cake* or the *white typewriter*, this monument was built from 1885 to 1911 to immortalize the unification of Italy in 1870, in particular the nominal leader and the new country's first king, **Victor**

Emmanuel II. After World War I the **Tomb of the Unknown Soldier** was added at the top of the steps beneath a statue of the goddess Roma. The tomb is guarded night and day by sentries. The monument is also officially called the **Altar of the Fatherland**. After more than 70 years, the Romans' hope that the pile of marble would lose its blinding luster has vanished and it remains out of harmony with its surroundings. The 2 **Eternal Flames** added in the 1970s were the final touch. Reports at that time that the monument was in danger of sinking under its own weight brought fresh hopes that it might be vanquished by gravity. A recent proposal was made to cover it with vines. Until the advent of terrorism, visitors could climb up to the top gallery for a view. Now the iron gate at the foot of the steps is

Via Dei Fori Imperiali

lowered out of sight to allow only visiting heads of state to place a wreath on the Tomb of the Unknown Soldier. Victor Emmanuel is buried in the Pantheon and is depicted on this monument in bronze on a horse. The 2 fountains represent the 2 seas that bathe the Italian peninsula: the Adriatic on the right and the Tyrrhenian on the left. A fragment of the top of the 1st-century BC tomb is next to the fountain on the left. The only redeemable features here are the 2 bronze chariots transporting a *Winged Victory* lady (1908 works by **Carlo Fontana** and **Paolo Bartolini**), which can be seen from various high parts of the city. You may find the *wedding cake* useful for orientation. The **Risorgiamento Museum**, within the monument, occasionally presents theme exhibitions.

39 Piazza Venezia This square takes its name from the imposing palace that dominates it on the left. It is modern in its present form, dating from the demolition of a jumble of old houses at the turn of the last century in order to complement the Victor Emmanuel monument with a large open space. Today it is the crossroads of Rome's tumultuous traffic, with 4 main thoroughfares disgorging their Fiats and Alfa Romeos into the square. No traffic light could cope, and the performance of the sole courageous police officer directing the traffic at the main intersection is a show to watch; he or she uses a flick of each finger to discipline a different flow of traffic. The fake Renaissance palace opposite the **Palazzo Venezia**, dating from 1911 (**A. Manassei**), was built for a Venice-based insurance company. The Venetian emblem, the Lion of St. Mark's, seen on the facade, is 16th century. The genuine Renaissance palace that stood here was demolished to make the Victor Emmanuel monument more painfully visible; the demolishers tactfully placed a plaque on the wall of the insurance building to indicate where they also had destroyed the house in which **Michelangelo** died in 1564. Recently an unsightly parking area in the square's center was replaced with large grassy islands.

The question on each Roman's mind is with what could we replace that white elephant monument to Victor Emmanuel?

40 Palazzo Venezia (1467, sometimes attributed to **Leon Battista Alberti**) Combines the strength of a medieval fortress with hints of the Renaissance's more graceful lines. **Pietro Barbo**, upon being made a cardinal by his uncle, commissioned the building before he became **Pope Paul II**. In 1564, another pope gave the palace, in exchange for other favors, to the *Most Serene Republic of Venice* to be used as the republic's embassy—hence the name. It remained such until Venice was seized by **Napoleon**, who gave the palace to the Austrians as their embassy in 1797.

During World War I, when Italy was fighting against Austria, the building was expropriated by the Italian king. **Benito Mussolini**, the Italian dictator, later took over the **Map Room** (Sala del Mappamondo), so called because of the painting of the world as it was imagined in 1495. It was perhaps the biggest single-occupant office in the world, measuring about 70 feet long and 40 feet wide. It also occupied 2 floors of the original structure, the ceiling of the lower floor having been demolished, and thus had 2 rows of windows on the square. Visitors were meant to be intimidated by the long walk they had to make to reach *Il Duce*'s desk. His various mistresses reported that he liked to dally with them on the floor or on the stone steps leading to the windows. From the palace's central balcony Mussolini declared war on France and then on the United States as thousands cheered him below.

When the Allied troops liberated Rome in June 1944, the palace was opened to the public for the first time. Today it houses a permanent museum of tapestries, ancient arms, medieval sculpture, silver and ceramic artworks, and paintings.

Some masterpieces from the temporarily closed Borghese Museum can be seen here. The palace also displays temporary exhibitions, advertised by large banners on the facade. ◆ M-Sa 9AM-1:30PM; Su, holidays 9AM-12:30PM. Piazza Venezia 3 (alternative entrance on Via del Plebiscito 10) 6798865

41 Vecchia Roma ★★★$$$ Arguably the most delicious antipasto in central Rome—including seafood and green-vegetable salads. The *alici* (raw white anchovies marinated in lemon juice and oil) are among the best anywhere. Spaghetti *alle vongole veraci* is one of the great Roman dishes—and here you can observe these special clams while they are still alive and spitting before being boiled to your taste. This restaurant is the best of its species, unspoiled despite its success among tourists. ◆ Closed Wednesday and half of August. Piazza Campitelli 18. Reservations recommended. No credit cards. 6864604

Little Shop of Horrors

According to legend and sources of varying authenticity, the following martyrs were killed in the following ways.

During the reign of Nero

St. Peter crucified.
St. Paul beheaded.
St. Vitale buried alive.
St. Theela tossed by a bull.
St. Gevase beaten to death.
St. Martin beheaded.
St. Faustus clothed in animal skins and torn to pieces by dogs.

During the reign of Domitian

St. John boiled in oil.
St. Cletus beheaded.
St. Denis beheaded.
St. Domitilla roasted alive.
Sts. Nereus and Achilles beheaded.

During the reign of Trajan

St. Ignatius, Bishop of Antioch, eaten by lions in the Colosseum.
St. Clement, Pope, tied to an anchor and thrown in the sea.
St. Simon, Bishop of Jerusalem, crucified.

During the reign of Hadrian

St. Eustachio and his family burnt in a brazen bull.
St. Alexander, Pope, beheaded.
St. Sinforosa drowned.
St. Pius, Pope, beheaded.

During the reign of Antoninus Pius and Marcus Aurelius

St. Felicitas and her 7 sons martyred in various ways.
St. Justus beheaded.
St. Margaret stretched on a rack and torn to pieces with iron forks.

During the reign of Antoninus and Verus

St. Blandina tossed by a bull in a net.
St. Attalus roasted on a red-hot chair.
St. Pothinus burned alive.

During the reign of Septimius Severus and Caracalla

Sts. Peropetua and Felicitas torn to pieces by lions.
Sts. Victor, Zephyrinus, Leonida, and Basil beheaded.
St. Alexandrina covered with boiling pitch.

During the reign of Alexander Severus

St. Calixtus, Pope, thrown into a well with a stone around his neck.
St. Calepodius dragged through Rome by wild horses and thrown into the Tiber.
St. Martina torn with iron forks.
St. Cecilia, failing to be suffocated with hot water, was stabbed in the throat.
St. Urban, Pope, beheaded.

During the reign of Valerianus and Gallienus

St. Pontianus, Pope, beheaded.
St. Agatha had her breasts cut off.
Sts. Fabrian and Cornelius, Popes, and St. Cyptian beheaded.
St. Tryphon burnt.
Sts. Ablon and Sennen torn by lions.

Ambassador Rinaldo Petrignani

Is it possible to have one favorite place in Rome, which is not only a bewildering city as a whole, but also a site of the spirit where visual image is inseparable from cultural and historical meaning?

The **Campidoglio** is the place that comes to my mind, among many others, because it has reflected the vigorous continuity of life and history for over 2 millennia.

From the Republican Era right through the Middle Ages and the Renaissance to our modern time, the Campidoglio has been the lifelong heart and seat of the city's government, and it seems to me to represent the best of the incredible beauty and significance of Rome.

Millicent Fenwick
Former Ambassador to the UN Food and Agriculture Organization

The **Church of San Clemente**

Go in through the entrance below street level, which was built in the late 12th century, and see the fine mosaics on display. Go down one flight to the **Old Basilica** (c. 500) showing the humble beginnings of Christianity. Go down another flight, and you will experience Rome of the classic 150 BC period. Pitch dark. Narrow streets, the same pavements the ancient Romans knew. A small temple of **Mithras**—no altar. A stone shows the bull's throat being cut, a ritual of the Eastern cult that came in toward the end of the Empire. San Clemente is on Via San Giovanni Laterano. It's capsule history.

On the bright side—my favorite restaurant. Right across the street from my office—a family place—informal, rapid service, good food, inexpensive. The proprietor is always on hand, overseeing sons and nephews. It's a completely *Italian* place—**The Pizzeria Pub** (Via Sardegna 34-36—two blocks off Via Veneto). Good pizza, too, I'm told, although I go in for spaghetti with clams.

Cow's milk mixed with whitewash will save the ancient monuments; the Belle Arte are using this all over town.

In ancient days, the **lighting of Rome** was created by Roman candles, long-burning candles with many wicks. Architectural highlights were revealed by the gently flickering lights placed along the ramps, stairs, and tops of buildings. The effect was magical. Before the war, the colonnade of St. Peter's Square and the cathedral itself were still lit in this manner. Two runners would stand poised at either end of the colonnade with a flaming brand in one hand. At the firing of a pistol they would start to run, dipping their torch at every step to light the candles as they passed. It was a race to see who would arrive first at the very top of the dome of St. Peter's. By the end of the race the facade and the square were bathed in glowing light. Today, the Capitoline Hill is lit this way on Rome's birthday (21 April).

On A Typical Roman Day in Ancient Times, the Romans got up at the crack of dawn; there was a law that delivery carts could only circulate at night, bringing provisions into the city for its needs—so it wasn't a particularly silent night. Upon waking, the only early-morning ablutions were to throw cold water on the hands and face and then rinse out the mouth.

Husband and wife, if well-to-do, slept on a matrimonial bed or kept separate bedrooms. Twin beds were frowned upon. The poor had palets made of masonry with straw or cotton mattresses thrown on top.

A tunic, a toga, or both were added on top of the loin cloth and tunic worn during the night. Some people

Via Dei Fori Imperiali

wore up to 3 or 4 tunics over the under-tunic. The men's tunics were usually made of linen or wool, short-sleeved, cut at the knees, and belted. The women's tunics were made of cotton, short-sleeved, and often down to the ankle. The toga, an elegant cloak, was a circle of pure-white wool that served as ceremonial dress, but it was difficult to drape, heavy to wear, and required frequent washings to keep it white. People came to detest the toga because it was difficult to keep oneself looking smart as it would constantly bunch to one side.

In Imperial times, many Romans adopted a garment that had a tunic top with a pleated skirt; instead of the toga, they wore a synthesis of a Greek cloak cut on the square. The short tunic made for chilly legs and arms. Slaves wore the same style as their masters but were permitted gloves in cold weather. After a quick glass of water, the men went to get a shave or have their beards trimmed, which was painful as the razors were made of blunt iron. No one shaved himself, not even slaves. Barbers became prima donnas and the shave became a rite. The men also, perhaps, had their hair dressed. In Republican times, the style was to wear the hair short in the back and on the sides. Only senators or consuls had their hair oiled or combed around a laurel wreath. Later, in Imperial times (Republican ended with Augustus' reign in 27 BC and Imperial times started then and lasted until the fall of the Empire in AD 476), curls came into fashion and curling irons were heated to mold the hair. (The men even went so far as to hide pimples with opaque cream!)

After her minimal ablutions, a wife had her hair dressed. (With wings it sometimes reached 3 tiers.) She used powdered horn to clean her teeth and many pots of creams and colors to make up her face. Over her under-tunic, she put on another long tunic with a belt, then a shawl and jewelry. She preferred brightly colored cottons with heavy gold braids and rare, supple silk. If she could not afford a tiara, she wore a headband.

In the city, apart from the expanse of public buildings, patricians and plebs lived side by side in the crowded streets. A great man's large house and garden (with private hot baths and sometimes even a lavatory) could be found next to an apartment block with 5 floors. In these buildings the ground floor was divided into shops and taverns with apartments on the upper 4 floors. These tenements were often badly constructed; throughout the city, one could hear the noise of buildings crashing down.

Only the very rich of the city escaped the need to go to the public lavatories. These had no doors or walls between the seats, and people met there without embarrassment, chatting and exchanging dinner invitations. Some had central heating to warm up the marble seats! Even in the Imperial Palace, the domed lavatory with precious wood and marble carvings had a 3-holer. However, the existence of these public lavatories did not mean that pedestrians were spared the indignity of receiving the unwelcome contents of a chamber pot on their heads from an upstairs window.

Breakfast was a bite of bread and cheese around 9AM. Then the work (or play) of the day began. There weren't many women in the working world and the women did not even do the shopping. In the 1st century BC it was rare for a household to have more than one slave. By the 2nd century AD one freed man (once a slave) had 4000 slaves! Owning 500 slaves seems to have been the norm. The Romans were rarely cruel to their slaves and would spur them to work harder by offering bonuses and nest eggs, which would enable the slaves to buy their freedom. Pliny the Younger, for example, would discuss important matters with his slaves. There were laws to free slaves if their master had died or treated them inhumanly. Poor women did housework until ladies' hour at the public baths. Rich women stayed home, visited friends, or went to plays. After the baths they often went out to dinner.

Every man was either a patron or a client. The poor man went to his patron for handouts. The client to his lawyer, the artist or artisan to his benefactor (in whose palace he might be working), the laborer to his workshop. The rich man went to see *his* patron in his litter (carried by at least 2 slaves). All had to pay court and wait their turn to give greetings. The laborer was second to last and the slave was last in line. The whole fabric of society, from ropemakers and pastry cooks to bureaucrats and senators, revolved around this patron-client phenomenon. Everybody had a patron higher than himself, even the richest man. The emperor was the sole exception.

Lunch was perhaps the leftovers from the night before. The children took some of this to eat at school. Cold meat and a little fruit were eaten as a snack before going to the baths.

When there were trials or court cases, the din was deafening in the basilicas. The cases lasted hours;

sometimes a consul or judge spoke for 5 hours non-stop with the emperor listening and even participating. However, the courts, like the Senate, had months of mandatory holidays. Business in this complicated society took place in the forums: Julia, Trajan, Augustus, Nerva, etc. The Romans were supreme merchants. The working day, as such, usually finished at midday (our time). Merchants, shopkeepers, and artisans, in summer and winter alike, didn't work the whole afternoon. Laborers downed tools between 11AM and noon. Only barbers stayed open late (approximately 12:30PM) to accommodate their customers' schedules. Wine bars and antique dealers might occasionally stay open until 2:30PM in the Forum Julia to try to get the last little piece of business.

Everybody went to the giant baths (*terme*) for one hot bath a day, even the most miserably poor and the slaves. It cost one penny to enter. Ladies' Hour at the baths was at the 6th hour (approximately 11:15AM). The Men's Hour was at the 9th hour (approximately 1:25PM). Within the baths were changing rooms, cold baths, a room with heated benches to get the body's temperature up slowly, hot baths, a swimming pool (Romans were excellent swimmers), a small room for saunas, a large amphitheater for nude gymnastics, and a room for oiling the body and for scraping off excess sweat after the gym and ball games that were played first. There were even medicinal baths and perfumed baths. And, of course, there were lavatories. Cubicles were provided for those who didn't want to mix. Massage, depilation, iron, and soda to cleanse the skin (they didn't have soap) were also provided. Romans believed in the sun's beneficial properties and took sunbaths. The baths were a center of social life. There were even libraries, drink and snack vendors, walkways with beautiful sculptures to admire, and great fountains such as those now in Piazza Farnese, which came from the Baths of Caracalla.

These activities were followed by the real meal of the day: dinner. This meal was held at the 11th or 12th hour (approximately 3PM). Some meals lasted 2 hours while others lasted until midnight with time out for acts, such as jugglers or dancers, between the courses. Guests took off their shoes at the entrance, where they had their feet washed upon arrival. Then they entered barefoot. Dinner was eaten reclining on sloping couches with the left elbow leaning on a cushion. It was considered terribly unchic to sit at a table, and only small children and slaves ate in that manner. Slaves often sat on stools and dined at their master's table, but they were only allowed to recline on holidays. A full dinner consisted of 7 courses with one's hands being washed with perfumed water between each course.

Everything you've ever heard in regard to a Roman banquet is true. They had teams of relay runners who rushed fresh oysters down from Brittany and Colchester in 24 hours. Other goodies included peacock pie, swan stuffed with live frogs, ice cream of a sort (they kept snow and ice in underground caves for use in the summer), and for the really debauched—a feather down the throat so one could start all over again. And let's not forget some serious and uninhibited dallying with slave girls, prostitutes, or slave boys between the courses.

The excesses weren't an everyday occurrence, and the majority of households ate frugally. They used a condiment called *garum*, which was a marinade of fish left to saturate in oil or vinegar in the sun. It was like Vietnamese *nuoc mam* or Thai fish sauce. For a sweetener, they used honey because sugar was not discovered until centuries later. They always cut wine with water and often laced it with honey and drank it hot, much like mead, which remained popular in England until 100 years ago.

Via Dei Fori Imperiali

Theater began to lose its charm when the Romans got an appetite for bloodier fun. Plays began to be liberally sprinkled with chorus and song, and the acting became exaggerated pantomime. The Italian art form, opera, is the modern version of these theatrics. The plays had become so well known that people could sing along. They were either horrifying tragedies or sleazy sex tales. (At a certain point, to revise interest in the theater, they even made it real: when the hero in a tragedy died, he really died. This sort of live theater finally moved to the Colosseum in the form of the Gladiator Games.) The smallest theater in Rome was twice the size of the largest modern American theater. A small one would hold 8000 seats. The Theater of Pompey, the first and most famous, built in 55 BC, held 27,000.

Marcus Aurelius (AD 161-180) tried to restore the work ethic by reducing holidays and returning the business year to 235 days. The remaining 130 days were devoted to public spectacles. Romans loved betting of all kinds, but chariot racing generated the most passionate response. The horses and the jockeys were famous throughout the Empire. The Circus Maximus, where the chariot races took place, had 255,000 seats. Games and spectacles often lasted an entire day, and some gladiatorial games continued for up to 9 days. Gladiators were culled from wayward sons, prisoners of war, and men condemned to death.

By the 3rd century AD, there was one day of holiday for every day of work. Some were justified as religious holidays, others celebrated the triumphs of commanding officers, and still others were simply the whim of the emperor. When circuses became more important than bread, the end of the Roman Empire was in sight. *By Vanessa Somers McConnell*

doric

ionic

corinthian

via Sacra

is excerpted from the rare and ancient guide *SPQRACCESS**, published in AD 313, almost 1700 years ago. Via Sacra is the best-known street in ancient Rome because triumphant generals ride along here on their way to the **Capitoline Hill**, where they give thanks to Jupiter for their victory. Follow their path as Rome's ancient past unwinds. The shopkeepers are hawking their wares, the senators are debating in the **Curia**, the lawyers are arguing in the **basilica**, and the young men and women are off exercising at the **baths**.

1 Meta Sudans Fountain If you can drag yourself away from the screams and shouts at the **Flavian Amphitheater** (Colosseum), walk past the Meta Sudans Fountain, where you might catch a glimpse of some gladiators washing after a combat—naturally the winners because the losers would be dead. Try to ignore the hideous statue of the **Colossus**, 120 feet high, built by **Nero**, of Nero. When the whole of Rome had turned against him and was out to kill him, Nero, not having enough courage to take the gentleman's way out, got his slave to help him commit suicide by thrusting his sword into his abdomen. Subsequently, the head of the statue was knocked off and those of other emperors added.

*SPQR—*Senatus Populusque Romanus*, which translates as the Senate and People of Rome.

2 Temple of Venus and Rome This is the largest of all the temples and can actually be considered 2 temples: one to Rome, facing the Forum, and one to Venus, facing the Flavian Amphitheater. This great edifice dominates the valleys on either side of it. **Hadrian** designed the temple and sent the designs to the great architect **Apollodorus**, whom he had exiled upon becoming emperor. Apollodorus was so scathing in his criticism of the project that he paid with his life for the pleasure of his comments. It was built 200 years ago (AD 135), and the giant statue that stood at the entrance to Nero's house, *Domus Aurea* (Golden House), had to be moved. It took 24 elephants to drag it down into the valley. On a

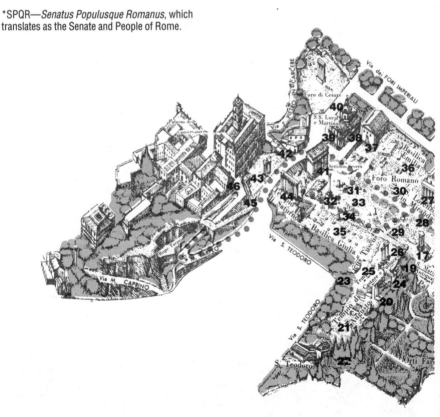

Holy Day watch the priests' procession as they come chanting down toward the tethered bull. Rome's birthday (21 April) is an exciting date, especially since they give the first 50 people a slice of roasted meat. This is an especially propitious temple for newlyweds to offer sacrifice.

3 Arch of Titus There are many triumphal arches along the Via Sacra, but only emperors, or generals having a *triumph* or victory procession, are allowed to go through them. So go around the side! This one was erected by **Domitian** to record **Vespasian**'s victory over the pharaoh and **Titus**' destruction of Jerusalem 230 years earlier. Look at the walls on the right side of the arch—the sculpted procession is carrying the spoils of the great **Temple of Solomon**. Also note the giant candelabra.

4 Temple of Jupitor Stator Don't miss this ancient temple built in 700 BC by **Romulus**, the founder of Rome, after he conquered the Sabines and kidnapped and raped their women.

5 Lupanaria-Brothels Near the tavern are the state-run houses of ill repute. There is also, of course, a plethora of free-lance *Hetaerae* who can be recognized by their yellow dresses. Young boys, here for the men who fancy them, are usually of Greek origin. The "Greek vice" is frowned upon if practiced openly, but tolerated between an owner and one of his slaves in the privacy of his own home.

6 Old House of Julius Caesar Now covered with shops since the last 2 fires. You are at the top of the rise of the Via Sacra. The grandeur of this road will knock you out; nowhere in the world is there anything to compare with it. Temple after temple gleams in its marble finery. With 700 places of worship throughout Rome, hardly a day goes by without the lowing of oxen being heard as they are taken to one temple or another to be sacrificed.

7 Chic Shops Precious goods, perfumes, spices, and fashionable shops. This whole area through to the little road behind is the smart part of town. Browse through it and admire the beautiful women of Rome choosing silks, buying fine jewelry, or bargaining for some ancient work of art.

8 Porticus Margaritaria Arcades of the *margarita* (pearl) dealers. This whole street on the left-hand side (abutting onto the House of the Vestal Virgins) is the pearl traders' market. Pearls are the most admired jewels in Rome—the bigger the better. These dealers have their pearls shipped in from all over the world. Some of the nouveaux riches like to throw pearls into their wine, watch them dissolve, and then drink the liquid. Sometimes an emperor will arrange a "rainfall" of pearls onto his guests at a banquet, but most Roman matrons prefer their pearls in necklaces, *diadems* (crowns), or hanging earrings. The shop at the north end will make jewels to order within 8 days (if there are no intervening holidays). **Quintius Curtius** at **No. 17** does wonders with seed pearls.

Light Red indicates buildings no longer standing. Black indicates buildings or ruins still visible

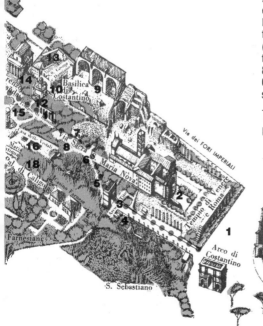

9 Basilica of Maxentius (Constantine)
This courthouse is 84 feet wide and 333 feet long (about the length of a modern football field). The 8 great columns hold up the gilded bronze roof, and all around you will be able to admire statues and works of art. The statue of the **Great Constantine** is being sculpted *in situ* because it's so heavy. His foot is as long as your leg! This place is far from finished, but it is already on a grander scale than most other basilicas. It will have a tribunal, nave, and aisles. The prisoner, or defendant, will stand on a round stone in front of the tribunal, where the judge will be seated; railings and the **Altar of Apollo** will separate him from the judge.

10 Vicus Sandaliarius Fine leather shoe and sandalmakers along a winding street peppered with statues, including the statue of **Apollo Sandaliarius**, which gave the street its name and was donated by **Augustus** himself.

11 Temple of the Penates This is the small temple situated to the right of the **Temple of**

Romulus. Penates are the gods brought back from Troy by **Aeneas** (753 BC). It is an extremely old rite—it is whispered that they used to sacrifice babies 800 years ago!

12 Temple of Romulus A lovely circular building built 11 years ago by **Maxentius** to honor his son Romulus, who died young. Its beautiful bronze doors are worth noting.

13 Temple (Library) of Peace Right behind the Temple of Romulus is the dazzling **Temple of Peace** built by **Vespasian** around 230 years ago (AD 80) in the hopes that peace was here to stay. The whole **Forum of Peace** stretches over half a mile. This part of the vast complex houses the library and survey office and the most impressive spoils from the sack of **Jerusalem**, including a curiously beautiful 7-branched candelabra shown on the Arch of Titus. It also houses the treasures from the hated despot **Nero**'s house. Soothsayers predict that these 2 sacred temples will become a place of worship for the new-fangled religion, Christianity: the **Church of Cosmos and Damiano**.

14 Temple of Vicaporta (Victory) The Temple of Victory right next door to the Forum of Peace! But this was built almost 200 years before the Forum. It is constructed on a small piece of land, in the shape of a 3-leaf clover. It covers the ruins of a house **Publicola** had originally built on higher ground overlooking the Forum, but people passed such snide comments that he tore down the house and rebuilt it on a lower site with no view. He died a pauper.

Tourists from Greece to Imperial Rome (64 BC to AD 400) often scoffed that its magnificence was fake as most houses had marble facades for the ground and 1st floors, only. All the other stories had trompe l'oeil paintings of marble.

15 Tapicieon An honorary momument put up by the citizens of **Tarsus** (St. Paul's city) proclaiming the close friendship between Rome and Tarsus—a sort of twinning. Its podium and the columns protect the life-size statue of **Emperor Gorlain**. On this section of Via Sacra one can often hear the sound of muffled footsteps and clanking chains as the prisoners from **Britain** go past.

16 House of the Vestal Virgins The site started a few hundred years ago. The vestals were expected to serve 7 years, starting from puberty. When the 7 years were up they were free to leave and marry. Today a vestal serves 30 years and is chosen between the ages of 5 and 10. As she enters the order her hair is shaved off and hung from a tree. The hair is then allowed to grow back and can be worn quite long. The first 10 years are devoted to learning, the next 10 to performing the rites, and the last 10 to teaching the newcomers. After the 30 years she can resign and even marry—but she'd be a bit old! Woe betide a vestal if caught with a man. Last year they found proof that one had misbehaved with a lover and she received the traditional punishment and was buried alive. There are only 6 vestal virgins and they are as revered as they are powerful; the mother superior is venerated. In order of precedence they come right after the empress and have seats of honor at the games, theater, and circus. Their lives are a mixture of austere tradition and great privilege. Just by passing a criminal in the street, they can stay his execution if they choose.

Emperors' wills and secret documents from the Senate are kept here, as no one would dare to enter. Peep through a hole in the back of **Q. Curtius**' shop (for a price) and you can glimpse part of the beautiful atrium (courtyard) of the vestals. The floor is covered with black-and-white mosaics; the center has a fountain and flower garden. Around the edge are 48 columns, green-and-white marble downstairs, coral upstairs, with statues between each column. Watch the vestals as they glide about their duties in pure-white sleeveless gowns that fall to the ankles with a simple girdle round the waist. Around their heads are 6 bands of twisted linen, like a coronet. On the ground floor there is a mill for grinding the salt used for sacred cleansings, rooms for guarding the secret documents, and a marble tank of the holy water. On the upper floor are the vestals apartments. They say the walls and floors are heated and that there is a private bath reached by a bridge. In winter, with the palace buildings now reaching almost 20 feet on top of the **Palatinus** (Palatine Hill), the building doesn't get as much sun as it used to. The **High Vestal** (Mother Superior) apartment, said to be covered with frescoes, is the most luxurious.

17 Temple of Vesta: Goddess of the Hearth This round building is a copy of the simple original building of thatched roof and reed walls. Here burns the *Sacred Fire*, which is allowed to go out only on New Year's Day (1 March), when the **Pontifex Maximus** (High Priest—in recent times usually the emperor) comes to relight the flame with 2 sticks. Then the blood from the tail of a horse that has been sacrificed to **Mars** is sprinkled on the altar. The sanctity of the fire that burns continually on the altar symbolizes the continuity of the state. The **Penus**, or Sacred Place, houses the **Palladium Statue of Minerva** from Troy.

The New Year's Day ceremony is too holy for tourists, but there are many other festivals you can watch, including the ceremonial emptying out of the **vestal dustbin** once a year. The burned bones and debris are taken down to the **Cloaca Maxima** (the large drain that keeps the Forum from flooding). When there is a sacrifice at the temple, the vestals put on a white wool hood bordered with purple. Their most important job is to tend the eternal flame. Other holy days at this temple are **Harvest, Vintage,** and **Lupercalia**. Don't forget that every offering at the temple must be accompanied by salt.

18 Grove of Vesta Behind the temple in the lea of the Palatinus is the **Sacred Grove** where the fruit and sweet-smelling trees grow. The **Via Nova** runs from this grove, under the Palatinus to the Arch of Titus.

19 Street of the Oxheads Between the **Temple of Castor** and **Pollux** and the **Temple of Vesta**.

19 Scala Annulariae (Ring Makers Stairs) Underneath the stairs that go from the east end of the Forum up to the **Palatinus** is where the precious rings are made: pearls, rubies, cameos, scarabs from Egypt, and even men's thumb rings in massive gold. The enormous edifice on the edge of the Palatinus is part of **Caligula**'s palace. And it is from the word *Palatinus* that the word *palace* came. For hundreds of years the whole hill has been one vast luxurious palace.

20 Oratory of the 40 Martyrs Probably built by **Hadrian**. These poor folk died in a frozen pond in Armenia—part of the Empire. But who they were and what they were doing has been lost in the mists of time.

21 Library and Temple of Augustus Atrium (garden courtyard) **of Minerva**. The goddess Minerva plays the same important role to the Romans as Athena played to the Greeks. Considered to be one of the 3 most beautiful buildings in Rome—along with the **Temple** (Library) **of Peace** and the **Basilica Aemilia.** The ramp that winds up to the Palatinus hill abutts on these buildings. They say it was here that the soldiers killed **Caligula**. Augustus has both a Greek and Latin library.

22 Horrea Agripiana (1st Century BC) Large merchandise warehouses.

23 Vicus Tuscus Named after the Etruscans who were allowed to settle here, this road goes to **Boarium** (cattle) **Forum** and **Circus Maximus**. The paving is terrible, but the

Etruscan artists, craftsmen, and dealers and the smell of perfume shops where Roman ladies order their special mixtures (oil of clove, musk from Persia, violet juice, and Egyptian spices) make this an interesting street.

24 Fountain Spring Lake of Juturna (named after a health-giving water goddess) is a long trough-shaped fountain, providing a last drink for the sheep, goats, pigs, and bulls on the way to their deaths. In memory of **Castor** and **Pollux**, 2 gods who saved Rome during a battle.

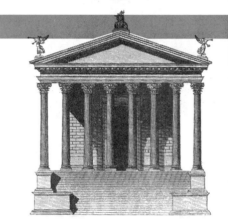

25 Temple of Castor and Pollux. They were called the **Dioscuri**—2 horsemen who came to Rome's aid in a battle against the Etruscans and Latini (499 BC). The temple was built 15 years later and is famous for its 8 lofty columns. The statues of the gods are in the *cella*, a walled inner sanctum that the eyes of the curious cannot penetrate.

26 Fornix Fabius Ruins of another arch that the Romans stole from the Etruscans. In the Etruscan language, *fornix* means arch.

26 Arch of Augustus This triumphal arch has one large central opening flanked by 2 smaller ones. Statues were put in the arches at a later date.

It was so painful to be crucified that the early Christians could not bring themselves to portray the Cross. Instead, they symbolized the Cross with the first two letters of Christ's name from the Greek alphabet. When Rome became the center of the Christian Church—and there were no more martyrs—then the Cross was represented as we know it today.

Light Red indicates buildings no longer standing.
Black indicates buildings or ruins still visible

27 Temple of Antonius and Faustina Built 150 years ago (AD 160), the temple has the most beautiful flight of stairs. For your ears alone it is said that **Faustina** was a faithless wife—and **Antonius** was very pious to put up with her. He even elevated her to a goddess!

28 The Regia This is where the high priests kept the lists of the annual acts, public events, and festivals of a religious nature. Here they

Via Sacra

exercised their functions. In one of the terrible thunderstorms, the river Tiber had a flash flood and washed away the Regia and other buildings. The site was later given to the **vestal virgins** whose first house was built here. They moved to the more spacious area across the road when their first house burned down (in yet another of the innumerable fires that rage constantly through Rome). They are proud of the fact that they can light up the night like the day with their oil lamps—the most sophisticated in existence with hundreds of flames within one lamp—but a gust of wind may cause a dreadful fire. **Nero**'s fire was only one of many; there's probably nary a building that hasn't suffered a dangerous fire at one time or another.

28 Ruins of Great Caesar's House Located right behind the **Regia**; since Caesar had been nominated **Pontifex Maximus**, it was handy to live next door. This house faced Via Sacra and had an elegant atrium at its center. He left his third wife, **Calpurnia**, on that fateful morning from this very spot to go to the Senate, which was meeting at the temple in the **Theater of Pompey** (due to redecoration of the Senate building). He was killed on the stairs of the theater on 15 March (44 BC). Who would have guessed that the *Ides of March* would be celebrated, at least for awhile, by the payment of taxes in a faraway land? This house, too, burned to the ground.

29 Temple of Julius Caesar (42 BC) This temple, built to honor the first mortal elevated to the rank of god, stands high overlooking the Forum on the very spot where Caesar's funeral pyre was lit. Hysterical people threw everything they could onto the fire in their grief—chairs, caskets, jewelry, and clothes—and almost burned down Rome. His house was just behind. People still give speeches from the **Rostra** in front of the temple, but the beaks of the boats captured at Antium have rotted away. At the time of the death of **Nero**, the last of Caesar's descendants, there was a great storm and the heads of the 4 statues of family members, which were on pedestals in front of the temple, were struck by lightning—and all 4 toppled to the ground. The butcher shops opposite are long gone, relocated in the **Market of Trajan**.

30 The Forum The Forum was the large open space where people met and justice was pronounced in Republican times. Serious events, happy times, great religious ceremonies, banquets for gladiators, orations, festivals, and dancing were all partaken here. Lawsuit re-

sults were also posted here. Little by little it became cluttered with the following:

Pillar of Phocas Look at the top and see the statue of the **Emperor**.

Lacus Curtius A wellhead enclosed by a railing: a holy spot since **Augustus'** time. Citizens would come to pray and throw some coins in for the Emperor's good health.

Statue of Marsyas Symbolizes civil liberty. A man with a pigskin of wine on one shoulder, a hand outstretched for justice. Brought from Greece 500 years ago (2nd century BC).

Comitium Where assemblies met to elect ministers and religious leaders, and to decide on punishments.

Janus A section where money changers transacted business.

Domitian's Monument Only the pedestal is left since the people destroyed the statue after **Domitian** was murdered 230 years ago. A violent storm sent the plaque on the base flying over the rooftops and it crashed on another monument.

Edicola Venere Cloacina Shrine to commemorate the construction of the great drain to dry up the swampy area of the Forum by the Etruscans 900 years ago.

Niger Lapis This black-marble slab marks a burial place of great antiquity, perhaps the tomb of **Romulus**.

Tunnels Located under the Forum with light shafts, they were probably for gladiatorial games years ago. When the **Flavian Amphitheater** was built these were filled in. The traditional fig tree, olive tree, and vine are always tended by a privileged gardener, a great honor as they are the symbols of Rome.

The Souvetaurilia An institution to purify Rome, it takes place every 5 years. A boar, a ram, and a bull are led 3 times around the assembly gathered in the Forum and sacrificed to **Mars** (god of war).

Tabularium The administrative headquarters of the Empire.

31 Rostra Named after the *beaks*—bronze rammers under the prows of ships used to ram and scuttle enemy ships. These were taken from boats that the navy had captured in battle, and were inserted into the stone dais, or platform. Nowadays the Romans fight on land more than at sea. Here, the great orators throughout the ages spoke so eloquently that they could change the course of history. In the old days there were statues of the ambassadors the **King of Veii** had put to death. When the great orator **Cicero** was assassinated, his head and hands were cut off and put on the Rostra, where he had so often addressed the Romans. The Rostra was moved to its present place about 100 years ago under **Septimius Severus**.

32 Umbilicus Urbis This marks the middle of the Roman world.

32 Volcanale Cult center of Vulcan. Corpses were burned here in years past.

33 The Golden Milestone Next to the ascent to the Capitol: **Clivus Capitolinus**. The stone records, in gold, the distance from this spot to all major cities in the Empire.

34 Arch of Tiberius Built by **Tiberius** in honor of **Germanicus** after he defeated the Germans; if a great soldier wins a battle against a terrible foe, he may take the name of the people he conquered.

Light Red indicates buildings no longer standing.
Black indicates buildings or ruins still visible

35 Basilica Giulia Started by **Julius Caesar**. The central hall is covered and a beautiful double row of columns runs around the entire perimeter—about the length of a football field. Civil cases, especially inheritance suits, are heard here. Large crowds love to come and listen to the judges and lawyers. Some of the audience have scratched games on the marble floor—for jacks or marbles—for a little betting between cases.

36 Basilica Aemilia A court of justice behind a row of banks where there used to be silversmiths, **Tabernae Argentariae**. Porticos were built on top of these shops so the crowd could watch the gladiator games in the Forum. **Paullus** rebuilt the basilica (53 BC) with money sent him as a bribe from **Julius Caesar**. A fish market used to be in the back section until it was relocated to the Trajan market.

37 Curia (The Senate) The fate of the world was decided here. It was destroyed by fire at least 5 times. It could hold 600 senators and each speaker rose in turn to speak from his

Via Sacra

seat (which had comfortable cushions on top of a wooden chair). At the end of the hall is a low podium for the president. The statues are of citizens who have helped the *Urbs* (State). Not much goes on here now; the senators meet mainly out of formalistic tradition. The emperor is supreme.

38 Graecostatis A raised platform for receiving foreign ambassadors.

39 Senaculum Senators and magistrates (who cannot enter the Senate House) can deliberate on thorny matters in this building.

40 Clivus Argentarius (money lenders) From here, during a triumphal procession, the emperors and generals proceed up to the Capitol—the prisoners to the **Tullian Prison** (Mammertine) and death.

41 Arch of Septimius Severus (AD 205) A beautiful arch with a bronze chariot on top pulled by 6 snorting horses; the emperor and his sons are riding in the chariot.

Light Red indicates buildings no longer standing.
Black indicates buildings or ruins still visible

42 Temple of Concord Built to commemorate the reconciliation after the civil war between the upper classes and the ordinary Roman citizens (*plebs*). There are 4 large statues of elephants inside, as well as many priceless works of art. In the back is the **Basilica Optimio**, which became **Basilica Argentaria**, frequented today by silversmiths and clerks of the exchequer.

43 Temple of Vespasian Built by his son **Titus**, the smallness of this building is masked by a clever architect. It looks bigger than it really is—of course, since every emperor built a temple or statue in this valley the place was filling up, even 200 years ago. In the shops you can buy some *tanagras* (votive offering figurines), take them into the temple, break them against the altar, and make a prayer.

44 Temple of Saturn Here the generals swear that they have been honest and have not kept any of the booty or prisoners in a successful war. A lot of the treasure of Rome is stored here—hundreds of thousands of gold and silver ingots. Constructed in early Republican times (497 BC) after the defeat of **Tarquinius Superbus**, the hated last king of Rome and an Etruscan as well! It was rebuilt with the booty from the defeated Syrians (30 BC).

45 Portico of the 12 gods All the household gods are represented in pairs in this covered archway. Every year there is a sacred banquet here to honor them. Just below is the headquarters of the scribes and heralds of **Aediles**: *Schola Xantha*, a small room with benches on 3 sides.

46 Tabularum A public records office constructed 400 years ago during the Republic, this magnificent building houses all the public records engraved on bronze plates. One of the ancient chroniclers, **Suitonius**, tells us the originals were lost in a fire and **Vespasian** had them all remade.

Roman Population

AD 250	2,000,000
500	50
1870	214,000
1970	2,000,000
1990	(over) 3,000,000

The Sacks of Rome

The Goths	AD	410
The Vandals		455
The Saracens		845
The Normans		1084
Charles V		1527

The Sack of Rome in 1527 was the bloodiest and most infamous. Emperor Charles V and King François I of France were vying for influence in Italy. Pope Clement VII, a weak member of the Medici family, had favored Charles V, but turned against him when he realized that Charles V was amassing more and more territories. To consolidate his power, Charles V sent a vast army under the command of the Duke of Bourbon to invade Rome. Thousands of German mercenaries (perhaps fired by Martin Luther's theses), Spanish imperial troops, and Italian Lombards had swelled Charles' army to nearly 40,000 men. Benevenuto Cellini, the sculptor who was already notorious for his criminal acts, claimed to have fired the shot that killed the Duke of Bourbon.

Without a leader, the troops let loose their fury. They defiled churches with orgies on top of altars, and the soldiers and prostitutes drank wine from the golden chalices. One hundred thirty palaces on the Aventine were gutted. The population shrank from 90,000 to 32,000. In this smoking inferno, the plague attacked. Pope Clement VII who was cowering in Castel Sant'Angelo, finally capitulated. In 1530, the Pope was humiliated even further when he had to crown Charles V as the Holy Roman Emperor.

The Malborghetto

Just over 2 miles out of Rome on the Via Flaminia (one of the ancient consular roads that radiate from the city) is the Malborghetto, an unimpressive brick building that looks like a farmhouse, but turns out to be filled with history.

The archeological superintendent of Rome, **Professor Adriano La Regina**, recently announced that this was almost certainly the place where **Constantine the Great** slept on the eve of his victorious battle of **Saxa Rubra** (AD 312). Here then, was the start of Constantine's conversion to Christianity—which would change the course of history and, according to the great historian **Edward Gibbon**, speed the *Decline and Fall of the Roman Empire*. For while sleeping here, Constantine had a vision that he must immediately attack the armies of his rival, **Maxentius**, with his soldiers' shields emblazoned with the sign of Christ. He attacked and defeated Maxentius the next day. Thus Constantine became emperor, and by the Edict of Milan he legitimized the Christian religion.

According to material published by *La Regina*, the Malborghetto, built by Constantine on the spot where he had the dream, was originally a triumphal arch faced much like the Arch of Constantine next to the Colosseum, except that it had openings on all 4 sides, like the Arch of Janus near Rome's Piazza Bocca della Verità.

This archeological revelation was published in the spring of 1986, and if you want permission to visit, write to Soprintendenza Archeologica di Roma, Servizio per la Didattica, Piazza delle Finanze 1 00186 Roma (4824181).

Enrico Sabbatini

The **Parione neighborhood**—that group of old houses, ancient palaces, winding little streets, and intimate lanes that run from Piazza Navona to Porta Sant'Angelo.

The small market in **Piazza del Fico**.

The artisans on **Vicolo delle Vacche**.

The old taverns between **Via del Corallo** and **Via di Monte Giordano**.

Piazza Navona and its fountains.

The **Church Santa Maria della Pace**.

Palazzo Boncompagni.

L'Oratorio Borromini.

La Torre dell'Orologio (The Clock Tower).

Piazza Pasquino and all of its history.

Rome is like living in a museum, and not the usual museum, which is a cemetery of history, but living history, alive, real, palpitating.

Via Sacra

Papal Audiences

The pope holds a general (public) audience every Wednesday unless he is out of the city. In winter, or in inclement weather, it takes place in the Vatican's 9000-seat auditorium (1971, designed by engineer **Pier Luigi Nervi**) or in **St. Peter's Basilica**. In good weather the audience is held in **St. Peter's Square**, with 24,000 seats. The starting hour varies with the season. Tickets are essential for the winter or indoor audience, while standing room in the square is usually plentiful but distant from the papal throne.

There are several ways to obtain a ticket. Two months in advance, ask your bishop's chancery to write to Rome for your tickets, or you may write to the Prefettura della Casa Pontificia, Citta del Vaticano, 00120 Roma (to the attention of **Father McGuire**), and pray that the post offices involved do their job within 60 days. You also may write to the Jesuit Curia, Borgo Santo Spirito, 00193 Roma, if you have Jesuit connections. If you are already in Rome, you can ask for help from the local American Catholic church, **Santa Susanna**, in **Largo Santa Susanna**. Probably the best bet for last-minute audience requests is the office at the **North American College** for seminarians, Via dell'Umilta 30, Rome 00187 (6789184), near the Trevi fountain. The office is supported by American bishops—but they do not claim to work miracles. You may also write far in advance to that office for tickets.

A general audience lasts about 2 hours; the best way to return to your hotel afterward is on foot. (The pope also appears at noon, sharp, at his library window to bless the crowd each Sunday he is in Rome, or at **Castel Gandolfo** if he is on summer holiday.)

A view of the city from a 1st century inhabitant: Smoke, wealth and noise.

Horace

Piazza del
Popolo

(Reshaped 1816-1820, **Giuseppe Valadier**) This square was the first part of Rome that pilgrims saw as they arrived from the north through **Porta del Popolo**. When **Queen Christina of Sweden** renounced her throne to become a Catholic and live in Rome, **Pope Alexander VII** had **Bernini** remodel the inner face of the porta for her arrival in 1655.

1 **Obelisk** The largest obelisk in Rome was brought here in 1589 from **Circus Maximus**. It was brought from Egypt by the first emperor of Rome, **Augustus**, around 10 BC and is over 3000 years old.

2 **Santa Maria del Popolo** (1099, architect unknown) This church is tucked into the Walls of Rome and built over the supposed tomb of **Nero** to chase away his ghost, which haunted the area. His wife was buried in a pyramid across the square, where **Rosati's** bar now stands. In 1477, during the reign of **Pope Sixtus IV**, this church was rebuilt. It contains a treasure chest of fabulous paintings from **Raphael** to **Pinturicchio**, from **Sansovino** to **Caravaggio**. The remains of **Cattanei Vanozza** and her murdered son, the **Duke of Gandia**, lie here. She was the mistress of **Alexander VI**, the Borgia pope; their other 2 children were **Cesare** and the beautiful **Lucrezia**. Cesare's ambition knew no bounds; he forced his attentions on his sister, murdered his brother, and finally perished because of it. The great *bon vivant* and brilliant patron of the arts, **Agostino Chigi**, is also buried here.

3 Rosati Enjoy the symmetry of Piazza del Popolo at what many say is the best café in Rome. The Rosati family has been serving visitors and Romans alike for 3 generations. They say there's a restaurant upstairs, but we've never heard of anyone going there. ♦ M, W-Su 7:30AM-midnight. Piazza del Popolo 5A. 3225859, 3611418

4 Canova The rival to Rosati's bar. Where the sun-lovers go to sit n' soak, in good weather. Named after the early 19th-century Venetian sculptor **Antonio Canova**, famed for his full frontal of Napoleon's sister Pauline (see **Villa Borghese** on page 29). Recently renovated. ♦ Piazza del Popolo 16. 3612231, 3612227

5 Santa Maria dei Miracoli and Santa Maria di Monte Santo (1679, C. **Rainaldi** with help from **Bernini** and **Fontana**) The design of these churches was based on the idea that as pilgrims entered Rome, these 2 seemingly identical buildings would welcome them with an example of the majestic quality of Rome. Rainaldi struggled and magnificently triumphed in making them appear the same, although the plots of land on which they stand are quite different—one church is round, the other elliptical.

6 Dal Bolognese ★★$$$ A chic restaurant where you can go and hope to be noticed, but failing that, you can look around and hope to see somebody worth noticing. Some critics claim that the fashion outshines the cooking, but the trolley of boiled meats with a delectable green sauce has earned its fame. Also good are figs (when in season) and prosciutto, pasta, and *carpaccio* (paper-thin raw beef with Parmesan and *rughetta*). To finish off the meal, try the gooey trifle. ♦ Closed Monday, Sunday night, and part of August. Piazza del Popolo 1. Reservations required. 3611426

7 Studio S Carmine Siniscalco presides over Rome's top gallery, where a vernissage is

Piazza del Popolo

both a social and an artistic event. ♦ Via della Penna 59. 3612086

8 Hotel Locarno $$ One of the most attractive of the intimate neighborhood hotels in downtown Rome. No restaurant, but a cozy bar. Here the décor is Art Nouveau. Thirty-eight rooms, one suite. ♦ Via della Penna 22. 3610841, 3610060; fax 3604898

9 Osteria St. Ana ★★$$ Rather "in" place with suave Italians and the international movie crowd. Rough, white-washed country walls and a plethora of pictures on the wall make this cozy celler feel like an art gallery. Know that the antipasto laid out on your table is not a gift—taste it and it will show up on your bill! This is not one of the restaurants that include a glass of bubbly or a bite of pâté in the cover charge. (Roman cover charges vary from one to 6000 lire and often are not marked on the menu as they should be.) Perhaps the best filet mignon in Rome. ♦ Via della Penna 68. 3610291

10 59 ★★$$$ Many people swear by this restaurant and rave about the food, but we find the ambiance cold and the service precious. The specialties are from Bologna, one of the meccas of Italian cuisine. The inspiration came from Rome's contemporary restaurateuse, **Ceasarina**, who has unfortunately gone on to the land of the great *grillade*. Ave! ♦ Closed Saturday (June-July), Sunday, and August. Via A. Brunetti 59. Reservations recommended. 3619019

Restaurants/Clubs: Red	Hotels: Blue
Shops/Parks: Green	**Sights/Culture:** Black

11 L'Artigiano On a quiet side street, a dedicated man plies his trade of working fine leather into one-of-a-kind belts or bags. ◆ Via del Vantaggio 36. 5314646

12 La Buca di Ripetta ★★★$$ A family-run place with simple, delicious food, including great mashed potatoes. Arrive early or late as there are no reservations and it's always crowded. Reasonable prices. ◆ Closed Monday, Sunday evening, and August. Via di Ripetta 36. 3219391

13 Galeria Gabbiano Sandro Manzo has moved to New York, but he always appears for the openings of his magnificently organized shows. ◆ Via della Frezza 51. 3227049

14 Pot Danish beauty **Merete Stenbock** heads a group of Italian connoisseurs who offer hand-painted plates, trompe l'oeil wooden panels, quilts, and hand-crafted terra-cotta pots. She herself designs the stunning wrought-iron furniture. Her tables can come with a beautiful mosaic designed especially for you. A very popular shop. ◆ Via della Frezza 11. 3227110

15 Canova's Studio Now a rather pedestrian art gallery, this is where the great sculptor **Antonio Canova** (1757-1822) created masterpieces that astounded and delighted. They are

Piazza del Popolo

extremely realistic, and the marble is so polished and smooth that it seems lifelike to the touch. ◆ Via delle Colonnette

16 Bar Maneschi Arguably the best ice cream in town, though not as well known as Tre Scalini in Piazza Navona. And, oh joy! There are lots of real fruit sherbets in at least 15 flavors. If you're feeling particularly hot and thirsty, try the *granita di caffè* (fresh iced coffee with optional whipped cream) or *granita di limone* (lemon literally crushed with ice). ◆ M-Sa 8AM-8PM. Via del Corso 66. No credit cards. 6784225

17 Via del Corso Italy's answer to the American shopping mall, this is Rome's longest and busiest supermarket. But it is highly repetitive: mostly jeans, sneakers, and other clothes for the young. Recently made into a pedestrian island with crowds of youths at virtually every hour, the shops and the merchandise change too frequently for us to chronicle. Enjoy yourself.

18 Cesari Fabrics Wall hangings, curtain materials, sofa covers. This elegant house almost invites you in with its curving staircase and candle lamps on the facade. The Cesari flag shop is on Via Barberini (see page 20). ◆ Via del Babuino 16. 3611441

19 Cesari/Vivai del Sud A brand new venture combining the chic of elegant outdoor furniture and flower power with Cesari's matchless furnishings. ◆ Via del Babuino 195

20 L'Artistica Artists' Supplies If you prefer to create your own paintings rather than buy those old ones in the nearby antique shops. ◆ Via del Babuino 23. 6792182

21 Ritz Why don't you step inside and do a bit of *putting on the Ritz*? Inestimably smart, ultra-conservative leisure clothes. ◆ Via del Babuino 188. 3612057

22 Hotel Valadier $$$ One of those charming, intimate hotels. Forty rooms (6 suites). All modern conveniences in a moderne setting. According to the prospectus *the perfect equilibrium of this concordance will stylize, from now on, every gesture, every request.* ◆ Via della Fontanella 15. 3610592, 362344, 3510059; fax 3601558

23 Lion Bookshop English-language stock with the accent on English. A large selection of travel books—including this one, but they've usually just run out of it. Cookbooks and novels and a nice literary atmosphere. ◆ Via del Babuino 181. 3605837

23 Fava *Favoloso!* Fava specializes in 17th- and 18th-century pictures of Vesuvius eruptions. These were the postcards of those times. Englishmen would tour the peninsula and the Neapolitans would churn out volcanic paintings. Eye-catching dark-of-night renditions of this local disaster kept the pounds sterling pouring in; no one could resist these colorful conflagrations—and it's difficult to do so today. ◆ Via del Babuino 180. 3610817

24 Arturo Ferrante Antiques Large still lifes of weird fish. Eighteenth-century bas-reliefs in pale-pink clay. And some micromosaics; one particularly fine example has a view of Rome in the center, surrounded by a Greek key design in perspective. But not cheap. ◆ Via del Babuino 42. 6783613

25 Armeria Antiquaria Marvelous little shop crammed with ancient guns, sabers, old military uniforms, a plethora of helmets, lead soldiers, and...a penny-farthing bicycle. ◆ Via del Babuino 161. 3614158

25 Café Notegen A nice place to rest your weary feet. Whereas a Roman bar rarely has places to sit, this is a *caffè*. Like a tearoom, with lots of tables and chairs. ◆ Via del Babuino 159. 3600855

26 Il Cortile Inside the courtyard of this attractive palazzo are 2 art galleries. The important one is Il Cortile, on the right of the fountain, run by the daughter of top contemporary Italian painter **Monachesi**. When **Luce** stages an opening the courtyard fills with the cream of Roman society, who drink her wine and gaze at her latest avant-garde art show. ◆ Via del Babuino 51. 6785724

27 All Saints Anglican Church (1882, **George E. Street**) Gothic revival. Protestant communion services in English every Sunday morning at 8:30 and 10:30. For some reason this Church of England parish comes under the diocese of Gibraltar. (The Catholic English-language church is Santa Susana, in the square of the same name.) ◆ Via del Babuino 153B (entrance on Via Gesù e Maria) 6794357

28 Stildomus Very modern furniture that's pretty expensive, but worth it. Top-of-the-line Italian design gives you useful items not otherwise available, such as a self-contained desk-and-bureau and halogen lamps. ♦ Via del Babuino 54. 6798645

29 Carlo Lampronti A small temple of Chinese antiques and porcelain figurines. The China figurines with detachable heads that wag—and stick out their tongues—are increasingly hard to find, according to Carlo, and cost a bomb. ♦ Via del Babuino 152 and 69. 6790306

30 Scuola di Arti Ornamentali If you are able to gain admission from the Rome commune, you may study frescoes, tapestry, weaving, and jewelry, as well as traditional painting, graphics, and sculpture. Geared to the working person, it is open in the afternoon and evening. But you can only apply on one day of the year and it is on a first-come, first-served basis. ♦ Via San Giacomo. 6790602

31 Livio di Simone Hand-painted canvas is worked into suitcases of all sizes with the softest leather corners you ever did espy. Expensive. ♦ Via San Giacomo 23. 6783906

31 Pitti Contemporary decorative objects. Animal cushions and boxes, cat *portemanteaux* made of tole. Funny, unusual, sometimes even useful presents for him, her, and you. ♦ Via San Giacomo 19. 6795930

32 Church of San Atanasio (1583, **Giacomo della Porta**) The Greek Catholic Church of Rome. ♦ Via del Babuino at Via San Giacomo

33 Oliver Valentino's ready-to-wear for chic young men and women. But you don't have to be that young—or that chic—to enjoy these clothes. ♦ Via del Babuino 61. 6798314

34 Fountain of the Baboon (Pre-1581) This is one of the famous "talking statues" of Rome, so named because they were used for hanging placards criticizing the city's rich and powerful—mostly the pope and his coterie. Witty and subversive, they filled the same role as the billboard in Tienanmen Square once filled for the restless citizens of Beijing. But Rome's were funnier. This was one of the first privately financed public fountains, originally placed near here by **Alessandro Grandi**, whose vast orchards stretched up the hill to the Pincio. In 1572 he had helped pay for mending the ancient Acqua Vergine aqueduct, which he needed to water his grapevines. The basin was from one of the classical Roman baths. The reclining figure behind the waterspout was originally supposed to be a Silenus, the mythological figure with a horse's ears and tail—but the local wits quickly dubbed it a baboon; this lead to the street being changed to Via del Babuino from the original Via Paolina. Just imagine the beauty of this area in the 16th century when there were only a few noble houses in the lee of the rolling farmland. Behind the fountain is the oldest artist's studio in the area, belonging to 4 generations of sculptors from the **Tadolini** family. ♦ Via del Babuino at Via dei Greci

35 Hotel Mozart $$ The rooms are not vast, but their ceilings are higher than in most Hil-tons. And with 31 rooms the hotel is small enough to allow for personalized service. But there is satellite TV, and it's spanking clean. ♦ Via dei Greci 23B. 6787422, 6787426; fax 6784261

Within the Hotel Mozart:

La Luna d'Oro Attractive place to have a drink, but why do they call these places *American bars*? Perhaps because they are designed for people who want to stay a while and not rush off after one quick drink? ♦ 6788923

36 Granmercato Antiquario Babuino (GAB) Rome's miniversion of London's Silver Vaults, with a lot of Sheffield, well presented in glass showcases. Slews of Victorian teething rings and rattles made of ivory and coral trees with silver handles. Nutcrackers of all sizes and shapes. For the man who has everything, including ink in his pen: a silver roller for blotting paper. Most of these Sheffield items, and the mahogany furniture in Rome's antique stores, are imported from England. ♦ Via del Babuino 150. 6785903, 6783304; fax 6841402

37 Licia Romano There must have been an awful lot of painters doing still lifes for noble

patrons in the 17th and 18th centuries. A few of the best have ended up here. ♦ Via del Babuino 142. 6791198

37 Emporio Armani Effortlessly exorbitant gray-on-gray look. Where the superior go to keep looking superior. Vast open floors with no door and a milling crowd of clones wandering bright-eyed like Alice in Wonderland. ♦ Via del Babuino 140. 6796898, 6788454

38 Amadeo Di Castro Antique art objects such as bas-relief sculptures and large terra-cotta pieces. ♦ Via del Babuino 77. 6790393

39 Adolfo Di Castro Seven antique shops in this area carry the Di Castro name, 4 on this street alone, but Adolfo says they are no relation. Here we have a mix of good 19th-century oils, Napoleon III furniture, and some fine micromosaics. These pictures crafted from tiny, barely visible minichips of colored glass were, Adolfo claims, invented here on Via del Babuino in the late 18th or early 19th century by **Giacomo Rafaeli** of the Vatican mosaic studio. The process involves heating Murano glass until it can be pulled out into wire-thin ribbons of color, which are then cut into short pieces resembling inch-long leads from a pencil. These are hand-assembled chip-by-chip, like bundles of matches stood on their ends, into wondrous pictures, usually views of cities and landscapes. Being a Roman art form, they often depicted views of the Eternal City and were sold as souvenirs to the more discriminating tourists. Here, for millions of lire, you can buy large panels made by Rafaeli's contemporary **Michelangelo Barberi**. ♦ Via del Babuino 80. 6795792

40 Mario Oasi Two stunning 17th-century terra-cotta Turks guard the entrance corridor to this antique shop that looks small but goes through the whole block to Via Margutta. A highly ornate 18th-century mirror with almost life-size cherubs and Venuses that must have come from a cardinal's palace. ♦ Via del Babuino 83/Via Margutta 66. 6780177

41 Zoffoli Antique silver and tiny "Fabergé" eggs. Hat pin specialist. ♦ Via del Babuino 137. 6790628

41 Olivi Small treasure house of old prints and books. Prof. Olivi really knows Roman history through its lithographs and can answer your most obtuse questions. ♦ Via del Babuino 136

41 W. Apolloni The ultimate temple of antiques—red velvet, white-marble busts, and glistening fountains. Highly lacqered 17th-century convivial genre scenes complete the somewhat precious ensemble. Of note are a pair of early 19th-century sofas in embossed epoch leather and a fine marble scagliola table depicting a bright-orange pumpkin. ♦ Via del Babuino 133. 6792429

42 Pinci Brass everything. Good assortment of brass ornaments and fixtures from small statues to attractive hooks for your bathrobe. We

Piazza del Popolo

like their dull brass finish more than the shiny look one usually finds. ♦ Via del Babuino 128. 6795154

c.u.c.i.n.a.

43 C.U.C.I.N.A. This is no bargain basement kitchen outlet, but a serious array of professional utensils for practicing *la grande cucina*. Impressive, overpriced kitchen battery you just might find useful. ♦ Via del Babuino 118A. 6791275

GIORGIO ARMANI

44 Giorgio Armani Top of the line for men and women who understand. The Rolls-Royce of modern clothing. ♦ Via del Babuino 102. 6793777, 6788257

45 Missoni The famous high-style, high-colored, high-fashion knitwear. Some of the sweaters are so spectacular that your boyfriend is liable to snatch them when you aren't looking. ♦ Via del Babuino 97. 6797971

46 Alinari He was the great 19th-century Florentine photographer whose prints are as treasured as Boticellis. This store carries photos by him and by the other great chroniclers of their times. If you want a record of how some corner of Rome looked at various times since the invention of the Brownie, they will help you locate the photos in the extraordinary

archives, and will order prints from the Florence headquarters. Picture books as well. ♦ Via d'Alibert 16A. 6792923

47 Osteria Margutta ★$$$ An attractive restaurant reflecting the artists' studio atmosphere of this lovely street. **Piero Gabrielli** offers good salads and Roman food. ♦ Via Margutta 82. 6798190

48 Via Margutta 53A Step into this courtyard and see 2 beautiful black-and-white mosaics rendered in the antique Roman manner (on the right-hand wall). ♦ Via Margutta 53A

49 Roberto della Valle Another temple, we wondered? Yes, we decided. Roberto's mosaic floors, marble emperor's bust, and the theatricality of heavy red-silk curtains (that turn out to be trompe l'oeil wallpaper) merit the temple accolade reserved for really fine antique shops. ♦ Via Margutta 85. 6796809

50 Turchi Yet another temple. As you walk in you feel you're on hallowed ground. Everything around you is beautifully carved in marble, and very ancient. **Alfredo** and **Valerio Turchi** have collected superb Carthaginian-style mosaics from the 3rd century AD, some showing antelopes in polichrome marble. ♦ Via Margutta 91A. 6792792, 6120056

51 Avignonese **Attilio Amato** always has some new line of beautiful objects for your home: wonderful terra-cotta boxes, bowls, lamps; burnished wooden pots and columns; marble obelisks and balls; and great misty glass jars wired as lamps. He has impeccable taste. ♦ Via Margutta 16. 3614004

52 Margutta Vegeteriano ★$$ Even if you don't care for vegetarian restaurants you'll go for the peaceful ambiance of this upper-class veggy emporium, and for the great wine card. Margutta operates this and **Antico Bottaro** at Passegiata di Ripetta 15 (3612281). ♦ Via Margutta 119 (around the corner toward Via del Babuino) 6786033

53 Pincio An attractive public park that connects directly with the gardens of Villa Borgese (see page 29). The view of the city of Rome from the terrace looking down to Piazza del Popolo is magnificent. The garden is known for the busts of famous Italians that edge its lanes, as well as the unusual water clock.

Dining on Pincio Hill:

Casina Valadier $$ The view here is marvelous. Come early or pretty late when the weather is nice, as smart Romans flock here to soak up the sun. Antipasto of mozzarella balls and cured ham, then spaghetti and ravioli, veal cutlets, salad, and ice cream. The price isn't too high, and the kids can run around while the parents have coffee. After your meal, walk down the steps and pause to admire the 4 statues with their Phrygian caps—in 1789, the French revolutionaries took this cap as a symbol of the Revolution. ♦ Closed Monday. 6792083, 6796368

Restaurants/Clubs: Red   Hotels: Blue
Shops/Parks: Green   **Sights/Culture:** Black

Eating in Italy

In most countries food fuels the active population, whose function it is to produce goods and thus contribute to national growth. This pyramid is inverted in Italy, where heavy and light industry, the service sector of the economy, and, in fact, the entire national infrastructure are designed to promote eating. The automotive and public transportation industries are booming in Italy because they expidite the delivery of food to the eaters—and vice versa. Italians comprise the quintessential consumer society, dedicated to consuming the food they grow, distribute, and commercialize. For this is *the* activity about which they really care.

A typical Italian's day opens with coffee and the croissant-like *cornetto*. (Foreigners must avoid barking *cornutto* at café waiters, who may not want their wives' fidelity questioned publicly.) To compensate for the limited quantity on which they breakfast, Italians have developed the world's highest quality coffee. Although their physicist Enrico Fermi made an important contribution to atomic fission, most Italians are more concerned with the espresso machine, a major 20th-century contribution to culture in Western Europe. These geyserlike pressure cookers produce in as little as 12.5 seconds a tiny cup of coffee that is demonstrably fresh, never bitter, and has minimal effect on cardiac fibrillation.

The espresso machines are a major export item and contribute significantly to the economy of northern Italy, where they are designed, engineered, and mass-produced. It should be mentioned that Italians usually take their morning espresso not at a sit-down café but at a stand-up bar—so called despite the absence of a rail for foot-resting—since Italians remain on their feet throughout the coffee ritual, as they do in St. Peter's during Mass. The supernatural qualities of espresso coffee are illustrated by the fact that Italians drink it in the morning with the conviction that it will wake them up, and in the evening with equal certainty that it will put them right to sleep—and it does.

Pasta is the main feature of lunch. This meal is followed by a siesta, which guarantees Italian longevity and health. This tradition may be disappearing, but it was long believed that the pasta-siesta cause was championed by the Vatican in the belief that men who shared the midday break with their mistresses would return to their wives and children in the evening with avid (i.e., guilt-ridden) devotion and thus safeguard family values.

That workers still leave the office for lunch is proven by the 2 midday gridlocks that tie up Italian life, first on the telephone lines, then in the automobile lanes. In Rome, for several minutes just before 1:30PM, all phone circuits are hopelessly busy. A foreigner might assume that this is the moment of peak business activity when negotiations are intense and contracts are being settled. However, an Italian knows that this is when everybody phones the cook and cries out *Butta la pasta*! (Throw the spaghetti in boiling water!) Then follows a grand prix sprint as everyone tries to get to his or her pasta while it is still al dente—chewable, undercooked, perfect! Meanwhile, buses are bulging, taxis are unavailable, and subway trains are under siege by the entire working population traveling to that great midday meal (taken in Rome about 2:00PM, much earlier in the north, and still later in the south). Between 2:30 and 3:00PM Rome's streets are deserted; central areas officially closed to traffic are unpatrolled and freely passable. It is an ideal time to drive across town, although when you get there you will find everything closed, everyone away—eating.

Dinner comes much, much later (any time between 9-11PM); it's the big event for which lunch was only a prelude. Dinner is a social event, whether at home or at a restaurant. Note: a trattoria is also a restaurant, the difference being that it is less likely to have white tablecloths. Further note: if you want just one rule of thumb for choosing restaurants, avoid those with white tablecloths as they are likely to be either much more expensive than you anticipated or way below your standards.

Italian restaurants and trattorias are grand opera: noisy, colorful, and (often simultaneously) very serious as well as light-hearted. The quality of one performance may differ from another, because everyone, onstage and off, is a prima donna (or *primo uomo*).

Foreigners must not imagine that a waiter in Italy is a mere spear-carrier as in other countries, upstaged by the maître d'. No, in Italy it is the waiter who plays the leading role and deserves the applause. He memorizes the score and carries the whole performance from beginning to end without losing a note. It is he, not some captain or even owner, who tells you what you should eat, memorizes your order—and that of all his other customers—steps and fetches, shows concern for your enjoyment, and finally asks for and receives your payment. He is the real hero of Italy's central ritual and key economic endeavor.

Piazza del Popolo

Recommended Art Galleries

Studio S **Carmine Siniscalco** (his brother is the sculptor **Sinisca**) puts on a variety of high-caliber shows. **De Chirico** is a favorite, and Carmine S. helps organize exhibitions of his work throughout Europe. His artists are figurative but always have a touch of mystery. To help foster new talent Carmine tries to give young aspirants equal time with more established artists. ♦ Via della Penna 59. 3612086

Il Gabbiano The exuberant **Sandro Manzo** maintains this gallery's high quality season after season. **Botero** is a favorite of his, as is **Constance La Palombara**. The stable of artists is figurative, but there's a sense of humor lurking in the shadows. Sandro travels constantly and now spends part of his time in New York. ♦ Via della Frezza 51. 3607049

Il Cortile Spectacular **Luce Monachesi** is in the avant-garde of Roman art. Her shows are usually abstract, minimalist, preposterous, or happenings! She was brought up in an artistic milieu; her father is the well-known painter **Monachesi**. ♦ Via del Babulino 51. 6785724

Il Ponte Shows curated by **Marguerite Failone** are often outrageous, and she has an unerring eye for detail. She deals, in the best American style, all over the world, from Chicago to Tokyo. ♦ Via Sant'Ignazio 116. 6796114

Galleria 2 RC **Walter Rossi** and his wife have the best print studio in town. They've been working for famous artists, producing exactly the right tones for years. A recent series was by **Sutherland**. ♦ Via dei Delfini 16. 6792811

Phone in advance if you want to visit an art gallery in the morning—most are open only from 4-7:30PM.

via Condotti

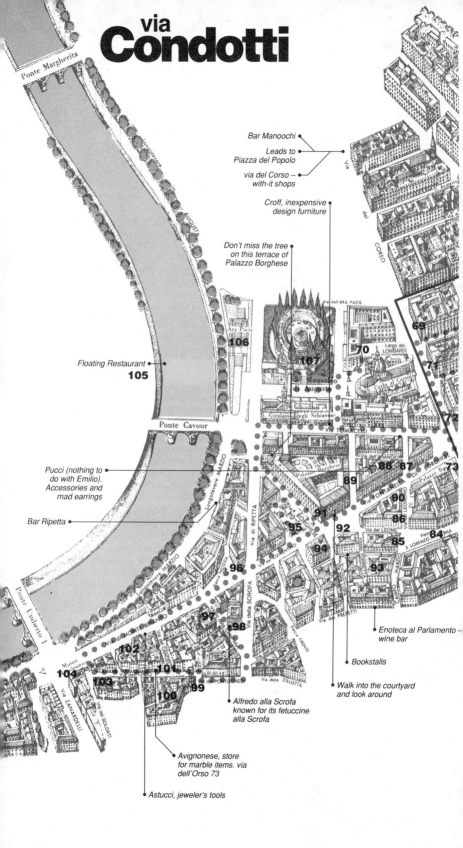

Bar Manoochi •

Leads to •
Piazza del Popolo

via del Corso –
with-it shops

Croff, inexpensive •
design furniture

Don't miss the tree •
on this terrace of
Palazzo Borghese

Floating Restaurant •
105

Pucci (nothing to •
do with Emilio).
Accessories and
mad earrings

Bar Ripetta •

Enoteca al Parlamento –
wine bar

Bookstalls

Walk into the courtyard
and look around

Alfredo alla Scrofa
known for its fetuccine
alla Scrofa

Avignonese, store
for marble items. via
dell'Orso 73

Astucci, jeweler's tools

via Babuino – an antique shop street

Outdoor snack bar in good weather

Flower and vegetable stand

via Margutta – the artist's street

Pet shop – parrots and hamsters

This aerial view may be the only view you get into this beautiful garden!

In blistering weather duck your feet in the fountain

Economy Bookstore

taxi stand

Fendi Lane

Clothes for Tots

Look up at the bee over each doorway

Laura Biagotti, elegant clothes

via Tritone leads up to via Veneto

Oringinal site of Ara Pacis Augustae

Shoes and boots

Great cafe-bar

Prime Minister's house – Palazzo Chigi

Rinascente Department Store for clothes and toiletries

Roller skating in the evening

Central post office

Cables and telex

SIP – phone operators

Quick photo developing/printing

Visit the Trevi Fountain at night when its full splendor is illuminated

= newsstands

See detail map of shopping area on page 99

65

Via Condotti is your day for self-indulgence. There are only a few monuments and historical places to visit. Instead, this area is known for its superlative shopping, Italian-style; some feel it even surpasses that of Paris. Certainly a lot of fine goods found in France are made here, and Italians have a flair for just about anything that's visual—and audible! Each time you walk through these streets you will be intrigued by places that you didn't see the first time.

The chic ambiance started when the **Spanish Steps** were built in 1721. The English milords moved in on the Roman leg of their Grand Tour to imbibe culture, and new hotels sprang up to accommodate them on their arrival from the north through nearby Porta Flaminia.

Via Condotti is named after the subterranean conduits of water from the **Aqueduct Acqua Virgine** (so named after a beautiful young girl who, in the 1st century BC, showed the engineers of Agrippa the spring for which they had been searching). This water fed many of the fountains, the Baths of the Pantheon, and the Baths of Agrippa (1st century AD).

Breakfast is usually included in the price of your hotel, but **Babington's**, at the bottom of the Spanish Steps, is a good place for your morning meal if you can hold out until after you've wandered around the top of the Steps. There are lots of places to eat lunch—just choose from the restaurants in the area in which you find yourself at lunchtime. But please check on museum hours—many are open only until 1PM.

1 **Obelisk** (1st century BC) In 1788 it was moved from **Sallust**'s nearby gardens (AD 100); the US Embassy now stands on a small part of these grounds. Said to be an ancient Roman copy of an Egyptian obelisk (i.e. an early fake—more recent fakes are Fendi and Gucci bags for sale on the steps below). There are 48 Egyptian obelisks in Rome. They were brought from Egypt in ancient Roman times (roughly between 200 BC and AD 200) on specially built boats—probably *quadriremes* (4 stories of oarsmen). During the latter period Roman emperors placed special orders for obelisks that were made to their specifications—some had the hieroglyphs added after delivery in Rome. ♦ Piazza Trinità dei Monti

2 **Trinità dei Monti Church** (1495) **Charles VIII** of France founded this twin-towered church of golden stone in memory of his stay in Rome in 1495. Today it may be Rome's most photographed church. Inside there are several chapels, including one endowed by the French ambassador who financed the Spanish Steps in 1660. There are 2 frescoes by **Federigo Zuccari**: one in the chapel to the left of the presbyter of the **Coronation of the Virgin Mary**, and the other in the 6th chapel on a large lunette of **Augustus** and **Sibyll** (1553). ♦ Piazza Trinità dei Monti

3 **Convent of the Sacré Coeur (Sacred Heart) and French Kindergarten** (17th Century) Built on the remains of the grandiose **Villa of General Lucullus** (AD 63), you can only get to see this pastoral spot if you send your child to the school. It is probably worth it. ♦ Piazza Trinità dei Monti 3. 6792245

4 **Villa Medici** (c. 1590, **Annibale Lippi**) **The French Academy** (similar to the British and American academies, and for that matter, the academies of all countries who have such cul-

tural establishments in Rome) houses the lucky Fellows who have won the *Prix de Rome* competition to study art, history, architecture, or archeology in Rome for 2 years. Good art shows are held periodically. Just a modest country house before **Cardinal Ricci** of Montepulciano converted it to its present magnificence on the designs of Lippi. Its imposing facade is quite spare of ornamentation except for a slight enhancing of the windows with discreet architraves. But on the garden side, the walls are covered by a solid tracery of sculpted decoration. **Pope Leo XI** (1605, a Medici from the famous Florentine family) lived in the palazzo and gave it his name. The splendid park is open to the public Wednesday 9-11AM. ♦ Viale Trinità dei Monti. 6798381

5 Hotel Hassler & Villa Medici $$$$ The top hotel in Rome. **Mrs. Carmen Wirth**, the owner, is Swiss-American and combines the best of both traditions. Her son, **Roberto Wirth**, who manages the hotel, was recently honored as *Best Hotel Director in the World*. The nicest apartments, abutting onto the church belfry at the top of the Spanish Steps, all have great views, and some have balconies. The ground-floor lounge and bar are vast period pieces with a pianist tinkling out live Muzak late afternoon and evening. The barman makes a mean Bloody Mary. In summer the inner courtyard becomes an open-air restaurant. The hotel prides itself on being elegant, so don't turn up in scruffy jeans! ♦ Deluxe ♦ Piazza Trinità dei Monti 6. 6782651, 6792651; fax 6799278

Within the Hotel Hassler & Villa Medici:

The Hassler Roof Restaurant ★★★$$$$ Serves fine food, including à la carte lobster and caviar. ♦ Piazza Trinità dei Monti 6. Reservations required. 6782651, 6792651

6 Hotel de la Ville $$$ Right next door to the Hassler is another first-rate hotel. Each of the reasonably priced rooms has a television, a direct-dial telephone, and air conditioning. There is even a garage for guests' cars. The building is old, which gives it the advantage of varied rooms, so your choice is wide open. Hollywood actress **Valerie Perrine** always manages to get one of the rooms with a sensational terrace. Within the hotel is a bar and a restaurant. (You eat in the courtyard during summer.) Beautiful view from the roof. ♦ Via Sistina 67. 6733; fax 6784213

7 La Scalinata di Spagna $$ Lovely little pension of 14 roomlets. The best to ask for are Nos. 15 and 16, which open directly onto the terrace, where you can have breakfast in the summer. Don't miss the tame parrot—

he's divine! Some people book in advance—for their honeymoon. No restaurant. ♦ Piazza Trinità dei Monti 17. 6793006; fax 6840896

8 Valentino Haute Couture This place is not for the timid, and rightly so. Those with pocketbooks of capacious dimensions, and a lot of taste, come here to order a favorite suit, cocktail dress, or ball gown. If you can't afford the high fashion, don't worry, you can go to his ready-to-wear boutiques: **Boutique Donna** (ladies), Via Bocca di Leone 15/18 (6795862), and **Boutique Uomo** (men), Via Condotti at Via Mario de' Fiori (6783656). ♦ Piazza Mignanelli 22 or Via Gregoriana 24. 67391, 6789638

9 Palazzetto of the Grotesque Masque (1591, **Federigo Zuccari**) A glorious rococo facade of a monstrous face; the door forms a mouth, the windows form the eyes. Designed by artist Federigo Zuccari, the younger of 2 painter brothers, it was destined to be a school for artists. Some of his paintings are in the **Trinità dei Monti Church**. Federigo went to England in 1574 and painted **Elizabeth I, Mary Tudor**, and nobles of their courts. It is now the **Hertzian Library for the Study of Art History**. ♦ Via Gregoriana 30

 Via Condotti

10 Hotel Gregoriana $$ Small 19-room hotel tucked away just a stone's throw from the top of the Spanish Steps. It is clean and cozy. Rooms R and S have the best views. No restaurant or bar. ♦ Via Gregoriana 18. No credit cards. 6794269, 6797988; fax 6784268

11 L'Isola Art Gallery This beautiful and spacious gallery used to be the **Marlborough Gallery**. L'Isola continues the high level of excellence with famous painters and sculptors such as **Pomodoro**. The gallery preference leans towards the abstract. The up-and-coming painters are personified in **Carlo Battaglia**, whose abstract seascapes have a pulsing, repetitive rhythm. Exhibitions change every 3 weeks. ♦ Closed Monday AM, Sunday, and Saturday PM, 1 June-15 Sep. Via Gregoriana 5. No credit cards. 6784678, 6790029

Restaurants/Clubs: Red   Hotels: Blue
Shops/Parks: Green   **Sights/Culture:** Black

12 Papirus: Art Paper Shop Everything here is colored by hand and a lot of the paper is handmade as well. Glorious swirls of yellow and blue (and every other color for that matter) make this paper unique. No 2 designs are the same. Marbleized paper was invented by a Frenchman in the court of **Louis XIII**. He quickly became personal bookbinder to the King. Today, Florence is the center for this type of artwork. Here at Papirus this paper is made up into a variety of gifts: jewel cases with velvet linings, book covers, diary covers, little sculptures, obelisks, photo frames, etc. It's difficult to resist buying something. ♦ Closed Monday AM and Sunday. Via di Capo le Case 55a. 6780418

13 Spanish Steps (1721, **Specchi and de Santis**) Since these were built thanks to a Frenchman's largesse, it is rather unfair to call them Spanish. (The Italians refer to them as the *Scalinata della Trinità dei Monti*—*never* the Spanish Steps!) Old engravings show the church on the crest of a hill with small trees descending to the piazza. The French ambassador **Monsieur Gouffier** financed the 137 steps, which were designed by **Alessandro Specchi** and **Francesco de Santis**. Throughout the centuries beggars had to buy a license to hustle travelers on the steps, and some of them became famous. The most beautiful women from all over the Italian peninsula would come to the steps to be discovered by the art-

Via Condotti

ists and sculptors working in nearby **Via Margutta**. (Still a street of artists, with 2 annual art shows in June and October.) The view from the top, over the roofs of Rome, is breathtaking, but the view from Via Condotti looking up the soaring stairs to the church is equally lovely—especially when they are massed with hot-pink azaleas at Easter time. It's a mob scene in the summer, on weekends, and in good weather.

14 Fontana della Barcaccia (The Old Barge, or Leaking Boat Fountain) (1629, **Pietro Bernini**) Because of lack of water pressure in the **Aqueduct Acqua Virgine**, which feeds it, this fountain, designed by **Bernini**'s father, was made to wallow under street level. Some say the Tiber's flooding in 1598, when a boat was washed up on this spot, is the true reason for this unusually shaped fountain. Don't miss the Barberini bees. They indicate that the patron was **Urbano VIII** from the Barberini family—elected to the papal throne only 4 years before the fountain was built. This was the height of the Roman Baroque, and many spectacular buildings, sculptures, and fountains were built during his reign.

15 Babington's Tea Room ★$$ A relic from the time when so many English lords stayed in this area on arrival in Rome during their Grand Tour—Via delle Carrozze, just opposite, is where they had their carriages repaired (*carrozza*=carriage). You can get an English breakfast of scrambled eggs here—the tea and crumpets are just as good as at home. But one may encounter grumpiness, slow service, and prices that aren't low. The dinky tables and seats are uncomfortable. ♦ M, W-Su 9AM-8PM. Piazza di Spagna 23. 6786027

16 Metro Station The metro is a relatively new and wonderful thing in Rome. It was difficult building it, as they were constantly stumbling on some great temple or other. It doesn't have too many stops but can be useful if you're not living in the center. It's also the best way to get to the Vatican (stop Ottaviano). ♦ Piazza di Spagna

17 Bottega Veneta Beautiful, elegant leather goods. **Vittorio Moltedo** prides himself on not having the eternal initials splashed everywhere. These goods are so finely made and so chic, one can immediately recognize them as coming from the Bottega. But they are not cheap. ♦ Via San Sebastianello 16b. 6796068

18 Pratesi Superb linen and cotton sheets, towels, and everything for the bath and bedroom. Expensive. ♦ Closed Monday AM and Sunday. Piazza di Spagna 10. 6790673

19 Keats and Shelley Memorial Museum Keats lived out the last few months of his young life in these cramped lodgings. In 1821, at age 27, he died painfully of tuberculosis in the little room over the Spanish Steps. You can see his death mask, many engravings, and a fine library of 19th-century books on Keats, **Shelley**, **Byron**, and the others. A lot of English poets, including **Elizabeth Barrett Browning, Thackeray**, and **Tennyson**, came to Rome for inspiration in the 19th century. These romantic poets were lured here to plunge into a rediscovery of the classics. They fell for the lyric beauty of the city, the ancient ruins, and the gentle countryside. Attractive souvenir ashtrays for sale. ♦ M-F 9AM-1PM, 3-6PM; Sa 9AM-1PM. Closed August. Piazza di Spagna 26. 6784235

20 Spagna 35 Quick Photo Service Your photos developed and printed within one hour. ♦ Piazza di Spagna 35 or Piazza Mignanelli 3. 6840317, 6840318

20 Maurizio Righini Caries Etro's luxury line of bags, slippers, robes, and throws from Milan. Also Hermès and Chanel bag rip-offs. ♦ Piazza di Spagna 36. 6783579, 679966

20 American Express Travel agent, money changer, mail holding service. ♦ M-F 9AM-5:30PM; Sa 9AM-12:30PM. Piazza di Spagna 38. Credit card service 549121, travel services 67641, lost or stolen cards (24 hrs) 72281, 72282

Horse-drawn carriages can be found in Piazza di Spagna and in St. Peter's Square.

Via Condotti Area Shopping Map

VIA DEL CORSO

VIA DEL GAMBERO

VIA MARIO DE'FIORI

VIA PROPAGANDA

PIAZZA DI SPAGNA

69 Simona

68 Cilli
68 Pape Satan
68 Sorelle Macalle

67 Vertecchi

66 Delucchi
66 Nectar
66 Wine Shop & Bar

65 Otello

VIA DELLA CROCE

71 Bruscoli

Il Sogno 68

59 Lilia Leoni

59 Toto alla Carrozze
Beltramme 67
Vertecchi scatole 67
Re Degli Amica 67
Angelo 67

Wiener Bierhaus 65
Fior Fiori 65
Hotel Condotti

61 Hotel Carriage
34 Restaurant
Hotel Piazza di Spagna

64

VIA BOCCA DI LEONE

VIA DELLE CARROZZE

• Nectar 72 Hotel Plaza
37 Max Mara

58 58 58
Bea I Numeri Moroni
36 Condotti Fine Art
• Battistoni
33 Benetton
33 Battistoni
• Ferragamo Gianni (Men's) 61 Versace

60 Serra

32 Cucci

30 ——— Ferragamo (Women's)
• Gucci
Bottega di Lungavita Ranieri 62
62

Siragusa 63

28 Caffé Greco

26 Richard Ginori

VIA BELSIANA

VIA MARIO DE'FIORI

VIA DEI CONDOTTI

Merola 74

Massoni •

Desmo 35
40 Franco Maria Ricci
40 Fendi Buccellati 35
40 De Paolo
Burma 34
Hotel d'Inghilterra Valentino
42 42

42 Palazzo Torlonio

Beltrami 31
Louis Vuitton 29
Gianni Carita 29
Valentino Uomo 29

45 Carlo Palazzi
45 Nino
Sergio Valente 27
Bulgari 27
Gucci 27
Newspaper
25 Kiosk

VIA BORGOGNONA

Diego della Valle 38
Laura Biagotti 38

52 Ramirez

Ferre 39

50 Santini
50 Cartotechnica
50 Company
LiO Bazaar 41
48 Bozart Flood Water
Plaque 41

Fendi 40
Fendi 40
Fendi 40

Moda 43
Gianni Versace 43
Uomo

Number 22 44
Givenchy 44
47 Bar dei Fiori

VIA BOCCA DI LEONE

VIA FRATTINA

53 Grilli

54 Fabi

54 Vanina
55 Anticoli

51 James Joyce Plaque

Benetton •

Saggiorno 49 in Frattina

56 Anglo-American Bookshop
56 Mario

Max Mara 47

Arimo 46

57 Onelli

VIA DELLA VITE

PIAZZA DI SPAGNA

Nipponya 57

21 **Apollodoro: Art, Architecture, Design**
A truly amazing art gallery and design shop with a range of objects from exquisite functional sculptures, such as **Michael Graves**' tea service in a Postmodern vein, to painting exhibitions; the pictures hang from trendy blue pipes with brass finials. **Paolo Portoghesi**, the top Italian architect, designed the space at the behest of his wife, who dreamed up the idea. **Giovanna Portoghesi Massobrio** and her husband were inspired by **Trajan's Forum** (1st century AD), designed by **Apollodorus** of Damascus, believing it to be one of the most superb architectural triumphs in the world. The trompe l'oeil entrance is marvelous—one is convinced there is a long glass gallery with marble floors stretching out ahead; in reality it is a deft painting on the front entrance. This theme is carried through the whole shop with great success. Highly

Via Condotti

recommended. ◆ M-Sa 10AM-2PM, 5-8:30PM. Closed August. Piazza Mignanelli 17. 6787557

21 **La Rampa** ★★$$ Terrific food and prices make this attractive restaurant one of our favorites. Reservations aren't accepted, but the wait is worth it. The antipasta is a must for lunch. Also great pasta and particularly good *abbacchio* (lamb). In summer, the restaurant spills out into the piazza under some beguiling vines. Inside, the décor makes you feel as if you are on a medieval Roman street. ◆ Closed Monday lunch, Sunday, and holidays. Piazza Mignanelli 18. No credit cards. 6782621

22 **Column of the Immaculate Conception** An antique column of marble discovered in the nearby **Via di Campo Marzio**. It was erected in 1857 and crowned with a statue of the Virgin Mary. Every year on 8 December the pope meets with the mayor to hold a prayer service, watched by a cast of thousands. This date commemorates the Feast of the Immaculate Conception.

23 **Catello d'Auria** Glove emporium with elegant Louis XV furniture and mirrors in which to admire your clad hands. In the family since 1894. Gloves are coming back! ◆ Via Due Macelli 55. 6793364

23 **Saglio Merceria** Buttons from Valentino, Chanel, St. Laurent, etc. Exclusive accessories. Upgrade your Bloomies suit! ◆ Via Due Macelli 71. 6784011

24 **Palace of the Congregation of the Propaganda Fide** (Propagation of the Faith) (1622, **Bernini** and **Borromini**) The 2 arch rivals worked jointly on the outside of the building. Bernini did the facade facing the square, Borromini the concave and convex side on Via di Propaganda just before committing suicide in 1667. The vast expanse of dark-red brick makes some people wax eloquent, but it seems a bit heavy and oppressive. **Pope Urbano VIII**'s ubiquitous bees can be seen on the Via dei due Macelli side. ◆ Piazza di Spagna (Via dei due Macelli-Via di Propaganda)

25 **Spanish Embassy to the Holy See (Vatican)** (1624) This stolid Baroque palace passed into Spanish possession in 1647. **Borromini** did many designs for remodeling it and was given a Spanish knighthood for his pains, but only his stairs and vestibule were executed, and in the 19th century the stairs were changed. **Antonio del Grande** is responsible for other alterations. **Bernini** did 2 busts, but none of this is visible unless you're Spanish. This embassy is the reason everything around here is called *Spanish*. It used to be the only Spanish Embassy when Rome was capital of the Papal States; but when **Garibaldi** finally conquered them in 1870, 10 years after the unification of the rest of Italy, Rome then became the capital of the new state. From then on there were 2 sets of embassies in Rome—one for Italy and one for the Vatican. ◆ Piazza di Spagna 56

25 **Newspaper Kiosk** Largest selection of US and foreign magazines in the area. ◆ Piazza di Spagna (Via Borgognona)

26 **Richard Ginori** A large range of porcelain, glass, tableware; some surprising designs and bright colors. ◆ Via Condotti 87/90. 6781013

27 **Gucci** Predictably beautiful leather goods known the world over. There's always a mob scene of tourists swaying backward and forward trying to get at the counter for some status symbol or other. The *Gs* abound on everything from leather suitcases to cigarette lighters. ◆ Closed Monday AM and Sunday. Via Condotti 8. 6790405, 6793888, 6789340. Also at: Via Condotti 77. 6796147, 6798343

The Italian chapter of the **Federation of Housewives**, whose membership exceeds 30,000, was formed in 1982 to campaign for the rights of housewives. Their priorities include financial remuneration for their work, life insurance, pension plans, and social security.

BVLGARI

27 Bulgari This upscale jewelry shop is famous the world over for its beautiful settings of BIG, BIG stones. Italian Style personified in luxurious glittering necklaces, rings, bracelets—something for everywhere a woman's body can be adorned! Plus heavy gold watches for men and women and various lovely jewels for men. The most unusual are the *filati* microchip mosaics of views of antique Rome, made into cufflinks. Superb. Have a look at the expensive solid-gold and platinum evening bags. Although the triple windows look forbidding, there are a few items that are affordable. Push on in. A beautifully worked pen at about $100, or a delicately chiseled key chain for only 3 times that, show that it is possible to buy something from the *Prince of Jewels* at a fairly reasonable price. ♦ M-Sa 10AM-7:30PM. Closed 12-19 August. Via Condotti 11. 6793876

27 Sergio Valente Great haircuts plus beauty and health care. This beauty center (for men and women) has been completely redesigned and expanded. Sergio has added a **Beauty Farm** by combining with **Dominique Chenot**, who created the **Villa Eden** spa in Merano. So you can have massage, face and body treatments, algae application, sauna, and sun, each taking place in a room decorated with heavenly flowers to help alleviate your stress. Escape the madding crowd and have a light, tasteful lunch prepared while having your beauty needs attended. ♦ Tu-Sa 9:30AM-7PM. Via Condotti 11. 2nd fl. 6791268, 6794515

28 Caffè Greco Some say that—even though it wasn't known as Greco until 1760—this is the same establishment that **Casanova** wrote about in his memoirs, where in 1743 he waited and waited for an amorous assignation with a lady-love who never appeared. You might do better. An attractive paneled place. The sandwiches are delicious, even if the waiters are a mite supercilious. **Ex-President Pertini** of Italy was a regular until his recent death. ♦ M-Sa 8AM-8:30PM. Via Condotti 86. No credit cards. 6791700

29 Valentino Uomo Every man longs to wear Valentino's 4 Ss: suits, shirts, sportswear, and sweaters; so come in and browse. ♦ Via Condotti at Via Mario de' Fiori. 6783656

29 Gianni Carita One of Milan's finest jewelers has installed himself in this gorgeous dual-level high-tech store. ♦ Via Condotti 13. 6840047

29 Louis Vuitton The initials are familiar. Since 1854 Louis Vuitton has been making great steamer trunks and other essentials for the traveler. It has become increasingly difficult to find street vendors hawking the fakes, so it's lucky the mother house in Paris finally opened a Rome branch. But don't expect bargains. ♦ Via Condotti 15. 6791086, 6840000

30 Ferragamo This Florentine shoe and bag dynasty has shops all over Italy. It has branched out into clothes, too, and all is in good taste and well made. Expensive, but so are all the others. ♦ Via Condotti 74. 6798402, 6791565. Also at: Via Condotti 66. 6781130

31 Beltrami Rather frighteningly large shop for men's and women's shoes, bags, and some clothes. Quite racy styles and hardly less expensive than their better-known competition. ♦ Via Condotti 19. 6791330

32 Cucci Couldn't resist putting this one in because of the name. What with Gucci, Pucci, and Cucci, you may just about have had it! This is a serious shop for men's ties, but it also sells men's and women's shoes and leather clothes. The colognes are good and affordable. ♦ Via Condotti 67. 6791882

33 Battistoni The finest men's shirts in the world. Colorful cotton cambrics, Egyptian gossamer-weight silks in stripes and checks. And shoes, suits, etc. And **Gianni Battistoni**, the genial shirt king, has brought out a fabulous men's cologne named *Marte* (Mars, the god of war)—essential for anyone out to conquer. There is a women's store at No. 57.

Via Condotti

♦ Via Condotti 61a (in the inner courtyard) 6786241

33 Benetton Sports clothes with a young and trendy look. Very successful conglomerate doing business worldwide. Strong colors. In this area alone there are 2 other Benetton clones. ♦ Via Condotti 60. 6790524

34 Burma Fake jewels with a capital F. If you can't go into Bulgari, come here. The settings are well done and the big stones look real, even if they aren't. ♦ Via Condotti 27. 6798285

35 Buccellati The most gorgeous jewelry. The favorite of anyone who understands painstaking quality. The look is the brushed-gold *Florentine* finish. It must take a silversmith months with the aid of a microscope to chisel these fine, understated works of art. Very expensive, but this didn't frighten off the poet **Gabrielle d'Annunzio**, who was a faithful client in the last century. ♦ Via Condotti 32. 6790329, 6786784

35 Desmo Shoes and bags. This used to be a good place to get Bottega Veneta-type leather goods at bargain prices. Now we find it's no longer a bargain and the look isn't as refined. ♦ Closed Monday AM and Sunday. Via Condotti 34. 6791122

Restaurants/Clubs: Red   **Hotels:** Blue
Shops/Parks: Green   **Sights/Culture:** Black

36 Condotti Fine Arts One of the most amusing, unusual antique shops in Rome. From large stone fountains to a plaster sculpture of a young girl and her monkey (18th-century Neapolitan and a cool 4,000,000 lire). ♦ Via Condotti 56. 6791973

37 Max Mara Another of mad Max's clones has invaded Condotti! See also the original on Via Frattina. ♦ Via Condotti 46. 6787946

38 Diego della Valle Fashionable men's and women's shoes. Open during lunchtime. ♦ Via Borgognona 45

38 Laura Biagiotti Beautiful duds for the working woman. Many of the clothes are in luxurious cashmere—including sweaters for the nonworking man. Laura finds inspiration in her medieval château on the edge of town, but her sizzling silks and calorific cashmeres look great in the cool urbanity of this vast showroom. ♦ Via Borgognona 43. 6791205

39 Gianfranco Ferre Ready-to-wear. Smart as only the Italians know how to be. This is the women's department; men are further up the same street. ♦ Via Borgignona 42B. 6790050, 6780256

40 Fendi *Elegantissimo*! Clothes, bags, suitcases, and shoes in leather as well as great fur

Via Condotti

coats. This street might have to be renamed Via Fendi because there are as many Fendi shops as there are Fendi sisters: **Anna, Carla, Paola, Franca**, and **Alda**—plus **Karl Lagerfeld** (their designer). ♦ Ready-to-wear boutique: Via Borgognona 40. Furs: 39. Regimental-striped accessories: 38B. Bags and leather articles: 36B. Shoes: 4/E. **Fendissime**, for the young (from the third Fendi generation): 4/L. ♦ 6797641

40 Franco Maria Ricci Fine bookstore. The coffee-table books about works of art *are* works of art! Ricci also publishes the fine art magazine *FMR*. ♦ Via Borgognona 4/D. 6793466

40 Profumeria De Paolo Pay cash and you'll get a discount on perfumes and body cosmetics. Open during lunchtime. ♦ Via Borgognona 4F. 6784018

41 Lio Bazaar Funny footwear and unusual shoes. Unique features include sneakers in silver or gold and lace hightop sneakers. ♦ Via Borgognona 35. 6784020

41 Flood Water Height Plaque In December 1870, the rain-swollen Tiber river reached this height (4 feet). ♦ Via Borgognona 33

42 Hotel d'Inghilterra $$$ One of our favorite hotels in Rome. Once a guest house for the **Torlonia Palace** (opposite at No. 78), the building became a hotel in 1850. From the **King of Portugal** to **Mark Twain, Henry James**, and **Ernest Hemingway**, the hotel has housed important guests. Situated slapdash in the great shopping area, it even has **Valentino** right next door. There are 4 suites on the top floor, each decorated differently, with lovely views of the city. There are 2 drawing rooms with exquisite 18th- and 19th-century paintings, some of the prettiest on glass. The Roman Garden—a suite of rooms with trompe l'oeil painting, as if one were outside in a garden—is a good place for a private business meeting. No restaurant, but there is a cozy bar—and our Condotti-watcher, **Andrea**, says the chic group from the **No-name** bar (formerly on the corner of Condotti and Belsiana) has moved its perpetual party here. One hundred two rooms. ♦ Via Bocca di Leone (Lion's Mouth) 14. 672161; fax 6840828

42 Valentino This is the women's boutique, so imagine what the couture clothes cost! But the quality is right. ♦ Via Bocca di Leone 15. 6795862

42 Palazzo Torlonia (1660, **G.A. de Rossi**) Sneak in and admire the large inner courtyard with its moss-covered fountain and Roman marble statue. The **Princely House of Torlonia** is quite a recently ennobled family. A certain gentleman from Toulon accompanied **Napoleon** on his wars and ended up in Italy owning a lot of real estate. Toulon was Italianized into Torlonia. ♦ Via Bocca di Leone 78

43 Moda This new women's shop is the sensation of the '90s. Moda's buyers relentlessly haunt London, Rome, Madrid, and New York day and night, on the lookout for the newest classic chic. Sonya Rykiel, Tarlazzi, Instante, Versace—all reasonably priced. ♦ Via Borgognona 31. 6790951

43 Gianni Versace Uomo You'll see the diff! These are designer clothes, and the design is Italian. ♦ Via Borgognona 29. 6795292

44 No name but the street number Very fine embroidered sweaters. ♦ Via Borgognona 22

44 Hubert de Givenchy The utter sophistication and understated quality of truly French fashion, at prices that are still less than in the US. Givenchy trained under **Balanciaga** and inherited his mastery of cutting. You might just bump into **Audrey Hepburn**; she often wears Givenchy clothes. ♦ M 3-7PM; Tu-Sa 10AM-7PM. Via Borgognona 21. 6784058

In Rome, every mansion with a court is called a *palazzo*.

45 Carlo Palazzi A wonderful setting in a Baroque palace for some wonderful men's clothes. Palazzi has been ahead of the pack for 20 years and isn't lagging yet. The ultimate in men's wear. ♦ Via Borgognona 7/C. 6791508, 6789143

45 Nino ★★$$$ An "in" place to go after a tiring day at the nearby fashion houses. This restaurant serves Florentine food: *zuppa di fagioli* (white-bean soup), *bistecca alla Fiorentina* (a tender T-bone steak), and a great crème caramel. House wine is more than adequate. ♦ M-Sa 1-3:30PM, 8-11PM. Via Borgognona 11. Reservations recommended. 6795676

46 Arimo Lingerie for women—and men. Young, practical, and reasonably priced. ♦ Via Frattina 16. 6780577

47 Bar dei Fiori Strangely shaped baby liquor bottles and fine ice creams. ♦ M-Sa 8AM-9PM. Via Frattina 135. 6783335

47 Max Mara Unusual medium-priced fashions with a zing. ♦ Via Frattina 28. 6793638

48 Bozart Costume jewelry. Not so much the big diamond or emerald, but lots of fun chains and earrings that are very much in style. ♦ Via Bocca di Leone 4. 6781025

49 Soggiorno in Frattina $ Rooms for long stays with partial use of kitchen. ♦ Via Frattina 41. 6382495 (phone 9AM-10PM)

50 Company Men's clothes—from jeans to tuxedos. ♦ Via Frattina 126. 6780304

50 Cartotechnica Romana Attractive writing paper, expensive pens, funny gifts. ♦ Via Frattina 124. 6791029, 6789830

50 Santini Brilliant window display of elegant shoes for both sexes. Women's are mostly flat or with a small heel. ♦ Via Frattina 120. 6784114

51 Plaque on Wall **James Joyce**, the greatest Irish novelist of our century, stayed here from August to December in 1906. ♦ Via Frattina 51

52 Ramirez If you're looking for the last word in shoes and don't want to spend a bundle, go to one of the 5 Ramirez shops in Rome (or the 7 in southern Italy). ♦ Via Frattina 85A. 6792467

Grilli

53 Grilli Shoes If you want to be comfortable *and* elegant, get Grilli's version of the high-heeled sneaker: rubber wedges and fine tailoring at reasonable prices. ♦ Via del Corso 166. 6793650

54 Vanina Quality inexpensive clothes for him and her. Known for classic pants, fashionable dresses, and coats. ♦ Via del Gambero 39. 6794264

54 Fabi For those "last gasp" accessories just before you leave Rome, when you want to bring home the "latest" thing from the Eternal City. ♦ Via del Gambero 24. 6791210

55 Anticoli Very reasonable sweater shop, pretty designs. ♦ Via della Vite 28. 6784496

56 Anglo American Bookshop Bestsellers; particularly well stocked on travel books. But do they have **Rome**ACCESS®? ♦ Closed Sunday. Via della Vite 57. 6795222

56 Mario ★★$$$ Another Tuscan restaurant, so you can expect good beef and steaks. It has game in season with *pappardelle* (long, flat pasta) *alle lepre* (supposedly hare, but perhaps it's only rabbit). Duck and wild boar are also on the menu. Try the ricotta tart (like cheesecake, but lighter and less fatty) with hot-chocolate sauce! Reasonable prices when you don't order steak. The 20 tables are a little bit squeezed. ♦ Closed Monday lunch; Saturday, 1 June-15 Sep; Sunday; and August. Via della Vite 55. Reservations recommended. 6783818

57 Nipponya ★$$ (Japanese Pub) Lots of plastic food in the window, even some inside. However, one can have real food and it's simple and good. Wooden bar for express service. The Japanese have invaded this area with the more expensive **Tokyo** up the road at Via di Propaganda 22 (6783942), and **Hamasei** at Via Mercede 35 (6792134). They are all good, since Japanese tourists help to keep the cooking authentic. ♦ Closed Wednesday. Via della Vite 102. 6799550

57 Onelli Everything for shoes and slippers. If your feet need help, Onelli has pads, liners, shoe trees, and laces. ♦ Via della Vite 78. 6792971

Via Condotti

58 Bea Light Shop All sorts of modern lights and an especially wonderful present for children: a mouse that lights up. ♦ Via Belsiana 27. 6795386

58 I Numeri ★$$ Breezy young luncheon place open at night as well. Simple fare, colorfully presented. Habitat furniture look. Roast beef, hamburgers, spaghetti *al limone*, and lots of salads; unpretentious and fast. Not really an Italian ambiance, but full of Italians, with few tourists. ♦ M-Sa noon-midnight. Via Belsiana 30. 6794969

58 Filippo Moroni One-of-a-kind jewels. Very unusual Italian creations. At his lab on nearby Via del Corso, Filipo will work to your drawings and specifications. ♦ Via Belsiana 32A. 6780466

59 Lilia Leoni Decor Stop by, if only to take a look at this new decorator's shop with beautiful mosaics and a floor of antique tiles. ♦ Via Belsiana 86. 6783210

59 Toto alle Carrozze ★★$$ A superb restaurant with antipasto in every variety imaginable. As part of the "clean look," Toto has become all white and glistening, but don't be put off. The specialties, posted daily on a high-

tech bulletin board are low-tech delights.
♦ Closed Saturday dinner and Sunday. Via
delle Carrozze 10. 6785558

60 Serra Boutique A nice little place where you
can get **Valentino** copies at half price. ♦ Via
Bocca di Leone 51. 6795354

60 Gianni Versace Another of the great Italian
clothes designers. His look was sturdily mas-
culine for years, but now some more feminine
items are creeping in. The clothes have flair—
so get a shawl if you can't afford the whole
ensemble. ♦ M-Sa 10AM-7:30PM. Via Bocca
di Leone 26. 6780521

61 Hotel Carriage $ Charming hotel with
lovely, ornate gilded furniture downstairs.
Within a stone's throw of **Piazza di Spagna**.
The 20 rooms are on the smallish side but
perfectly adequate. Some attractive and
slightly bigger rooms are on the top floor
around a terrace; ask for No. 46. ♦ Via delle
Carrozze 36. 6793312, 6794106; fax 6799106

Via Condotti

Bottega di Lungavita

62 Bottega di Lungavita (Longlife Boutique)
There are a few herbal shops in Rome and the
olde worlde variety are the most satisfying.
Herbalist **Donatella Piccioli** only works in the
afternoon, so if you want a cure for a specific
illness don't pop in early. Do you have gout
caused by too much meat and alcohol? Sting-
ing nettle, elderberry, and juniper, with a
sprinkle of sarsaparilla brewed in boiling water and drunk immediately will cure it. All sorts
of herb teas for all sorts of maladies. Opera
singers are faithful clients for the tea made of
sage and erisimo, which soothes the vocal
chords. Red eyes? Eufrasia and meliloto will
calm the strain and eliminate the bloodshot
look. Of course, there are lots of other things
for your health as well: natural food products,
whole rice, brown spaghetti, honey, royal jelly,
ginseng. And a beauty line with everything for
the hair, gorgeous soaps, and sweet-smelling
flower colognes. The best potpourri ever. Can
you resist it? ♦ Via Mario de' Fiori 24A.
6791454

62 Via Mario de' Fiori Named after a painter
(1603-73). Some of his work is in the Galleria
Palazzo Colonna, and appropriately enough it
depicts flowers painted on Venetian mirrors.
(*Fiori* means flowers.)

62 Ranieri ★★$$$ This is where the **Fendi**
crowd comes between fittings for a long, el-
egant, old-fashioned meal in a plush setting.
Another Roman landmark where the food isn't
really the point. If you're not a regular, the
help may be a little snooty. ♦ Closed Sunday.
Via Mario de' Fiori 26. 6791592, 6786505

SIRAGUSA

63 Siragusa An unusual jewelry shop specializ-
ing in archaeological pieces and ancient
carved stones. Fabulous 3rd- and 4th-century
BC coins and ancient beads, all dug up in Asia
Minor, Greece, and Egypt, are set into hand-
made chains. This shop is like a precious little
museum. The staff speaks 4 languages—En-
glish, of course, is one of them. **Mr. Siragusa**
comes from Siragusa in Sicily (this was
Magna Grecia from 700 BC to 300 BC, until
the Romans took over). ♦ Closed Saturday.
Via delle Carrozze 64. 6797085

64 Hotel Piazza di Spagna $$$ This minihotel
has been completely modernized. Only break-
fast, but there is fine eating right around the
corner. It was a house of ill-repute in the good
old days—yes, even up to 20 years ago. Six-
teen bedrooms. ♦ Via Mario de' Fiori 61.
6793061, 6790654

65 Fior Fiori Cheeses, pastas, and salty goodies. See if you can walk past this one—the
mouth waters just to think of it. ♦ Closed
Thursday PM (as all food shops) and Sunday.
Via della Croce 17/18. No credit cards.
6791386

65 Ristorante Otello ★★$$ Quite famous
now as an extremely reasonable restaurant
with good food. This restaurant follows the
seasons as all good restaurants should, and
every season has its specialty. In early June,
sample melon with raspberries tucked inside
the half shell; you'll never forget it! The décor
is rather simplistic, with paintings one sus-
pects were done by local artists from Via
Margutta in lieu of payment for meals enjoyed.
Charming courtyard for summer eating, but
there may be a short wait for your table.
♦ Closed Sunday and 2 weeks at Christmas.
Via della Croce 81. 6791178

65 Wiener Bierhaus (Birreria Viennese)
★$$ Viennese sausage and sauerkraut restaurant started in 1939 by **Hans** and **Luise
Geissauf**. Luise still runs the show with her
daughter. If you crave a good beer, either light
Munich or a Dark Forst from Austria's old vas-
sal state, the Alto Adige (in northern Italy),
and a good *weiss wurst* (white sausage),
come here. There is also Hungarian gou-
lash—shades of the old Austro-Hungarian
Empire—and a wicked Steinhagen (a traditional shot of pure alcohol before your beer).

Luise is justly proud to have the only restaurant in Rome that, in winter at least, serves roast goose; ask for *oca arrosto con krauti rossi e spatzle* (roast goose with red cabbage and roast potatoes). There are 13 tables downstairs and 20 upstairs, with private rooms available for parties. The décor is resolutely Alpine. ◆ M-Tu, Th-Su noon-midnight. Via della Croce 21. 6795569

66 Wine Shop & Bar Nineteenth-century atmosphere; in the back it's almost like a club, with a zinc bar and various bubbly wine tastings—and also some tables for more serious eaters/drinkers. Cheese croquettes to whet your appetite for more. You can learn about Italian wines here. 1985 was a great year in most of Italy's provinces—wait 6 to 19 years and come back! ◆ Closed Sunday. Via della Croce 76. 6790896

66 Nectar Ecological body-care products. *Pamper your bod without harming nature* is the slogan. Nothing here has been tested on animals! An English firm has opened this, and a clone shop at Via del Corso 132 (6792537). In both you'll find the most delectable assortment of soaps, perfumes, bath oils, and lotions, all packed in dainty baskets and looking like candy. Nectar will make up a basket to your taste. Great gifts. ◆ Via della Croce 76A. 6781862

66 Delucchi Beautiful fruit-and-nut shop with some tinned food besides. Fresh mangoes, guavas, and even lychees in season. Try the dried fruit—pear, apricot, etc. ◆ Closed Thursday PM and Sunday. Via della Croce 74-75. No credit cards. 6791630

67 Angelo's Pasticceria Bar for breakfast, lunch, tea, or snack with a croissant (*cornetto*), sandwiches (*tramezzino*), or gooey cakes and ice cream. In Italy you cannot just go up to the counter and order, you have to buy your *scontrino* (receipt) first. ◆ Closed Sunday. Via della Croce 30. No credit cards. 6782556

67 Vertecchi Artists' supplies plus. Here you can buy watercolors to paint some views of Rome. This shop is complete with pens, pads of all kinds, paints, plastic folders—you name it! Yes, it even has Filofax refills. ◆ Via della Croce 70. 6783110

67 Re Degli Amici ★★$$ Classic Roman cuisine plus meat specialties, including steak *au poivre vert* and steak tartare. The waiters are renowned for being cheeky, funny, and making you feel at home. Try the smashing hors d'oeuvre trays (antipasto); there must easily be 20 and you can help yourself. Wonderful service and, in the evening, great pizzas. ◆ Closed Monday-Tuesday lunch. Via della Croce 33/B. 6782555

Daily Specials
Monday through Wednesday you're on your own, but Thursday is gnocchi day, Friday is fish—especially filet of *bacala* (fried, dried salted cod)—Saturday's special is tripe, and Sunday's is lasagna.

67 Vertecchi scatole (boxes) All sorts of paper things for the home. Color-coded napkins, little bags and boxes, shiny plasticized wallpaper, unusual gifts. The same management as the artists' supply store across the road. ◆ Via della Croce 38. 6790100

67 Fiaschetteria Beltramme ★$$ What neighborhood restaurants used to be like: small, wholesome food, no frills. A favorite with journalists, who like to sit at one of the half-dozen oval tables, joining whomever is already installed here—like a private club. So if you speak Italian, come to this "in" group. But it's not a fun place; the setting is somewhat drab and the waiters long-faced. Food is okay but secondary. A delicious exception is the raspberries served in half a cantaloupe—the best marriage of the year but only in summer. ◆ Closed Sunday and 2 wks in August. Via della Croce 39. No phone

68 Il Sogno (The Dream) Baby shop and nightclothes for *la mamma*. Reasonable prices. ◆ Via della Croce 45. 6796501

68 Sorelle Macalle Chic, unusual fashion shop. The mix of furs, wools, silks, and fake tiger stripes is delicious. Moderate to expensive, but you won't see these styles anywhere else. ◆ Via della Croce 68. 6784284

68 Pape Satan Silks and satins; no cottons, but lots of embroidered mad rags. ◆ Via della Croce No credit cards. 63. 6798281

Via Condotti

68 Cilli Unusual bags; well worth popping in to have a look. ◆ Via della Croce 58. 6783157

69 Simona Gorgeous undies and (in the summer) swimsuits. Here are all the latest styles from *outré* to cover-up conservative. Not as expensive as **Cesare** and really very pretty. ◆ Via del Corso 83. 6790077

70 Pizzeria La Capricciosa Large, bustling restaurant with over 25 tables. Typically Italian with a big selection of antipasto, all sorts of prepared vegetables, hams and salamis, and mozzarellas. (Either cow's milk or the delicate waterbuffalo's milk, which is, of course, the real mozzarella.) Large selection of pastas and the specialty (only at night): pizza. It was here that **Pizza Capricciosa** was created—more or less everything, plus an egg. ◆ Closed Tuesday and 15 days in August. Largo dei Lombardi 8. 6878636, 6878480

71 Bruscoli Stockings galore! Go down into **Aladdin**'s cave and be amazed at the variety. Socks and gloves, too. ◆ Via del Corso 112. 6795715

Restaurants/Clubs: Red **Hotels:** Blue
Shops/Parks: Green **Sights/Culture:** Black

72 Hotel Plaza $$$ This large hotel has been catering to the discerning public since 1860. And it, too, has had royalty among its guests. When the hotel first opened, the **Queen of Mexico** came to lodge for several months. Its old-world grandeur has not dimmed, but that doesn't stop today's staff from being attractive and knowledgeable. Especially notable are the telephone operators; the only ones in town who do not leave you hanging on the line for minutes on end while they presumably ring your party. Here, miracle of miracles, they buzz the room and immediately get back to you to take a message if the room doesn't answer. The downstairs reception rooms are magnificent, and there are salons to rent for private parties. The central salon has a turn-of-the-century stained-glass ceiling. The rooms on the courtyard (about 100) are all very quiet and the old-fashioned bathrooms are a joy. A mammoth facelift is underway, which will not distrub the great public rooms. There is a bar tucked in behind all the magnificence, with deep-padded chairs to flop into after a harrowing morning spent deciding between a Fendi bag and a Bottega Veneto purse. There is even a beauty shop—and a minister. Two hundred forty rooms. ◆ Via del Corso 126. 6783364; fax 672101

73 Palazzo Ruspoli (1586, **Bartolomeo Ammannati**) This large palace, most of its frontage on Via del Corso, was built for the **Ruccellai** family. It took 30 years to complete. In 1776 it was bought by the Ruspolis. Note the elegant windows of the *piano nobile* (noble floor—one flight up, where the princes live; larger windows, more carving, higher ceilings). After the fall of **Napoleon** in France, his sister **Hortense**, ex-Queen of Holland, lived here with her family. One of her sons left this palazzo to go back to Paris and became **Napoleon III**. Closed to the public. ◆ Largo Carlo Goldoni 56

74 Merola This is the third generation of glove purveyors since 1885, and they have been officially recognized for their service to the nation. Don't forget, gloves are coming back. ◆ Via del Corso 143. 6791961

75 La Rinascente Rome's only real department store. The clothing department occupies 4 floors of this building; the other general departments are in **Piazza Fiume** (8841231). Good-quality clothes for men, women, and children, with some designer names. Medium prices but no bargaining. ◆ Largo Chigi (Via del Corso) 6797691

76 Rizzoli Bookshop Largest general bookstore in Rome, with a section of foreign-language books and a quantity of fine art books. Related to the store of the same name in New York. The Rizzoli publishing house is the parent company, but books of all Italian publishers are available. Good selection of coffee table embellishers and guidebooks—who knows, you might even find **Rome**ACCESS®. ◆ Largo Chigi 15. 6796641

77 Palazzo Carpegna The **Accademia di San Luca**, which occupies this building, is a 15th-century confraternity of artists and art appreciators originally housed on Via Sacra. **Cardinal Carpegna** had bought the houses on this site with the intention of incorporating **Borromini**'s plans (1640). The Cardinal was a sure bet for becoming the next pope, and he wanted a palace grand enough for his imminent high station. There was to be an extraordinary circular courtyard with a bridge linking the 2 halves of the palace—as he was not able to get dispensation from the incumbent pope to close the intervening public thoroughfare. The Cardinal died before being elected pope. The only parts of Borromini's plans that were executed were the magnificent oval ramp and, in the entrance way, Baroque stucco curlicues—out of the center of which emerges a handsome face resembling, to a striking extent, the current head of the Carpegna family. (Although everyone believes such ramps were for horses, it is more likely they were for mules to bring water up to the top floors.) The **Accademia Gallery** contains paintings by **Raphael, Guercino, Titian, Piazetta** and **Rubens**. ◆ Admission. M, W, F 10AM-1PM. Closed August. Piazza dell'Accademia di San Luca 77. 6789243

78 Er Buco ★★$$ A tiny club for a circle of friends who eat here daily—and they're trying to keep it a secret. **Danilo Petrini** will let you in if there's room left at one of the 7 tables. He'll bring you a real straw-wrapped fiasco of Chianti if you ask for the house red, or a carafe of sparkling white (both drop-dead desirable). He'll bring you hand-cut slices from the various types of ham and wild boar hanging from the rafters. He'll suggest freshly made pasta with mushrooms, followed by game. Be game. But also, be kind to those of us who would like to keep the club to ourselves (and know it deserves more stars)—don't come. ◆ Closed Sunday. Via del Lavatore 91. 6790011

79 Piccolo Arancio ★★$$ This is the little sister of the **Arancio d'Oro** and **Trattoria da Settimio al Arancio** (see page 78). Dependably good cuisine in a glistening setting. ◆ Closed Monday. Vicolo Scanderberg 112. 6786139

80 Trevi Fountain (1762, **Nicola Salvi**) There are lithographs showing this square empty, waiting for the fountain. Houses had been torn down to make room for it, and the whole wall of the **Palazzo Poli,** behind it, was erected as a backdrop. The fountain is so vast, and the High Baroque sculpture so vivid, that one feels the horses are splashing their way out of the fountain and will careen past at any minute. Trevi is a shortening of *Tre Vie* (3 streets), and the large body of water dominates the small square in which the 3 streets come together. **Acqua Virgine**, the water source that dates back to the year 19 BC, runs for only 14 miles, which makes it the city's shortest aqueduct. Its pipes run mostly underground, but like Rome's other external water sources, it had been cut off during the barbarian invasions—speeding the fall of the Roman Empire in the 5th and 6th centuries. The popes, who picked up the pieces from the emperors, did not get around to repairing the aqueducts for 800 years. They reinstated the emperors' custom of decorating the spot where the water appears within the city with a great fountain—called the *mostra* (show). When **Pope Nicholas V** finally reinstated the Acqua Virgine in 1453, he ordered a modest monument (to himself) built at the arrival point, and the original basin was built by **Leon Battista Alberti.** Two centuries later **Pope Urban VIII** commissioned **Bernini** to build a major fountain, but this urban renewal came to a halt when the Pope died, and still another century went by before **Pope Clement XII** finally approved the present plan—completed 2 popes later, under **Clement XIII.** This account illustrates why Rome has so many monumental fountains (so many popes opening up so many aqueducts and congratulating themselves by having a monument built) and also why the Romans don't expect things to get done in a day. (*Pazienza,* they will murmur—patience, take your time, no hurry.)

Salvi was commissioned to build this fountain on the basis of a contest. (He lost but the pope chose him anyway.) He died before it was finished—but not before putting up a large urn to obstruct the shop of the local barber who had made rude remarks about the fountain. The water was most appreciated by the locals as it was sweet. The rite of drinking the water to assure your return to Rome was gradually changed to throwing in a coin. Now the superstition requires you to toss the coin over your left shoulder if you want to come back. In this

Via Condotti

way the city makes quite a lot of money, which it gives to charity—unless the urchins get there first to clean out the fountain when the police are looking the other way. A night stroll is really the most spectacular way to see Neptune and his chariot surging out of the gushing water. Even though in the movie *La Dolce Vita* you saw **Anita Ekberg** leap in here for a late, late dip, don't try it—police are waiting to arrest you. ♦ Piazza di Trevi

80 Giusti Right opposite the Trevi Fountain is the equally famous home of the "car shoe" (pronounced *cashew* here). This is the very lightweight loafer, with rubber bubbles sweeping along the sole and up the back, favored by Fiat's **Gianni Agnelli** since his racing driver days. This is a high-quality sporting goods clothing store, but Signor Giusti just happened to make it big with the *cashew.* ♦ Piazza Fontana di Trevi 91. 6790726

81 Al Moro ★★$$$ A favorite with politicians. **Franco Romagnoli**, the son of the legendary **Moro**, now runs the place. *Carciofi alla romana* (whole artichokes cooked in garlic and wild mint), scampi *al Moro, capretto al forno* (roast kid), or a great pork-loin roast. For dessert, profiteroles or chestnut mousse. Some good Gavi Chianti wines and a superb Barolo Brunate. ♦ Closed Sunday and August. Vicolo delle Bollette 13. Reservations required. No credit cards. 6783495

82 Er Tartufo $$ Simple restaurant for a quick lunch near the Fountain of Trevi. In winter the specialties include the highly perfumed white truffle. ♦ Closed Sunday. Via Sciarra 59. No credit cards. 6780226

83 Piazza Colonna A busy square near the confluence of 2 important shopping streets, Via del Corso and Via Tritone. It is also the center of Rome's principal industry—government, since the Palazzo Chigi, on the corner of Via del Corso closest to La Rinascente department store, is the office of the prime minister. It was designed by **Maderno** in the 16th century.

At the Piazza Colonna:

The Marcus Aurelius Column (AD 193) In the center of the square. This metal column has bas-relief sculpted comic strips winding up to the crowning statue; it's similar to Trajan's column but not as artistically fine. Marcus Aurelius was a peace-loving philosopher who, as emperor, had to fight the bloody battles depicted on this column. He encouraged the arts and letters and was adored by the Romans. They put his statue at the top of this column, where it remained until 1589, when **Pope Sixtus V**, the city planner of Rome, replaced it with the present effigy of **St. Paul**.

84 Europeo Snack Bar & Ice Cream Parlor It is a rare good fortune to find a small snack

Via Condotti

bar with tables and chairs both inside and outside. (Most Roman bars are stand-up affairs.) Many flavors of tea, alcoholic drinks, as many different ice creams as Baskin Robbins, but with the accent on Sicilian specialties such as *cassata*. There are both hot and cold sandwiches, cakes (the ones from Sicily stuffed with ricotta), and chocolates and sweets by the gram. This is the place that has everything, including ice-cream cakes to take away and balls of string that are actually chestnut paste. ♦ M-Tu, Th-Su 8:30AM-8:30PM. Piazza San Lorenzo in Lucina 33. No credit cards. 6876300

85 Suzuki Flower Shop This gaily colored shop is full of the most exotic flowers—only by touching them do you realize they're fake! The peonies and zinnias are amazingly lifelike. What a wonderful, lasting impression to give a bunch of these eternal flowers to a hostess after a delicious meal. ♦ Via del Leone 2. No credit cards. 6876454

86 Aureli The Romans call this the Bulgari of the fruit shops. Everything you can imagine in the way of fresh fruit, dried fruit, and other exotic groceries. ♦ Closed Thursday PM and Sunday. Via del Leoncino 23. No credit cards. 6878582

87 Pizzeria al Leoncino ★$ A spartan little dive for the young and those whose money has run out. **Signora Livia Signorini** serves only at night, and only pizzas—which happen

to be very thin, crunchy, and absolutely delicious. The pizza oven is a relic from some ancient time when marble was used in abundance. The wood fire glows invitingly. Order 2 you can afford it. There are some pies and cakes for the sweet tooth whose meal isn't complete without the taste of sugar. ♦ M-Tu, Th-Su 6PM-midnight. Via del Leoncino 28. No credit cards. 6876306

88 Trattoria da Settimio all'Arancio ★★$$ A brightly lit neighborhood place that is full all the time. The crowd is varied. Roman princes mingle with trade union leaders and there are a lot of young Italians as the prices are very reasonable. *Fusilli alla melanzana* (macaroni with eggplant), *carpaccio* (paper-thin raw beef with oil, Parmesan cheese, and tart *rughetta* salad), and crème caramel would make a good meal; but if you go on Friday there is fresh fish at low prices (normally very expensive in Rome—maybe because the Mediterranean is getting so polluted the fish have to come from afar). The owner of New York's beloved Russian Tea Room was drawn here by our previous edition of **Rome**ACCESS®, and loved it. ♦ Closed Sunday. Via dell'Arancio 50. 6876119

89 Arancio d'Oro ★★$$ The second of this small family chain of Arancio (orange) restaurants (see **Trattoria da Settimio all'Arancio** just above—and **Piccolo Arancio** on page 76). Montepulciano d'Abruzzo wine by the liter. Pizza in the evening, as it should be. Spaghetti with clams, mussels, and *rughetta*. Tagliatelli with baby squid. Grilled steak and vegetables arrive sizzling on a metal griddle. Lemon mousse. ♦ Closed Sunday. Via Monte d'Oro 17. 6878571

89 Stefano Ganbini Stefano will make any belt you want, if indeed you can't find your dream already here. ♦ Via Monte d'Oro 18. 6876198

90 Delettré In a small shop that looks like a velvet jewel case is some of the most fantastic jewelry we've ever seen. Precious stones, invisible floating settings, sculpted rock crystal; clips that have a vague nostalgia for the '30s, yet have 2001 in mind; little lizards that creep up the wrist inquisitively. A cosmopolitan Frenchman, **Bernard Delettré** of Paris, Los Angeles, Rio de Janeiro, and Rome, is the gemologist and supervises the cutting. His wife, **Sylvia V. Fendi**, daughter of **Anna Fendi**, designs these unusual, beautiful pieces. Highly recommended. ♦ Via Fontanella Borghese 39. 6877722, 6781912

90 Invisible Mending All the invisible menders are closing down, so this is a precious exception. **Signora Durastante** can mend a tear in both natural and synthetic fibers; she also repairs lace or spangled net. ♦ Closed August. Via Fontanella Borghese 70. No credit cards. 6871092

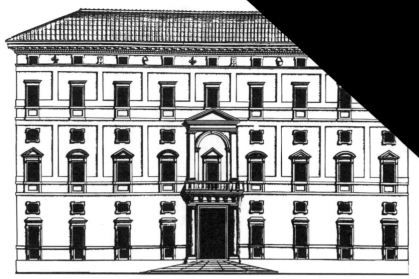

91 Palazzo Borghese (Front block, 1578) This enormous palace is known as the *ciambella* (biscuit with a hole in the middle). Building was started by **Monsignor Tommaso del Giglio**. Because he was from Bologna, it is thought that he used the Bolognese architect **Giacomo da Vignola**, who designed Villa Giulia, now the Etruscan Museum. The building passed into the hands of a Spanish cardinal, **Pedro Deza**. At the time of his death in 1600 the front part had been roofed over and one wing completed. Four years later the building again changed families when **Cardinal Camillo Borghese** bought it. When he became **Pope Paul V** one year later in 1605, he gave the palace to his 2 brothers, but he continued to preside over the grandiose building proceedings. Construction did not stop through the years as other wings, courtyards, and friezes were added. **Carlo Rainaldi** did extensive work on the palace and built the part that reaches the river front and looks like a galleon. In the old days, before the high embankment was built to protect the city from flooding, the galleon was moored next to the Port of Ripetta, a beautiful series of curving stairs down to the water's edge. Inside this palazzo is a magnificent courtyard with colossal antique statues, including *The Bath of Venus* and 3 fountains. The ground floor used to house the family art collection, now in Villa Borghese. One flight up, in the grand salons of the *piano nobile*, is the exclusive **Caccia Club**. The ceilings are so high that there is a tale that the first inhabitants were giants. The building on the opposite side of the piazza was for the legion of domestics. ♦ Largo Fontanella Borghese 19

92 La Fontanella $$$ This restaurant has changed hands yet again. The regulars have all fled to the nearby **Due Ladroni**, along with the former owner. In the summer there are tables outside, and it is open in August—very rare for Rome. Tuscan cooking: *fiorentino* (T-bone steak), *penne alla vodka* (macaroni vodka), *vitello tonnato* (cold veal with creamy tuna sauce). The wine selection includes, in the whites, a good Gavi di Gavi, and the reds boast a superb but expensive Brunello (Brunello di Montalcino has to be 5 years old to be called Brunello). ♦ Closed Saturday lunch and Sunday. Largo Fontanella Borghese 86. 6783849

93 Azienda Agricola Presents for the gourmet. Perhaps the tiniest shop in town, with the

Via Condotti

best honey and olive oil. Try the thick olive paste on country bread, and you'll never forget it. ♦ Vicolo della Toretta 3. 6875808

93 Vini Birra Buffet ★★$ Paper tablecloths printed with *bambini* and grapes set the tone. Fine wine bar with great soups, salads, *crostini*. Also—oh, yum, yum, yum—polenta from the Veneto with Gorgonzola, 4 cheeses, or just plain sausages. Presentation with pleasing colors is part of the care taken to accompany a great cellar; but they don't blink an eye if you ask for beer or just water. A hit with the locals and the young. You might have to wait. ♦ Closed Sunday. Piazza della Toretta 60. 6871445

94 El Toula ★★★$$$$ If you must go to the most frankly swanky trattoria in town and are prepared to pay for it, okay. This is all yours. The seating is arranged so you have total privacy for your conversation, yet you can see and be seen. Perhaps that's why there is always a sprinkling of Italian cabinet ministers. In Italy it is unheard of for a host to be expected to maintain high quality in more than one restaurant, but host **Alfredo Bettrane** seems to have managed here as well as in Milan and Turin. So gorge yourself on *pappardelle* pasta with oysters, goose breast, and other exotic dishes, many of them Venetian. ♦ Closed Saturday-Sunday lunch and August. Via della Lupa 29. Reservations required. 6783498

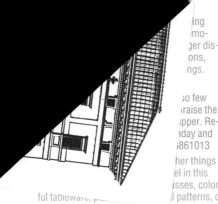

...ing ...mo- ...ger dis- ...ons, ...ngs.

...so few ...raise the ...pper. Re- ...day and ...861013

...her things ...el in this ...sses, color- ful tableware, ...l patterns, or the ubiquitous large juice pitcher with a silver cover and handle. Modest prices on the whole. Specializes in export shipments. ♦ Tu-Sa 10AM-6PM. Piazza Nicosia 30. No credit cards. No phone

97 La Campana ★★★$$ (1450) In spite of a mysterious murder in the family, this restaurant is highly recommended. **Romolo**, a

Via Condotti

nephew of the owner, has taken over and kept up the standards. La Campana has been serving high-quality Roman cuisine at modest prices for over 100 years. *Vignarola* is one of the specialties: a soup with generous lashings of thick green vegetables that is without peer. Excellent fresh fish, meats, good al dente spaghetti and rice, and one of the best *torta di ricotta* (type of cheese cake but almost as light as a creamy soufflé) ever tasted. In the old days this was a favorite haunt of priests and well-known personalities who, after eating, would slip out the back door, across a courtyard, and into a house of ill-repute. The doors of the house would then close and no one was allowed inside until the customer had left, thus guarding his anonymity. Then he would retrace his footsteps back to the restaurant and leave by the front door as if he had been in the restaurant all the time. ♦ Closed Monday and August. Vicolo della Campana 18. 6875273, 6867820

Have you ever stopped to think how boring Italian cuisine must have been during the centuries before the lowly **tomato** made its appearance among the old-world staples at the turn of the 16th century? We have never seen a full-course meal in Rome that didn't depend on the tomato at some stage. Italians tend to choose the smaller, thinner, less brilliant orange tomato over the fat, round, red variety favored by Americans.

98 Boccondivino ★$$ This tiny jewel of a restaurant is charmingly decorated. It literally means Heavenly Mouthful, which might be a little ambitious, but the food is good. Don't take the surly service personally. ♦ Closed Monday. Vicolo della Campana 11. No credit cards. 6547129

98 Alfredo alla Scrofa ★$$$ Just come here for that fettucine with triple butter (*al triplo burro*), which made the name of Alfredo synonymous with fine Roman cuisine. Don't worry about whether this is—as it claims—the original Alfredo, as opposed to **Alfredo al Augustea**. They both lay claim to the continuation of the originator's 50-year tradition. The other dishes are undistinguished; but those fettucine, served with the golden spoon and fork, are very good. We also recommend the fresh vegetables in season. ♦ Closed Tuesday. Via della Scrofa 104. 6540163

99 Church of Sant'Antonio dei Portoghesi (1695, **Martino Longhi** and **Carlo Rainaldi**) Designers of buildings during and before the 17th century were artists. **Bernini** was first a sculptor, then an architect, just as **Michelangelo** was first a painter and sculptor, then an architect. This small, beautifully ornate Baroque church took almost 50 years to build. It was the church of the Portuguese community in Rome and you can see the shield and the arms of the royal Portuguese house of **Braganca** on the facade. It is built in the shape of a Latin cross with 2 chapels on either side of the cupola. To the right is a sculpture of **Canova** (1806-1808). ♦ Via dei Portoghesi

99 Albergo Portoghesi—Hotel Meuble $ A hotel for 150 years. There are 27 rooms with baths and heating in this small, slightly gloomy hotel. But many people like its no fuss attitude and its central location near the historic parts of the city. Breakfast but no restaurant. ♦ Via dei Portoghesi 1. 6545133, 6864231; fax 6876976

99 Casa Frangipane Don't miss the original 15th-century doorway of this Frangipane family citadel, in recent centuries owned by the **Anselmis**. In the old days, Rome was peppered with fortified towers—as **San Gimignano** still is. (Try to spot these towers today—many of them have been incorporated into the fabric of later buildings, but are still visible.) This has been called the *Monkey Tower* since the 17th century, when a monkey snatched the proprietor's newborn baby and scampered up to the tower with the baby in its arms. When the monkey was finally recaptured, with the baby unhurt, the owner built this statue to the Virgin Mary in thanks. ♦ Via Palomba at Via dell'Orso

100 Opificio Romano Exquisite mosaics inspired by the ancient Roman variety. Can you afford them? But can you afford not to have them? ♦ Via de' Gigli d'Oro 9. 6542762

101 L'Orso 80 ★★$$ The antipasto arrives like an AMTRAK train. Leave lots of room as the menu is varied and portions are generous.

You might ask them to hold the salt. For the discerning *stracciatelli* lover, your hunt stops here. Chef **Tonino**, bedecked in whites and wearing his toque at that jaunty angle only Italians can get away with, pops in and out constantly making sure all is well—and it is! ♦ Closed Monday and part of August. Via dell'Orso 33. 6864904

102 Antique Shop You could easily walk past this small shop as there is nothing outside to tell you either the name or what it specializes in. But a tiny window with a few lovely pieces might catch a sharp eye. **Sergio Scarapazzi** has a fine collection of silver, ivory, and bronze. He is interested only in the years between 1700 and 1860 (Louis XIV, Louis XVI, Napoleon I, Napoleon III). There are superb Empire candlesticks, and Scarapazzi has a predilection for porcelain with a history behind it. The cups, jugs, and plates with exquisite painted views are masterpieces. A collector's delight. ♦ Closed Saturday PM, Sunday, and August. Via di Monte Brianzo 73. 6543021

103 Hostaria dell'Orso ★★★$$$$ **Blu Bar** on the ground floor, restaurant on the 1st, **La Cabala** nightclub on the top floor. This place is for those who are tired of the neighborhood trattoria and want to get all dressed up to go somewhere elegant and live it up. The building is ancient and for over 600 years has been an upper-class hostelry. **Dante** stayed here when he came to see the Jubilee of **Pope Bonifacio VIII** (1294-1303); **Montaigne**, the French man of letters, stayed here when he was made honorary burgher of the city in 1581. Cardinals and envoys to the pope stayed here when on missions to the Vatican. Today you can dine on caviar, foie gras, tender meats, and sweets in an authentic medieval palace. Sip champagne or *spumante* (Italian bubbly) at the charming piano bar, or dance to a live orchestra in La Cabala nightclub. Suave owner, **Franco**, can be seen dancing with his favorite *principessa*. In 1936, architects doing some restoration tore down a small room that had been added centuries ago over the street. It turned out to be a medieval lavatory and they found, to their horror, the skeleton of a young man who had been walled up inside. What had happened? Had it been a trap and directly after he went to the bathroom he was locked in to die? Or was it a murder or a sudden death and to get rid of the body they bricked it up all those centuries ago? ♦ Restaurant: M-Sa 8PM-midnight. Nightclub: daily 10PM-dawn. Via dei Soldati 25. Reservations required. 6864250, 6864221

104 Napoleon Museum This museum contains paintings and bibelots that commemorate the Napoleonic era in Rome. The 1st and 2nd rooms honor **Napoleon I**; the 3rd room memorializes **Napoleon III** (Second Empire). The 4th room is devoted to **Pauline Bonaparte Borghese**. Souvenirs from Napoleon's 2 funerals (1821 and 1840) can be found in the 10th room, while the other rooms have memorabilia of Napoleon's mother, **Letizia**,

and nobles and personages of the Second Empire. Don't forget that Napoleon cut quite a swathe through Italy, repeatedly invading various duchies and city-states. He even named his only son King of Rome. And his admiration for the ancient Romans gave birth to the so-called Empire look, which was inspired by Imperial Rome. ♦ Admission. Tu, Th 9AM-2PM; W, F-Sa 9AM-2PM; 5-8PM; Su, holidays 9AM-1PM. Closed August. Via Zanardelli 1. 6540286

105 Old Map and Photograph Shop Here you will find much testimony to Rome's past. A positive motherlode of fascinating views of a Rome now gone forever: multitudes of horse-drawn carriages fill up the whole of St. Peter's Square; aerial views of the crowded little streets leading up to St. Peter's, which Mussolini demolished; bridges that were torn down or swept away. ♦ Lungotevere Mellini 2

106 Ara Pacis Augustae (Altar of Augustus' Peace) (9 BC) The story of the excavation of the Ara Pacis is as interesting as the monument itself. **Cardinal Andrea della Valle** was a great art connoisseur of the 16th century. In 1525, some superb high reliefs from pagan times entered his collection. Nobody knew what they were, but some guessed they might be from **Domitian's Triumphal Arch**. These ended up in the gardens of Villa Medici. Twenty years later **Cardinal Ricci** of Montepulciano bought some large panels,

Via Condotti

which he sawed into 3 pieces for easy transportation to the Medicis of Florence. These had come to light when the foundations of a palace were being dug in Via in Lucina. The panels depicted marvelous figures in a procession, the drapery of their garments so natural it was lifelike. Other panels went into other great houses—and eventually one frieze ended up in the Louvre, another in Vienna, and yet another in the Vatican Museum. Three hundred years passed, and then, while reinforcing the substructure of a palace (they didn't know it, but it was the same one on the corner of Via del Corso and Via in Lucina), more slabs of the same exquisite work were found. In 1898, 50 years later, the new Italian government started to acquire these high-relief panels from all over the world. By now it had dawned on the experts that these giant marble pictures might well be, and later they realized they definitely were, part of the legendary **Ara Pacis Augustae**. More excavations were undertaken but with great difficulty as the present-day road was several yards above the level of the altar's foundation. The houses and palaces in the surrounding area were in danger of collapsing if the last great sculptures were extracted, so they were left behind. In 1937, the totalitarian Fascist government passed Draconian laws that enabled the freezing of the ground, making it possible to delicately dislodge the last remaining pieces and to shore up the rotten wood pilings that had been put into the earth as foundations 500 years previously to hold the weight of the palace above.

The 2 front reliefs represent the world of legend. **Aeneas**, looking austere, sacrifices on a country altar on the right; on the left was the **Lupercal**, the cave where **Romulus** and **Remus** were suckled by the she-wolf. (This panel has, unfortunately, been destroyed.)

The 2 exterior sides are the highlight of this monumental visit. They represent the 4th of July parade in 43 BC. On that precise day, **Emperor Augustus** was given a hero's welcome upon his return from war in Spain and Gaul. He had been so successful in pacifying these fringes of the Empire that the Senate ordered the construction of the **Altar of Augustus' Peace** at a place consecrated that same day during his triumphal parade. The figures visible today are in the artists' 3-dimensional and precise record of Emperor Augustus leading his family and followers during the parade and the consecration ceremony of this Altar of Peace in this city 2000 years ago. Executed during the 4 years right after the event, the giant screen figures must have seemed like a Second Augustan Triumph when the completed altar was dedicated in 9 BC.

The parade begins—in the badly broken left section of the side panel facing Augustus' Mausoleum—with 3 or 4 Lictors, bearers of

the ceremonial fasces, or bundles of sticks, marching just ahead of the Emperor. (Fasces symbolized obedience to the Law and thus fascism was named after this sign of imperial authoritarianism.) That's Augustus himself, taller than the others, whose face appears as the last one in that broken left section of this picture. Unfortunately, the whole front of his body cannot be seen, and the image breaks across his face—but you can see that he is young and handsome. His left arm and shoulder are clearly visible to the right. **Tiberius**—who is to be the next emperor—is right next to him in the foreground, almost touching the imperial left arm.

Those next couple of fellows with the strange beanies on their heads are the *flamens*, or lighters of the ceremonial fires. After the old man with the Imperial Ax on his shoulder, that tall one with his right fist clenched is **Agrippa**, Augustus' best friend and son-in-law; then the Emperor's wife, **Livia**, his daughter **Julia**, and his friends. Notice the children: Agrippa's child is tugging at his toga for attention and another imperial child, with a very serious face, is holding his own offering on this auspicious day.

On the side facing the Tiber River you will see the other VIPs of this same procession: the

priests, magistrates, and some of the senators who voted for the monument and ceremony. The **Pontifex Maximus**, high priest, is recognizable by the toga lightly covering his laurel-wreathed head. This was before the emperor took over the awesome title of Pontifex Maximus. That title eventually passed to the popes, which is why they are still called pontiff.

Now look at the back of the altar's outer wall. These 2 sculptural panels are symbolic of the 2 entities Romans hold most dear. One depicts **Roma** (almost wholly destroyed) and the other **Tellus** (Italy). Tellus is a serene mother figure, looking lovingly down at her 2 *bambini*. On either side are the deities of air and water. Air is sailing on a swan and Water is on a sea monster. Inside the inner sanctum, on either side of where the altar would have been, are scroll-shaped carvings with exquisite high reliefs of a sacrificial procession, with the ill-fated animals being led by priests. Don't forget to look closely at the stylized flower and leaf scrolls, both inside and outside the enclosure. These sculptures represent the very highest degree of perfection Roman art ever attained. ◆ Tu, Th, Sa 4:30-8PM, Su 9AM-1PM, Apr-Oct; Tu-Sa 9AM-2PM, Su 9AM-1PM, Nov-Mar. Via di Ripetta

107 Mausoleum of Augustus (28 BC) The most important ancient building in **Campus Martius**, a large area between the Quirinal and the Tiber, the Capitoline and the Porta Flaminia. The river often inundated this low, flat ground forming ponds and swamps. There was even a hot spring that was used for *termae* (medicinal baths).

Although the early Romans used the land to graze sheep and horses or to grow corn and wheat, the Campus Martius was named after and consecrated to Mars, god of war. Soon after, Roman youths and soldiers practiced athletics and military exercises here. Before the mausoleum was built, temples to foreign gods were permitted here because the area was outside the city proper. There was even a grandiose temple to Mars himself. Over 20 temples sprouted here. Then in 221 BC the Circus Flaminius was built. In 55 BC **Pompeius** (Pompey) built the first stone theater nearby (see **Pompey's Theater** on page 111), ignoring an edict that no theater could be made of stone. (One explanation for this edict is that the senators and consuls were frightened that an eloquent actor might rally the people against them, so all theaters had to be makeshift affairs in wood. Pompey got around this by putting a temple at the top of his theater and adding gardens and bars.)

To solve the problem of flooding, Caesar had wanted to change the course of the Tiber by making it go behind the Janiculum Hill, but he died before he could realize this dream. Augustus built his mausoleum here despite the floods—perhaps because this was the place closest to the center of Rome where he could have a large, flat, open area for what was to be a vast dynastic monument.

Restaurants/Clubs: Red	Hotels: Blue
Shops/Parks: Green	Sights/Culture: Black

The large circular drum of Augustus' tomb was faced with marble. On this was built an arcade, and the roof of this arcade supported other arcading that had conical cypress trees placed on the 3rd and 4th stories. This magical mix of nature interlocking with architecture for very important buildings was a Roman first and last. (Nobody has since conceived of nature in architecture on such a grand and sumptuous scale.) On the very top of this birthday cake, a 50-foot bronze statue of Augustus looked out regally and benignly. Two obelisks enhanced the entrance, and beautiful parks and gardens surrounded the tomb. Tombs weren't the dead places they are today. On the date of the person's death and/or birth, feasts would be held inside the tomb. The mourners became gently sloshed as they toasted the person's accomplishments. Augustus' designated heir, **Marcellus**, who died in his youth, was the first person to be buried here. Over 15 urns of ashes of the great and near-great were placed here—among them at least 6 emperors—so there were a lot of parties. The **Colonna** family converted the ruins into one of the stronghold towers of Rome in the 10th century. Four hundred years later, in 1354, **Cola di Rienzo**'s body was burned here. He had tried to reestablish Rome's imperial sovereignty under his own leadership during the time the papacy moved to Avignon, but he was killed by a servant of the princely Colonna family while delivering a speech. These families were all-powerful during this desolate time and an amazing amount of tit-for-tat murdering went on until the pope was reinstated in Rome. During the Renaissance (16th century) the tomb became an ornamental garden. In the 18th century it became a bull ring for intimate corridas, and in the late 19th century a roof was added and it became the most unusual concert hall in the world! In the 1930s **Mussolini** reexcavated the original building and envisioned his own ashes reposing here in glory as Rome's present-day savior and uncrowned emperor. However, Mussolini met a traitor's death at the hands of anti-Fascist partisans in 1945. He and his mistress, **Clara Petacci**, were shot and hung upside down naked in the center of Milan. No visits. ♦ Via di Ripetta

---

Most Romans flee town during scorching August; but those who stay benefit from the munificence of the Roman authorities, who have been known to drape a huge screen from a large monument and set up thousands of chairs in the streets for an all-night Roman version of the drive-in movie. These open-air festivals cost only a small fee.

Up until 50 years ago, Italians washed their linens in the age-old way of their Roman forefathers: Place all the sheets in a large clay pot. Tie a cloth securely over the top, using the lip to fix it. Dump all the ash from the fireplace into the center of the cloth and pour boiling water on top; allow to ferment for 3 days. Then rinse abundantly and dry. The linens will have a sweet smell.

Gianni Bulgari
Proprietor, Bulgari Jewelry

A city remains a city on credit from the tide that flows among its rocks, a sea of men, mused the English poet Ruth van Todd. The tide of Western man has shaped the *rocks* of Rome so that they act as its uninterrupted witness.

This witness has had his ups and downs but never failed to be there with some proper piece of testimonial. The layers are stratified with uneven conspicuousness: the withdrawn severity of the Middle Age millennium squeezed between the mundane grandeur of both the Empire and the Renaissance, or the pomp of the Baroque followed by the parochial 19th century.

Rome is an open-air biography of the 25 centuries of life and deeds of Western man, a colossal emporium of memorabilia superimposed one atop another in puzzling and whimsical chaos.

Reading, deciphering, and living within that chaos is still the most inspiring exercise for anyone interested to know how man did shape the environment. Rome is the eternity of the ephemeral, the everlasting witness of how man has been and a subdued inspiration of how he might be.

There is, strangely enough, an ecumenical affinity between Rome and New York; while the latter is the place of all palaces, Rome is the place of all times.

Ten Unusual Dishes

Bresaola—like the exquisite cured ham, *prosciutto crudo*, but made from beef.

Rigatoni alla pagliata—the intestines of newborn calves, with the curdled milk inside. Specialty at **Er Galetto**.

Insalata puntarelle—a strange wild grass skinned into spirals with anchovy sauce. Served in many restaurants.

Gnocchi alla Romana—gnocchi made with semolina (corn rather than potatoes). Hard to find even in Rome, but you might try **Sora Lella**.

Olive ripiene all'ascolana—olives filled with chopped meat.

Carciofi alla Giudea—fried artichokes. Try them at **Da Costanza**.

Gelato Ficchi d'India—Prickly-pear ice cream at **Il Drappo**.

Fragole al limone—Strawberries with lemon or white wine, widely available.

Sorbetto agli asparagi—Asparagus sherbet at the **Hilton La Pergola**.

Risotto alle fragole—Rice cooked in broth with Parmesan cheese and strawberries. This is a salty dish!

The **cats of Rome** love spaghetti with tomato sauce. They literally live on handouts from little old ladies.

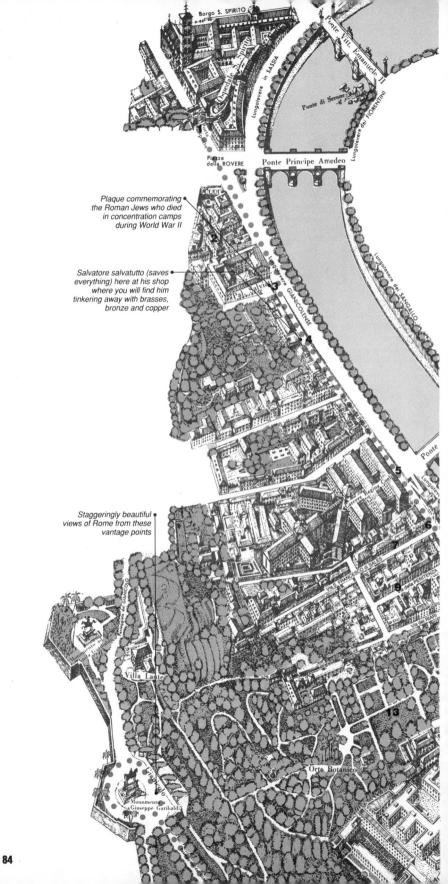

Plaque commemorating
the Roman Jews who died
in concentration camps
during World War II

Salvatore salvatutto (saves
everything) here at his shop
where you will find him
tinkering away with brasses,
bronze and copper

Staggeringly beautiful
views of Rome from these
vantage points

Trastevere

Literally *across the Tevere* (Tiber)—this part of Rome is closest to the Etruscan cities of the northwest. Apparently the early Romans, who were mostly sheep and cattle farmers, were impressed with the suave and elegant Etruscans and made the Etruscan **Lars Porsenna** their king. A few hundred years later, in 509 BC, the Romans turned against the last Etruscan king, **Tarquinius Superbus** (he thought he was the greatest), who killed someone by kicking him down the Curia steps. Superbus looked to his Etruscan cousins for help and the enmity flared between Rome and Etruria. Finally, Rome won and declared itself a Republic. At the height of Rome's power, Trastevere was peopled by sailors from Ravenna who worked the giant awning to keep the sun and rain out of the Colosseum. The experience and precision of sailors was needed to pull the ellipse-shaped tenting over the spectators. Trastevere was still predominantly a sailor's quarter as late as AD 872, when **Pope John VIII** recruited men for the Battle of Circeo (fought at Mount Circe of Ulysses fame), which he won against the Saracen Moslems. Tradesmen, who until recently practiced exclusively here, included tanners, potters, cabinetmakers, and gardeners.

1 Porta Santo Spirito (Fortification of the Vatican) (1538, **Antonio Sangallo**) Sangallo (1483-1546) designed this massive entrance to the Vatican and rebuilt the ancient **Hospice of Santo Spirito in Sassia**. Inside the walls and out, this was the quarter where the Saxon pilgrims lived. The original church was started in AD 689, and finished in 720 by **King Ina of Wessex** and his queen, **Ethelburga**. There was an adjoining school, **Schola Saxonum**, for priests, and a hostel for pilgrims with kitchen gardens and a vineyard. The famous 11th-century **King Canute** was the last reigning monarch from Southern England to make the pilgrimage to Rome. (He also ruled over Denmark and Norway, but he couldn't turn back the tides.) In the 12th century the area decayed and the pope took the property from the English and made it into a hospital. **Sixtus IV** added a hospice for foundling children in the 15th century. The hospice had a turntable with an open hatch

Entrance to Botanical Garden – watch for announcements of jazz concerts in the park

Villa Farnesina – don't miss Raphael's frescoes nor the upper floor which houses the Gabinetto Nazionale delle Stampe

Raphael courted La Fornarina (the baker's daughter) here at Romolo Restaurant

Fabrizio

Don't be put off by the nondescript entrance to Checco er Carrettiere, a wonderful restaurant tucked away on this tiny side street

Small fountain which was moved from the other end of Ponte Sisto to this location in Piazza Trilussa

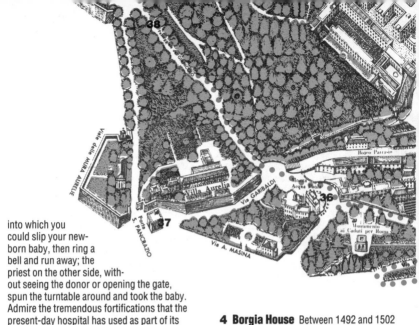

into which you could slip your new-born baby, then ring a bell and run away; the priest on the other side, without seeing the donor or opening the gate, spun the turntable around and took the baby. Admire the tremendous fortifications that the present-day hospital has used as part of its courtyard. This is now a modern hospital with an emergency department, **Pronto Soccorso**, which we hope you won't need. Its entrance is on Lungotevere in Sassia.

2 Pensione La Rovere $ A modest little room-and-board pension just a stone's throw from the Vatican. Rooms are spartan but clean! Extra charge for the shower. The upper bedrooms have terraces and good views. ♦ Vicolo San Onofrio 5. 6540739

3 Palazzo Salviati Not open to the public since it, along with the adjoining gardens, has become an army enclave—not a big loss, since **Prince Borghese**, who bought the building from the Salviatis, took all the paintings and put them into Palazzo Borghese. ♦ Piazza della Rovere 83

3 Plaque to the Jewish dead A poignant testimony to the 1000 Jews who were rounded up here and sent to the concentration camps. Only 16 returned. ♦ Piazza della Rovere 83

4 Church of San Giovanni alla Lungara It was started in AD 847, during the reign of **Pope Leo IV**, and modernized in the early 19th century. This whole area had been gardens (and earlier, emperors' vineyards) before the last part of the 16th century, when **Pope Julius II** built Via della Lungara, which cut straight through the gardens from Porta Santo Spirito south to Porta Settimiano. ♦ Via della Lungara 50

4 Borgia House Between 1492 and 1502 **Pope Alexander VI** reigned and his bastard son, **Cesare Borgia**, terrified the good citizens of Rome and the lands he set out to conquer—in pursuance of the Pope's desire to perpetuate his dynasty and keep the papacy permanently in the family. Cesare owned this simple building, which was outside the city walls. There were 2 underground passages, one to the Vatican and one to the riverbank. Imagine this monstrous bully, after a night of carousing and bloodletting, having the bodies he wished to do away with (including his own brother) carried by his accomplices down the tunnel to the water's edge, where a boat with muffled oars waited to remove the corpses. And if things ever got too hot for him or his sister **Lucrezia**, they could take flight along the other tunnel, which brought them into the protective arms of their scheming father in whose eyes they could do no wrong. ♦ Via della Lungara 46

4 Salvatore Salvatutto Tinker's Shop Pinocchio's bottega, with an interesting collection of these long-nosed Italian naughty boys. Old brasses, bronzes, and copper. Salvatore, whose name means *fixes everything*, is constantly tinkering inside—welding, mending, gluing—and in general, fiddling. He describes his shop as filled with *curiosities and strangenesses; surprises from the past; small creations; all things that today, alas, are extinct; restoration of every type of object and material.* ♦ Via della Lungara 44

5 Jail of Regina Coeli (Queen of the Heavens) Having taken your life in your hands and braved the speeding traffic hurtling toward you down this canyonlike street, look up at the new road on the embankment to see how high the embankments were built in order to protect the city from the destructive Tiber River floods. Even as late as the beginning of this century, boats were used on this street after a

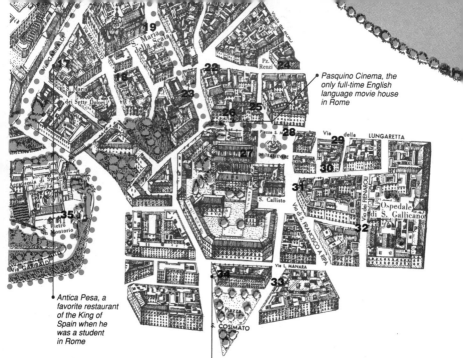

Antica Pesa, a favorite restaurant of the King of Spain when he was a student in Rome

Pasquino Cinema, the only full-time English language movie house in Rome

Alberto Ciarla is an elegant fish restaurant in Piazza San Cosimato

deluge. (The latest deluge, in 1986, caused a mudslide down the Gianicolo Hill, and for a few hours Via della Lungara was back in the last century with Fiats almost completely submerged.) The large undistinguished mass of the prison now assails you. This is where defendants are kept while awaiting trial and sentencing. There is no shame or embarrassment in the case of these inmates (usually in for fraud or extortion, not for murder) or their loved ones, who wait outside for visiting hours. The atmosphere is convivial and chatty. On various side streets one can often see an inmate's son or daughter climb up on parked cars for better audibility and shout the family news or announce the impending visit of a lawyer to their incarcerated father—then hear the muffled response of the prisoner. At night one can hear the mournful cry *Ci vuole una donna!* (I need a woman!), and sometimes *Ci vuole la mamma!* (I want my Mom!) ♦ Via della Lungara 29

6 Convento del Buon Pastore (Convent of the Good Shepherd) This whole block was once a convent that took care of unwed mothers and their children. In 1980 the nuns, whose numbers had dwindled to a handful, were chased out of the building by the municipality. Feminists have taken over 3 rooms in the building and there are plans to make it a cultural center. There is an experimental theater in the back, a children's playground in the courtyard, and on the side, a restaurant that hasn't paid any rent since the nuns left! ♦ Via della Lungara

7 da Benito ★$$ Lots of parking space inside and an equally large vaulted dining hall make for an airy atmosphere. The usual cooked-vegetable antipasto trays, with ham and seafood salad, are starters. Spaghetti *alle vongole*

(with little clams) is good, although the fettucine *al funghi porcini* (fresh egg pasta with wild mushrooms) is a mite gluelike. But the risotto *ai scampi* is just right: al dente (not overcooked—literally *to the tooth*). The veal cutlet smothered in sauce and mushrooms could do with less cornstarch. Efficient ser-

Trastevere

vice, good open house wine, and all sorts of sticky no-no cakes. ♦ Closed Monday. Via San Francesco di Sales 1. 6548063

8 San Giacomo alla Lungara Church (1560) This church, opposite the Buon Pastore convent, is all that is left of a convent for reformed prostitutes founded by **Pope Pius IV** of the **Medici** family. It was later given to the Augustine nuns by **Urban VIII** (1623-1644) of the **Barberini** family—look for the bees. The building was rebuilt in 1642 by a Barberini cardinal; the great Baroque artist **Bernini** designed a memorial. With a hospital, a jail, churches galore, convents for the repentant, and—until they built the high embankments along the river—a lunatic asylum, this area of town could be called self-sufficient. ♦ Via della Lungara

L'ARTUSIANA

9 L'Artusiana Restaurant ★$$ Artusi was a 19th-century gourmet who wrote *Science in the Kitchen* and *The Art of Eating Well*. He was the Italian equivalent of Escoffier. This restaurant tries to emulate the fine palate of Artusi, and does it pretty well. The menu changes often. They serve only fresh fish and a cross section of taste treats: toast with various meat and vegetable pâtés; *fusilli provençale* (serrated macaroni with chopped black olives—salty but good; *tonarelli* (thin, square spaghetti) with sage and saffron—excellent; a quiche-type soufflé—good; *ovolini fritti* (small mozzarella balls fried lightly with an anchovy sauce—very good). Perhaps the chef is a bit too ambitious and should simplify the menu. ♦ Closed Tuesday. Via della Penitenza 7. Reservations required. 6547053

10 Da Luigi In this corner bar and café, Luigi carries on in a modest way the tradition of good coffee and *tramezzini* (sandwiches) that his father established before him. ♦ Closed Sunday. Via della Lungara 14

10 F.ORMA Cabinetmakers. Two young master craftsmen in fine woods, American **Douglas Andrews** and Italian **Guido Orsini**, have taken over the art gallery that used to be here. The space has become their workshop and exhibition hall. They make highly lacquered geometrically shaped tables and trays. ♦ Via della Lungara 15. 6541351

11 Villa Farnesina (1511, **Baldassare Peruzzi**) An exquisite small palace designed for the multimillionaire international banker **Agostino Chigi** on a tiny part of the site of **Julius Caesar**'s country house where **Cleopatra** stayed in 44 BC, and from where she fled

Trastevere

when Caesar was murdered. Caesar could not bring her into Rome itself since his wife, **Calpurnia**, a respectable Roman matron, lived here. So he bent the rules by lodging her here, just outside of what was technically Rome. It was a terrible scandal for Caesar, especially as Cleopatra had brought their illegitimate child, **Caesarion**, with her. (She was the first woman to have a Caesarean operation—named after him. Egyptian doctors were very advanced.) These gardens of Caesar's country house extended all the way down the Lungara and up the Gianicolo hill. In his will, Caesar left part of the gardens to the Roman people. During Imperial times (27 BC-AD 476) this became the center of a large wine industry. The highest land commanding the best view was kept by various emperors. The ancient Roman *Pizzutelli* grape (pink lozenge with pale green) grows wild today and does not exist anywhere else in the world.

Chigi gave superb, extravagant dinners here for his friend and patron **Pope Leo X** and a star-studded cast of characters. He especially liked the former waterside pavilion. (When this was being destroyed to make room for the river embankment, engineers found remnants of a Republican-era house, presumably

Caesar's hideaway for Cleopatra, with delicate frescoes painted on the walls.) It was here, during important dinners, that the great Renaisance banker Chigi would have the silver plates tossed into the river after every course in a fit of luxurious bravura. (Bad tongues maintain that they were easily fished out afterward as he had planted large nets just beneath the surface of the water.) Chigi was a great art patron and commissioned various artists, especially **Raffaello** (Raphael, 1483-1520), to do the frescoes. Raphael worked here on and off from 1512 to 1518. In fact, Chigi allowed the artist to house his mistress here in order to get more work out of him. According to the biographer and artist **Vasari**, Raphael was killed by over-exertion as *he continued his amorous pleasures to an inordinate degree.*

Within the Villa Farnesina:

The Loggia is now in the back. A garden pergola and the real entrance to the villas. Raphael, along with **Giulio Romano** and other students, painted the 12 frescoes of the *Story of Psyche* to bring the garden into the building. Don't miss the erotic symbolism above Mercury's hand. The whole porch seems overgrown with plants. (No glass in between the arches in those days.) In the second room downstairs—which was originally another loggia open on the river side—is a whole scene painted only by Raphael. One can immediately see the difference in the quality of the painting—the people look more real and the skin tones glow. Galatea, floating on her shell pulled by impish dolphins, is having a wonderful time. **Peruzzi**, who designed the building, also painted the ceiling in this room. (In those days, painters and sculptors were also architects.) An oft-told tale about **Michelangelo** involves the painting he left behind in this same room. When he dropped in, Raphael was out (probably making a gallant visit to his love, **La Fornarina**); in his absence Michelangelo painted a large head (left wall) as a sign of his visit—and supposedly a hint to Raphael that his work was too small in scale for the size of the room!

The **upper floor**, where special exhibitions are occasionally held, also houses the **Gabinetto Nazionale delle Stampe** (Print Room). In Chigi's bedroom, there are more frescoes; those by **Sodoma** are said to be his best. In 1580, due to bad management, the Chigi fortune frittered away and the villa was sold to the **Farnese** family—hence its name. Nobody knows why the plan to join it by a bridge across the river to the Farnese palace on the opposite bank was never accomplished.

 The gardens suffered at the hands of the new 1870 government. Designed in 1506 to be an extension of the building, they were torn apart and the giant trees cut down to make way for the roadway that separates the villa from the river. But to the right one can walk, sit on a bench, and enjoy the fountain. ♦ Tu-Sa 9AM-1PM; F 9AM-1PM, 4-6PM. Via della Lungara 230. 6540565, 6561375

12 Palazzo Corsini (Facade 1736, **Ferdinando Fuga**) **Girolamo Riario**, nephew of **Sixtus IV**, was given the property by his uncle. The Pope was very much a self-made man, a fisherman's son with brains who had risen in the church to the supreme office. He was ambitious and one could almost say he invented nepotism; he amassed a fortune for his family with gifts of costly properties. The whole area was a giant garden right up to the top of the Gianicolo hill with thousands of rows of vines for wine, fruit orchards, and wild nature. Girolamo married **Caterina Sforza**, whose beauty was legendary and whose father was the strong man of Milan. **Cesare Borgia**, the detested son of **Pope Alexander VI**, defeated Caterina's armies at Forli and was so impressed by her bravery during the battle that he had her brought back to Rome fettered in golden chains. After she had languished in prison for a year (Castel Sant'Angelo) the French persuaded him to release her.

Michelangelo stayed one year but never got a commission from Cardinal Riario, because, as **Vasari** said, *Riario has a small understanding of art.*

One of Rome's great figures, **Queen Christina of Sweden**, moved here in 1662 after abdicating her throne and embracing the Catholic religion. She died in the room with 2 wooden columns overlooking the gardens on 19 April 1689. (Some say she was madly in love with a cardinal and that's the reason she embraced Catholicism.) She created the Queen's academy, *Accademia Reale*, which later became the Arcadia. In this connection she commissioned a series of beautiful medals inspired by the arts and sciences, of which she was an enthusiastic patron. Today this is the seat of the **Accademia dei Luncei**, a distinguished scientific institute so ancient that Galileo was among the founders. She also enjoyed the fabulous life of Rome, with its pageants, processions (see the 17th-century paintings in Palazzo Braschi), banquets, and the like. Although converted to Catholicism, she still utterly detested the bigotry of the father confessors. In 1729, 140 years after her death, **Clement XII** gave the modest palace to his nephew **Cardinal Neri Corsini**, who transformed it into a princely palazzo; the vast facade is **Fuga**'s best work.

Here, in 1797, **Joseph Bonaparte** narrowly escaped death when his sister-in-law's fiancé, **General Duphot**, was shot dead by papal guards during an attempted coup against Napoleonic power. This led to yet another French invasion—this one by **Bertheas**—and the imprisonment of **Pope Pius VI**. (Don't forget that the French captured the papacy for almost 70 years and brought it to Avignon from 1309-1377.)

Within the Palazzo Corsini:

The Corsini Library One of the oldest libraries still in situ the way it was conceived in the 18th century by the studious **Monsignore Lorenzo Corsini.** Accademia dei Lincei is a learned society of scientists, scholars, and men of letters, including several Noble laureates, some of them American.

The National Art Gallery The gallery contains many paintings of the 16th and 17th centuries. Especially noteworthy is a portrait of **Beatrice Cenci** by **Guido Reni** (1575-1642). She was executed after she murdered her father, who had raped her, even though her whole family testified what an ogre he had been (see **Palazzo Cenci** on page 131). Another interesting painting is a rare portrait of the prolific **Bernini** by **Baciccia** (1639-1709), who was more noted for his interior design and frescoes in the Church of the Gesù (Jesus). There are also paintings by **Caravaggio, Murillo, Van Dyck** and **Rubens**. ♦ M, Sa 9AM-1:30PM; Tu-F 9AM-6:30PM; Su 9AM-12:30PM. Via della Lungara 10. 6542323

13 Botanical Gardens Entrance gate at the end of the Via Corsini—one of the prettiest and shortest streets in Rome. The giant magnolia tree in the middle is so old that it used to look into **Queen Christina**'s torrid bedroom next door. Once the private gardens of the **Palazzo Riario/Corsini**, although in those days they were much larger. Before the municipality took it over, there had been some magnificent avenues of hundred-year-old illexes topiaried into a dense canopy (like the ones in Villa Aldobrandini in Frascati), under which Queen Christina had strolled with the

Trastevere

Arcadians. The municipality disgracefully—and despite the intercession of **Queen Margherita**—sold these ancient trees for firewood in 1878. Still, the garden is lovely, even after the severe winter of 1984-5, which did terrible damage to the tropical tree section, wiping out a whole quarter of the garden where parrot and African acacia trees stood side by side with rubber trees from the Amazon. ♦ M-Sa 9AM-6:30PM. Largo Cristina di Svezia 24. 6864193

14 Palazzo Torlonia **Prince Torlonia** (whose ancestor had been in Napoleon's entourage as a simple furnisher of cloth and who originally came from Toulon) housed his fabulous art collection here in his private museum. The family got rich under Napoleon, rose to be bankers under Pius VI, and finally, princes and marquises. But they made their big money draining the malarial swamps all over Italy (after having bought them for a song), and in some of them unearthed ancient artworks. There are 2 Torlonia families, one of which is indigenous to Rome. Now private residences. ♦ Via della Lungara 1

Restaurants/Clubs: Red	**Hotels:** Blue
Shops/Parks: Green	**Sights/Culture:** Black

15 Porta Settimiana (Present facade of gate, 15th century) This magnificent gate to the city was named after **Emperor Septimius Severus** to whose country estate it once led. It was incorporated into the **Aurelian Wall** in the 3rd century AD; notice how thick the wall is at this point. Modifications of the doorway were made during the reign of **Alexander VI** (the Borgia pope, 1492-1503). It was the city boundary until 1633. On the far side of the wall (looking down on the Caffè Settimiano and the punks in the adjoining pub) is a recently restored but badly damaged Baroque fresco, the *Sermon on the Mount.*

You are now entering Trastevere—quarter of artists and whores! Having been cut off from the mainstream of the city until the unification of Italy in 1860 (Rome became the capital in 1870), Trastevere is the least changed part of Rome, and until very recently the people did not speak Italian but a local dialect that was impossible for most Italians to understand. Poets who wrote in this patois are remembered because their names grace a square or 2. Trastevere is a rabbit warren of little streets and *piazzete* (small squares). Look up to the rooftops and see one of the miracles of Rome—the roof gardens and verdant terraces, which become extra living rooms during the warmer months of the year.

15 Romolo Restaurant ★★$$$ This is where **Raphael** courted and adored **La Fornarina** (the baker's daughter). Some of his most famous

Trastevere

paintings are portraits of her. Goodies to savor in this ancient tavern (at least 400 years old) are *bresaola*—the beef equivalent of prosciutto (raw cured ham); *amburghese alla diavolo*—not devilish burgers, but a juicy cornish hen flattened and cooked on the grill until crispy; any green vegetable reheated in olive oil with garlic and red peppers; and the tempting *tartufo*—vanilla ice cream with flaming chocolate coating. The garden—with the 1700-year-old wall of Rome to one side and the medieval walls on the other and giant *ombrelloni* (parasols) covering the tables from direct sun—is very attractive for summer dining. Reserve if over 4 people. ♦ Closed Monday and part of August. Via Porta Settimiana 8. 5813873, 5818284

15 Sarti Ceramic Art Master ceramicist **Domenico** and his daughter **Lavinia** are so talented that they can braid clay into small, medium, or large cachepots of great elegance. Statues and shell fountains for the millionaires; useful and beautiful lamps, bowls, and trays for the rest of us. ♦ Via San Dorotea 21. 5892079

A city greater than any on earth, whose amplitude no eye can measure, whose beauty no imagination can picture.
Claudian

16 Da Gildo Pizzeria ★★$$ All pizzerias are traditionally open only in the evening, when they light the giant wood fires. Da Gildo is owned and run by 2 young men who also wait on the tables, flying through the 3 little rooms with delicious pizzas crowding the edges of their plates. The place is attractive with an unusual choice of posters on the walls and a lovely little marble fountain that keeps the vegetables crunchy and cool. You might take the hors d'oeuvres (antipasto) and then indulge in scrumptious pizza. Wine by the bottle, not carafe. ♦ M-Tu, Th-Su 8PM-1AM. Via della Scala 31A. No credit cards. 5800733

17 Antica Pesa ★★$$$ This restaurant is definitely upscale. When the **King of Spain** was a student at the Spanish Academy up the road, he used to come here, and he returned a few years ago to savor his old haunt with then **President Pertini**. An Italian critic says it is full of American professors, rich pilgrims, and ladies in sparkling paillettes dresses. An abundance of fish is laid out as you come in, and the fire for grilling immediately gives you ideas of what you'd like to eat. In the winter, the long hall filled with modern paintings is an attractive frame for the business of eating, but outside, in the paved garden under trees and giant parasols, is where the restaurant really comes into its own. ♦ Closed Sunday. Via Garibaldi 18. Reservations recommended. 5809236

18 Lucia ★★$ A sign on the wall, repeated on the menu, announces *The kitchen cannot serve clients in a great hurry; all our food is freshly cooked to your order.* In other words: slow food, friend, no fast food here. Fine, authentic Roman peasant dishes in an authentic atmosphere. Where else can you still find cow's tails and dry, spicy sausages dangling overhead, not for decoration but because that's where **Silvana** keeps them until she reaches up with her broomstick and pitches them down into **Paolo**'s waiting arms? A mom-and-pop shop where pop—**Ennio** to the *habitués*, and most customers are *habitués*—looks in the summer as if he were on a boat, serving in crisp white shorts. You sit out in the middle of the street, as do the neighboring Trasteverini who come down from their hot apartments to cool off in the evening air. We cannot claim to have discovered this uncut gem. **Veronelli**, Italy's prime connoisseur of fine wines and food has recommended it, and Lucia has won prizes for the no-frills, no-disappointments cooking. But we have to be careful not to give too many stars, lest we ruin this wonderful, unspoiled delight. ♦ Closed Monday. Vicolo Mattonato 2/B. 5803601

19 Church of Santa Maria della Scala and Vecchia Farmacia (Pharmacy) In 1592 the church was built from designs by **Francesco da Volterra** to house a miracle-working picture that used to be on the stairway (*scala*) of a medieval house. A lovely canopy altar on columns was added in 1650, designed by **Carlo Rainaldi**. Long before, Carmelite monks founded the adjoining pharmacy for the poor. During one of the plagues that afflicted the city in 1523 the monks saved many lives—and made their reputation and fortune—with the ruby-colored *Acqua della Scala*. Plagues referred to a variety of terrifying mass deaths: bubonic (brought by fleas who had bitten infected rats); typhus and dysentery (dirty drinking water and flooding of the Tiber river with its subsequent contamination); and malaria (which every summer was a hazard since the ancient Roman waterways had been allowed to get silted up, and stagnant waters in low-lying areas were ideal breeding grounds for mosquitoes). Famines also cut a swath through the population. So the High Renaissance period in Rome, from 1500-1560, which inspired man to build and paint the most beautiful palaces and artworks, had a grim side of death and destruction. Plagues afflicted the city in 1523, 1527-1529, 1538-1539, and 1558-1559. From 1726-1804, **Fra Basilio** invented many herbal remedies and was visited by kings and cardinals who marveled, as did his students, at his sagacity. You can visit the upstairs shop, still faithfully kept as it used to be. The marble urns were used to store remedies in honey or oil, such as *Teriaca* (made with viper's heads) for stomachaches, *Acqua Antipestilenziale* for severe internal disorders, and *Antisterica* for headaches. The modern pharmacy on the ground floor keeps normal hours. ♦ M-F 9-11AM. Piazza Santa Maria della Scala. 5806217

19 Piazza Santa Maria della Scala Opposite the church, the buildings with street **Nos. 53-57** will give you an idea of how Trastevere looked earlier in this century—a series of cottages with their inhabitants milling around among the barnyard animals in the unpaved streets below.

da CHECCO

20 Checco er Carrettiere ★★★$$ (When you see *er* instead of *al* in the name of a restaurant you know it's Roman cooking.) Don't be put off by the nothing entrance. This is a fine Roman place tucked away from the glare of the common hordes. A large countrified room, like an old farmhouse, with garlic and peppers hanging from the beams, and through the glass doors an outdoor patio for dining when the weather is warm. Seafood arrives daily but you can order meat if you prefer, or if your budget won't stretch to fish (which is expensive in Rome). The antipasto table is a real treat with every sort of prepared shellfish and vegetable imaginable. Our favorite is a potato-and-tomato mix that we've never found in another restaurant. Very thick, it is neither a whip nor a purée—but a smash! We found the house pasta specialty too oily, but there are many other spaghetti dishes that are delicious. Roman spaghetti *alle vongole* (a type of baby clam) with bits of chili peppers thrown in to liven it up is particularly good. Go on to a vegetable or straight to dessert if the starters and pasta have filled you up. In Rome you don't have to order a main course if you

Trastevere

don't want one. Good fruit, such as pineapple cut in an attractive way—of course it's fresh, no Roman wants anything canned or frozen—strawberries and raspberries in season, and ice creams. Reserve if more than 4. ♦ Closed Monday and Sunday dinner. Via Benedetta 10/13. No credit cards. 5817018

21 Da Gigi Il Moro ★$ The bread is so fresh, it's still moist. The servings are so abundant, you can't see the plates. The beer is on draft. The *fettuccine boscaiolo* with mushrooms and sausage is almost sweet. The fish is fresh. The pizza is only at night. A Roman trattoria! ♦ Closed Monday. Via del Moro 43. 5809165

22 Da Otello ★★$$ Specialties from the region of Umbria, the center of Italy's pasta production. This popular tavern, which becomes a pizzeria at night, has recently been upgraded—good food at reasonable prices. The narrow street becomes its dining room in summer. This is the sort of place that in France would have paper tablecloths, but the French could never equal these grilled eggplant with Parmesan—or the blueberry pie with crust as thin and flaky as the succulent pizzas. ♦ Closed Monday. Via della Pelliccia 49 (Piazza San Egidio) 5896848

23 Museum of Folklore and Romaneschi Poets Located in the old **Convent of the Carmelites of San Egidio in Trastevere**, the museum features copies of famous Roman sculptures such as the "speaking" statues, sketches of life in old Rome, and information about the Trastevere poets who wrote in the old dialect. Recommended for children are the "tableaux" of Roman life in the 18th century, one flight up. This whole area is most like Rome used to be 200 years ago. Old Trastevere, where Renaissance houses, Baroque churches, and humble dwellings are all cheek by jowl with small open squares wedged in between. Count how many churches you can spot between the Vatican walls and Piazza Santa Maria in Trastevere. ♦ Tu, Th 9AM-1PM, 5-7PM; W, F-Sa 9AM-1PM; Su 9AM-12:30PM. Piazza San Egidio 1/b. 5816563

24 Galeria del Batik Painted ceramics by **Clotilde Sambuco** and **Maria De Santis**. The lessons in batik and ceramics have disappeared into the woodwork in favor of sales of sensational ceramics from the deep south of Italy. Great jugs representing knights and their damsels in 17th-century style, vast spaghetti plates and soup tureens, all joyously painted by hand. Also fine woven table linen from Sardinia. ♦ Via della Pelliccia 30. 5816614

25 Ci-Lin ★$ If your diet includes an obligatory visit once a week to a Chinese restaurant, this isn't a bad place to go. The soups are excellent, as are the fried bananas and apple fritters. The usual sweet-and-sour pork, shredded beef, and deep-fried shrimp are tasty. (Ci-Lin's twin, **Oriental**, at Via Calatafimi 27 (4746820), is a good place to go if you're

Trastevere

stuck near the Stazione Termini—Central Railway Station. It is more beautiful and some *satays* have been added to the menu.) ♦ Closed Wednesday. Via Fonte d'Olio 6. No credit cards. 5813930

26 La Canonica Restaurant ★$$ (per the inscription MDCLXXV) Here in the capital of the Catholic world is an amazing sight: a trattoria inside a deconsecrated chapel, hence the name! The facade is wonderfully Baroque, if you can see it through the parasols. A sweet place with a menu predominantly of fish and spaghetti. Red tablecloths, tables outside in summer. Reserve if over 6 people. ♦ Closed Monday. Vicolo del Piede 13. 5803845

26 Pasquino Cinema There were many "speaking" statues in Rome, from Republican times (BC) to the present. When Romans were dissatisfied or angry about something, a placard in rhyme would mysteriously appear hanging from the statues' necks, berating and lamenting, sometimes in savage verse. Pasquino was a rich 16th-century tailor by appointment to the Holy See, and so renowned was his bitter wit—particularly at the expense of the papacy—that the nearby antique statue

on which he would place his criticisms was moved upon his death to its present location outside his shop in Piazza Pasquino. His name was immortalized forever: *Pasquinades* (satirical writing).

So Pasquino seems a good name for a cinema. This is the only full-time English-language movie house in Rome. The films are not the latest and the prints are not the greatest, but if you don't want to hear **Meryl Streep** or **Warren Beatty** spouting Italian—come here. In the summer, as in the greatest of the emperors' salons, the ceiling rolls open to let in the stars—natural air conditioning. ♦ Daily 4-11PM. Vicolo del Piede 19. 5803622

27 Libreria Lungaretta Nova Falco stocks lots of children's books, and some English books. ♦ Via della Lungaretta. 90.5890860

27 Piazza Santa Maria in Trastevere In the center of the square is a large fountain designed by **Carlo Fontana**, who also added the portico to the church in 1702. A lot of people designed fountains for this spot, among them **Girolamo Rainaldi** (1570-1655). His was modified by **Bernini** (1598-1680), who added shells at the corners (he was mad about shells), and this in turn was torn down and rebuilt with the same design but in gray marble. Pity. To the left of the church is a vast closed palace. This is **Palazzo Moroni**. It used to be the summer palace of Benedictine monks who in the hot months were driven from their monastery because of malaria-carrying mosquitoes.

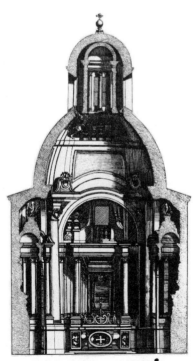

27 Church of Santa Maria in Trastevere
This church is on a site where, in Imperial times, a fountain of oil sprang up and ran

down to the Tiber. There was a squabble between tavern keepers and the new Christian church for ownership of the site, and the **Emperor Alexander Severus** decided it *was better God should be worshipped in whatever form* rather than let the tavern keepers have the place. And so this was the site of the first church to be officially opened for the Cult of Christianity. It was founded in AD 222 in honor of **San Calisto** (Saint Calixtus), who, in one of those rare shots, was thrown out of a window and landed head first in a well. He drowned and therefore was canonized. **Pope Innocent II**, who came from a famous Trastevere family, the **Papareschi**, rebuilt the church from 1130 to 1143. On the facade the splendid mosaic of the Virgin and Child enthroned, surrounded by 10 virgins—although they look like 4 girls and 6 men—was made in 1290 by **Pietro Cavallini** on a commission by **Stefaneschi**. (He is in the picture being presented to Mary by St. Peter.) Inside the church there are more magnificent mosaics; the ones at the top of the apse are 12th-century Byzantine, and Cavallini did the comic strip depicting the life of the Virgin and Christ. The magnificent pavement of multicolored marbles is Cosmatesque; the **Cosmati** family were marble artists who made geometric floors out of chopped up ancient columns and statues (in the 12th and 13th centuries) until the vogue faded. Two cardinals' sarcophagi are beautifully sculpted. Five popes are presumed to be buried beneath the high altar. An old *Scola Cantorum* (Liturgical Singing School) used to be on the right side of the church. ♦ Piazza Santa Maria in Trastavere

28 Sabatini ★$$$ There are many restaurants on this square—some of you will insist on going to the well-known Sabatini (2 separate restaurants) and others will find **Galeassi** convenient as it's right in the piazza, too. We can't really recommend the expensive Sabatini, and the other is adequate but not thrilling. Though Sabatini's fish restaurant has been dropped from most gourmet books on Rome, the view while sitting outside and looking toward the 13th-century mosaics on the church is unbeatable. The food is tolerable and the atmosphere festive. A lot of the fish is frozen. Beware of the bag snatchers. Reserve if over 4 people. The other Sabatini (closed Tuesday and 2 weeks in August when the other is

open) is around the corner at Vicolo Santa Maria in Trastevere 18. ♦ Closed Wednesday and 2 wks in August. Piazza Santa Maria in Trastevere 13. Reservations recommended. 582026

28 Galeassi ★$$ Adequate Roman food with a nice terrace in the square for summer lunching and dining with a splendid view of the church's 13th-century mosaics on the facade. Beware of the purse snatchers while dining outside. ♦ Piazza Santa Maria in Trastevere 3. 5803775, 5809898

29 Nino Salomone Leather Workshop Bags and soft moccasins made to measure. Belts and wallets. You can actually watch Nino making his fine wares. This is the start of **Lungaretta**, the leather-and-jewelry street. ♦ Via della Lungaretta 89/A

LO SCRIGNO

29 Lo Scrigno Tapestry and leather bags and ornate 19th-century-looking costume jewelry. ♦ Via della Lungaretta 78. 5899828

29 Marinucci A lady from Argentina designs her own one-of-a-kind handbags, pouches, and suitcases. ♦ Via della Lungaretta 65/A. 5894877

29 Artiginato Argentino The local gaucho, **Roberto Graziano**, offers consistently high quality in original designs from Argentina and Brazil. Silver jewelry made in Italy, leather goods, handmade sweaters, toy parrots. Reasonable prices. ♦ Via della Lungaretta 96. 5891886

Arco di S. Calisto in Trastevere

30 Arco di San Calisto ★$$ Raucous singing (no need to talk or think) with the owner, **Signor Fioravanti**, belting out a few himself and playing a mean harmonica. This conviviality makes for a restaurant with lots of local color. Long tables full of Swiss or Italian tourists. (Italy was divided into city-states for over 1000 years, so anyone who's not from Rome is a *straniero*—foreigner.) Nineteenth-century grisaille frescoes with medallions and shells on the walls and ceiling. Charming landscapes painted on glass on the walls. Roman fare includes *carciofi* (artichokes cooked with garlic and mint), *carciofi alla giudea* (in the Jewish manner, which means the old Roman recipe, double-fried). Prosciutto ham cut by hand—much tastier. Fettucine *con vongole rose* (with clams in a light tomato sauce). Grilled swordfish steak, grilled meat, fried sole. Ice cream covered with chocolate paillettes and the best *canarino* (lemon-peel digestive tea) in Rome. ♦ Via dell'Arco di San Calisto 45. Reservations recommended. 5818323, 5806991

31 Paris ★★★$$$ Not French food, but Roman—and scrumptious. Small whitebait marinated in lemon or deep-fried, pasta, chickpea soup, tagliolini *al pesto*, ravioli with ricotta, *riso rosa*—all make good starters. Then there are 3 categories of main courses: meat grilled or cooked with a sauce, fresh fish, or fried goodies such as mozzarella, *baccala*, and artichokes. Save some room for the vegetable, fruit, and zuppa inglese. ♦ Closed Monday and Sunday PM. Piazza San Calisto 7/A. 585378

32 Camillo a Trastevere ★$$ Hidden in a side street cut off from the tourist bustle around Santa Maria in Trastevere lies a spa-

Trastevere

cious restaurant with a flaming grill that serves as an open fire to give atmosphere in the winter. Camillo and his family get top marks for cutting your prosciutto *crudo*, by hand, and serving it with *carciofi alla giudea*, artichokes Jewish style—soft in the center with crunchy leaves. *Puntarelle* with anchovy sauce is a wild and wonderful salad. Tagliolini are served with baby scampi so small you weep for them. The fish is not only fresh, but fixed-priced (whereas most Roman restaurants charge by the *etto*, or tenth of a kilo, making it hard for you to know what your bill might come to in the seafood department). ♦ Closed Monday. Via dei Fienaroli 7. 5892860

The Italian government's wine labeling laws take the guesswork out of selecting a good wine: a label of D.O.C. (*Denominazione di Origine Controllata*) means the wine meets the quality control standards; D.O.C.G. (*Denominazione di Origine Controllata e Garantita*) means the wine is of the best quality.

Restaurants/Clubs: Red   Hotels: Blue
Shops/Parks: Green   **Sights/Culture:** Black

33 Il Forno Amico Bakery If you want a round brown loaf of perhaps the best bread in the world, come in the early morning and ask for *pane di grano*. The secret is that it's baked from a mixture that is half wheat grain and half wholemeal flour. All baking is done on the premises overnight, and when they're out of bread, you're out of luck. ♦ Piazza San Cosimato 53. 5810720

34 Istituto di Belezza Tiziano and Fiorina, who sell natural beauty products, recently opened this beauty salon with massage, manicure, and pedicure. ♦ Via Agostino Bertani 12. 5809471

ALBERTO CIARLA

34 Alberto Ciarla ★★★$$$$ An elegant, elite fish restaurant near a Trastevere square where great elm trees once provided shade. Live fish and shellfish fill the tanks in the window and peer at their relatives, who've been prepared in a succulent fashion. Noteworthy dishes include the fish *ceviche* (raw-fish salad marinated in lemon), ravioli stuffed with fish instead of the usual spinach and ricotta, the restaurant's own green olive oil, sea bass with almonds, oysters *fondo oro* (from Normandy), and raw sea bream with ginger. Dinner begins with a complimentary drink. Service and food are excellent, though Alberto's success sometimes shows in a supercilious attitude with resulting imperfections in the cuisine. ♦ Closed Sunday, 15 days at Christmas, and 15 days in August. Piazza San Cosimato 40. Reservations required 5818668

35 San Pietro in Montorio To get to this church, walk uphill along the Via Garibaldi. Rebuilt at the end of the 15th century for **Ferdinand** and **Isabella of Spain**, the facade is typical of Renaissance simplicity. The remains of **Beatrice Cenci** (see **Palazzo Cenci** on page 131) are buried under the high altar. The view from the front of the church is among the best in Rome.

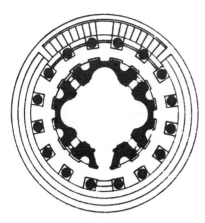

In the courtyard is **Bramante**'s well-known **Tempietto**, constructed in 1499 on the spot where **St. Peter** is believed to have been crucified. The perfectly proportioned simplicity of this small-scale temple places it among the best examples of Italian Renaissance architecture.

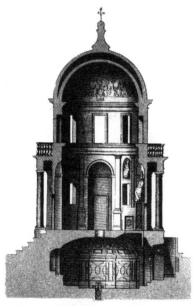

Now it is one of the preferred places for young couples to get married. Don't be surprised to see antique Rolls-Royces or horse-drawn carriages outside, especially on Saturday morning.

Walking uphill along **Via Garibaldi** leads to the **Gianicolo Hill**. This hill is 270 feet high, but it is not considered one of the Seven Hills of Rome.

The name *pasta puttanesca* reflects the earthy origins of the spicy sauce of tomatoes, garlic, capers, olives, and anchovies. Italian prostitutes (the *puttane*) had little time or money for cooking a fancy meal, and this sauce was quick and cheap to prepare.

On the Gianicolo Hill:

36 **Fontana Acqua Paola** (1612, Fontana and Ponzio) When **Pope Paul V** of the **Borghese** family mended the Aqueduct of Trajan, he pillaged the Forum for marble with which this magnificent giant fountain was built. The basin was carved in stone in 1690 by Fontana. Four of the columns of the old St. Peter's were used here. There is a lovely view of the city from the parapet on the other side of the road. During the **Summer Festival of Rome**, theatrical pieces are staged in the fountain by stopping the water flow and covering the basin with planks of wood. Chairs are set up in the street for spectators. The fountain provides a marvelously regal backdrop for an open-air theater.

37 Porta San Pancrazio Built by **Pope Urban VIII** of the **Barberini** family (denoted by the bees), who reigned from 1623-1644. The massive gate was joined by the **Aurelian Walls** on either side but **General Oudinot** of the French army managed to breach it in 1849.

38 **Passeggiata del Gianicolo** This large park on the hill enables you to enjoy the city and get away from the hustle and bustle at the same time. Telescopes provide a better view of the panorama below. A small fun-fair with a mechanical merry-go-round and Shetland pony rides, an open-air *Punch and Judy Show*, and kiosks selling coffee, ice cream, and sandwiches make this a fun place for both adults and children. A glorious monument to **Garibaldi** depicts him on horseback here, near the battleground where he fought the French.

Trastevere

Counting, Roman Style

I	=	1	**LX**	=	60
II	=	2	**LXX**	=	70
III	=	3	**LXXX**	=	80
IV	=	4	**XC**	=	90
V	=	5	**C**	=	100
VI	=	6	**CI**	=	101
VII	=	7	**CC**	=	200
VIII	=	8	**CCC**	=	300
IX	=	9	**CD**	=	400
X	=	10	**D**	=	500
XI	=	11	**DC**	=	600
XII	=	12	**DCC**	=	700
XX	=	20	**DCCC**	=	800
XXX	=	30	**CM**	=	900
XL	=	40	**M**	=	1000
L	=	50	**MM**	=	2000

Corso
Vittorio Emanuele II

(called *Corso Vittorio*, with stress on the first *o*) is a broad, winding avenue that was punched through the maze of tiny streets after Rome became the capital of united Italy in 1870. Corso Vittorio must not be confused with Via del Corso, that long, straight avenue that leads from Piazza del Popolo to Piazza Venezia. Walking the length of Corso Vittorio today, from where it starts at the **Piazza del Gesù**, you will be parallel to the medieval but now obscured **Via Papalis,** the road of the popes' cavalcade when they rode in procession between the **Vatican** and the **Palace and Church of San Giovanni in Laterano**—which used to be their residence and is still their *official* cathedral (a little-known fact). The popes' processions followed smaller byways on either side of what is now Corso Vittorio; this route was also called the **Via Peregrinorum** (Pilgrims' Way) since it was followed by the faithful from the Capitoline Hill to St. Peter's.

So this was the secular center of Papal Rome. On either side of Corso Vittorio are the principal sights not only of Renaissance Rome, mainly to the south, but also of Baroque Rome, mainly to the north of the artery. With the very notable exception of the **Pantheon** and **Largo Argentina**, this is not a route for classical monuments. By the end of the Roman Empire almost the whole area was covered with magnificent public buildings—circuses, theaters, baths, and temples—but after the Barbarian invasions, the dwindling and impoverished population started pillaging these monuments for their more immediate needs. By the Middle Ages the heart of the city had shifted here from its earlier concentration around the Roman Forum. Today you will still see the narrow alleys of the medieval city, cobblestoned and without sidewalks, the streets where artisans were grouped according to their skills, and the room-wide houses jumbled one upon the other, especially in the older area between Corso Vittorio and the Tiber River.

1 **Piazza del Gesù** Said to be the windiest square in Rome because the Devil, out walking with the Wind one day, excused himself while he went into the Jesuit Church—and the Wind has waited there for him ever since!

2 **Church of the Gesù** (1575, **Vignola**; facade **Giacomo della Porta**) Except for its exuberant High Baroque interior decoration, this church typifies the serious religious demands of the Catholic Church in the Counter Reformation period, when it was responding to the challenge of the Protestant revolt against Rome. The facade is sober, with heavy scrolls on the sides holding together the Greek temple front and the lower, wide array of engaged columns. This used to be called the *Jesuit Style* of church architecture. ♦ Piazza del Gesù

Church of the Gesù

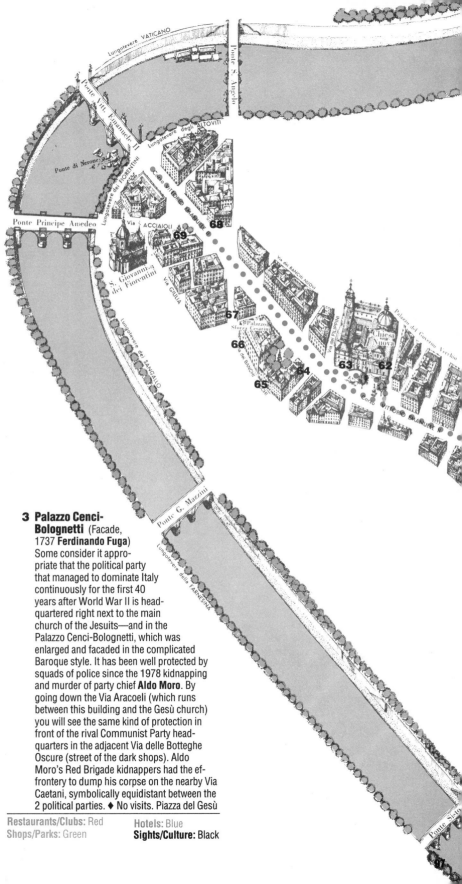

3 Palazzo Cenci-Bolognetti (Facade, 1737 **Ferdinando Fuga**) Some consider it appropriate that the political party that managed to dominate Italy continuously for the first 40 years after World War II is headquartered right next to the main church of the Jesuits—and in the Palazzo Cenci-Bolognetti, which was enlarged and facaded in the complicated Baroque style. It has been well protected by squads of police since the 1978 kidnapping and murder of party chief **Aldo Moro**. By going down the Via Aracoeli (which runs between this building and the Gesù church) you will see the same kind of protection in front of the rival Communist Party headquarters in the adjacent Via delle Botteghe Oscure (street of the dark shops). Aldo Moro's Red Brigade kidnappers had the effrontery to dump his corpse on the nearby Via Caetani, symbolically equidistant between the 2 political parties. ♦ No visits. Piazza del Gesù

Restaurants/Clubs: Red
Shops/Parks: Green

Hotels: Blue
Sights/Culture: Black

Look over the fresh produce on the table as you enter La Maiella, a serious 3 star restaurant

Premier Craxi liked to stay at the luxurious Raphael hotel

Palazzo Madama has housed the Senate since 1871

Campo dei Fiori, the fresh produce market, is open everyday except Sunday from 6AM to 1PM

Theater of Pompey is the fateful site where Caesar was murdered on the Ides of March

Costanza, ★★★★, not many restaurants earn a 4 star rating but this one ranks for its outstanding grilled dishes, terrific ambiance and attentive service

Note that there is only one angel on the facade of Sant'Andrea della Valle, as Pope Alexander VII criticized the first one so much that artist Cosimo Fancelli refused to make another

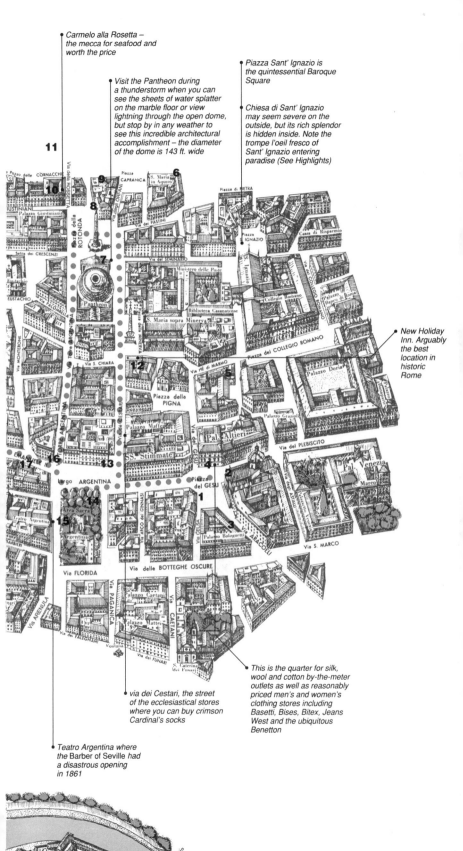

Carmelo alla Rosetta –
the mecca for seafood and
worth the price

Piazza Sant' Ignazio is
the quintessential Baroque
Square

Visit the Pantheon during
a thunderstorm when you can
see the sheets of water splatter
on the marble floor or view
lightning through the open dome,
but stop by in any weather to
see this incredible architectural
accomplishment – the diameter
of the dome is 143 ft. wide

Chiesa di Sant' Ignazio
may seem severe on the
outside, but its rich splendor
is hidden inside. Note the
trompe l'oeil fresco of
Sant' Ignazio entering
paradise (See Highlights)

New Holiday
Inn. Arguably
the best
location in
historic
Rome

This is the quarter for silk,
wool and cotton by-the-meter
outlets as well as reasonably
priced men's and women's
clothing stores including
Basetti, Bises, Bitex, Jeans
West and the ubiquitous
Benetton

via dei Cestari, the street
of the ecclesiastical stores
where you can buy crimson
Cardinal's socks

Teatro Argentina where
the Barber of Seville had
a disastrous opening
in 1861

4 Bises (**Palazzo Altieri**, 1670, **G.A. de Rossi**) Within this vast, late 17th-century palace of **Pope Clement X** is one of the many shops of the textile firm Bises; the others are nearby. This is the quarter of the silk, wool, and cotton by-the-meter outlets. Bring home a bolt of some of Italy's greatest luxury products— silk-making is concentrated near Lake Como, other textiles around Tuscany, but you can buy them all at reasonable prices within a block of here. Bises also sells ready-to-wear suits at its **Boutique Uomo**, next door at Corso Vittorio Emanuele I, and there are reasonably priced men's and women's clothing stores on both sides of this first block of Corso Vittorio, including **Abitex, Basetti, Jeans West,** and the ubiquitous **Benetton.** ♦ Via del Gesù 93. 6780941

5 Al Piedone ★$ This tiny restaurant, with 2 rooms hidden in back, is named after the nearby giant marble 4th-century foot that is thought to have been part of Constantine's colossal statue. Simple but tasty, with tasty prices, too. House wine comes in flasks, but they are the no-nonsense one-liter size. Stuffed olives and head cheese make a good antipasto. *Pasta nera* is the specialty, its color supplied by small-grain black caviar. The olive oil is so upper class it's blue! ♦ Via del Pie' di Marmo 28. 6798628

6 Curiosita e Magia Mysterious shop with tricks for children and professional magicians. Antique games. Magic shows are held here occasionally. ♦ Piazza Montecitorio 70. 6784228

7 Pantheon (AD 125, **Hadrian**) The only perfectly preserved ancient building in Rome, and perhaps the single most perfect building in the world. **Emperor Hadrian**, no mean hand at architecture, as shown by the villa he designed in Tivoli, built the harmonious temple we see today. Although the bricks with which it was built are stamped with his seal, Hadrian did not put his name on the temple. On the pediment he ascribed the building to **Consul Marco Agrippa**, the son-in-law of **Augustus**, who in 27 BC had built a smaller square temple here that is now incorporated into the pillared front porch. Agrippa's entrance had been on the south side, facing his complex of baths, basilica, and gardens, but Hadrian moved it around to the north, and on the other side he grafted the main circular chamber to it. The simplicity of the design is impressive, for it consists only of one round and one quadrangular element, their dimensions in perfect harmony with one another and their junction uncluttered by any decorative element. Hadrian added a Roman dome on a circular base to the form of the Greek temple. It sounds easy, but no one has equaled it in the intervening milleniums. It deserves to be contemplated slowly inside and out, so take time for an ice cream or espresso at one of the bars in the **Piazza della Rotonda** that face the en-

trance. You can also contemplate the fact that while the original temple was dedicated to all the various Roman gods (*pantheon*), it became the **Roman Catholic Church of Santa Maria ad Martyres** in 609 and was briefly the official burial place of Italy's now disenfranchised royal family. Just think, this vast dome was originally gilded with bronze both inside and out; imagine it shining in the southern sunlight. How it must have dazzled the northern Barbarians during their successive invasions in the 5th and 6th centuries.

One of the marvels of this building is that it remains virtually as Hadrian built it. The Pantheon escaped despoliation, unlike all the other Roman buildings in this area, because in 608 the **Emperor Phocas**, who was ruling from Byzantium, gave the Pantheon to **Pope Boniface IV**, who consecrated it as a church, thus making it a mortal sin to remove as much as one stone. Nevertheless when **Constantius II**, a subsequent Byzantine emperor, visited Rome in 655, he took the gilded bronze roof tiles for his own capital of Constantinople. However, they were hijacked by Arabs and ended up in Alexandria, Egypt. In the 8th century, **Pope Gregory III**, worried about the tileless dome, sheathed it with lead sheets in 735—as you see it today. Even the great bronze doors are the originals, as are 13 of the 16 immense granite columns that hold up the front porch of the Greek temple. Incidentally, the beams under that porch roof were originally wrapped in bronze, but the bronze was taken by **Pope Urban VIII** for the construction of the **Baldacchino** in **St. Peter's**—giving rise to the accusation *what the Barbarians didn't do, the Barberini family did!*

Perhaps the most fascinating thing about the Pantheon is how that enormous 143-foot

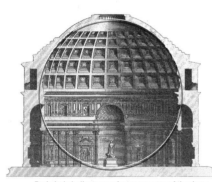

Red circle indicates perfect symmetry of the dome

Corso Vittorio Emanuele

diameter dome—wider even than St. Peter's and with a hole in the middle (called the oculus)—was held up without any sustaining columns or flying buttresses. It is a completely new round form for a temple. Hadrian was daringly innovative in his construction methods. The rotunda rests on a brick-faced concrete drum 20 feet thick, and the dome itself is increasingly thin, diminishing to 4.5 feet at the top. It also becomes increasingly lighter, with heavy travertine mixed in the concrete at the base, then the lighter tufa stone, and, finally, feather-light pumice at the summit. On the outside of the dome you can see semicircular brick arches that you might think were originally openings; these relieving or discharge arches help overcome the immense problem of retaining the thrusts of the dome. In fact, during construction huge cracks started to appear; the building was probably sinking into the swamp on which it stood. The builders hurriedly added to the foundations

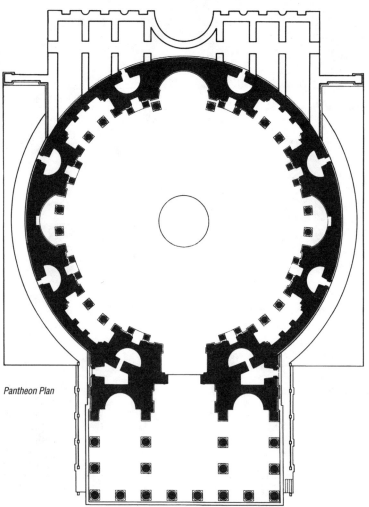

Pantheon Plan

and reinforced the back and sides by encasing the round drum on 3 sides in a boxlike base that somewhat marred the purity of Hadrian's design. One result is that you feel the sense of roundness much more strongly inside than outside. From inside, also, you can appreciate the perfect proportion. Note that the diameter of the dome is identical to its height, so that in theory a giant orb would fit snugly inside the rotunda. The roundness is further emphasized by the circular opening at the top, which is its only source of light. The beautiful coffering, or lacunars, indented inside the dome, were made by pouring the concrete dome over molds. The lower niches in the walls, of alternating sizes and shapes, are all Hadrian's original designs, and have since inspired hundreds of generations of architects, as will be seen particularly in the nearby Baroque masterpieces of **Bernini** and **Borromini**.

The few modern additions include some unremarkable paintings and sculpture. Between the second and third chapels on the left are the tombs of **Raphael** and of his official mistress (whom he had so scandalously betrayed); his is the one with an ever-present fresh flower. The first king of Italy, **Vittorio Emanuele II** (after whom this walk is named), is buried in the round niche on the far right, and his son **King Umberto I** (assassinated at Monza in 1900) lies in the opposite niche on the left along with his widow, **Queen Margherita**.

The ideal time to visit the Pantheon is during a rainstorm, when you will be surprised how pleasant it is to see sheets of water splattering on the colorful marble floor. But best of all, we are told, is to be there during a violent thunderstorm, when the effect of the lightning zigzagging through the open roof is so awe-inspiring as to make one understand why the ancients worshipped the violent gods of the elements. ♦ Piazza della Rotonda. Tu-Su 9AM-1PM, 2PM-1 hr before sunset, 4PM in winter. Closed Monday and Sunday morning, 15 August, 25, 26 December

Restaurants/Clubs: Red   **Hotels:** Blue
Shops/Parks: Green   **Sights/Culture:** Black

8 Sole al Pantheon $$ (1467) Newly renovated 4-star hotel in one of the most glorious settings imaginable. Located in the square across from the Pantheon, this impeccable hotel may be Rome's oldest. For 500 years, the restaurantless inn has been catering to theater people and tourists. When the poet/playwright **Ludovico Ariosto** stayed here in 1513 on the eve of a papal audience it was called **Albergo Montone**. **Pietro Mascagni** celebrated the triumphant opening of his opera *Cavaleria Rusticana* here in 1870. So try to reserve one of the 30 rooms. Though there isn't the bustling traffic of nearby Corso Vittorio Emanuele, the crowds of young people here tend to carouse late into the night. ♦ Via del Pantheon 63. 6780441; fax 6840689

9 Da Fortunato: Trattoria del Pantheon ★★★$$$ America's favorite storyteller tells a story of his favorite trattoria owner being *fortunato* (lucky) because he, **Gore Vidal**, comes here regularly. Many Americans do, but they are always in the minority because this *trat* is besieged by politicians from the nearby Parliament buildings seeking the perfect risotto or pasta with porcini mushrooms, followed by the perfect Roman-style tripe (only on Saturday) or fresh grilled seabass. *Godfather* producer **Fred Roos** comes here for strawberries in winter! Smart restaurants like this no longer follow the seasons the way we think they should; your maddest wishes can now be granted. Prickly pears in February, anyone? But luckily, *puntarelle* (wild, curly salad with anchovy sauce) is also on the menu in season, as well as polenta with country sausages, carpaccio of raw salmon, and, if you ask for it, *arancio tagliato a spicchi* (orange cut at the table into bite-size wedges—a finger ballet executed with pride by your waiter). ♦ Closed Sunday and half of August. Via del Pantheon 55. Reservations required. 6792788

10 Carmelo alla Rosetta ★★★$$$$ Fish is expensive here, as it is in most Roman restaurants, but many consider this the mecca for seafood and worth any price. The fish soup is purer than bouillabaise and just as generous. Everything is fresh, including the sardines in the pastas, so what Carmelo has to offer you will depend on which boat came in. And they do arrive daily, whereas most Rome restaurants only have fresh fish Tuesday and Friday. Wash it all down with a very dry *Gavi di Gavi*. Attractive, fishy locale. ♦ Closed Saturday lunch, Sunday, and August. Via della Rosetta 9. Reservations required. 6861002

11 Quinzi e Gabrielli ★★★$$$$ Very upmarket. "Gourmet Jack" from Los Angeles swears it's the best seafood he's ever tasted: lobster with all the trimmings and such subtle sauces.

We like the counter where you can have an antipasto *di mare* and a glass of sizzling cold spumanti. Full of fat cats at lunch. ♦ Closed Sunday. Via delle Coppelle 5. 6879389, 6874940; fax 6871740

12 Piazza della Minerva In the center of this square diagonally in back of the Pantheon is the delightful little monument consisting of an obelisk mounted on an elephant's back, designed in 1667 by **Bernini** for **Pope Alexander VII**, of the **Chigi** family. The Pope wrote the monument's inscription, which explains that the elephant symbolizes the massive intelligence needed as a base for wisdom. The obelisk was one of many brought from Egypt by the ancient Romans, who, being polytheists, even dedicated temples to Egyptian gods. This obelisk was erected at the nearby site of the Roman temple of the goddess **Minerva**, which gave its name to this square and the church.

12 Santa Maria Sopra Minerva (1280; portals 1453; interior restored 1848-1855) Famed as the only Gothic church in Rome, it has been attributed to the architects of Santa Maria Novella in Florence, **Fra Sisto** and **Fra Ristoro** of the Dominican order to which both churches belong. Its other ties with Florence: the great 15th-century painter **Fra Angelico** is buried in the floor of the first chapel to the left of the altar; **Michelangelo** created the statue of Christ between this chapel and the altar; **Filippino Lippi** painted the superb frescoes (1489) in the **Carafa Chapel** at the south transept. These 3 great Renaissance artists came to Rome from Florence because commissions from the popes and their families were even more remunerative than those of the **Medici** family. The Renaissance started moving from Florence to Rome in the middle of the 15th century, and the Medicis themselves came to Rome toward the end of the century. Here, in the Carafa Chapel, Lippi's stunningly lifelike

Corso Vittorio Emanuele

paintings are dedicated to **St. Thomas Aquinas**, whose life is depicted on the right-hand wall—along with portraits of 2 young Medicis who became popes **Clement VII** and **Leo X**, and who are entombed behind the high altar. The Gothicism of this church was compromised in the 19th century, when gray marble was wrapped around the 8 pairs of piers that go down the central nave. This was particularly unfortunate for **Bernini**, whose contribution to this church, on the second pier from the altar on the north side, was the High Baroque tomb of the venerable **Sister Maria Raggi** (1653) with her look of religious ecstasy. Accessible from the nearby sacristy is the chapel of **St. Catherine of Siena**, who had arranged the popes' return from their long exile at Avignon in the 14th century. She died in 1380 and her room in the nearby Dominican convent was moved here in 1637, adding another chapter to this history-packed church. ♦ Closed noon-4 PM. Piazza della Minerva

13 Via dei Cestari Turn north off the Corso Vittorio Emanuele onto this narrow street behind the newspaper kiosk on the corner of Largo Argentina. This is the street of the ecclesiastical vestments. Priests, cardinals, nuns, and monks from around the globe come here to fit themselves with glorious costumes—or just to look at the golden embroidered cassocks, the burnished miters, and silver soutanes. You can get crimson cardinals' socks here. Anyone can buy, and the secret is that prices are extraordinarily low for such secular items as underwear and black shoes. There are a half-dozen good surplice stores on this street, primarily for clerics, and one unisex boutique called **Barbican** around the corner to the right at Santa Caterina da Siena 70, which also caters to nuns. The first segment of this street was formerly called **Via del Calcalari** (street of the lime kilns), for it was in this area that the magnificent marble of ancient Rome was boiled in caldrons and reduced to lime in the Middle Ages—which makes one think that the real Vandals were sometimes the Romans themselves.

14 Area Sacra del Largo Argentina (Ruins of 4 Roman Temples, 6th to 2nd centuries BC) In 1928, **Mussolini** scrawled an *Imperial Act* safeguarding these newly excavated temples and forbidding any new construction over them, for *archaeology and for hygiene*! The Little Dictator's real motive in uncovering this and other Roman sites was to glorify what he liked to think of as his empire by association with ancient Rome. These temples were not Imperial, but built in the Republican period, which lasted 500 years leading up to the ascension in 27 BC of **Augustus**, who became the first emperor. Notice that the 4 temples were built on what was then ground level, but is now 3 or 4 yards below the present streets; this is generally true of the ruins of ancient

Corso Vittorio Emanuele

Rome. In subsequent centuries, especially the Middle Ages, accumulated dirt and neglect caused the street level to rise about a yard every 500 years. Unfortunately for you, but to the great pleasure of Rome's enormous cat population, you cannot go down to examine these ruins, but must observe them from above, preferably from the eastern edge of the square, closest to the Piazza del Gesù, where you started this walk.

Little remains of the 4 temples and even less is known about them. They are always referred to by letters, reading from right to left or north to south. **Temple A** is in the best shape, having been restored under the first emperors. Do not be misled by indications of round construction; this is left over from the 2 churches subsequently built here one above the other. **Temple B**, in the center, was consecrated in 101 BC by **Catulo**. It is the only originally round structure and has a handsome mosaic floor. Between Temples A and B is an

addition (currently referred to as **Temple E**) constructed during the Empire; only 3 broken walls remain. **Temple C**, the last fully visible podium on the left, dates back to the 4th and 3rd centuries BC. During most of the 6th century BC, Rome had been a monarchy under Etruscan rule. This period is documented at the extraordinary **Villa Giulia National Museum** (see page 30). **Temple D** is three-fourths covered by Via Florida, an important traffic street to the south, but its partly visible north wall dates back to the 2nd century BC. If you now walk around to the opposite side of the excavations, the Via di Torre Argentina, and look over the edge near the bus stop, you will see that right behind Temple A are the remains of one of ancient Rome's magnificent public toilets, with rows of marble seats unpartitioned so that the citizens could use this time to be sociable and exchange the news and gossip of the day. ♦ Largo di Torre Argentina

15 Teatro Argentina (1731, **Girolamo Theodoli**; facade, 1826 **Pietro Holl**) Built on the site of the **Pompey Theater** colonnade. In 1861, at the disastrous opening of the *Barber of Seville*, the audience booed and hissed, apparently on orders of **Napoleon**'s sister **Pauline Borghese**, who had it in for the composer **Gioachino Rossini** for being mean to a friend who wanted Rossini to rework the part of the tenor. International theater festivals are held here and sometimes plays are in English. Also called **Teatro di Roma**. ♦ Largo di Torre Argentina 52. 6544601, 6545006

16 Il Delfino $ Not only do we shun fast food, but we hesitate to list any *tavola calda* (literally hot table or cafeteria) because we hope our readers do not come to Italy to rush through meals. Instead, we hope you will adopt the Italian habit of taking an hour or 2 to savor a carefully prepared, individually cuisined feast for both lunch and supper. But, we understand that sometimes you may have to emulate the other Italian habit—fast food from the hot plate; and in a place like this you will find it not so bad. Il Delfino has recently been spruced up, and, of course, its location at this busy intersection in central Rome is unbeatable. ♦ Closed Monday and August. Corso Vittorio Emanuele 67. No credit cards. 6864053

16 Pascucci *Frullati* are fruit shakes—delicious whipped-up mixtures of any fruit you want with ice, milk, and syrup. The young blades come from far and wide to have their daily delight here. ♦ Closed Sunday. Via Torre Argentina 20

17 Tiziano $ One of the few hotels in the heart of Baroque Rome is located in an appropriately grand palazzo. There is a new restaurant and a cocktail bar for those without the energy—or imagination—to explore the neighborhood pubs. Rooms over the Corso Vittorio can be noisy, so bring earplugs or plead for a back room. Sweet dreams! ♦ Corso Vittorio Emanuele 110. 6865087, 6875087; fax 6543861

18 Archimede ★★$$ This is **Bruno Luci**'s original Archimede, with arguably the slowest service in Rome. It has moved twice in the last few years, but now Bruno has cleaned up his act, beautified the premises, and seems to have found the right location. So stay right here, indoors, or in summer get a table overlooking this tiny square, which is an extension of Piazza di Sant'Eustachio, behind the Pantheon. Crisp artichokes, Jewish style (*carciofi alla giudea*), and fried zucchini flowers stuffed with cheese and anchovies (*fiori di* zucchini) remind you that you are just a few blocks from the Rome Ghetto. ◆ Closed Sunday and half of August. Piazza dei Caprettari 63. 6861616, 6785216

18 Travailleuses Missionnaires/L'Eau Vive ★$$$ There is something disconcerting about all these exotic, nubile waitresses being members of the *Order of Christian Virgins of Catholic Missionary Action Through Work*, as is the interruption for hymns just when you are settling down to enjoy your dinner. These girls come from all over the French-speaking Third World to wait (presumably unsalaried) on you, gliding around with poise and grace in their long skirts. It used to be called simply **L'Eau Vive**, but the order got into trouble with the authorities and "reopened" with the new name, meaning working missionaries—but people still call it by its shorter moniker. Too much French food, not enough spicy, exotic dishes. In fact, other than the daily specials from faraway places, there's no spice. There is a reasonable fixed-price menu at lunch. ◆ Closed Sunday and part of August. Via Monterone 85. Reservations required. 6541095

19 Sant'Eustachio Cafe Universally acclaimed the best cup of coffee in Rome! All evening exuberant natives swarm into the little square of the same name and jam into this tiny bar to get that perfect espresso. The mystical quality of this potion must be noted by visitors to the Eternal City. The Romans take their coffee standing up, as they do Mass at St. Peter's. They drink it on arising with the certainty it will wake them up, and again just before going to bed with equal faith that it will put them to sleep! The square is best reached from the right rear corner of the Pantheon by the tiny Via Palombella. ◆ Closed Monday. Piazza di Sant'Eustachio 82. 6861309

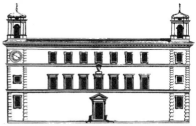

20 Sant'Ivo alla Sapienza Church (1660, **Borromini**) This is the first of 4 masterpieces by Borromini that you will encounter on this walk, and these—along with **San Carlo alle Quattro Fontane** (see page 24)—are the essential works you must see to realize his genius. The problem is that they are usually closed and few people have been able to see them all in a brief visit to Rome. Churches, like most monuments of Rome, are frequently closed in the afternoon, and as far as we know this one is officially open only on Sunday morning for Mass. At other times, track down the *portière* (guardian) of the **Palazzo della Sapienza**, in which this church is enclosed, and thrust a fat tip into his palm.

Borromini seems to have been frequently stimulated to invent new forms by the challenging limitations of the sites on which he had to construct for his demanding clients. Here the client was **Sapienza** (meaning wisdom), which became the University of Rome in 1303. The site was a square box at the back of the college building, hemmed in by 2 cloisters that ran the length of the building. Since he owed this commission to **Pope Urban VIII** of the **Barberini** family, Borromini first planned a church based on the form of a bee—the Barberini family symbol. The final floor plan is even more ingenious; it is based on 2 intersecting triangles that make a 6-pointed star and a hexagon. If you stand at the

Corso Vittorio Emanuele

center of this small church and look up at the soaring dome, you will see the 6 points of the star have been converted by Borromini into alternately round and straight-lined shapes. Your eye will automatically be drawn around this endless loop of concave and convex forms—which are Borromini's hallmark and that make him the prophet of the rococo architectural style, which carried the Baroque one step further. As with arabesque tracery, the eye never comes to rest in Borromini's churches. You may find the stark white of this interior and the endless 8-pointed stars climbing the dome oppressive, but you will realize that you are as far from the Gothic as one can get. And from the courtyard you will see the famous spiral top—like a ziggurat recalling the biblical Tower of Babel! Enter Palazzo della Sapienza from Corso del Rinascimento or Via del Teatro Valle.

Restaurants/Clubs: Red   **Hotels:** Blue
Shops/Parks: Green   **Sights/Culture:** Black

21 Da Papa Giovanni $$$ Kitsch red-plastic banquettes, affable service with a glass of Prosecco on the house, and an intimate club atmosphere. Prices are high, food a little too inventive (spaghetti served in empty cheese shells for example), but it's a wonderful place to take a wonderful girl for a treat. ♦ Closed Sunday. Via dei Sediari 4. 6865308

22 Piazza Sant'Andrea della Valle The charming Renaissance fountain, attributed to **Carlo Maderno**, is in the middle of what used to be an artificial lake made by **Agrippa** in the 1st century BC. Hence the name *Valle* (valley). Hence also the water games that the notoriously naughty **Emperor Nero** invented a century later. The aristocratic ladies of Rome had to loll around by the lake shore playing the role of Roman prostitutes for the benefit of the Emperor and his friends, who bobbed by on a raft as they chose their woman.

22 Sant'Andrea della Valle (1665, **Carlo Maderno, Carlo Rainaldi, and Carlo Fontana**) The soaring dome by Maderno is the

Corso Vittorio Emanuele

second highest in Rome after St. Peter's. Rainaldi designed an elegant Baroque facade, set in motion by the thrust and counter-thrust of columns and overhangs, and he decided to use sculpted angels instead of scrolls at the corners to tie the upper and lower halves together. **Cosimo Fancelli** was commissioned to make 2 angels. But to this day there is only one—Fancelli was so hurt when he heard that the first angel had been criticized by **Pope Alexander VII** that he dug in his heels, declaring *if he wants another, he'll have to make it himself!* The Pope didn't, and you may be charmed by this little note of asymmetry on an otherwise carefully balanced facade. Inside, there is not so much balance but rather the energy-packed motion of the early 17th century. Here in this cavernous church you can literally see the painting style of Rome's Baroque evolving from the earlier, more classical High Renaissance. Observe the frescoes of **Domenichino** (1581-1641) and of **Giovanni**

Lanfranco (1582-1647). First look at Domenichino's fine early paintings on the vault of the apse representing the life of **St. Andrew**. They are rendered statically, as if they were easel paintings designed to be looked at on a gallery wall. Then contrast these with the frescoes on the dome by Domenichino's archrival Lanfranco, who solved the difficult problem of adapting to the necessities of painting trompe l'oeil figures on a curved surface. He imitated the great **Correggio** (1489-1534), whose domes in Parma used foreshortening and bright colors to create the illusion of endless space leading up to heaven. Here, Lanfranco's *Assumption of the Virgin* even uses real light from the windows above as an element of his painted composition (effects later used so successfully by Bernini). Now, look carefully at Domenichino's adjacent pendentives representing the evangelists, which he executed after he had seen Lanfranco's work above. Here the vigor of these figures is comparable to **Michelangelo's Sistine Chapel** frescoes, but it is obvious that Domenichino has progressed from the Renaissance toward the Baroque, provoked by the successful dome frescoes of his rival. ♦ Piazza Sant'Andrea della Valle

23 Pisoni Candles Our favorites are the superb *fiaccole*, which since ancient times have been used at festive occasions to light the outside of buildings. This brilliant way of lighting buildings has been practiced for over 2000 years, and until recently the Vatican would have 2 atheletes poised with burning torches in hand at the end of either wing of St. Peter's front colonnade. At the bang of a gun they would start running toward the center, dipping their torches as they went in order to light each of the thousands of Roman candles placed along the edge; crowds would watch the runners to see who would arrive first to light the ultimate candle on the tippity top of St. Peter's dome. All palaces, theaters, monumental buildings, and churches were lit in this way. For almost 200 years **Costantino Pisoni** and his heirs have been supplying every conceivable kind of candle for Rome's leading families. ♦ Corso Vittorio Emanuele 127. 6543531

24 Palazzo Massimo alle Colonne (1536, **Baldassare Peruzzi**) Owned by the **Massimo** family, which traces its lineage back further than any other family in Rome. It's built on one of the most ancient sites, the **Odeon of Emperor Domitian** (who also built the adjoining stadium, which is now the Piazza Navona). The Odeon, a small theater, was built in a semicircular form. This explains the curved front of this central section of Palazzo Massimo, which follows the same arc as the adjacent **Church of San Pantaleo** (unfortunately broken by the intervening building, which also belongs to the Massimo family). The main palazzo is called *alle Colonne* because of the Doric columns of the portico at the main entrance, where traditionally anyone without lodging can sleep. In fact, in the late 1970s there was an indigent distant member of the Massimo family who spent every night in that open loggia along with his equally scruffy-looking lady-friend. Each year on 16 March everyone is welcomed into the palazzo to visit the chapel on the upper floor in order to commemorate the anniversary of the miraculous resuscitation of young **Paolo Massimo**, who had been given up for dead until the visit in 1583 of **St. Philip Neri**, founder of the Oratorian religious order (see Borromini's Oratory of San Filippo Neri on page 117). This annual chance to see a real Roman prince's private digs is worth waiting for. ♦ Corso Vittorio Emanuele 141

24 **Luciano Mattei Foto Ottica** Film, cameras, spectacles. Signor Mattei has been on this site for over 25 years. ♦ Corso Vittorio Emanuele 160. 6877305

25 **Souvenir—Cornici e Stampe** Although a tourist shop for souvenirs and guidebooks, this is a quality place with fine original prints of Rome and good modern copies. ♦ Via Cuccagna 19. 6875822

26 **Palazzo Braschi** (1792, **Cosimo Morelli**) This huge, roughly triangular pile is the last palace in Rome erected for the family of a pope. **Pius VI,** of the Braschi family, followed a long papal tradition in building a palace for his nephews. But times had changed, both morally and esthetically. Palazzo Braschi represents the triumph of quantity over quality. In addition to the **Rome Museum**, listed below, this palazzo houses occasional cultural exhibitions, such as drawings of Rome by the famous and less famous, foreign and domestic.

Within Palazzo Braschi:

Rome Museum The pope's open railroad train, used by **Pius IX**, is a perennial favorite. Paintings of the popes' entertainment through the years are also fascinating. There is a large painting here of a vast spectacle staged by the **Barberini** family for **Queen Christina of Sweden**'s first carnival, showing that the tradition of Bread and Circuses was still active in papal Rome. Carriages in the flooded Piazza Navona, and jousting in the same locale, are portrayed with understanding and humor. Travel writer **Georgina Masson** hopes that an appreciation of the color and good humor of such scenes will enable the visitor to empathize with the theatricality of Baroque architecture. Perhaps. But it should at least enable us to relate that most maligned of architectural styles to the city where it found the strongest and most individualistic flowering. Roman Baroque may not exist or even be understandable anywhere else. Pity all this is in such a drab palazzo when so many great ones seem to be unused. ♦ Admission. Tu-Su 9AM-1PM, holidays (June Tu-W, F-Sa 9AM-1PM; Th 5-8PM) Piazza di San Pantaleo 10. 688855

Corso Vittorio Emanuele

27 **Piazza Navona** The name Navona is a corruption of its Latin name, *Circus Agonalis*—meaning the arena for athletic games—which in Medieval Latin was rendered first as *in agone*, then *n'agona*. The current piazza has the exact elliptical shape of the original circus built by the **Emperor Domitian** on this spot in AD 86; only the harmonious buildings now surrounding it have replaced the original tiers of stone bleacher seats. Those seats were still used in the mid-15th century, when the sport-loving Romans came here to watch jousts between knights in armor, the Renaissance successor to the original Olympic-type games of the Roman Empire. To see the remnants of this stadium, walk out the exit furthest from

Plan, Piazza Navona

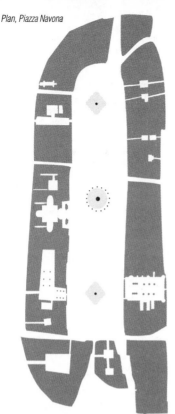

Corso Vittorio, turn left into Piazza Tor San-guina, and after 30 or 40 paces you can look through glass on your left to an area under the existing buildings where the 1st-century sta-dium construction is still visible. Now that you have imagined how the original Roman Circus must have looked, come back into the piazza and take in the wonders of this Baroque plea-

Corso Vittorio Emanuele

sure-place. Two of the 3 fountains in the pi-azza are by **Bernini** and the principal palace and church are by **Borromini**. Most important, this piazza, day and night, is a perpetual fun fair. It is a pedestrian island rather than a thor-oughfare; its various restaurants and ice-cream parlors are open from early in the morning to late at night. And like all of Italy's great piazzas, it is a giant stage set—a back-drop against which the theater of daily life is played with such brio that the actors and spectators have become one. Here everything is for display: the fabulous fountains, the buildings, the tourists, the artists and artisans hawking their works. The ancient Romans flooded it to stage mock sea battles, and in the 17th and 18th centuries, during the stifling heat of August, cardinals and princes had their gilded carriages driven around the water-filled piazza. Nowadays, December is the busi-est month, when children stream in to patron-ize booths set up around the piazza, including Christmas decoration shops and shooting galleries. It's a bit commercial, but it brings the carnival spirit back to Piazza Navona—and you may still be able to find small figures of shepherds, wisemen, and Madonna-and-child to make up a Nativity scene like the traditional ones from Naples.

Look around the piazza again and you will start to understand the fascination of the Ba-roque, a very Roman style of architecture—or rather of decoration, for this style is intended more to delight the eye than to be functional. This piazza became a Baroque showplace in 1644 when **Innocent X** was elected pope and went on a building spree, starting with a small building that his family, the **Pamphili**, owned here. Like most building sprees, this one was motivated by his desire to keep up with the Joneses—or in this case, the rival **Barberini** family, whose favorite son, **Urban VIII**, had just ceased being pope. Luckily for us, Inno-cent's drive to outshine his predecessor came at the height of this new and exciting style—rather than at a time like the late 19th century when Rome had more money than taste. One element of continuity between the Rome of the popes and that of their predecessors 1500 years earlier is that Innocent, like Diocletian before him, wanted to create a place of public pleasure as well as private glory. In one sense of the word or another, the Piazza Navona has always been a circus—and always will be.

28 Fountain of the Moor (1653, **Bernini**) At **Pope Innocent X**'s request, Bernini added the Moor pinching a dolphin's tail to an earlier fountain that was raised up on a pediment and had 4 figures of tritons blowing into shells. (They can now be seen in the Villa Borghese gardens.) The secret of Bernini's prodigious activity is that he made sketches that were carried out by his assistants.

29 Palazzo Pamphili (1650, **Rainaldi** and **Borromini**) Too big and too flat, but it is lighter in feeling than the Palazzo Barberini, which it was intended to outshine. Inside, Bor-romini was able to reduce some of the heavi-ness of Rainaldi's original design, and the great salon, with its ceiling painting by **Pietro da Cortona**, is less pompous than that in Ber-nini's Palazzo Barberini. But you can only look around inside if you know the Brazilian am-bassador, whose residence and embassy this has been since 1960. **Pope Innocent X** (who apparently did not live up to his name) built this for his sister-in-law and confidante, **Olympia Maidalchini** (who certainly was not innocent).

Restaurants/Clubs: Red   **Hotels:** Blue
Shops/Parks: Green   **Sights/Culture:** Black

30 Sant'Agnese in Agone Church (Facade, 1657 **Borromini**) **Pope Innocent X** decided to add to his adjoining **Palazzo Pamphili** a family chapel that would incorporate the shrine built on the spot where the 13-year-old saint had been martyred in AD 304. In fact, this had originally been a neighborhood bordello where the child was forced to strip in front of the clients; so great was her piety that her hair suddenly grew sufficiently to hide her embarrassment. Borromini did much the same when he was commissioned to complete the church that had just been started by **Girolamo** and **Carlo Rainaldi** (1652). He covered it with a facade so original and daring that the shallow and elongated site to which he was limited is not even noticed by the admiring throngs. Rather than having the central pediment come forward as in most churches, Borromini has pushed it in back of the flanking belfries in a concave thrust that is echoed in the repetition of concaves and convexes throughout the facade.

31 Fountain of the Four Rivers (1651, **Bernini**) An Egyptian obelisk balanced above figures representing the great rivers of 4 continents: the Danube, Ganges, Nile, and Plate. Don't believe the anecdotes guides tell about these figures; the River Plate is not holding up

his hand to keep **Borromini's Sant'Agnese Church** from falling on him, nor is the River Nile's face covered so he won't have to look at that facade.

In fact, Borromini was hired to work on that church a couple of years after this fountain was finished. Truth is stranger than fiction. The obelisk was brought to this 1st-century arena from **Emperor Maxentius'** great antique circus that was built out on the Via Appia, where **Pope Innocent X** had seen the obelisk broken in 4. Bernini stole the commission for this fountain away from Borromini—who by then had become his arch rival—by bribing the Pope's lady-friend, **Olympia Maidalchini**. Bernini gave this unscrupulous papal sister-in-law a solid silver model of his design for the fountain, insisting that it must be left out so that Innocent X would see it, which he did. The Pope then incurred the wrath of the Roman population by taxing bread to raise a vast sum in gold coins (29,000 scudi) to finance the fountain. Both Innocent and Donna Olympia were publicly reviled (her name being written in 2 words as *olim pia*, meaning once virtuous in Latin). The Pope's reputation never quite recovered from this expensive folly, but now, 230 years later, we realize that the Pamphili family had made a brilliant investment of public funds in embellishing the most enjoyable piazza in Rome.

32 Mastrostefano ★★$$$ The late, beloved **Luigi Barzini**, who chronicled *The Italians* for all time, liked to sit here in the sun, savoring the Piazza Navona all around him with the same gusto with which he relished **Signora Mastrostefano**'s food. We can only add that it is certainly the best available in this square. The cheese crêpes are good as openers, the ricotta cheesecake is a great closer, and in between you can't go wrong with the grilled swordfish steak and white wine. Reserve for an outside table. ♦ Closed Monday and part of August. Piazza Navona 94. 6542855

33 Palazzo Madama (Facade, 1610 **Ludovico Cardi** and **Paolo Marucelli**) This Baroque block surrounded by police has housed the Senate since 1871. The original building was a

palazzo built for the **Crescenzi** family and passed in a dowry to the Medicis. It was the residence of **Catherine de Medici** before she set off to Paris to marry the king—taking with her the greatest chefs of the age, and thus introducing fine cuisine for the first time in France. But it was named for the woman who then inherited it, **Margaret of Parma**, the wife of **Alessandro de' Medici**. Margaret was the illegitimate daughter of **Charles V** of Austria, so she only had the title *Madame*. Be sure to see the beautiful 16th-century granite fountain in the alley just behind the building. In the late 1980s, when an underground passage was built connecting Palazzo Madama with an adjoining Senate office building, the diggers found this enormous basin—and realized that it is the twin of the one in front of the Villa Medici (see page 66). ◆ Corso del Rinascimento at Piazza Madama

Al Sogno

34 Al Sogno An extraordinary toy shop. A Noah's Arc of every conceivable stuffed animal. All the dolls and toys imaginable to spoil the kids rotten. ◆ Piazza Navona 53. 6864198

35 La Maiella ★★★$$$ A serious restaurant. Not that your host, **Antonio**, won't exchange a joke or 2 with you like all great Roman restaurateurs, but the perfection of the cooking is the most important objective here, more so than the décor, which is straightforward no-frills. And the waiters treat your order with due solemnity. Try risotto with zucchini flowers, filet of turkey with mushrooms, or a fresh-grilled sea bass with olives that could follow a pasta dish such as *raviolini* with artichokes. Look over the fresh produce on the table as you come in for inspiration, but you really can't go wrong. The regional specialties are from Abruzzi—east of Rome. In summer you'll be out of doors under the large umbrel-

Corso Vittorio Emanuele

las, drinking the open white wine and wondering how long this bliss can last. Reserve, especially for a table outdoors. ◆ Closed Sunday and part of August. Piazza di Sant'Apollinare 45. 6864174

36 Passetto $$$ Another snob restaurant that rests on its past glories. The white tablecloths in the large white hall do not create an inviting atmosphere. But in winter, when the truffles are being sniffed out of the humid earth by trained pigs or dogs (better, as they don't try to gobble them up), *fonduta alla Piemontese con tartufi* is a great refinement—but not given away! ◆ Closed Monday lunch and Sunday. Via Zanardelli 14. Reservations required. 6540569, 6543696

37 Raphael $$$ Also known as **Government House**, as former **Prime Minister Bettino** (his original name was **Benito**) **Craxi** slept here. Judging from the number of cops, he still does, and is expected to be premier again. The location, right next to Piazza Navona, is

dreamy. The service is usually what you would expect of such a luxurious small hotel. The ivy-covered facade and the curious antiques in the lobby and adjacent bar area make you hope that this is the perfect Roman hotel you've been looking for. Many guests are disappointed because the rooms are small and not luxurious. But some of the views from upper floors are unforgettable. ◆ Largo Febo 2. 650881, 6869051; fax 6878993

38 Umberto Buceti Antichita Aladdin's Cave. Dirty windows hide mountains of Sheffield silver spilling onto the floor from half-open crates. Mostly to the trade, but you, too, with a sharp eye, can spot a beautiful object to buy. **Andrew** (among silver experts "Andrew" is a reference point) suggests haggling a bit. ◆ Piazza Monte Vecchio 16. 6546604

38 Antico Caffè della Pace Wonderful antique coffee bar-cum-tearoom with a 2000-year-old Roman column holding things up. Sitting at a table is pricey but the fruitcakes are superb. ◆ Via della Pace 4. 6561216

39 L'Insalata Ricca 2 $$ This restaurant specializes in antipasto and pasta. We love the idea because those are always the most scrumptious parts of the meal anyway. ◆ Piazza Pasquino 72. 6547881

40 Piccola Farnesina ai Baullari (1546, **Antonio Sangallo the Younger**) Delightful small Renaissance palace housing a delightful small museum. The name Farnesina is a misnomer as it never had anything to do with the Farnese family—whose much larger palace just down the Via Baullari carries the family crest of iris flowers. The confusion resulted from the fact that this palace was built for a French emissary to the Holy See, **Thomas Le Roy**, who having been ennobled by **François I**, had a facade decorated with the fleur-de-lis (flower of the lily).

This French royal flower emblem so closely resembles the Farnese iris that everyone assumed this must be another of the Farnese's many real-estate holdings. In our minds the confusion is compounded by the fact that the Farnese Palace now houses the French Embassy, and everyone assumes that those irises are fleurs-de-lis. Also, **Pope Leo X**, to whom Thomas Le Roy was the French king's emissary, was a member of the **Medici** family and therefore had the fleur-de-lis on his crest as well. Except for the fact that the original facade on **Vicolo del'Aquila** is crammed up against 2 other buildings and therefore is difficult to see, we prefer this little jewel to the hulking Farnese. The museum entrance side, facing Corso Vittorio Emanuele, is a 19th-century addition, grafted on after that end of the palazzo was sliced off to make room for the corso. ◆ Corso Vittorio Emanuele 168

Within the Piccola Farnesina ai Baullari:

Museo Barracco Baron **Giovanni Barracco** collected classical, Egyptian, and Assyrian art and donated these superb works to the city in 1902. In **Room II**, one flight up, is the oldest Egyptian statue in Italy, a relief of the court official **Nofer** (c. 2750 BC). In the same room is a series of later but very fine Egyptian portraits including a 3rd-millenium pharaoh. Another room on this floor, **Room III**, is usually locked, but ask the attendant in Room II to open it so you can see the late 6th-century BC Greek *Head of a Youth* with a know-it-all smile and curly hair. Up another flight of stairs are more fine Greek portraits. ◆ Admission. Tu-Th 9AM-2PM, 5-8PM; W-F, Sa 9AM-2PM; Su 9AM-1PM. 6540848

41 Deconsecrated Church The hall upstairs for the local confraternity, or guild, is largely empty (see **Oratorio del Gonfalone** on page 127 for explanation of these groups). The 4 caryatids holding up the roof look down in a melancholy manner, while the family that lives in the penthouse smiles in the sun. ◆ Via dei Baullari 144

41 Fornaio Bakery with breads in wonderful shapes, such as alligators, pastries you never dreamed possible, and abundant fruit tarts. The MOST fabulous breadery we know. Take the kids at Christmas to admire the edible manger with marzipan villages and roofs dripping with "snow" icing. ◆ M-F 7:30AM-2PM, 4:30-8PM. Via dei Baullari 4

42 Angeli Here on Via dei Baullari—that means *street of the trunk makers*—is the only shop that still sells luggage. Soft bags for visitors who have bought so many Italian goodies that they won't fit into their suitcases for the trip home. ◆ Via dei Baullari 139. 6875835

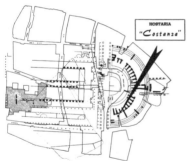

43 Costanza ★★★★$$$ Aptly located in **Paradise Piazza**. What more could you want? Venetian friends have complained that the risotto is a mite overdone. But Costanza still deserves that fourth star because the food is superior, the waiter/owners *simpatico*, and the place unforgettable. The main dining area is an entrance passage of the 2000-year-old **Theater of Pompey**, as you will see by looking up at the diamond-patterned brick work in the monumental vaulting. Arguably the best Jewish artichokes in town, ditto for the spaghetti *alle vongole veraci* and the skewers of either prawns or meat with rosemary and basil. Trust the suggestions, including the house wines, and the description of this ancient historic area, where 2000 years ago history finally caught up with **Julius Caesar**. In summer, the outdoor tables are poised precariously in the entrance alley. ◆ Closed Sunday. Piazza del Paradiso 63. 6861717, 6541002

44 Grotte del Teatro di Pompeo ★★★$$ A few years ago, when this was a pizzeria without a name, it was referred to as the *French restaurant* because the employees of the nearby French Embassy usually chose this, of all the notable tables in the area. There are no more pizzas, but the pasta is worthy of your attention and the **Marchis** (the owners) are right to underline that this is a restaurant. In fact, the green fettuccine with Gorgonzola sauce and the risotto *al radicchio* (rice dish with red lettuce) are superb. The third star is due to the great price/quality ratio. A simple restaurant where everything seems to turn out wonderfully. ◆ Closed Monday. Via del Biscione 73. 6543686

45 Theater of Pompey (53 BC) Only underground traces remain of this U-shaped theater, which stretched almost a quarter-mile from the **Campo dei Fiori** down to the **Largo Argentina**. The rounded end was just off the Campo dei Fiori, where Piazza del Biscione and Via del Biscione meet. To get a feel for the theater layout, slip through the passageway leading from the back corner of Piazza del Biscione (closed at night) and you will emerge on the Via di Grottapinta. This curved street follows the outline of the ancient theater's semicircular auditorium—and is now the site of the **Teatro dei Satiri**, which carries on the thespian tradition but on a comparatively minuscule scale. All previous theaters in Rome had been built of wood in accordance with a senatorial decree. Pompey only managed to get this vast stone construction accepted by incorporating a temple to **Venus Victrix** at the top of the auditorium in such a way as to make the rows of seats appear to be the steps leading up to that place of worship—and he had the entire construction dedicated as a temple.

This did not prevent him from including some of the bloody sports favored by the Romans

Corso Vittorio Emanuele

as part of the dedication ceremonies; 500 lions and 18 elephants were killed in the auditorium on opening day. The theater's capacity is variously estimated at between 10,000 and 40,000 seats that rose on 3 tiers while the arms of the theater that lead away from the hemicycle enclosed a vast covered portico surrounding public gardens. The toga-wearing spectators would hang around this early Shubert Alley, patronizing the various taverns—precursors of the excellent restaurants now enclosed in the former theater's outline. Like the great baths (which later included theaters), this complex of buildings provided diverse entertainment possibilities. So it is not surprising that when the **Curia** (where the Senate held its meetings in the Roman Forum) was temporarily closed for restoration in the spring of 44 BC, the senators moved into the theater—occupying the Hecatostylon, or portico, of 100 columns that had been adorned by Pompey with many wonderful sculptures only 9 years earlier.

The irony of choosing Pompey's theater for those Senate sessions in 44 BC may not have escaped that leading Roman citizen who earlier that year had gotten himself appointed consul and dictator for life. He had weakened the power of the Senate by reducing their number to 900, and in redesigning the calendar named the month of his birth after himself—July, for **Julius Caesar**. The fates of Pompey and Caesar had been inextricably interwoven. Pompey had been married to Caesar's daughter **Julia**, and the 2 had been close political allies; along with **Crassus**, they had formed the original triumvirate that ruled over the fortunes of the still technically Republican Rome. When he built this theater to enhance his popularity with the Roman masses, Pompey had in fact been ruler of the greater part of the Roman world, while father-in-law Julius had only the 2 provinces of Gaul. The third triumvir, Crassus, died the year Pompey built the theater. Even more important, Julia had died the year before. So these 2 great men faced each other without any buffer between them except the natural geographic divides. The Senate distrusted Pompey—as they distrusted any unbridled autocrat—and by an overwhelming majority had ordered both Pompey and Caesar to disband their armies. Pompey's refusal to comply gave Caesar the pretext to declare war and march his army down from Gaul into Italy. In 49 BC he had crossed the Rubicon River at the northern end of the peninsula and headed south. Pompey had suffered some military losses, then had fled—to military defeat in Greece and to death by stabbing in Egypt in 48 BC. In the intervening 4 years, Caesar had made himself the only show in town, proclaiming his own divinity, and was expecting that the Senate on that 15th of March would proclaim him *King of the Orient*. He had not learned the les-

Corso Vittorio Emanuele

son of Pompey's downfall. He walked into Pompey's theater that morning without heeding the warnings and was stabbed to death by a group of senators, including **Brutus**, his adopted son (some say natural son), and died here at the base of Pompey's statue. ♦ Via del Biscione

45 Hotel Campo Dei Fiori $$ Once a simple inn, this place has been modernized. It is the hotel closest to the Baroque heart of Rome. But with only 27 rooms, less than half with bath or shower, you must hurry to secure your reservation. Roof garden but no restaurant; which is fine because lunching or sup-

ping in one's hotel is always a mistake, and in an area surrounded by taste treats, it would be criminal. ♦ Via del Biscione 6. 6540865, 6874886

45 Da Pancrazio $$ When you go down into the lower cavelike room that looks as if it had been carved out of the native rock, you know you are reliving history. **Caesar**'s death is very immediate here in the remains of **Pompey**'s vast stone theater in which 2000 years ago the recently divinified Julius gasped, *You too, Brutus*, in bitter disappointment. Well, you, too, might be disappointed if you expect the food to be of the same quality as the setting. Nothing could be. So relax, drink in the ambiance and the open house white wine, and eat up the history and the seafood specialties. You can't go wrong with the risotto. **Signor Pancrazio, Sr.**, moved here in 1911 and has been going strong ever since. Large rooms on the ground floor for groups. Don't miss the antique art pieces in a display case, some real and others fake. ♦ Closed Wednesday and part of August. Piazza del Biscione 92. 6861246

46 Hostaria Romanesca ★$ **Enzo** and **Lucio** run the other simple restaurant in the square, which gets masses of sun even in winter. When he's in town they also get **Ben Gazzara**, with his massive cigar and his beautiful wife. Sundays are good for a peaceful and sunny lunch as the market is closed. A real bargain, but there are only 8 tables, so come early. We usually warn against ordering seafood in a very inexpensive place, but with the fish market at the door it would be difficult for the *vongole* to not be fresh. ♦ Closed Monday. Piazza Campo dei Fiori 40. 6864024

THEATRVM POMPEI

47 Hotel Teatro di Pompeo $$ This attractive 12-room minihostel opened in 1988 on the site of Great Caesar's assassination. But don't let that deter you. You will sleep soundly and the price is right. There are a couple of meeting rooms and a bar situated in the 2000-year-old remains of the original theater, air conditioning, and rooms with wood beams. All rooms are double or twin with minibar, radio, TV, and a direct-dial phone. ♦ Largo del Pallaro 8. 6872566, 6545531; fax 6872812

47 Campo dei Fiori From 6AM to 1PM, every day except Sunday, this is the most beautiful food market in the world. Mostly fruit and vegetables, with fish down at the end by the Farnese movie theater (a second-run smeller) and meat at the other end in the fixed stalls. The name means *field of flowers*. The flower market was moved some time ago to the end of Via Angelica on the other side of the Vatican, but there are still a few colorful floral stalls in the center, where Via Baullari carries the vista down to the Piazza Farnese a few paces away.

In sun or rain, the stalls are covered with the famous Roman *ombrellone* (big umbrellas), or with tarpaulins, depending on the wealth of the merchants. Here there are no fixed prices for the produce; some stands will give you a discount on the posted price, while all will indulge your proclivity to do a little good-natured haggling. The vegetables are so fresh you can assume they were in the ground a few days ago. Don't expect to get wild strawberries in November or chestnuts in May. You will discover dozens of vegetables you never knew existed; for instance, there are a half-dozen distinct varieties of broccoli. Because each one has its own season and the Italians respect seasons, they haven't insisted on standardizing a single broccoli and forced it to grow outside its natural season the way Americans have. They have let a hundred flowers bloom—and if they don't see the one that they love, they love the one they see.

If you get here long before 9AM you may find things still in a state of confusion, with sawhorses, poles, and awnings not yet assembled within the market's stalls. After 1:30PM, the stalls will be stored for the next day's market. The shops inside the buildings remain open throughout the afternoon. That gloomy sculpture in the square's center is **Giordano Bruno**, a monk and philosopher who was burned alive here for heresy by the Counter Reformation papacy in 1600. The more famous **Galileo Galilei** was no martyr to his scientific conclusions; he survived, thanks to his friendship with **Pope Urban VII**, despite condemnation by the Inquisition for his belief that the sun was the center of the universe and the earth moved around it. Unlike Bruno, who stuck to his beliefs and burned for them, Galileo actually recanted during his interrogation by agreeing with the Church that the earth did not move; according to popular legend he added *and yet it does move!* ♦ Piazza Campo dei Fiori

47 Om Shanti $ Light refreshments and *pizette* (pizza bread filled with cheese or ham—the real Roman sandwich, toasted or cold). The other sandwiches and fruit tarts are served cold. Charming little room in the back with tables and chairs. But Roman cafés are called bars to remind you that you are supposed to stand up—or pay a lot more for anything consumed sitting down. You can rent this little place on its day off. ♦ Closed Monday. Piazza Campo dei Fiori 53. 6875530

48 Ruggeri Mozzarella *di buffala* (the authentic kind has to be from water buffalo, not the common cow—and don't forget that in Italy this is not a kind of cheese, it's a mozzarella, period), salami, and hard-to-find specialties such as peanut butter for the Yanks, marmite for the Brits, and *knäkebrot* for the the Nordics. ♦ Piazza Campo dei Fiori 2

49 Palazzo Spada (1550, **Merisi da Caravaggio** and **Giulio Mazzoni**) Perhaps the most exciting of all the 16th-century buildings. Experts disagree on whom to give credit. The exuberant stuccos are surely Mazzoni's—but they don't think he designed the whole palazzo. Built for **Cardinal Gerolamo Capo di Ferro**, it was acquired in 1632 by **Cardinal Bernardino Spada**, whose descendants sold it to the government in 1926. Some consider the stucco Mannerist decorations on the facade and in the courtyard frivolous. They depict cavorting centaurs and tritons and generous festoons of fruit and flowers. The most extraordinary feature is the trompe l'oeil perspective in a small formal garden on your left as you enter, which can be glimpsed from the center courtyard through the library doors. There seems to be a magnificent colonnade leading majestically to a distant clearing with a life-size statue. For a modest tip the porter will take you in so you can judge for yourself the actual size of the passage leading to the pint-size statue. **Borromini**, the great Baroque master, designed this in 1652 for his friend **Virgilio Spada**, Cardinal Bernardino's brother. To visit the Cardinal's private collection in its original surroundings, go up the steps to the

Galleria Spada. Four sumptuous rooms with paintings by **Titian, Andrea del Sarto, Breughel**, and others, as well as some of the original furniture and curiosities. The palace is now home of the **Italian Council of State**, so visiting the state rooms requires special permission. Don't miss the statue of **Pompey**, at the base of which **Julius Caesar** was said to have been killed. Experts may disagree about its authenticity. Everyone agrees, however, that the palazzo's throne room is of special interest because such rooms were limited to the palaces of princes, dukes, and a few marquises, the only homes the pope actually visited—and which therefore had to have thrones upon which he could sit! The fountain in the small square in front of the entrance used to have water spouting from the bosoms of a buxom female nude. For permission to visit the state rooms write to Ufficio Intendenza, Palazzo Spada, Via Capo di Ferro 3, 00186 Roma; or call Mr. Cuomo at 6861158. ♦ Galleries M-Sa 9AM-2PM; Su, holidays 9AM-1PM. 6861158

50 Palazzo Farnese (1514-1589, **Sangallo, Michelangelo**, and **della Porta**) This is now the French Embassy, but if you can get in, through diplomatic contacts, it is certainly a palace worth visiting. A bit on the massive side for some people's taste (its astronomical building costs were the butt of many jokes scrawled on placards hung around the talking statues' necks (see **Pasquino Cinema** on page 92). The architectural style is High Renaissance, but some of Michelangelo's designs

Corso Vittorio Emanuele

for the top floor and all the great frescoes are Mannerist, the style that acted as a transition to Baroque. The French Embassy rents this vast building from the Italian government for the nominal fee of one lire per year, and the Italians pay a similar token amount for their palatial quarters in Paris (although not so large—and one franc is worth more than one lire!).

Pope Paul III (1534-49) was a Farnese and had grandiose ideas for his family mansion, but he did not live long enough to see it completed. Travel writer **Georgina Masson** describes it as *sober magnificence*. The Farnese family was modest enough, coming from Bolsena, but they could trace their lineage back to Rome's 11th century. In the 15th century, a son married a **Caetani** and was catapulted into Rome's high society. One hundred years later the future Pope Paul III, still just **Cardinal Alessandro Farnese**, wanted an adequate lodging for himself and his children near **Campo dei Fiori**, the business district. He

asked **Antonio da Sangallo** to start building. Work proceeded normally until Alessandro suddenly became Pope Paul III. Then Sangallo changed his designs and the "adequate lodging" had to become the most fabulous palace ever. Three large houses were bought and torn down to make enough room to build something special. In 1546 Sangallo died, but his designs for most of the facade and courtyard were carried out. Michelangelo contributed to the top floor, including the grandiose roof cornice, as well as the now glazed-over loggia in the center of the facade. The Pope died in 1549, but work continued for another 40 years. One of the sons, **Cardinal Ranuccio Farnese**, was the first person to live continuously in the palace. This just meant the work had proceeded enough to have comfortable, and that means very comfortable, suites already finished. **della Porta** was called in to continue in 1573. He carried out most of Michelangelo's ideas, including the archway over Via Giulia and the buildings and gardens leading down to the river. One flight up, the great fresco artist **Annibale Carracci** (with some help from family and friends) painted giant classic figures on the ceilings of the famous **Galleria** and what is now the ambassador's private dining room. The superb Galleria paintings, which depict the gods' love affairs, must have been quite risqué for a cardinal's ceiling. In 1626, when **Cardinal Odoardo Farnese** died, the palace was deserted because his heirs could not afford the maintenance. In 1635 they accepted the French proposal to convert the building into the French Embassy. Famous Frenchmen such as **Cardi-**

nal **Richelieu** and the **Duc d'Estrées** held court here, and for 6 months former **Queen Christina of Sweden** (page 89) lived here; she removed the fig leaves from all the nude male sculptures when she first arrived in Rome in December 1655. Apply to the French Embassy's Cultural Section for permission to visit, with a passport, a few days in advance.
♦ Piazza Farnese. 6542152, 6879054

51 Farnese Floor and wall tiles in antique or modern styles, all gorgeous. Sold by the square meter, but not cheap. Mosaics in marble—everything you need to make your elegant palazzo (or split-level ranch house) a faultless setting. Designed by **Tullio Di Donato**, who launched the white-on-white tile vogue. ♦ M-F 9AM-3PM, irregularly in the afternoon. Piazza Farnese 50. 6896109, 6896205; fax 6874793

51 Sergio De Benedetti An exciting grotto where marble is restored and old tiles sold. Rooting around among the dusty antiques, statues, terra-cotta bowls, and ancient tiles, you may chance upon some magic find.
♦ Vicolo dei Venti 5. 6870810

52 Restauro Farnese Lab for repairing ceramics; also glass and crystal although the card says they take no responsiblity for the latter. Wood restoring next door. ♦ Piazza Farnese 43. 6869294

52 Come Nuovo means *like new*. In fact, these sensible baby clothes are so attractive and impeccable that you would never guess they are all secondhand. You can also make arrangements here for your child's portrait in pastels.
♦ M-F 11AM-6PM. Piazza Farnese 45. 6872577

53 Piazza Farnese One of the wonders of Rome is the dramatic difference between this square and the Campo dei Fiori, only paces away. This is Baroque and as delightfully incandescent as the fountains at either end, whereas the *campo* is medieval and as brooding as the statue in the center. The style is set by the architectural preponderance. Here it is the **Palazzo Farnese** that dominates the square with its grandeur (so fitting for the French Embassy). The fountains are like bathtubs for the gods; they were found in the ruins of the **Baths of Caracalla**, but the silky, sensual granite was brought from Egypt at the time when Roman emperors were importing the magical obelisks and the divine **Cleopatra**.

54 Hostaria Farnese $ Cheap and cheerful, halfway between Piazza Farnese and Campo dei Fiori. We suggest *penne alla arrabiata* (angry macaroni), *faraone* (guineafowl), and *zuppa inglese* (English trifle pudding). ♦ Closed Thursday. Via Baullari 109. 6541595

55 Er Galletto ★$$ **Giovanni** has been known to get as pickled on his good house white as on the *alici* (whitebait) that he marinates so successfully in olive oil and lemon juice. But nobody can surpass him at hand-cutting the prosciutto; and one can always tell the difference between the machine-cut ham and the real thing. Everything with Giovanni is authentic, and thus he has gained the patronage of the American Academy professors, whose profession it is to distinguish the real from the fake. ♦ Closed Sunday. Vicolo del Gallo 1. 6861714

56 La Vacca (15th century) Formerly an inn and one of the 4 luxury hotels owned at the start of the 16th century by the very beautiful **Vanozza Cattanei**, who had been the notorious mistress of **Pope Alexander VI** and mother of his even more notorious children, **Lucrezia** and **Cesare Borgia**. La Vanazza had amassed a sizable fortune due to papal connections by the time Alexander VI switched his attentions to another local beauty, **Giulia Farnese**, so she invested in this hotel chain and lived happily ever after with her third husband—even getting an exemption from the wine tax, thanks to her old lover. Once Alexander was dead and buried she affixed the still visible shield, which combines the coats of arms of her husband and of the Borgias—who made it all possible. ♦ Vicolo del Gallo 13

57 La Carbonara ★$$$ Elegant restaurant where noble Romans like to dine in the square on a summer night. In winter, the 2 floors are comfortable and the service upper class.
♦ Closed Tuesday. Piazza Campo dei Fiori 23. Reservations recommended. 6864783

57 La Barese ★$ In summer, the tables are set next to those of the Carbonara, so you can position yourself next to your rich friends and enjoy the same sun and the same great view and the same...well, there is some question about whether the quality of cuisine is the same. Known as a *bruschetta*-and-pizza joint, this simple restaurant serves specialties from the Bari region (hence the name). Try *orechiette alla Barese*, ear-shaped hand pasta (pasta made in the restaurant by pressing one's thumb into a circle of freshly prepared dough) with green Italian broccoli and hot peppers. Peasant food, but some of us like peasant food very much. The house white is an open pure-grape wine with no additives or headaches. We like that, too. And we like the aged lady in the kitchen, and **Kumar**, a burly Sri Lankan who distributes the dishes and the laughter. ♦ Closed Sunday. Piazza Campo dei Fiori 28. 6861312

58 Palazzo della Cancelleria (1513, **Bregno** and/or **Bramante**) One pope's nephew won the price of this vast palace in a night of gambling with another pope's nephew. Must have been high stakes in that nepotistic group because this is the largest single building unit of its epoch in Rome. It's also very beautiful and harmonious—a pure product of the Renaissance. In fact, art historians praise this as the first monument of the Renaissance in Rome. The only problem is that the tons and tons of marble that went into it were plundered from one of the great monuments of ancient Rome: Pompey's Theater, which stood just a couple of hundred yards from here—where **Julius Caesar** was killed. Other art historians decry the very existence of this building. Whatever the merits of this controversy, it is worth walking into the courtyard to admire the delicacy of the superimposed arcades surrounding it. The proportions are so carefully worked out that the gigantic size is never oppressive. Renaissance architects strove to have every part of their building in perfect scale with every other part, even working out precise mathematical formulas to determine what was harmonious and what was not. Notice this building is extremely harmonious despite the fact that it is asymmetrical, which is true of almost all of Rome's big palaces, presumably be-

Corso Vittorio Emanuele

cause they were built to cover the entire building plot, and such plots, by medieval heritage, were simply not quadrangular. The first owner/gambler was **Cardinal Raffaele Riario**, of the great Riario and **Pazzi** families, who conspired to murder **Lorenzo dei Medici** in his native Florence and did kill his brother **Giuliano. Uncle Sixtus IV** claimed ignorance of the conspiracy, but none believed the Pope was innocent. In any case, within a couple of centuries this palace was in the hands of another cardinal from another noble family: **Cardinal Henry**, Duke of York and brother of the Catholic pretender to the British throne, **Bonnie Prince Charlie**. When **Napoleon** occupied Rome (1809-1814) it housed the law courts, and it subsequently became the Papal Chancellery—hence its name and the fact that it is Vatican territory. Even today it is not subject to Italian sovereignty. Ask your hotel concierge when there will be a classical music concert.

Within the Palazzo della Cancelleria:

San Lorenzo in Damaso (1495, door by **Vignola**) Built as part of the palace for Cardinal Riario, it replaced a 4th-century church founded by **Pope Damasus I**.

59 Grappolo d'Oro ★$$ **Andrea** and **Carlo**'s restaurant is favored by resident foreign artists. Few frills, few thrills. But some unusual Roman specialties, such as *puntarelle*, local curly salad with anchovy sauce; bitter but good. ♦ Piazza della Cancelleria 80. 6897080

59 Essences—Creazioni di Profumo The perfume maestro, **Giovanni Daga**, young and handsome, comes in the afternoon to make up a scent especially for you. All the Oriental and floral essences. ♦ M-F 9AM-1PM, 3-8PM. Piazza della Cancelleria 88. 6872536

59 Fotoforniture De Bernardis The freshest Kodak film in town, plus professional services to help if you have a problem with your Brownie or Leica. ♦ M-F 9AM-7:30PM. Piazza della Cancelleria 63. 6864047, 6864143

60 MozArt's A specialist in lutes, **Enrico Baldi** mends mandolins, guitars, and harps, builds violins, and sells all the above plus unusual pianos. For instance, the piano that is a twin to **Beethoven**'s own; it has only 6 octaves and less height than a standard grand, but is beautiful. Turn left as you leave the door, and don't miss the first lane on your left, **Via Acetari**, alley of the mirrors. ♦ Via del Pellegrino 10. 6875488

If you are in Rome during **Carnival** and do not have the resources to make a costume, rent one at either of these famous costume houses: **Neri Teatro Moda** (Viale Giulio Cesare 21, 319747), or **M. Ferroni** (Arco della Pace 5, 6541831), near Piazza Navona. The latter specializes in historical costumes and outfits for children.

Restaurants/Clubs: Red	**Hotels:** Blue
Shops/Parks: Green	**Sights/Culture:** Black

Maresci & Notari
gioielli

60 **Maresci & Notari** Jewelry-making and selling. **Elio Maresci** and **Mario Notari** design and craft these beautiful bangles on the premises. There are 3 categories: silver with tiny precious stones; silver and gold with small rubies, etc; and gold-plated silver with semiprecious stones. Delicate styles with seed pearls and lapis lazuli in antique-inspired designs. Or chunky, with 1930s-style filigree. ♦ Via del Pellegrino 48. 6865570

61 **No name sandwich bar** ★$ We promised to write the minimum on this recent discovery, and you'll understand why. Open red and white wines rest on the counter while crowds mill about waiting for hot-from-the-oven made-to-order sandwiches on Roman pizza bread. ♦ Closed Thursday, Sunday, daily 2-5PM. Via Governo Vecchio 25

61 **Via Governo Vecchio 104** On the gorgeous facade of this 15th-century palazzo, ancient frescoes of the owner, his secretary, and his pet parrot are just barely discernable between 18th-century bas-reliefs of nineteen worthies in festooned frames. The present inhabitants talk darkly of this having been a Vatican prison for clergy, whereas moth-eaten books identify it as the **Confraternity of the Stigmata**. ♦ Via Governo Vecchio 104

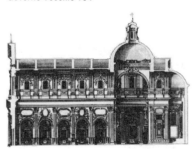

62 **Chiesa Nuova—Santa Maria in Vallicella** (1605, **Matteo di Citta di Castello** and **Martino Longhi**). Called the *New Church* since the 16th century, when it was begun as a replacement for the small medieval Franciscan Church and **Convent of Santa Maria in Vallicella** (referring to the small valley of a former tributary of the Tiber). This and the adjoining, architecturally more significant **Oratory** were built for the **Congregation of Oratorians**, a Counter Reformation religious order founded in 1561 by **St. Philip Neri**. The new church was built wide in keeping with the precepts of Neri, who believed that Catholicism had to be preached to the masses as a defense against the inroads of the Protestant Reformation. Once Neri died, his decree that churches should be spartanly plain was ignored by his followers and the exuberantly Baroque interior

decoration we see today was carried out by the then in vogue **Pietro da Cortona**, whose exploding ceiling painting is one of the artistic highlights of the church. It depicts a vision Neri had in which he saw the Virgin Mary holding up part of the old church when it threatened to fall down on the congregation. There are also 3 early 17th-century paintings on slate (to prevent reflections) by **Rubens** over and on either side of the altar. ♦ Piazza della Chiesa Nuova

62 **The Oratory (Oratorio dei Filippini)** (1662, **Borromini**) The original plan called for a richly undulating facade, very 3-dimensional, like a stage set. But Borromini had to compromise because he was denied permission for the facade to jut out into the square and was forced to build in brick, which gives this now greatly flattened facade the appearance of having been built to last only temporarily while awaiting a finish in the traditional marble facing. Also, the central part is topped by a curious pediment of straight and curved sections that is slightly more Islamic than Christian. The inside of the oratory chamber itself has interesting examples of Borromini's banded ribbons running up the walls into the ceiling—and it is still used for musical events, including oratories. But the high point of this building, around the corner in the **Piazza del Orologio**, is the clock tower where Borromini's genius for convex and concave surfaces reached an apogee of almost musical, rhythmic undulations. As he rings all the possible changes in a relatively small area, this tower is worth far more than a casual glance. ♦ Piazza della Chiesa Nuova

63 **QSS Laboratorio Fotografico** Your color photos developed and printed within an hour by **Raffaella** and her happy crew. ♦ Corso Vittorio Emanuele 227. 6869658

63 **Bella Napoli** An ice-cream parlor specializing in treats from Naples, where they claim to have invented ice cream. Large and spacious, with a tearoom in back so you can gorge in private. ♦ Corso Vittorio Emanuele 246

64 **Da Luigi** ★★$$ In the lovely tree-lined **Piazza Sforza Cesarini** you have your choice between 2 excellent trattorias, this and **Polese**. But it doesn't seem to be cut-throat competition; the knives are too busy with the food. So choose either one and you won't be disappointed. Luigi caters to a slightly younger, more with-it group. But in summer, especially under the *ombrellones*, with flickering lights and passing minstrels, everyone feels at home in this crazy square. ♦ Closed Monday. Piazza Sforza Cesarini 24. 6545463

64 Polese ★★$$ When we first settled in Rome we thought **Da Luigi** was the hotest act in town and Polese was a bore. Now we're coming around. Less youth-oriented doesn't mean less good. These are not formula dinners with quick turnover, but sensible Roman food. Risotto *radichio e gamberi*; thick, fresh veggy soup; *bresaola* and *rughetta*. In fact, the whole menu, typed up daily in the shape of a wine carafe, is a delight to all the senses. ◆ Piazza Sforza Cesarini 40

65 Pietro Simonelli Mask Lab For Carnival, for the theater, or as a wall decoration, you need a mask. Pietro can be seen making these artistic face-coverings out of papier-mâché or plaster. None of them will remind you of *Phantom of the Opera*. ◆ Via Banchi Vecchi 125. 6868912

65 Gazza Ladra Cane Shop Although this antique shop has stylish 1930s statues and plaques, the real treasure is a most spectacular collection of unusual walking sticks. Imagine strolling the boulevards holding in your grip a magnificent naked lady carved in ivory, or a Japanese theatrical mask in miniature, or a griffin. Arcane! ◆ Closed Monday AM. Via Banchi Vecchi 29. 6541689

65 La Riggiola Ancient tiles as tables. An ingenious interior decorator has designed elegant tables using old tiles from Southern Italian palaces and castles; we fear the rape must have cleaned out the whole of lower Italia. Used with slate, the black-and-white effect is stunning. ◆ Via Banchi Vecchi 110. 6544127

66 Cavaliere Pacitti Etchings and lithographs. Browse through the unusual print selection; you won't be disappointed. ◆ Via Banchi Vecchi 59. 6540391

67 Santucci Marcello Engraver Whether it's a bathroom sign for that restaurant you're going to open, or an engraved visiting card with your heraldic coat of arms, Marcello will incise—before your very eyes. ◆ Via Banchi Vecchi 103. 6543211

68 Mekong ★$ Since Vietnamese cuisine is perhaps the most delicately refined in the world—with unexpected *trompe la bouche* (fool the mouth) surprises—it is worth an occasional night out, even in Rome, where the essential ingredients are difficult to find. This bamboo-decorated corner dining room is youthful in its spirit and personnel. You can speak French with **Monique**, the co-owner, and with the many Vietnamese who wait on you with courtesy and good humor. Ask for pâté *impériale* (hot, crunchy spring roll to be eaten with your fingers in a lettuce leaf with fresh mint) or *poulet à la citronelle* (stir-fried chicken with lemon grass). ◆ Closed Tuesday. Corso Vittorio Emanuele 333. 6869651

69 Taverna Giulia ★★$$$ An eating emporium so upscale that you might feel a little nervous about going in. The décor is somewhat intimidating, and most of the diners seem to be refined connoisseurs discussing the cuisine in hushed Gallic phrases. But food critics praise it for being faithful to the high principles of Ligurian (Genoa) cooking. You cannot go wrong sampling whatever has just arrived from Genoa. We also recommend that you try the pasta *al pesto*, which is the specialty. ◆ Closed Sunday and August. Vicolo del Oro 23. Reservations required. 6869768

Nightlife

One of the criticisms of the Eternal City is that there's very little *Dolce Vita* left. We think you can still have a ball here, but you have to use your imagination.

Theaters

Occasionally, there are productions in English, if few and far between. Foreign dance companies come for a week or less at a time.

Teatro di Roma ◆ Largo Torre Argentina. 6875640

Olimpico ◆ Piazza Gentile da Fabriano 17. 399036, 3962635

Sistina ◆ Via Sistina 120. 4756841

Valle ◆ Via Teatro Valley 23. 6869049, 6879028

Teatro Giulio Cesare You can get tickets for the Spoleto Festival here as well. ◆ Viale Giulio Cesare 229. 353360, 384454

Opera Roma And, of course, the great Roman Opera! ◆ Via Viminale. 4825597

Sometimes you can see local English-language plays at:

Teatro Goldoni ◆ Vicolo dei Soldati. 561156

Workshop Theatre ◆ St. Paul's Church. Via Napoli 58. 3275886, 860503

Your hotel concierge can help you with all the above.

Cinema

All movies are dubbed in Italian except at these 2 cinemas:

Pasquino Cinema (see page 92)

Alcazar (English-language original, Monday night, only) ◆ Via Cardinal Merry del Val 14. 588099

Late-night Restaurants

Osteria St. Ana (see page 59)

mai di domenica (see page 127)

Da Albino il Sardo (see page 141)

Hostaria dell'Orso (see page 81)

Osteria Margutta (see page 62)

Nightclubs

Floor shows:

Night Carousel ♦ Closed Su and July-August. Via Emilia 54. 4740629

Club 1001 ♦ Closed Su and August. Via Lazio 31. 4825974

Dancing:

Open Gate Luxury nightclub where you dine as well. Lots of beautiful people. ♦ Closed Su and July-September. Via San Nicola da Tolentino 4. 4750464

Bella Blu Intimate dining; **Maria Letizia Rapetti** has a nightclub in the next room if you feel like dancing. ♦ Via Saluzzo 30. 7010981

Gilda Italy's nightlife aficionado, Foreign Minister **Gianni De Michelis**, gives Gilda his highest rating in Rome. ♦ Closed M and July-August. Via Mario de' Fiori 97. 6797936, 6784838

Notorious Newest spot for dining and cabaret. This is where the Terpsichorean foreign minister is likely to be. ♦ Closed Tu and August. Via San Nicola de Tolentina 22. 47468

Jazz Clubs

Alexanderplatz Traditional. New band every night. ♦ Closed July-August. Via Ostia 9. 3599398

Saint Louis Music City Traditional, salsa, modern combos, changing every night or 2. ♦ Closed M and July-September. Via del Cardello 13/1. 4745076

Rock Clubs

Alien For the young and not faint-hearted; good head-banging stuff. ♦ Via Vellitri 15. 8551112

Piper Often has English bands come over for a stint. ♦ Via Tagliamento 9. 8449254

Euritmia Caribbean and rhythm-and-blues. ♦ Via R. Murri. 5915600

Piano Bars

Tartarughina Restaurant on the premises. ♦ Via della Scrofa 1. 6783067

Chef du Village A piano and lots of candles. ♦ Via Governo Vecchio 125. 6868693

Bars

Hemingway Same square as Quinzi Gabrielli. A charming, traditional bar that spills out onto the street in summer. ♦ Piazza delle Coppolle 10. 6544135

La Cornacchie Young bar/restaurant that also goes out in good weather. ♦ Closed Monday and August. Piazza Rondanini 53. 6864485

Free Shows

Fontana di Trevi This spectacular fountain looks best at night, when the spotlights play on the just-cleaned marble statues and the gushing water (see page 77).

The **Colosseum** with a full moon rising behind and through its arches.

Summertimes

Villa Medici (French Academy) Open-air movie festivals in the lush gardens. Afterward, dine on the elegant terrace under the trees (see page 66).

Opera at the Baths of Caracalla (see page 163, Monthly Specials).

Ostia Antica Plays in the ancient Roman theater. The 1700-year-old city becomes very mysterious at night (see page 151).

Concerts in the Campidoglio Classical music in this superb setting designed by **Michelangelo** (see page 163, Monthly Specials).

Walter Stait
Advertising Executive

Best hotel:
Hotel de la Ville Roma, Via Sistina 67-71. The nicest rooms are on the garden side. Lunch at the bar off the lobby is great. For assistance, ask general manager Emilio Biagini and the morning *portiére*, Nicola.

Best restaurant:
Il Pasetto, Via Zanardelli 14, located just before Piazza Navona on the river side.

Best tailor and men's clothes:
Peppino Scarapazzi at Carlo Palazzi, Via Borgognona 7B-77C.

Best place to rent mopeds and vespas:
Barberini Agency, Via della Purificazione 66.

Best barber:
Pino at **Modafferi**, Via del Cappucini 21, at the bottom of Via Sistina near Piazza Barberini.
In search of a good barber during a recent visit to Rome, I did the right thing by asking the advice of the *portière* at my hotel. He sent me to Modafferi, *a small barbiere signore,* but of the first class, just off the Via Sistina. After Pino seated me in one of his chairs, he asked what I wanted done, and I asked him what choices I had. I'm not sure I understood everything he said in Italian, but with his emphasis on certain words and with his gestures he made it all sound so necessary and, above all, so intriguing, that I felt compelled to have the works, which turned out to be a haircut, a shampoo, a facial, and a manicure.

The superb technique, the careful attention to detail, the interest shown in the final results, and the time devoted to me were a far cry from the rush and indif-

Corso Vittorio Emanuele

ference that characterize my barbershop. Pino sent me forth feeling every inch an elegant Roman. The trip to the barber's turned out to be one of those thoroughly Roman experiences, and I look forward to renewing it on every Roman holiday I take in the future.

Paulo Buitoni
Businessman

I like to walk through the little streets near **Campo dei Fiori**, with the Roman artisans in their small shops and many people in the streets on my way to **Piazza Navona** to have an apéritif in a bar and later to eat at **Sesto Gitrone di Marcello**. Then I have coffee at the bar in **Piazza Sant'Eustacchio** and continue to walk through the small streets in the center of medieval, Renaissance, Baroque, Neoclassical, and modern Rome, where I am under its fascinating spell.

Restaurants/Clubs: Red   **Hotels:** Blue
Shops/Parks: Green   **Sights/Culture:** Black

The Tiber

(*Tevere* in Italian) is the most historically famous river in Europe because it cuts through the center of Rome. It begins in Tuscany, north of Rome, and travels 252 miles before spilling into the Mediterranean Sea. (The last 21 miles are between Rome and the sea.) The natural mouth of the Tiber is at Ostia, but the emperors **Claudius** and **Trajan** created a second mouth by digging a canal to Fiumicino—now the site of Rome's major airport. The depth of the Tiber varies between 7 and 20 feet and sometimes goes as low as 4 feet in the dry months. The ancient Romans described the Tiber as being tawny in color because of the sediment. Today it is still tawny—because of the pollution. (Perhaps that's why they call Rome eternal.)

From the beginning of recorded history to the Fall of Rome, 10 bridges were built across the Tiber within the city. **Pons Sublicius**, the first bridge, was made of wood. Around 179 BC the **Aemilius** bridge was built with stone foundations. It finally collapsed in 1598, but part of it, now called **Ponte Rotto**, can still be seen near **Ponte Palatino**. **Ponte Milvio** was open to cars and trolleys until 1965, but today it is only for pedestrians, as the vibration caused by heavy traffic had threatened its stability.

The 2 bridges connecting the **Tiber Island** (near the **Ghetto**) date from the 1st century BC. Today's **Ponte Sant'Angelo** was originally built by **Hadrian** (AD 134) as an accessible route to his mausoleum, now **Castel Sant'Angelo**. The arches nearest the 2 shores were built in the 17th century and altered in 1892 when the embankments were constructed; the others were built by Hadrian's imperial masons.

Cleopatra entered Rome on a river barge, as did all the obelisks stolen from Egypt and most of the marble from Tuscany. The commercial docking areas in ancient times were near today's **Ponte Sisto** and **Ponte Testaccio**. The papal port on the Tiber was at **Porto di Ripetta**, demolished at the beginning of this century when the high embankments topped by broad roads were built to prevent the Tiber from

flooding the city. As a flood control measure, the construction of these embankments has been successful. (The last serious flood was in 1870.) Also, they now provide the main traffic arteries—called *Lungotevere* (literally, along the Tiber)—since the city center was largely closed to vehicles in 1988. The embankments, however, are so much higher than the water level that one can no longer enjoy the river's beauty except by strolling under the trees on the river side of the Lungotevere. The intrepid visitor who descends to walk along the quai at the water's edge finds him or herself in a country within the city, but rarely gets a good view of Rome.

Stashed away on the banks of the Tiber, just beyond the city center, are endless private clubs where members and their guests can feel as though they are escaping from reality as they swim in blue-tiled pools set in green gardens and play tennis and bridge amid the lofty pines filled with leg-sawing cicadas.

Until the 1960s, swimming and fishing in the Tiber were popular in the heart of the city. However, industrial pollution has put an end to both. In recent years, a few seagulls have been seen over the Tiber indicating that some fish are returning to its waters. The **Associazione Amici del Tevere** (Friends of the Tiber, 6370268) has started summer cruises between Rome and Ostia Antica (with return by bus).

Another way to enjoy the river is by dining at **Canto del Riso** or **Isola del Sole**, 2 houseboats that have been converted to restaurants.

Because of the swerves in the Tiber's course (particularly near the Olympic Stadium and the Vatican), it is difficult, even for natives, to always know which side of the river you are on. This walk also does some zigzagging as it takes you to the most interesting places along the Tiber.

1 Castel Sant'Angelo (AD 139, **Antonino Pio**) A one-hour visit to this splendid fort is the best illustration of how Rome has been built up layer upon layer over the last couple of thousand years. Originally designed by **Hadrian** as his tomb, it was turned into a medieval fortress by the warrior popes, whose late Renaissance successors topped it with an ex-

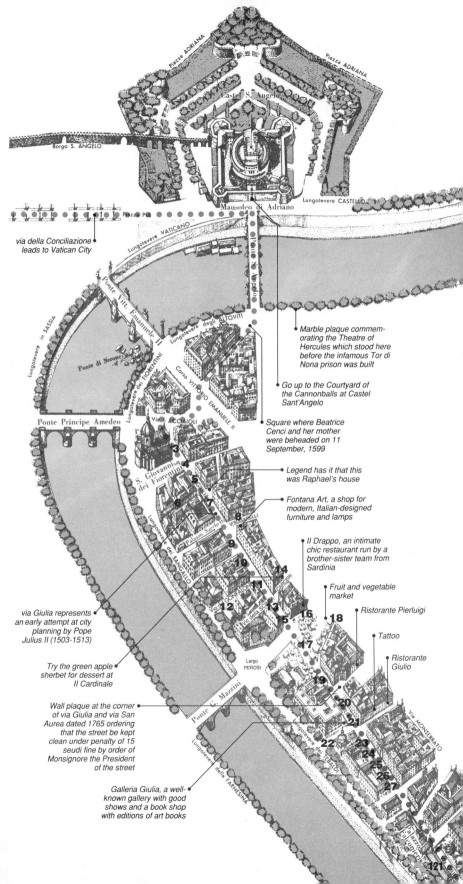

Piazza ADRIANA

Piazza ADRIANA

Castel S. Angelo

Borgo S. ANGELO

Lungotevere CASTELLO

Mausoleo di Adriano

Piazza Pia

via della Conciliazione leads to Vatican City

Lungotevere VATICANO

Ponte S. Angelo

Marble plaque commemorating the Theatre of Hercules which stood here before the infamous Tor di Nona prison was built

Lungotevere degli ALTOVITI

Ponte Vitt. Emanuele II

Lungotevere in SASSIA

Ponte di Nerone

Lungotevere dei FIORENTINI

Corso VITTORIO EMANUELE II

Via ACCIAIOLI

Go up to the Courtyard of the Cannonballs at Castel Sant'Angelo

Square where Beatrice Cenci and her mother were beheaded on 11 September, 1599

Ponte Principe Amedeo

S. Giovanni dei Fiorentini

3
4
5
6
7
8

Legend has it that this was Raphael's house

Fontana Art, a shop for modern, Italian-designed furniture and lamps

Palazzo Sacchetti

Via BUOCCLLI

9
10
14

Il Drappo, an intimate chic restaurant run by a brother-sister team from Sardinia

Fruit and vegetable market

Lungotevere dei SANGALLO

11
12
13
15
16
17
18

Via dei GONFALONIERI

Via della SC

Via dei MECENE

Ristorante Pierluigi

Tattoo

Ristorante Giulio

via Giulia represents an early attempt at city planning by Pope Julius II (1503-1513)

Largo PEROSI

19
20
21

Try the green apple sherbet for dessert at Il Cardinale

Ponte G. Mazzini

22
23
24
25
26
27

Via MONSERRATO

Wall plaque at the corner of via Giulia and via San Aurea dated 1765 ordering that the street be kept clean under penalty of 15 seudi fine by order of Monsignore the President of the street

Lungotevere della FARNESINA

Galleria Giulia, a well-known gallery with good shows and a book shop with editions of art books

121

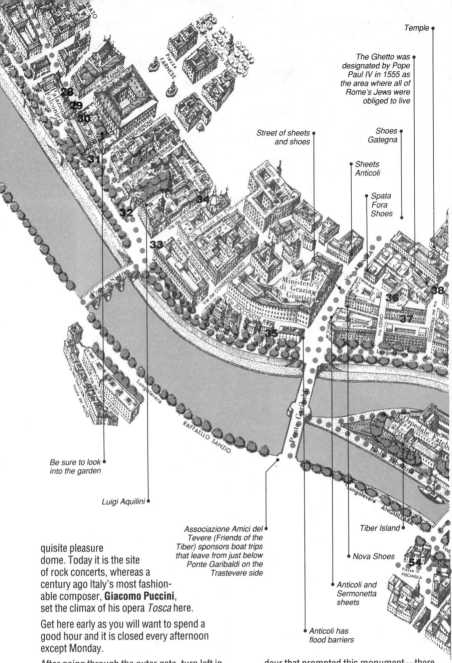

Temple •

The Ghetto was • designated by Pope Paul IV in 1555 as the area where all of Rome's Jews were obliged to live

Street of sheets and shoes •

Shoes Gategna •

• Sheets Anticoli

• Spata Fora Shoes

Ministero di Grazia Giustizia

Be sure to look • into the garden

Luigi Aquilini •

Associazione Amici del • Tevere (Friends of the Tiber) sponsors boat trips that leave from just below Ponte Garibaldi on the Trastevere side

Tiber Island •

• Nova Shoes

• Anticoli and Sermonetta sheets

• Anticoli has flood barriers

quisite pleasure dome. Today it is the site of rock concerts, whereas a century ago Italy's most fashionable composer, **Giacomo Puccini**, set the climax of his opera *Tosca* here.

Get here early as you will want to spend a good hour and it is closed every afternoon except Monday.

After going through the outer gate, turn left in the courtyard, which flanks the Castel. In the low building on your left, built against the outer wall, you will first find the ticket window and then, 50 paces further, a most important room containing 3 models representing the building in the ancient, medieval, and Renaissance periods. Only after studying these models should you enter the Castel and mount the long winding ramp up through history.

Formerly a papal fortress (which saved at least one pope's life), the main part of the structure dates from AD 135, when the Emperor Hadrian designed it to be his family's mausoleum. It wasn't personal or family gran-

deur that prompted this monument—there was simply no space left in the older Imperial Mausoleum built by Augustus. Construction started just 3 years before Hadrian's death and was completed in 139. The square foundation, about 275 feet wide, supported a circular tomb 164 feet high and 210 feet in circumference. The brick was faced with marble, and cypresses were planted on the top of this gigantic mass. The center core of the building was hollow except for the imperial tombs.

The upper parapets were decorated with large statues, including one of Hadrian as a sun god driving a 4-horse chariot. In AD 271 the mausoleum was included within the **Aurelian Walls** and Romans fled here during the siege by the Goths in 410; some of Hadrian's statues were hurled down on the enemies below. *The Dancing Faun*, now in Florence's Uffizi Gallery, and *The Sleeping Faun*, now in Munich, were among the surviving statues.

During a plague in the year 590, **Pope Gregory the Great** ordered everyone in Rome to take part in a religious procession to tell heaven to stop the plague. Hundreds died in the march toward the Vatican, but the Pope saw a vision of the **Archangel Michael** hovering over Ha-

drian's tomb, sheathing his sword, which the Pope took as a signal that their prayers had been answered. Eventually a chapel and finally a statue of St. Michael were built on the tomb, hence the change in name to Castel Sant'Angelo.

In the 14th century, perhaps because it was realized that the mausoleum would make a great fortress, it was converted into one so as to coincide with the popes moving their residence from the building next to Rome's official cathedral, **San Giovanni in Lateran**, to the Vatican Palace. At that time the secret passageway, which snakes for half a mile from the Vatican atop the Leonine Wall (see page 6), was built specifically to allow the pope and

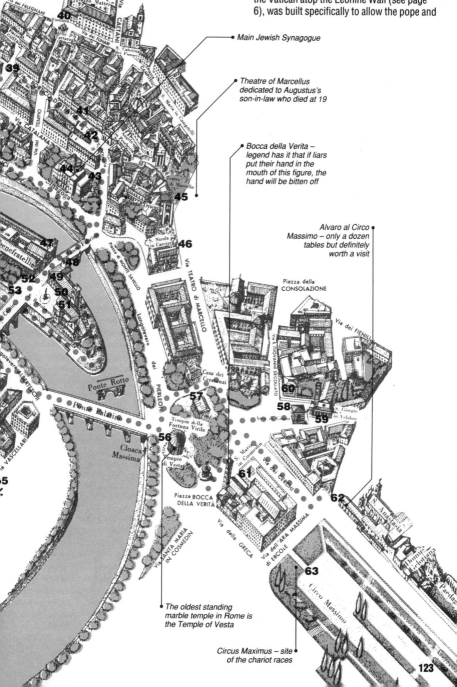

Main Jewish Synagogue

Theatre of Marcellus
dedicated to Augustus's
son-in-law who died at 19

Bocca della Verita –
legend has it that if liars
put their hand in the
mouth of this figure, the
hand will be bitten off

*Alvaro al Circo
Massimo* – only a dozen
tables but definitely
worth a visit

The oldest standing
marble temple in Rome is
the Temple of Vesta

Circus Maximus – site
of the chariot races

his aides to reach Castel Sant'Angelo without running into hostile elements on the ground. In the 1527 seige of Rome, **Pope Clement VII**'s life was saved because he was able to reach the safety of the former pagan tomb.

Life was not too grim inside. In 1492, the Borgia pope **Alexander VI** built a rather sumptuous residence in the fortress with all the comforts he required, including handsome frescoed walls. For obvious reasons, the fortress was also used as a place where the popes kept their gold coins—the Vatican Bank, in other words. It later became the papal prison, a place of execution, an air-raid shelter, and now a museum. To opera buffs, the monument's terrace is the setting of the final scene in Puccini's *Tosca*. You will note that when the 19th-century heroine jumped over the parapet she could not possibly have landed in the Tiber.

After entering, one must descend a few steps to Hadrian's ground level, and then start the ascending ramp with vestiges of the original mosaic pavement. It leads past the sepulchral

chamber and finally up to the **Courtyard of the Cannonballs**. The cannonballs are stacked according to weight. A great but dubious legend has it that when Sweden's **Queen Christina** came here (having abdicated in order to become a Roman Catholic) she was in a frisky mood and fired one of the still operative can-

The Tiber

nons in the direction of the **Villa Medici** (today's French Academy). No deaths or damages were reported, and the royal cannonball is now part of the fountain in front of the Villa Medici.

Upon entering the papal apartments, note the painted trompe l'oeil doorway and flight of steps with a mysterious figure looking over his shoulder as he climbs them. There are also 3 curious paintings. The first depicts a cardinal receiving **James II of England** in 1717, at Imola, near Bologna. The other 2 illustrate bacchanalian revelry; the one on the right is by **Dosso Dossi**, and the one opposite, a copy by **Poussin** of a picture started by **Bellini** but finished by **Titian**. Also on this level are 3 huge 14th-century treasure chests where the pa-

pacy's jewels and crowns were kept until 1870 when the new Italian government claimed the papal fortress as state property. Be sure to ask for the Renaissance **popes' bathroom**, perhaps the first private tub after the Decline and Fall of the Empire. The walls have delightful frescoes by **Raphael**'s students and the water was heated by a log fire under a giant caldron behind the wall. At the very top of the Castel, the Baroque statue of St. Michael is by a Dutch sculptor named **van Vershaffelt**, and is best seen from ground level across the river. In the dry moats around the Castel Sant'Angelo, boys often play soccer by day and other mixed games by night. ◆ Ticket booths M 2-5:30PM; Tu-Sa 9AM-1PM; Su 9AM-noon. Lungotevere Castello. 6875036

Within Castel Sant'Angelo:

Michael's Sandwich Bar $ Light refreshments and drinks on the upper terrace. ◆ M 2 6:30PM; Tu-Sa 9AM-2PM; Su 9AM-1PM. 6875036

2 **Ponte Sant'Angelo** This bridge, originally designed by **Hadrian**, is the best approach to his mausoleum. The 3 central arches are the original ones, those at either end were added in the 17th century and took their present form in 1892. The bridge was the scene of a tragedy during the 1450 Holy Year. Tens of thousands of pilgrims came to Rome. In fact, by the year's end **Pope Nicholas V** had deposited 100,000 golden florins in the Medici Bank. On 19 December, the pilgrims gathered to see **St. Veronica**'s veil exhibited. When they were returning to the city center across this, the only bridge, horses took fright at the far end of the bridge, blocking passage while the pilgrims continued to shove their way onto the bridge. The bridge, like Florence's **Ponte Vecchio**, was lined with wooden shops. In the crush and panic, 170 people were killed. The shops were removed. The later statues (1672) come from **Bernini**'s workshop. The bridge carried speeding Fiats until 1960; now it's reserved for walking, gawking, and photo opportunities.

Dining on the River:

Canto del Riso ★★$$ Just below **Ponte Cavour** is a charming restaurant actually floating on the river. In the summer it is open for both lunch and dinner. Although the service is a little slow, nothing could be nicer on a balmy summer night than to dine on a gently swaying *peniche*. The starters—prosciutto and mozzarella, spaghetti, or an exotic salad—are good, and grilled meat or fish make a nice main course. Ice cream and fruit salad are refreshing desserts. Formerly, amusingly shaped houseboats housed swimming and rowing clubs along the river, but this is one of the few barges still operating. Now the river is too polluted for swimming; a well-known TV personality died as a result of the dirty water during a New Year's Eve jump into the river. It used to be a regular end-of-the-year feat—a show of bravery to dive into the cold waters of the river. If and when the river is cleaned up, perhaps this ritual will be revived. ♦ Closed Monday; Sunday evening in winter. Lungotevere Mellini 7. Reservations recommended. No credit cards. 3610430

Isola del Sole ★$$ Near the **Ponte Metropolitana**. The other restaurant on a houseboat. From the springtime until the autumn, movie stars, musicians, and just ordinary folks enjoy the magic of floating and eating together. Gnocchi with gorgonzola and spinach, *orrechiete al pesto* (ear-shaped spaghetti with garlic and basil), turkey steaks with nut sauce, chicken, and sweet corn, fresh fruit, a blisteringly cold dry white wine, and the sun-dappled water with rowing sculls to round off the experience. ♦ Closed Monday and December. Lungotevere Arnaldo da Brescia. Reservations recommended. 3601400

Via Giulia

In medieval times the only access to St. Peter's for the swarms of pious pilgrims from all over Europe was through the narrow and tortuous streets **Via del Pelegrino** and **Via dei Banchi Vecchi**. To take the strain off the **Ponte Sant'Angelo**, the **Vatican Bridge** (near the present **Ponte Vittorio Emanuele**) was constructed on the foundations of Nero's ancient *ponte*, but it was soon swept away during one of the seasonal floods. As **Benvenuto Cellini**'s autobiography makes vividly clear, brigands, pickpockets, slops from chamber pots, and unscrupulous curio hawkers made the narrow pilgrim route into another calvary.

Via Giulia was cut through the mass of medieval hovels by, and named after, **Pope Julius II** (1503-1513) of the **della Rovere** family to make St. Peter's more accessible to pilgrims. For many, Via Giulia, which stretches straight as an arrow for nearly a mile, is the most beautiful street in Rome.

It represents an early attempt at city planning. The Pope created a new approach to St. Peter's but died before he could rebuild the broken Vatican bridge to which this street was supposed to lead. When the street was newly opened, artists rushed to buy property, as the real estate was cheap; **Sangallo** the architect, **Cellini** the sculptor, and **Raphael** the painter lived here. One hundred years later it had become the smartest street in town. **Borromini** lived in nearby Vicolo Orbitelli. Originally, **Bramante** was going to design all the buildings to create a uniformity of architecture. Those buildings on the right once had gardens in the back trailing down to the Tiber. Today the street is Rome's second capital for antiques, after Via dei Coronari (see page 141). The shops, which vary in styles and epochs, are too numerous to review here, but you can count on the quality to be uniformly high. Just window-ogle the whole way down the street.

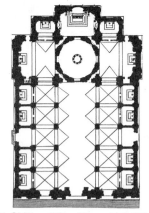

3 Chiesa di San Giovanni dei Fiorentini (The Florentine Church) (1620, **Sansovino, Sangallo**, and **Maderno**) Each Italian city-state, or duchy, in Renaissance times had its own church in Rome, and this section of town was Florentine. **Raphael, Peruzzi**, and **Michelangelo** also submitted drawings for the church. Sansovino won the competition to design it, but he later had a falling out with **Pope Leo X**, so Sangallo took over building it. Then the Pope died. Finally, in 1620—a century after the original competition—**Carlo Maderno** put on the cupola and the church was finished. The facade was added in the 18th century by **Lorenzo Corsini**. ♦ Via Giulia

3 Le Antiquarie Appropriately located just off Piazza dell'Oro, this tiny shop sells antiques and art objects. The furniture, some old, some not so old, is mostly from the Venice region, the sparkling dishes are from Faenza, and the cult jewelry is from...Hollywood! ♦ Via del Consolato 19. 6896898

4 Number 82 This house on the corner of Via Giulia and Via dei Cimatori is one of the oldest and most artistic of the area. Built at the end of the 15th century, it was given to the **Confraternity of the Fiorentini** by **Pope Julius II**. Its style is admirably pure with a small courtyard and a large rustic doorway. Don't miss the el-

egant balcony on the 1st floor, or the remains of the facades, which were usually decorated in those days—the heraldic swirls and geometric triangles in gray-on-gray were scratched into fresh cement. ♦ Via Giulia 82

5 Raphael's House Legend says this house belonged to the great High Renaissance painter. Actually, he owned the land, but died before he could build the home for which he had already made plans. ♦ Via Giulia 85

5 Palazzetto (Little Palace) of Antonio da Sangallo (1536, **Sangallo**) This artist had 3 real-estate lots on the street and was also called upon to finish the Florentine Church, which he worked on for only a few years; but how convenient to live so close to one's work!

Restaurants/Clubs: Red   Hotels: Blue
Shops/Parks: Green   **Sights/Culture:** Black

This house that the artist built for himself was so lovely that when he died it was quickly bought by a son of **Cosimo de'Medici**, Grand Duke of Tuscany and ruler of Florence. All the scrambled egg on the facade was added to glorify the Medicis. ◆ Via Giulia 79

6 Preistorici ★$$$ A smart, tucked-away restaurant where one can sample bizarre recipes as well as some of the owner's specialties from Venice. Truly inventive cuisine and a good place to go if you are tired of normal Italian fare and want a cozy nook to dine in. And remember, if you don't feel like going on to a main course, it's quite all right in Italy just to keep ordering starters (antipasto and pasta). Risotto, a Venetian specialty, can be enjoyed here with a large variety of vegetable-and meat-based sauces. ◆ Closed Sunday. Vicolo Orbitelli 13. 6892796

7 Palazzo Sacchetti (1542, **Sangallo** and **Vasari**) Because the back of the palace gives onto the river, it was often flooded when the waters of the Tiber rose. Vasari, the late Renaissance painter and chronicler, wrote of this to a friend when he succeeded Sangallo as the building's architect. A **Medici** also bought this house but resold it to **Cardinal Ricci** of Montepulciano in 1552. It wasn't entirely finished by Vasari until 1554. The **Sacchettis** fell out with their fellow Florentines, the ruling Medicis, and so they moved to Rome and bought the palazzo, giving it their name. It is vast, with a courtyard in the middle, and on the river side it has an enclosed formal Italian gar-

The Tiber

den with giant antique sculpted heads. See if you can spot the remains of a marble fountain (which no other guidebook will tell you about) on the corner of **Via Giulia** and **Vicolo del Cefalo**. It is an easily recognizable boy on a dolphin, and it doesn't take an expert to understand where the water once came out! ◆ Via Giulia 66

8 Fontana Art Beautiful modern Italian furniture and lamps. The windows are on Via Giulia, but the entrance is around the corner. ◆ Vicolo Sugarelli 96. 6864148

9 Sculptor Jeweler Sergio Passafiume makes lovely little precious pieces where a blacksmith shod horses in times gone by. Sculptures in gold and bronze as well as earrings and bracelets are all designed and made

by this fine artist. Another jewel is to be found in the adjacent courtyard of Via Giulia 102, where a trompe l'oeil perspective is topped by a family coat of arms and a marquis' coronet. ◆ Via Giulia 101. 6877216

9 Church of San Biagio (Facade 1730, **G.A. Perfetti**) This church is so old that it was rebuilt (!) in 1072. It is under the tutelage of the Armenians on their island in Venice. (A few Armenians fled to Italy when Armenia was overrun by the Turks, and their island was the only part of Venice that Napoleon didn't conquer since it was too minuscule for the great conqueror to bother with.) Next door, on the corner of Vicolo del Cefalo and Via Giulia, is the third house **Sangallo** built, but it is rather dilapidated today. It houses the Armenians who rented out their monastery on the other side of the church. A bit of **St. Biagio's** throat is preserved in a reliquary and has always been considered to have miraculous properties for healing tonsilitis. Vicks, watch out! ◆ Via Giulia

10 Cardinal Hotel $$ (Started last half of 15th century, **Bramante**) Bramante had been asked by **Pope Julius II** to design a magnificent **Palace of the Tribunals** with a massive entrance gate. The medal, which was struck on the basis of the plans, shows the building more like a fortress with turreted towers in the middle and at the 4 corners. Though it was never completed, the work was started by pillaging giant cut stones from the Forum. After a few years, it was suspended because of the death of the Pope (1513), the death of the artist (1514), or because funds ran out. Choose your favorite version as all 3 exist in the history books. All that remain are the masonry "cushions" outside and the massive stones on the corner of Via Giulia and Via dei Bresciani that, seen from inside the hotel, make a nice, if heavy, decoration in the attractive bar. The unfinished building finally was ceded to the **Confraternity of the People of Brescia**. It eventually passed into the hands of the Armenians. In the late 1970s the transformation into a hotel began. Perhaps there is a little too much red felt everywhere, but it certainly gives a luxurious quality to the place. Most 5th-floor rooms have balconies. No food service, except breakfast, which is included in the room rate. Seventy-four rooms, half single, half double; 50 percent with baths, the others with showers, all air-conditioned. ◆ Via Giulia 62 (main entrance Via dei Bresciani 35) 6542719, 6542787; fax 6799809

11 Prison for Minors (1827, G. Valadier) Large building with no entrance on Via Giulia, only barred windows for naughty children. In the old days, when this and the prison next door were in operation, this part of the street was cut off by 2 heavy chains and wrought-iron palings guarded by sentries. This building is being restored and will open as the **Museum of Criminality**. Ask your hotel concierge for up-to-the-minute details. ◆ Via del Gonfalone at Vicolo della Scimia

12 mai di domenica (never on Sunday)
★★★★$$ This charming, cozy restaurant, tucked away in a quiet back street, opened in 1989. Medieval meter-thick walls, old brick, wooden beams, blazing fireplaces, and pink-and-gray interiors are just the right recipe to soothe the eye and encourage the stomach. Tables out-of-doors in summer. The chef/co-host used to cook for a Vatican cardinal, whose loss is our gain. *Bianco della Casa* turns out to be *La Vela*, a light Tuscan white—reasonably priced, as are the other wine selections. The country-style bread is crunchy, and so fresh it's still moist. Antipasti include *torta di cipolle* and *di funghi* (onion or mushroom tart); ask for a half order of each and you will be amazed as they melt in your mouth. For pasta you could choose *pave di gnocchi* (oh joy! made of semolina instead of potato) in a white sauce with mushrooms. Fettucine *incappuciatte* are cloaked in thin slices of eggplant; normally served with a melted cheese topping, they can be ordered plain, in which case the hosts, who know how beneficial *pepperoncini* can be, bring you chilli flakes to excite your jaded palate. All this has been so light and tasty that you are ready for the delicious meat or fresh fish. Particularly superb is the *salmone valletana*, grilled to a T and served with a light tomato sauce. And you will still have room for the razor-thin apple pie with just a dash of custard. Our price/excellence yardstick would suggest 4 stars for this cross between a French bistro and a Roman osteria. Besides, the hosts are *simpatici* and they stay open late. Dinner only. ♦ Closed Sunday. Via del Gonfalone 7. Reservations recommended. 6872897

13 Oratorio del Gonfalone (1st facade, early 16th century; 2nd facade, early 17th century **Domenico Castelli**) Although these facades are on Via del Gonfalone, unless there is a concert you actually enter through the back door on Via della Scimia. The **Confraternity of the Gonfalone** was like a guild or protective association. In the Middle Ages people formed guilds to take care of their own interests and those of their fellow workers, priests, or citizens (Florentine, Genovese, etc). In medieval times, Gonfalone were standard bearers who carried the flags. Their charitable work gave money for medical assistance, mortuary costs, and dowries to poor spinsters. However, in the early 16th century a lot of their money went into decorating the interior of their oratory. In 1573, **Federigo Zuccari** (see **Palazetto of the Grotesque Masque** on page 67), along with other artists, painted the beautiful frescoes of the 12 images of the *Passion of Christ*; you can't miss Judas, looking worriedly around, his hand tightly clasped on a soft purse of money. In the frescoes, the ornate twisted columns that divide the pictures look like the Baldacchino in St. Peter's. The confraternity held many religious processions each year, and as they walked members would flagellate themselves to cleanse themselves of impurities. Others were hooded like the Ku Klux Klan and would march to the Colosseum where they held services. Religious processions in the Middle Ages played a similar role to that of circuses in the Roman Empire: show biz for the masses.

When Italy was united in 1870, the State confiscated many of the Church-owned buildings that were not consecrated. The **Capitolo di San Pietro**, a body of priests who run the Vatican's earthly holdings, sued the State over this building and won it back. Until 1955, a saintly priest used the place as a storage room for dried and tinned food that he gave away to the street sweepers of Rome. Ten years ago the laborious work of cleaning the frescoes, blackened by age and smoke from candles, began. Now it is a hall where classical and chamber music concerts are given. Don't miss the miniature organ that was carried in the processions, and if you are lucky enough to hear a concert you will be amazed by its sweet tones. The 4 superb candle holders, which were also used in the processions, have a pair of golden cherubs holding up the lanterns. And last but not least, the 2-tone terracotta tile floor is the original, laid in 1548. ♦ M-Sa 9:30AM-noon. Vicolo della Scimia 1B. 6875952

14 Il Cardinale ★★$$$ The marvelous, suggestive menu card hides a great list of dishes inside! The mousses should be tasted, as should the salad of raw artichokes (not those large French ones but delectable baby Italian ones), the lighter-than-air gnocchi with ricotta and spinach, and the strange plum ravioli. Try the green-apple sherbet or the crème brûlée for dessert. ♦ Closed Sunday. Via delle Carceri 6. No credit cards. 6869336

The Tiber

15 Carcere Nuove (New Prison) (1655, **A. del Grande**) Another forbidding edifice, built 200 years earlier than the nearby Prison for Minors. It was a model of humanitarianism in its time, as the sign on the building indicates: *for a safer and a more humane incarceration of the guilty*. It was closed down at the end of the 19th century, when **Regina Coeli Jail** opened on just the other side of the river (see page 86). ♦ Via Giulia 52

Many hostelries during the Renaissance had animal names. **Vicolo della Scimia** (Monkey Alley), for example, was named after the Hotel of the Monkey. There is still the famous **Hostaria dell'Orso** (Bear, see page 81). Pope Alexander's mistress owned 2 taverns: **Osteria della Vacca** (Cow) and **Osteria del Leone** (Lion).

16 Il Drappo ★★★$$$ **Paulo** and his sister **Valentina** are from Sardinia, hence the lovely, crunchy *carta di musica* (music sheets— large, thin, pizza-size bread disks). An intimate, chic restaurant with very good food. Try the scallops with vegetables as a main course, and for dessert, the *sebada* (lightly- fried batter filled with cheese accompanied by honey) or the prickly-pear sherbet, which should give you an idea of the unusual range. ◆ Closed Sunday and part of August. Vicolo del Malpasso 9. Reservations required. 6877365

17 Chiesa di San Filippo Neri (1728, F. Raguzzini) In 1623 **Rutilio Brandi** from San Gimignano, who suffered from terrible gout, built this now-ruined church to try to assuage the malady caused by his high living! The buildings also comprised a confraternity, an oratory, and an old pharmacy. Nothing but the facade remains. In 1940, Mussolini destroyed all the buildings in this area to prepare for a large road he planned to join the Ponte Mazzini with the Chiesa Nuova on nearby Corso Vittorio Emanuele. This was one of the few occasions when a dictator had to abandon a project because of the uproar it provoked. Today there is a good fruit and vegetable market behind the church in the little square. And no big road to anywhere. ◆ Via Giulia

18 La Moretta ★$ Good value, especially for summer lunches, when you can sit out on the sun-bathed street under an *ombrellone* and savor the *farfalle* (butterfly pasta) with pink sauce made of bell peppers. ◆ Closed Sunday. Via Monserrato 158 (Piazza della Moretta) 6861900

The Tiber

18 Casa di Pietro Paolo della Zecca In 1462 **Eleanor of Portugal** lodged here before marrying **Emperor Frederick of Austria**. Accordingly, a wall plaque, *Al Austria Spetta Dominare Tutto*, warns that Austria will rule all! The original owner had bought a triangular plot with an acute angle where Via Monserrato intersects Via dei Pellegrini; he intended to have this building occupy the whole plot, terminating in a point. The point was cut off by the municipal authorities, who forced him to loose a part of his real estate, in the public interest—a judgment that is sometimes cited as the earliest example of city planning. The resulting public "air space" was the beginning of **Piazza della Moretta**. ◆ Via Monserrato at Via dei Pellegrini

19 L'Ariete: Artists Cooperative Gallery A high standard of work is on view here every month. Because it is a cultural association, there is no gallery percentage added to the price of the paintings. The works of art are reserved during the show and sold directly by the artist afterward. There are some figurative painters, but the majority are abstract. Worth going in. ◆ M-Sa 4-8PM. Via Giulia 140E. 6874651

19 Spirito Santo dei Napolitani Church (1700, radical restoration by **Carlo Fontana**) Although there was an ancient church and convent for Dominican sisters on this site in the 14th century, and 200 years later it was rebuilt for the **Confraternity of the Neopolitans**, all that exists today is a rather mediocre example of the ornate Neopolitan Baroque. ◆ Via Giulia

20 Studio Punto Tre Luciano Ferella, an interior decorator, moved his studio to this storefront in the corner of the elegant Palazzo Ricci, and also shows delectable objects. The trompe l'oeil wooden screens are by Mastroani's daughter and the cubistic wood bottles are made by the son of another famous Italian. Shop around among the Italian elite. ◆ Closed Monday AM. Via Giulia 145. 6864321

20 Palazzo Ricci (1634, architect unknown) Perhaps the best address for a residence in Rome. A somewhat gloomy palace relieved by the frescoed and engraved facade on the other side of the building in Piazza Ricci—where you can sit out in summer and admire these frescoes while eating a fine meal at **Pierluigi's** (6858717). The 2 inner courtyards of this unaccountably famous palazzo have lovely proportions. ◆ Via Giulia 146

21 Galleria Giulia Well-known large picture gallery with editions of art books and a bookstore. The stable of artists includes **Domenico Gnoli**, **Pierre Klossovski**, and **Pedro Cano**. The gallery also has works by **Klee**, **Kokoschka**, and **Savinio**, among others. ◆ Via Giulia 148. 6542061, 6861443

Restaurants/Clubs: Red   Hotels: Blue
Shops/Parks: Green   Sights/Culture: Black

21 Via Della Barchetta The name means *small boat*, indicating that this street once ran down to the Tiber's edge where the water taxis stopped. Now the part of the street between Via Giulia and the Lungotevere has been re-named Via San Eligio. But this narrow, single-block lane leading to Via Monserrato is still action-packed. No. 16, **Paolo Monico's Tattoo Saloon** (6873206), is headquarters every afternoon except Sunday for the motorcycle and black-leather set, where they choose from an impressive display of colored or monochrome needlepoint illustrations. At No. 19, but spilling out into the street in summer, is **Hostaria Giulio** (6540466), which serves typical Roman dishes; like most restaurants in this quarter, it's closed Sunday.

22 Chiesa di San Eligio (1516, **Raphael**; finished 1575) Don't miss this little church down a small side street. Its full name is **Sant'Eligio degli Orefici** (The Gold and Silversmiths Guild's Church). Sant'Eligio was a goldsmith. It is generally accepted that Raphael started the building. The beautiful dome located over the intersection of the form of the church, a Greek cross, was added later and changed the style from High Renaissance to Baroque. ♦ Via San Eligio

23 Palazzo Varese (1618, **Carlo Maderno**) Built for **Monsignor Diomede Varese** from Milan. Inside is a lovely courtyard with a 2-story arcade within a 4-story loggia—an attractive Tuscan note. ♦ Via Giulia 16

24 Palazzo of the Spanish Establishment (Facade, 19th century **Antonio Sarti**) The ornate facade records the visit of **Queen Elizabeth of Spain,** who came here in 1862 to help the poor, the pilgrims, and the infirm. The delicate flower-and-leaf wrought-iron gates should not be missed. ♦ Via Giulia 151

25 Santa Caterina da Siena Church (1526, **Baldassare Peruzzi**) This building was the church, oratory, and rooms for Sienese priests. Note the coat of arms of Siena on the facade. The church was redesigned in 1770 by

Paolo Posi, a condition inflicted upon many great Renaissance buildings in later Baroque periods and not often successfully. There also used to be a defense watch tower nearby to protect the Sienese colony in Rome. ♦ Via Giulia

26 Palazzo Cisterna (c. 1560) Designed by **della Porta** for della Porta. The Latin inscription on the front makes it clear that this was his house. ♦ Via Giulia 163

27 Palazzo Baldoca, then **Muccioli,** then **Rodd** (1696, **Nolli**) The artist **della Porta** lived on this site at the end of the 16th century, 100 years before the present palazzo was built. **Lord Rennell of Rodd**, the British ambassador for 10 years after World War I, renovated the palace. However, he did not see much of his home during the loveliest months of the year, as the entire Italian government, with the diplomatic corps in hot pursuit, was wont to summer in Naples, where it was cooler. ♦ Via Giulia 167

28 Palazzo Falconieri (Beginning of the 16th century, architect unknown) The **Oldescalchi** coat of arms with an eagle, leopard, and incense burner are visible on the facade, but in 1606 a member of the **Farnese** family bought the palace. Then, in 1638, it became the property of the Falconieri family from Florence. In 1649 **Borromini** modernized parts of the palace, adding the beautiful, open, 3-arched loggia at the very top, a hawk's head on the facade, and interior stucco work of rare beauty. ♦ Via Giulia 1

29 Santa Maria dell'Orazione e Morte (1576; rebuilt,1737 **F. Fuga**) This church belongs to a monastery whose job was to collect the unclaimed dead and dispose of the bodies. Look at the facade loaded with skulls and this little reminder: *me today, thee tomorrow.* All but one of the passages to the river, with large underground halls for storing and unloading corpses, were sealed during the work on the embankment walls along the Tiber, except for one; this one has an artistic display of human bones worked into various objects, such as a

candelabra. More easily visible for the intrepid is the church of **Santa Maria della Concezione** (see page 25), which has a wealth of macabre sculptures also made with human bones. ♦ Via Giulia

30 Arch of Palazzo Farnese (1603, **Michelangelo**) Via Giulia's most exciting point is where the creeper-spangled overhead walkway connects Palazzo Farnese to its satellite houses, which were originally on the river's edge (now marred by the high embankment and the high road of the Lungotevere). Michelangelo had designed this whole right wing of the palazzo to be arcaded. He had wanted to adorn it with a fountain made of Greek statues found in 1545 at the Baths of Caracalla. This wing would have gone down to the river's edge and spanned the breadth of the river with a bridge to join Palazzo Farnese to its country house in Trastevere, **Villa Farnesina**. The private bridge was never built, but what a beautiful architectural conversation point it would have made to stand in the garden of the palace and see this walkway proceeding down to the river and then across it!

During Carnival on Via Giulia, which was the widest street in Rome when it was built, there used to be fabulous races with water buffaloes pulling carnival carts. They even organized jousts with this arch used to hang the effigy that the horsemen had to pierce with a lance while going at full gallop. And in these festive times the palace garden on the river side of Via Giulia was filled with classical statues and divided into 4 parts with different colored flowers massed in each section. Also, there was a large fishpond with a balustrade in *pepperino* (dark local stone) and a marble fountain, which had 4 shells, 4 tortoises, and 4 baby angels. If you peek through the railings to the garden of the palace proper you can see the wing on the left where the French ambassador has film showings; this French cinémathèque on the river side was where the Romans played the local game of *pallacorda* in centuries gone by. ♦ Via Giulia

31 Fountain of the Giant Mask (1626, **Carlo Rainaldi**) This used to be in a little square near the spot where one took the waterbus to go over to Trastevere. The fountain was started in 1570, but because at that time the water from the Aqueduct Acqua Virgine only got as far as Campo dei Fiori it was 50 years before the fountain was finally joined with the Acqua Paola, the only water that could reach it, via a cross-river pipe. In Carnival days, the mask would sometimes be spiked and spew out wine! ♦ Via Giulia

32 Thien Kim ★$$$ A small, darkish place said to be run by the wife of a former South Vietnamese diplomat. The food can be good and the ultrathin Vietnamese ravioli are light and delicious. But not too many people in Rome know much about exquisite Vietnamese food,

The Tiber

so they don't do the ravioli often enough. Since it is difficult to get Vietnamese ingredients in Rome, it is an uphill task to present authentic recipes. In the adjacent cul-de-sac, at Via dell'Arcaccio 14, **Luigi Aquilini** (6540219) has an old-fashioned store with great vats of olives, raisins, dried fruit, coconuts, and other nuts. ♦ Closed Sunday. Via Giulia 201. 6547832, 6861106

33 Maniglie (Handles) A wonderful shop that specializes in door handles and other brass hardware items. ♦ Via dei Pettinari 52. 6541255, 6543119

Restaurants/Clubs: Red
Shops/Parks: Green
Hotels: Blue
Sights/Culture: Black

33 Il Palloncino Rosso (Red Balloon) A light-hearted shop with bright-colored clothes for children up to 13—and their moms! ♦ Via dei Pettinari 49. 6864213

34 Ponte Sisto $ This establishment caters primarily to groups, though the street is too narrow to permit an enormous tour bus to drop passengers at the door. Individuals are welcome when space is available, but breakfast is the only meal served. However, they can arrange lunch or dinner for groups. The price and location are right and you can get a taxi or walk to anywhere in Rome. ♦ Via dei Pettinari 64. 6868843; fax 6548822

35 Evangelista ★★$$$ Newly remodeled, this modest restaurant has become *the* chic place to go for late supper with the movie stars and politicians. Evangelista put *carciofi al mattone* (artichoke under a brick) on the calling card, and he's right—this specialty is worth boasting about: squashed, succulent, and crisp. The house wines are, unfortunately, in bottles—rather than carafes filled from demijohns, which we consider more authentic—but good: a white *Pettignano* and a red Chianti from Val di Penna. On each table is a decanter of green olive oil with a curious wood stopper. *Suppa di farro* is a cereal soup dear to the Tuscans; so hearty and thick that it might take the edge off your appetite. *Orecchiette alla Giulia*—artichokes again, nestling in these Sardinian pasta "ears." *Trippa Fiorentina* is so delicate and sweet that even those who don't like innards will be delighted. But if the soup and pasta filled you up, take the *rughetta e parmigiano* salad and weep. ♦ Closed Sunday. Lungotevere Vallati 24 (back entrance Via delle Zoccolette 11/A) 6875810

36 Le Donne ★★$ The price/excellence ratio is high. Dinner only, but they stay open until 3AM! "Italian Modern" décor. Perhaps a bit too much spotlight from above, but our hostess, who created this *tavern* for her 3 daughters (*le donne*), says that's what the young folk like, and she's not about to change it. Aside from thin, crunchy pizzas (don't be surprised to see the Italian at the next table leave the best crispy parts) there is a table loaded with green vegetables as well as reasonably priced smoked salmon and prosciutto. The menu accommodates all tastes from pasta to pork chops. The risotto with white truffles is suitably aromatic and incredibly low priced; of course, the truffles are already baked into the rice, not shaved on at the table the way the more expensive restaurants do it. Tiramisù and crème brûlée for the sweet tooth. ♦ Closed Monday. Piazza Cenci 70. 6864008

36 Palazzo Cenci The attractive 17th-century entrance to this vast palace with its sinister family story begins, unusually, with a flight of stairs, because the rest of the palace is built on a small hill, beneath which lie the ruins of **Circus Flaminio** (221 BC).

The Cenci family had immense wealth when **Beatrice**, one of **Francesco Cenci**'s 12 children, was born in 1577. When he was 45 years old, he was tried before the papal courts on a sodomy charge but was pardoned on payment of 100,000 *scudi*. He became embroiled with his sons over that and other financial matters, so he moved his second wife and Beatrice to a castle outside Rome that he had rented in 1595. He was known for his violent temper and brutality toward his family, and there were rumors that he committed incest with Beatrice. She found solace with the castle-keep, **Olimpio**, whom she, together with her stepmother and her 2 brothers, hired to kill her father while he was sleeping in the castle in 1598. Francesco was killed, and all were arrested. Beatrice and her stepmother were beheaded near the Pont Sant'Angelo and the Castel Sant'Angelo served as a grandstand for the papal court. Her brother **Giacomo** was tortured with hot pincers, bludgeoned to death with a mace, and then his body was drawn and quartered. Her other brother was sentenced to life imprisonment but pardoned after one year. The family's large property holdings were confiscated by the pope. This papal action sent a message to the noble families that they had to behave better than the Cencis. A lot of tales have been inspired by poor Beatrice, including one by **Shelley**.

A walk around the palace takes you up Vicolo dei Cenci to a square where the palace's main entrance (late 15th century) is located. There is a small courtyard with doric columns on 2 sides and a loggia above with ionic columns. The **Via Monte Cenci**, going uphill, has another facade and a family chapel where Francesco intended to bury Beatrice and Giacomo. Instead, a requiem Mass is said each year for them, on the date of their executions, 11 September. Within the palazzo, at Santa Maria dei Calderari 38 (6868377, 6543142), is the upmarket restaurant **Al Pompiere**. Though skirted by the Ghetto, the Cenci Palace was not included within the Ghetto's confines.

The Ghetto

Mrs. Tullia Zevi, president of the **Union of Italian Jewish Communities**, told RomeAC-CESS® that this quarter was chosen by **Pope Paul IV** in 1555 as the area where all Rome's Jews were obliged to live and do their business. Because it was so difficult to live in and so unhealthy—it was flooded most of the time—it was considered the best place in Rome to keep the Jews in the forced state of humiliation that was his objective. Following the example of the Venice ghetto, the Jews at that time were only allowed to deal in used clothing and furniture and were limited in the jewelry they could wear outside the ghetto—no more than 3 rings for the women and only one for the men. The gates were shut at night. The ghetto rules continued until the Napoleonic occupation, but they became more lenient after Pope Paul died in 1559. (He was buried secretly in the Vatican out of fear of a public demonstration against him for his oppressive reign.) After some research, loopholes in the Ghetto laws were found by both Jews and Italians.

Mrs. Zevi referred us to a document dated 162 years before the birth of Christ in which a delegation of Macabees (i.e. Jews) asked the Roman authorities for help against the Syrians, and she added *nothing has changed!* On the basis of such documents, Rome's Jewish community is considered the oldest in Europe, having been in continuous existence for over 2000 years. When **St. Peter** came to Rome he probably stayed in the Jewish quarter in Trastevere where there were approximately 30,000 fellow Greek-speaking Jews and 15 synagogues. All non-Romans were expected to reside in Trastevere in those times, but during the day they could circulate and do business everywhere. The leading actor in Nero's court theater was a Jew, as were some of the Empress Poppea's lovers. But most were honest merchants attracted to Rome, the hub of the Empire. The bulk of the Jewish community remained in Trastevere for centuries. Today the Jewish population in all of Italy is what it was in Nero's time in Rome. The Rome community is the largest, with over 14,000 Jews and 6 synagogues. About 2000 Jews still live in the Ghetto and another 3000 have their businesses or jobs here. Romans still go to the Ghetto for bargains found even in stores owned by non-Jews. Many non-Jewish foreigners have acquired elegant penthouses in the Ghetto. While the **Main Synagogue** is the only one in Rome's Ghetto, it actually represents 2 places of worship since the separate **Sephardic Synagogue** is situated under the Main Synagogue itself. Though over 200 Jews joined Mussolini's 1922 March on Rome when he seized power, Il Duce passed oppressive racial laws in 1938, under pressure from his ally Adolf Hitler. These were ignored by the general public but Jews did lose jobs, especially in the civil service and as teachers. Not until the German occupation of Rome in 1943 were 2091 Roman Jews deported to Germany. Only 15 returned. In 1944, the Nazis executed 335 Roman males, 75 of them Jews. Though private citizens, particularly priests and nuns, hid many of them during the German occupation, all Jews suffered to some extent under the Nazi regime. Today, the Ghetto takes on a different air only on important Jewish holy days. The Ghetto's main street is **Via del Portico d'Ottavia**.

Mrs. Zevi expects to open to the public one of the Jewish catacombs in which the ancestors of the community she now leads buried their dead from the 1st to the 4th centuries AD. She says there were originally 6 but 4 have disappeared and the 2 remaining catacombs are particularly important, as the tombal inscriptions are our only source of information on these ancient communities, which she described as not rich, but hard working. One of the extant Jewish catacombs is near the main

The Tiber

Christian catacombs (see page 146). But the one she is opening to the public, Mrs. Zevi told us with irony, is in the garden of Mussolini's former residence, **Villa Torlonia**. For more information, contact the Union of Italian Jewish Communities (Lungotevere Sanzio 9. 5803670; fax 5803677).

37 Piperno ★$$$ If you like the greasy double-fried specialty called Jewish cuisine in Rome, this is the emporium. It can be good if eaten piping hot, but it's decidedly not kosher. The *carciofi alla Giudea*, artichokes deep-fried until crunchy and bitable, are excellent. Other vegetables done that way are a matter of taste. Oxtail and baked lamb are typically Roman courses. ♦ Closed Monday, Sunday night, August, and from Christmas to New Year's Eve.

Via Monte de' Cenci 9. Reservations required. No credit cards. 6540629

38 Santa Maria del Pianto (St. Mary in Tears) (1612, **Nicolo Sebregondi**) Contains a fresco of the **Madonna** that was seen shedding tears on 10 January 1546, when the painting was on the Portico d'Ottavia walls. At the time, the weeping was seen as a reaction to a nearby riot, the nature of which is not recorded. However, by the time the church was built to protect and honor the weeping image, now on the main altar, it was decided that the Virgin was mournful because her fellow Jews had not been converted. The Romans required the Jews to assemble inside the church to listen to sermons during Lent. ♦ Via del Pianto

39 Lorenzo Manilio's House (1468) There are several Renaissance dwellings here, including this one renovated in 1497 by Lorenzo Manilio, who proudly described the event in a travertine stone inscription running the length of his house. (It says that he had put up the inscription in the 2221st year after Rome's founding.) *Manilus*, as he wrote his name in Latin, also decorated the facade above the doors with his Greek name and with pieces of antique carvings found on the Via Appia a few years earlier. Don't miss the Jewish pastry shop on the corner; it is one of the prides of the Ghetto. ♦ Via del Portico d'Ottavia 1

39 Menorah 85 This bookshop specializes in Jewish lore. ♦ Via de Portico d'Ottavia 1/A. 6879297

39 Uno ★★$$ The only real restaurant in Rome serving strictly kosher food. (A cafeteria called **Meeting Meal**, 4 doors away, serves fast food of which the chief rabbi approves.) Many Roman restaurants are decorating in "Italian Modern," meaning black designer chairs and lots of white. **Gianni Zarfati**'s cozy place is no exception. Here it is enlivened by large splashy paintings of Orthodox candelabras and other symbols. The house white is a serviceable dry *Frascatti Superiore*. As expected, here are the Jewish artichokes, *carcioffi alla Giudeia*, surprisingly, about the best in town. The artichoke hearts are really soft and succulent, while the leaves are crunchy-brittle. The secret is that Gianni cooks them twice. Boiled in oil, medium heat, until half done, then taken out and dried; when you order, they are refried in boiling oil for a few seconds. *Carne secca con rughetta* is a type of *bresaola* (dried beef) with arugola salad. The meat is cured on the premises. Even the *grissini* breadsticks are marvelously crisp and rabbi-approved. For pasta you could order fettucine *straccotte* (beef spare ribs with tomato and cauliflower over squares of pasta in a fish broth)—quite a light dish if unexciting. Whiting with broccoli is delicious; balls of deboned fish with vegtables are good for cholesterol counters. ♦ Closed Friday dinner, Saturday lunch. Via del Portico d'Ottavia 1/E. 6547937

Restaurants/Clubs: Red	**Hotels:** Blue
Shops/Parks: Green	**Sights/Culture:** Black

40 Turtle Fountain (1585, Tadeo Landini) Probably from a design by **Giacomo della Porta**. An exquisite Florentine delight would be an understatement for this fountain, which can never fail to give pleasure. It depicts 4 boys, each holding in one hand a pet dolphin who is happily squirting water; while with the other hand, each nudges a turtle to take a drink from the fountain's upper basin. Not to be missed. ♦ Piazza Mattei

41 Da Giggetto ★$ The poor man's Piperno, but more authentic. A rabbit warren of dining rooms with solid tables, solid Roman-Jewish food and stolid, humorless waiters. In addition to the batter-fried specialties, try the baked mozzarella (*alla carrozza*) or stuffed veal. ♦ Closed Monday and July. Via del Portico d'Ottavia 21A. Reservations recommended. 6861105

42 Portico d'Ottavia (146 BC, **Celius Metellius the Macedonian**) Revamped by the **Emperor Augustus** in 27 BC as part of a covered passageway that was to link his **Theater of Marcellus** to the **Theater of Pompey** (near today's Campo dei Fiori). Augustus dedicated it to his sister **Octavia**. It was once enhanced with statues on top. In the early centuries of the Christian era, Octavia's porch became a fish market and to the right of the arch is an inscription in Latin regulating fish measurements—if the fish were a certain length the part above the fin had to be given to the caretakers, presumably for a fish soup. In the 8th century, a pope used the porch as an entranceway to a church that he called **San Angelo in Pescheria**, the Angel of the Fish Mongers.

43 Madonna della Divina Pietà (Our Lady of Heavenly Mercy) Tiny church behind the synagogue that never seems to be open for services. However, it continues to fulfill what may have been its main purpose as described in the inscription (Old Testament, Isaiah, verse 2) over the door: *I spread out my hands all the day unto a rebellious people which walketh in a way that was not good after their own thoughts.* The inscription on the door facing the synagogue is in Latin and Hebrew, serving as a permanent, censorious wagging finger directed at the Roman Jews. More than 20 years after the death of Pope John XXIII, the inscription in the Bishop of Rome's city seems more than a little out of step. ♦ Via Portico d'Ottavia

Grattachecchi This strange name refers to the opportune little bars that spring up throughout the hot summer. They serve cool drinks and granita (shaved ice in a variety of flavors, including lemon, coffee, and mint, with sugar sprinkled on top)—the same treat the ancient Romans ate to cool off. Try:

Ponte Cestio (corner of the Tiber Island) Until 3 AM.

Ponte Garibaldi (Trastevere side) the oldest *grattachecchi* in Rome, dating back to 1913. Try the choreographic fruit mix. Until 3 AM.

Ponte Cavour (Lungotevere in Augusta) Special orange tamarind-and-peach mix. Until 1:30 AM.

44 Main Synagogue (1904, **Costa** and **Armani**) Built in the Assyrian-Babylonian style. On its Tiber flank is a plaque commemorating Jews deported by the Germans during World War II. The synagogue's museum of ritual objects used in Roman synagogues in the last 300 years comprises the **Permanent Exhibition of the Jewish Community of Rome**. ♦ M-F, Su 10AM-2PM. Lungotevere Cenci (entrance to the exhibition next to the synagogue) 6864648

On 13 April 1986 **Pope John Paul II** participated in a special service at Rome's central synagogue, marking the first recorded papal visit to a Jewish place of worship.

A curious fresco can be found in the **Oratory of St. Sylvester**, next to the **Santissimi Quattro Coronati** church, near the Colosseum. It shows **Pope Sylvester** standing side by side with Rome's chief rabbi and other Jews who had been called together by the **Emperor Constantine**.

Savelli   Orsini   Caetani

45 Theater of Marcellus (11 BC) Construction started under **Julius Caesar** and was finished under Augustus, who dedicated it to his nephew and son-in-law, Marcellus, the Emperor's heir apparent who died at 19 in 23 BC. About half of the theater's ruins are still visible. The other half, on the Tiber side, was either demolished in the 4th century AD, when the stones were needed to repair the Ponte Cestio, or in the 12th century, when the theater's hunky ruins were used as a family fortress. Three rich papal families (**Savelli, Orsini, Caetani**) subsequently built their palaces on top of or into the theater with the entrance on the Tiber side. Today there are very posh apartments atop the ruins. On the ancient Ro-

The Tiber

man side, the visible doric archways at ground level (there were originally 41 arches) were rented out as shops until 1932. ♦ Via del Teatro di Marcello

46 San Nicola in Carcere (1599, **Giacomo della Porta**) Built out of the ruins of 3 Roman temples the church was given the name *in carcere* (in prison) presumably because there was a prison nearby prior to the 12th century. The interior is disappointing. Used occasionally for chamber music concerts. ♦ Via del Teatro di Marcello

Piano is not a musical instrument, but a floor in a building. In an elevator, push 1 (*Primo Piano*) if you want to go up one floor. *Piano Terro*, or simply *T*, means ground floor. If you want to practice your scales, ask for a pianoforte.

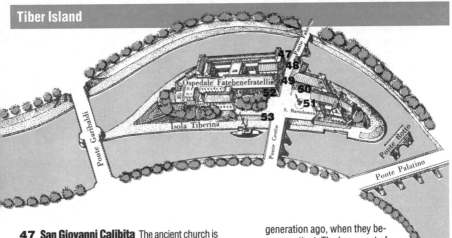

47 San Giovanni Calibita The ancient church is annexed to the hospital right opposite the Caetani Tower. Redone in the 18th century, it has a splendid marble interior and the best painting on the island, **Matia Preti**'s *The Flagellation of Christ.*

48 The Caetani Tower Built before the year 1000 by the **Pierleoni** family to command what was one of the main approaches to the city. The Pierleonis were Jewish in origin but produced a pope, **Anacletus II**, whose story is neatly embroidered in **Gertrud von Le Fort**'s novel *The Pope from the Ghetto.*

49 Sora Lella Trattoria $$ Located at the foot of the tower, this little restaurant run by its namesake, a vastly amiable matron who presides over the cash drawer and sees to it that the cuisine remains Roman. For the location alone, this quaint restaurant is worth mentioning. ♦ Closed Sunday. Via Ponte 4 Capi 16. Reservations recommended. No credit cards. 6861601

49 Alfonso's Bar Good coffee and sandwiches run by another imposing Roman, Alfonso, whose sideline is hiring out white limousines for weddings. (St. Bartolomeo is a favorite for romantically inclined, marriage-bent couples.) The adjacent mattress shop is the sole representative of the retail trade on the Island. ♦ Via Ponte 4 Capi

Tiber Island

50 Pierleoni-Caetani Castle In the Middle Ages, this served as a stronghold for the celebrated **Countess Matilda of Tuscany** and several fugitive popes. It became a Franciscan monastery in the 17th century, and after the unification of Italy it was a Jewish hospital and old folks home for 100 years. The municipal **Tiber Island History Museum** is to be here, to trace what its name implies and to preserve what is the third most important medieval monument in Rome after Castel Sant'Angelo and Torre delle Milizie.

50 Devotees of Jesus at Calvary On the front of the building, facing **Piazza S. Bartolomeo all'Isola**, an ornate doorway leads to the premises of this 18th-century marching and burial society. The red-hooded members held processions around the island until a

generation ago, when they became extinct. The basement of their oratory displays the bones of defunct members and of drowned bodies they recovered from the Tiber. Special permission needed for visiting.

51 Piazza San Bartolomeo In the middle of the square is a 19th-century monument commemorating Vatican Council I. San Bartolomeo has a deceptive Baroque facade that masks an ancient church built on the ruins of the **Temple of Aesculapius** around the year 1000 by the German emperor **Otto III**. He dedicated it to the memory of his friend **St. Adalbert of Prague**, whose altar stands in the millers' chapel where frescoes represent the floating flour mills that were moored around the island. Imagine getting your flour freshly milled daily—like espresso coffee today! A 12th-century wellhead on the steps to the main altar may be the last evidence of the medicinal spring that was always a feature of Aesculapius' temples.

51 Monastery The archway to the left of the church leads to a garden peopled with outsize, stylized religious sculptures that are the handiwork of **Father Martini**, one of 7 Franciscan monks who still serve San Bartolomeo. At the end of the garden, the River Police have their quarters in what used to be the city morgue. They have succeeded the Red Hoods in recovering bodies from the Tiber and rescuing people who fall or jump in.

52 Fatebenefratelli Hospital (Remodeled 1930) Occupying the entire upstream side of Tiber Island, this hospital is run by the **Order of St. John of God** (a Portuguese saint), whose monks established themselves here in the 16th century. It is known for its emergency ward, gynecology, and dermatology. Skin disorders are a recurrent theme in the island's healing tradition. Since the Middle Ages the tutelary saint here has been **St. Bartholomew**, who was martyred by flaying and by an association of ideas has skin complaints under his protection. In the 12th century, **Rahere**, favorite of **Henry II**, was cured of the itch on the island. On his return to England he founded **St. Bart's**, still one of the great London hospitals. San Bartolomeo and St. Bartholomew's celebrate their kinship with annual lectures and concerts given on Tiber Island.

The currents of international events have crossed the island unflaggingly all through its history. Besides Etruscans and Romans, Greeks, Jews, Germans, the English, Spanish, Portuguese, and the French have been here. Chinese and Arabic were taught by the Franciscans to prospective missionaries, and an American prophet of women's rights, the Transcendentalist **Margaret Fuller,** looked after the wounded at the Fatebenefratelli Hospital during the battles of the Roman Republic of 1848-1849 and sent her dispatches to the *New York Tribune* from the island in the Tiber.

53 Steps These lead down to the embankment, a place for one of the most romantic strolls in Rome, where concerts and dances are often held on summer nights. It combines dizzying vistas of millennial history and the sounds and sights of the lively young Roman fauna of today. Carved in the travertine blocks below the stairs is the stern (some say the bow) of a Roman galley with the bust of **Aesculapius** and his winged, twined serpents, **Caduceus,** all that remains visible of his temple. The idea of the island as a stone ship recalling the legend of the serpent has often been represented by artists. Ahead is a splendid view of the **Pons**

Fabricius with its dedicatory inscriptions. Beyond, toward the **Garibaldi Bridge**, the upstream end of the island has a pavement covered with spectacular contemporary graffiti on the theme of love.

54 Er Comparone ★★$$ The *er* (dialect for *il*) is the sign of a simple Roman restaurant without frills. But avoid those nearby traps where busloads of tourists go to experience Rome by night. This restaurant, with its large terrace for summer dining, serves authentic Roman fare, especially innards. Try the rigatoni *con pajata*; rigatoni are small macaroni and the *pajata* are lamb's intestines with the mother's milk curdled inside. Saturday is the traditional day to eat tripe in Rome, but you might find tripe or at least liver and sweetbreads here all week long. Charcoal-grilled meat is a specialty, and we suggest a *Dolcetto* red from Piedmont, but in Rome the open white wine is perfectly suitable even with meat courses. In the summer, especially, reserve a table on the terrace for a view of one of Rome's loveliest medieval houses. ♦ Closed Monday. Piazza in Piscinula 47. 5816249

55 Sandra Kennedy Coiffure Down a small medieval street near Santa Cecilia Church, a sassy Australian with golden scissors cuts hair superbly. For men and women. ♦ Via di Santa Cecilia 10. No credit cards. 5895793

56 Temple of Vesta (2nd century) Oldest standing marble temple in Rome, with 20 Corinthian columns and a cylindrical cell inside. It became a medieval church, **St. Stephen of the Carts**, so named perhaps because the ancient produce market was nearby. This pretty little temple has been misnamed for centuries because its circular form resembles the temple in the Roman Forum dedicated to Vesta—to whom this one has no connection. An inscription recently brought to light says that it was dedicated to **Hercules the**

Conqueror. A Baroque fountain (1715) stands nearby in this minipark. ♦ Piazza Bocca della Verità

57 Temple of Virile Fortune (2nd century BC) Strong Greek influence in design. Converted to a church in the 9th century, later became the official church of the Armenian community. The name it is best known by is incorrect but no male chauvinist will ever let that name vanish. It is now thought to have been a temple dedicated to **Portunus**, who in the Dark Ages became **Fortunus**, a river god. ♦ Piazza Bocca della Verità

58 Arch of Janus (Arco di Giano) (4th century AD) Janus was the god who protected crossroads. This is not the Emperor Constantine's triumphal arch, but a covering built at the same time to protect travelers at this important junction between the **Forum Boarium** (the ancient cattle market and the oldest of the fora), which occupied the present **Piazza Bocca della Verità**, and the **Forum Olitorio** (vegetable and fruit market in ancient times), a religiously important area north of here and the Roman Forum itself. ♦ Via del Velabro

59 Arch of the Money Changers (Arco degli Argentari) (AD 204) The guild of the money changers built this to honor the emperor **Septimius Severus**, his wife, **Domna**, and his 2 children, **Geta** and **Caracalla**—all of whom are depicted here in sculptured relief in the act of making a sacrificial offering in front of a tripod. Later, Caracalla killed his sister, so his portrait was broken off. This arch is now leaning against the corner of the adjacent church. ♦ Via del Velabro

Tiber Island

59 San Giorgio in Velabro (7th century with 12th-century portico and bell tower) The 13th-century altar has mosaic decorations by the **Cosmatis**; a fresco of Christ, the Virgin Mary, and 3 saints is from the school of **Pietro Cavallini** (1295). The charm of this carefully restored medieval jewel is its utter simplicity—so far from the richness that later became associated with churches in Rome and with monochrome gray sobriety. ♦ Via del Velabro

60 Palazzo al Velabro Residence $$ An apartment hotel built into a 16th-century palace. The elegance has remained and all modern conveniences have been added. Two- and 3-room apartments, each with kitchenette and direct phone. Available for a minimum of one week, no maximum. ♦ Via del Velabro 16 (just up the inclined street from the Arch of Janus) No credit cards. 6792758, 6793450; fax 6793790

61 Santa Maria in Cosmedin (6th century) Built on temples dedicated to **Hercules** and **Ceres**. Enlarged by **Pope Hadrian I** in the 7th century as the official church of the Greek community. (Via della Greca is the street to the right side of the church.) Uncertainty remains about the Cosmedin in the name, as it is Greek for ornament or embellishment (i.e. cosmetics). The facade (1899) is largely the work of **G.B. Giovenale** The 12th-century belfry, 7 stories tall, is the highest and most elegant of any ancient church in Rome. Embedded in the 12th-century portico (porch) on the left-hand wall is what may be the most famous stone manhole cover in the world. It was carved as a giant theatrical mask to cover a drain, enabling the water to enter through the hole of the figure's mouth. Some centuries ago, it was given the name **Bocca della Verità**

(the Mouth of Truth) along with the legend that if any liar put his hand in the mouth it would be chopped off. Another legend has it that a priest with a wooden cane would stand behind the Bocca della Verità and swat the hands thrust into the mouth by people known to be lying; we do not know whether this lie-detector test was sanctioned by church authorities. Mothers still bring their children for the test as do suspicious wives their husbands. No hands have been lost.

The church's interior has no major art but is considered a jewel of medieval church architecture. The crypt is a pagan hall. The polychrome mosaics in the floor and balustrade are by the studio of the famous Cosmati family, who, from the 12th to the 14th centuries, decorated churches all over Italy with ancient marble arranged in geometric shapes. ♦ Piazza Bocca della Verità

62 Alvaro al Circo Massimo ★★★$$$ Alvaro is the rotund and angelic host who welcomes you to this attractive but simply decorated tavern. Look carefully at the spread on your left as you enter: fresh fish and shellfish, today's vegetables and fruit, plus a few specialties you'll have to ask about as they are changed daily. The antipasto *di mare* (seafood salad) is memorable, as are the whitebait marinated in oil. Try Alvaro's pasta of the day with seafood; and if you still have room in your stomach and pocketbook, have the sea bass grilled with prawns on the side. There are only a dozen tables and a few more outside in the summer, so do phone ahead (some people call from America before flying to Rome). ♦ Closed Monday and half of August. Via dei Cerchi 53. Reservations recommended. No credit cards. 6786112

63 Circus Maximus (2nd century BC) Not where the movie *Ben Hur* was filmed, but where Ben actually raced his chariots a couple thousand years ago. This vast tract (2 football fields in width and a half-mile long) was ringed with marble bleachers from which 250,000 Romans screamed their encouragement. The emperor watched from his ornate box at the foot of the **Palatine Palace** and the magistrates, who refereed the races, had a special stand at the end nearest the Tiber River. Down the center ran the *spina* (spine), with obelisks to mark where the chariots had to wheel around and race in the other direction. Behind the stands were marble stables for the specially bred horses of the 4 color-coded teams that raced the golden chariots. Betting was the raison d'être of this stadium; Romans wagered fortunes on their favorites. The day's events might include races of 1-, 2-, 3-, and 4-horse chariots and there was the possibility, depending on who was currently emperor, that a losing charioteer might be put to death. The importance attached to these races makes the Indianapolis speedway seem tame. But all that remains is a vast grassy arena, with some ancient benches being excavated at the end furthest from the river. ♦ Via del Circo Massimo

Bests

Maria di Mase

What I like about Rome are its bridges on the **Tiber River**. Because the Tiber was regarded as a god, the river crossings were overseen by priests, which is why they were called *pontiffs*, meaning builders of bridges.

I especially like the **Ponte Sant'Angelo**, which was once named Ponte Elio. Emperor Hadrian, poet, artist, and architect, whose curiosity pushed him to spend most of his life traveling throughout the Empire, ordered the building of this bridge. There are new parapets surmounted by 10 angels with the symbols of Christ's passion designed by Bernini. The bridge provides a beautiful view of Rome. Another bridge from which one can enjoy a beautiful view is the **Ponte Cestio** that connects to the Tiber Island: seat of the Cult of the god, where one can admire the **Temple of Vesta** as well as the **Aventine** and **Gianicolo Hills**.

Milton Gendel
Art critic and idealogue of Tiber Island History Museum

Tiber Island is the most picturesque place in a city, with the highest rating for visual romanticism. The city rose at the river's only easy crossing point between Etruria to the north and the Latin lands to the south. Just downstream, Horatio held the bridge against the Etruscans—not so successfully after all, since they managed to king it over the Romans for generations.

Always known as a place of healing, the island entered medical history in 293 BC. Faced by an unabating plague, the Roman Senate sent a 12-man commission to Greece to consult the priests of the medical god, Aesculapius. On their return to Rome, the miracle-dispensing snake they were bringing back plunged overboard as their ship came abreast of the Tiber Island. Where the snake landed, the Temple of Aesculapius was built, and there it stood, serving as a hospital for many centuries until it was replaced

Tiber Island

by the forerunner of the present **Church of San Bartolomeo**—whose name is also used as an alternative appelation for the island.

In early times, the **Roman Forum** was a marsh between four of the **Seven Hills of Rome**: the Palatine, Caelius, Capitoline, and Esquiline (the other 3 are the Aventine, Quirinal, and Viminal). The **Cloaca Maxima** (a series of large underground water conduits) syphoned off all the water from the marshy Forum fields and provided the landfill on which the center of ancient Rome was built. The mouth of this amazing engineering feat can still be seen (it's almost as tall as the average man) on the Tiber banks near the Temple of Vesta, below the Ponte Palatino.

The city of all time, and of all the world.
Nathaniel Hawthorne

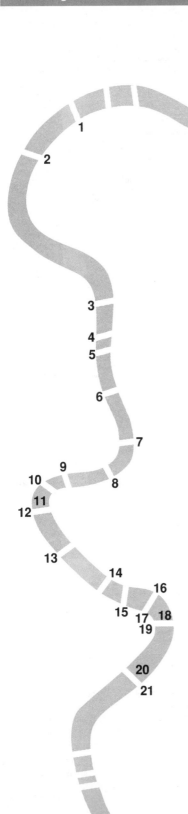

1 Ponte Milvio (Rebuilt 109 BC) This bridge played a strategic role in ancient times as it was the northern gateway to the consular roads of Flaminius, Cassius, Salaria, Clodia, and Veintana. It was also part of the **Aurelain Walls** fortification. The great battle of **Saxa Rubra** (AD 312), a decisive victory for **Constantine**, ended when **Maxentius** was killed on this bridge. The bridge has since been rebuilt and refortified often; the last 2 times were in 1805 by **Valadier**, and in 1850 under **Pius IX** after **Garibaldi** had blown up part of it to stop the French invasion. Vehicular traffic was abolished in 1980.

2 Ponte Duca D'Aosta (1939, **Vincente Fasolo** and **Antonio Aureli**) From the Foro Italico, a sports arena built under **Mussolini**, to the Lungotevere Flaminio. The bridge architecture, like the arena, is Fascist-style—massive, classically inspired, and pompous.

3 Ponte del Risorgimento (1910, **François Hennebique**) From Viale Mazzini to Piazza Belle Arti and on to Viale Belle Arti as it passes the Villa Giulia Etruscan Museum. The Risorgimento (Rebirth, or Resurging), Italy's 19th-century nationalist movement, led to the unification of the Italian states in 1870. Many of the Tiber bridges are named after the political leaders of this period, including the 3 great heroes: **Mazzini, Garibaldi, Cavour.**

4 Ponte Matteotti (1929, **A. Antonelli**) From Piazza Cinque Giornate to the Naval Ministry. Named after **Giacomo Matteotti**, a popular Socialist politician who was assassinated by Mussolini's brownshirted thugs in 1923 at the beginning of the Mussolini era. The public outcry for the Fascists to step down almost caused their demise, but instead **Mussolini** initiated a crackdown that abolished all remaining semblances of democratic government.

5 Ponte del Metropolitana Rome's youngest bridge, it carries the subway to 2 stations on the Vatican side of the Tiber.

6 Ponte Regina Margherita From Via Cola di Rienzo, a shopping street, on the Vatican side of the river to Piazza del Popolo. Named for **Queen Margherita**, who was only 19 when she married Italy's future **King Umberto I** in 1868. As the de facto queen—her father-in-law was a widower—she came to Rome to grace state occasions. When she was widowed in 1900, she moved to Palazzo Margherita (now the American Embassy), where she continued her sumptuous lifestyle.

7 Ponte Cavour (1901, **A. Vescovali**) From Via Colonna to the Ara Pacis. Named after **Count Camillo Benso Cavour** (1810-61), who was born in Turin, capital of Piedmont. Influenced by the French revolution of 1830, he started *Il Risorgimento* (the Rebirth, or Resurging), a newspaper in which he advocated a unified Italy with a constitutional monarchy. By 1848 a general frenzy for constitutional government broke into war in Italy and throughout Europe. Rulers were forced to let their subjects form some sort of self-government. Cavour masterminded the whole Italian unification as the prime minister of Piedmont, but he didn't live to see his dream come wholly true; he died in 1861. He was the greatest figure of the Risorgimento movement, which culminated in Italy's unification with the invasion of Rome in 1870.

8 Ponte Umberto I (1895, **Angelo Vescovali**) From Palazzo della Giustizia to Via Zanardelli and the Napoleonic Museum. Umberto I was the second member from the royal Savoia family to become king of Italy. He came to power in 1878, when his father, **Vittorio Emanuele II**, died, and reigned until he was assassinated in 1900.

9 Ponte Sant'Angelo (AD 134, **Hadrian**) Built by Emperor Hadrian to connect the city proper with his mausoleum (now Castel Sant'Angelo). After the bridge collapsed in the Holy Year of 1450, **Pope Nicholas V** rebuilt it. Another notorious event in the bridge's history was the execution of **Beatrice Cenci**. She and her mother and brother were incarcerated in the dreaded Tor di Nona prison after she killed her father, a cruel sadistic man who had terrorized his family and was rumored to have raped Beatrice. The entrance to this bridge was the site of her execution for the crime of patricide. In spite of its tragic history, this is the most beautiful of all the bridges; **Bernini** and his school sculpted the 10 angel statues between 1598 and 1660. Ideal "photo opportunity."

10 Ponte Vittorio Emanuele (1911) Stretches from Corso Vittorio Emanuele to Via della Conciliazione. Although **Vittorio Emanuele I** was king of the new state, Rome was by no means ready to welcome him with open arms. When he arrived on New Year's Eve 1870, he drove to his new residence at the Quirinal Palace, but the pope, who had left only the day before, had locked the palace and taken the key. The new king had to ask a locksmith to break open the door. What an inauspicious beginning for a new reign.

11 Pons Neronianus When it existed, this bridge was named for **Nero**, who reigned AD 54-68. It went from Campus Martius (the parade ground area between Corso Vittorio Emanuele and Piazza del Popolo) to the Vatican meadows (now the Hospital Santo Spirito in Sassia). Nero had his Circus just to the left of where St. Peter's Basilica now stands and needed a bridge to get there. The bridge fell down in the Middle Ages when there was a particularly high flood of the Tiber. One can still see the bridge foundation when the water level is low. The bridge was also called **Pons Vaticanus**.

12 Ponte Principe Amadeo di Savoia Aosta (Late 19th century) Named for **Prince Amadeo**, a member of the Savoia family from Piedmont. The bridge runs from the tunnel and Hospital Santa Spirito in Sassia on the Vatican side of the river to Via Giulia and Corso Vittorio Emanuele on the other.

13 Ponte Mazzini (Late 19th century) From the Regina Coeli Jail to Carerra Nuova on Via Giulia. Named after **Giuseppe Mazzini** (1805-72), who started his political career by joining the **Carbonari**, a secret society of patriots. While imprisoned for his activities with the Carbonari, he crystalized his decision to liberate Italy from foreign and domestic tyranny. From 1832 on, he lived a clandestine life, often in prison, and incited abortive revolutionary movements in Sardinia, Genoa, and Savoia. In 1848, he was one of the triumvirate that administered Rome for the brief time that city was a republic (when the pope fled during **Garibaldi's** abortive invasion). He wrote many papers on freedom as well as a letter urging Vittorio Emanuele to lead Italy to unity. In 1865, he was elected delegate from Messina. In 1870, 2 years before his death, he saw his dream become a reality—Italy was a unified country, ruled by **Vittorio Emanuele II**.

14 Ponte Sisto (Pons Aurelius) (4th or 5th century AD) Built during the late Roman Empire. After it was damaged in 1772, **Pope Sixtus IV** finally rebuilt it in preparation for Holy Year in 1475; it was subsequently renamed in his honor. Many Christian martyrs were thrown from this bridge into the Tiber. Superstition has it that you can only have good luck if you see a white horse, an old woman, and a priest crossing the bridge at the same time.

15 Ponte Garibaldi Named after **Giuseppe Garibaldi** (1807-82), a patriot who worked for national unity. He defended Rome from the French when the pope ran away in 1849. After several victories throughout Italy, the conquest

of Rome remained the major obstacle to unification. In 1861, his cry of *Roma o Morte* (Rome or Death) went unheeded as **Cavour** felt the timing wasn't right. Finally in 1867, he realized his dream of marching on Rome, but was defeated by papal troops aided by the French, and then exiled to Caprera. In 1870 he fought alongside the French against the Germans in the Franco-Prussian War. In that same year Rome was finally conquered, and by 31 December, **Victor Emmanuel II** of Piedmont had arrived in Rome to rule Italy. Garibaldi, Cavour, and Mazzini were the 3 who made the Italian unity a reality.

16 Pons Fabricius (Fabricio) (62 BC) This stone bridge, which links the left bank to the island, is the best preserved of the old bridges with much of its original structure still intact. In the Middle Ages it was also called **Pons Iudaeorum** because of its proximity to the Ghetto. The present parapet was added in 1679 under **Pope Innocent XI**. The original balustrade was bronze.

17 Pons Cestius (Cestio) (30 BC, **Cestius**) Today it's called **Ponte San Bartolomeo**. It was the first stone bridge from the island to the right bank (Trastevere). The pedestals had statues depicting the emperors **Valens** and **Gration**, who rebuilt the bridge in AD 369. It was reinforced from the 12th to the 18th centuries at various times. When the embankments were constructed in 1888, part of the bridge was yet again rebuilt, faithfully copying the old form.

18 Ponte Rotto (Pons Aemillus) The construction of this bridge was begun in 179 BC by **Fulvius Nobillor** and **Aemilius Lepidus**. Though the bridge itself was made of wood, they used stone to build the piers making this Rome's first stone bridge. **Scipio Africanus** and **Minuclus** finished the construction with stone arches in 146 BC. Today it's called *The Broken Bridge*, as only one arch remains.

19 Ponte Palatino This bridge stretches from Lungotevere Ripa to Lungotevere Pierleoni and is located right opposite the beautiful Temple of Fortuna Virili. The view of Tiber Island from the bridge enables you to see why the ancient Romans described it as the bow of a ship. The Ponte Rotto can also be seen best from this vantage point. Cross to the other side (if the cars don't mow you down—be especially careful as they are driving on the left here!) and look down to the water's edge, on your right, at the 2500-year-old **Cloaca Maxima**, the large arched opening of an underground drainage canal. In 600 BC, this great Etruscan engineering feat—a mighty drain built belowground to dry up the Roman Forum—diverted 7 underground streams, which in turn carried all the sewage away to the river. This drain is still in existence and functioning well as it keeps the Forum dry underfoot.

20 Pons Sublicius (c. 600 BC, **King Ancus Marcius**) The very first bridge to cross the Tiber in Rome helped to develop good relations between the Romans on the Palatine and the Etruscans on the right bank. Though the original bridge is no longer standing, it was built only of wood so that in the event of an attack it could be quickly scuttled to prevent the enemy from crossing. This bridge is the most historically famous—it was here that **Horatio** and his 2 companions held the bridge against the Etruscans.

21 Ponte Aventino From Porta Portese to Via della Marmorata. The modern maps also call it **Ponte Sublicio**. There is some discrepancy about where the first Pons Sublicius really was located.

Pons Caligulae A footbridge linking the Royal Palace on the Palatine with the most important place of worship, the **Temple of Jupiter** on the Capitoline Hill. It was torn down when **Caligula** was murdered.

Highlights

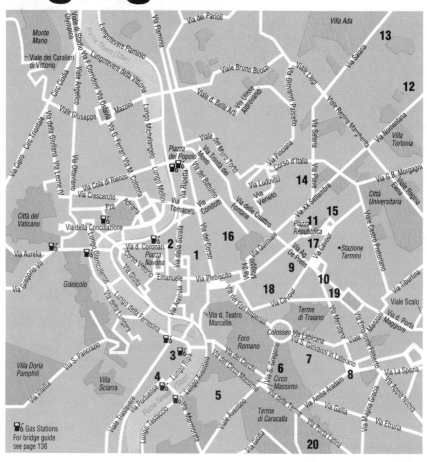

At the Piazza Sant'Ignazio:

Chiesa di Sant'Ignazio de Loyola (1626–1650, **Padre Orazio Grassi**) This church is named after the founder of the Jesuit order—he was a soldier and a saint! The Society of Jesus (Jesuit) has its main church, **Chiesa del Gesù**, nearby in Piazza del Gesù. The church is fittingly severe on the outside but really takes off inside in its rich splendor. The vaulted ceiling with a trompe l'oeil fresco depicting St. Ignazio entering paradise was painted by **Padre Andrea Pozzo**. His work makes the dome seem a hundred times higher than its actual size. Stand half way up the nave on the disk for the best view. Don't miss the lapis lazuli urn with relics of **St. Luigi Ganzaga** and the Baroque altar.

Nearby is another Jesuit stronghold, the little **Oratory of Caravita**, on the street of the same name. Less than 100 years ago, during Lent, the faithful were issued whips once the service had commenced. When the candles were snuffed out and the priest exhorted them from the pulpit, the congregation would disrobe their upper bodies (under cover of darkness)

1 Piazza Sant'Ignazio (1727, **Raguzzini**) The ultimate example of Baroque architecture, perhaps because it is on an accessible human scale. All the houses facing the church are harmonious and almost perfectly symmetrical. This is far and away the favorite Roman square among architects.

and flagellate themselves screaming or whimpering *Blessed Mary, forgive us.*

Le Cave di Sant'Ignazio ★★★$$$ A pizzeria at night, a regular restaurant during the day, this marvelous place can be full of tourists outside in the summer and packed with the old regulars inside. There's always a good sprinkling of parliamentarians as the House of Deputies is just around the corner. The place feels like a club: old men sit in corners, their silver-topped canes by their sides, as they pass around a bag of newly picked and freshly roasted chestnuts during the winter months. They banter with the owner or chat with another regular—perhaps the **Contessa**, who seems to spend every other evening here. The waiters know what she wants so well that she doesn't even have to order. If you are not a regular, you might be impressed with the wonderful display of fresh fish. It is brought from Fiumicino every evening at 7PM. The variety of starters are delicious—*ovolini di bufalo* (small egglike mozzarellas from buffalo milk), *focaccia* (a puffed up and crispy bread package), *suppli* (rice with meat or egg rolled in breadcrumbs and fried). Spaghetti and prawns with a light grazing of tomato sauce is one of the most delicious dishes. ♦ Closed Sunday. Piazza Sant'Ignazio 169. Reservations recommended. 6797821

2 Via dei Coronari A lovely meander down the antiques capital of the capital. Almost every shop here has some high-quality specialty: Baroque bookcases, Roman columns, an emperor's marble bust, inlaid wood, Neapolitan silver. As you wander from shop to shop, duck into the medieval cloister of the **Church of San Salvatore in Lauro**; the entrance is just to the left of the church at Piazza San Salvatore in Lauro 14. Then continue along toward Via di Panico, so named because an executioner lived here. Before you get to this street glimpse through the gate to **Palazzo Taverna**, just on your left up a ramp. Walk in if it's open; otherwise, try the main entry at the top of Via di Panico, at Via di Monte 36. The palazzo's tower, built in the 12th century, was mentioned in **Dante**'s *Inferno*. This palatial stronghold passed through several families, including the **Giordano** and the **Orsini**. See if you can spot the 2 marble bears that are enthroned in the bushes on either side of the present fountain. The bear is the logical family crest for the Orsinis as *orso* means bear.

3 Santa Cecilia in Trastevere (5th century AD; entrance by **A. Fuga**, 1725) This church was built above the house of **Valerianus**, a Roman patrician and husband of **Cecilia**. They were both martyred and made saints. Some historians believe that they were martyred under **Emperor Diocletian** around AD 303, but others believe that they were martyred much earlier, under **Marcus Aurelius**. Cecilia tried to kill herself by suffocation in her bath but was found alive. Then an executioner tried to chop off her head 3 times, but that also failed. She remained alive for 3

days, converting more people to Christianity before she finally died of her wounds. Go through the Baroque entrance and you will enter a vast garden. Pass the garden and walk into the church. Much of the original architecture has been ruined by reinforcements made in the 19th century. But many fine works of art still remain: the bell tower dates from 1113; there is a statue of Saint Cecilia by **Stefano Maderno** (1618); and a mosaic by **Pasquale** from the 9th century. ♦ Piazza di Santa Cecilia

4 Porta Portese Sunday Market Particularly noteworthy at this flea market are the wrought iron, the Neopolitan peasant furniture, the small glass chandeliers, the 19th-century brass odds and ends—and at **Malta** and **Pier Luigi**'s great stand, find 18th- and 19th-century boxes, bronzes, Tantric images, and furniture from India.

The entrance to Porta Portese is interesting for a couple of reasons: it is the exit from Rome through the city walls and is the site of the **Papal Arsenal** (the big building on the left), cautiously installed on the outside of the city in case there were any problems! ♦ Su 8AM-1PM

Places to eat nearby:

Panzanera, Hosteria and Pizzeria ★$$ After a tiring Sunday morning at the flea market, this is a good place to eat. Wine, lightly fermented grape juice, and delicious, simple things to sample. The sausage hanging from the ceiling as part of the decoration is sliced off before your eyes and put on your plate. *Ovolini di buffala* (miniature mozzarellas), great hunks of Castelli country bread, ravioli with spinach and ricotta, succulent fruit tart, and at night, pizza. ♦ Closed Wednesday. Viale Trastevere 84. No credit cards. 5818545

Oceano ★$$ Chinese/Malay restaurant. Sweet-and-sour pork, spring rolls, and excellent spicy Malay specialties. Fried bananas and apple crisp for dessert. ♦ Closed Monday. Viale Trastevere 132. No credit cards. 5817010

Da Albino il Sardo ★★★$$ A tall, dark, and handsome Scandinavian offers homemade ravioli, wild boar, Cannonau red. ♦ Closed Monday. Via della Luce 44. 5800846

5 Santa Prisca (4th century; facade, 1660 **C. Lombardi**) The rich history of this church makes it worthy of a visit even if the exterior architecture seems a bit drab. It was built in the 4th century over the house of **Aquila** and **Prisca**, mentioned in the Epistles of St. Paul. The Normans destroyed the church but it was rebuilt in 1456 and 1660. The antequarium is in the Roman house under the church, with one of Rome's best preserved **Temples of Mithras**, the pre-Christian cult (see **San Clemente Church** on page 32). The frescoes were discovered in 1940 and Dutch archeologists painstakingly put the fragments together to give new insight into this cult. ♦ M-F 10AM-noon. Piazza di Santa Prisca (Clivo dei Publicii)

6 Basilica Celimontana dei Santi Giovanni e Paolo Martiri (AD 410) The story behind the history of this church reads like a detective thriller. Two officers of the ancient Roman Imperial Army who were also functionaries of the State—the brothers **Giovanni** and **Paolo**—were converted to Christianity. They came from a wealthy noble family that owned a beautiful house near the **Temple of Claudius**, overlooking the valley of the **Colosseum** and the adjacent **Palatine** hill—one of the lovelier parts of Rome where real estate was at a premium. They followed Christ's teachings to the letter by giving away all that they had to the poor. They lived during the reign of **Julian the Apostate** (AD 361-363), the emperor who tried to turn the world back to paganism. The 2 brothers' action rubbed a lot of people the wrong way and took on political significance as flagrant nonsubmission to the Emperor's authority. Late one night, assassins broke into the brothers' house, killed them, and hid their bodies. Fearing their crime might be uncovered, the murderers also killed 2 other Christians, **Crispiano** and **Benedetta**, who learned of the killings and had begun to spread the word. The martyrdom earned the 2 brothers the titles of **Saints John** and **Paul**. One hundred years later **Pammachius** built an early Christian basilica above the 2 brothers' house where they had been buried—an exception to the Roman rule that burial had to be outside the city. There were many reconstructions in the 11th and 12th centuries, and the church's interior was redesigned in 1718 by **A. Garagni**. Thus, in **Clivo di Scauro**, a beautiful medieval square off Via di San Gregorio—not far from the Colosseum—stand the tombs, house, and basilica of these early Christian martyrs.

7 Santi Quattro Coronati (Church of the Four Crowned Saints) (4th century) Named after 4 Roman soldiers who were martyred: **Severo, Severiano, Carpoforo**, and **Vittorino**. To get to this church you must pass an ancient medieval tower, go across a courtyard, and follow the wall of the ancient convent where many popes lived. The church was used as part of a fortress during the Middle Ages to protect the popes in the nearby Lateran Palace. It was enlarged in the 7th and 9th centuries, ravaged by the Normans in 1084, and received its latest restructuring in 1914. Antique granite columns divide the church into 3 naves. A superb little 13th-century cloister, with capitals sculpted into lily leaves, lies beyond. The **Oratory of San Silvestro** has a lovely fresco painted in 1246. ♦ Via dei Santi Quattro Coronati ("SS Quatro Coronati")

8 San Giovanni in Laterano Basilica and Palace Complex A whole book could be written on the history of this church. In our limited space suffice it to say that it was the seat of the **Patriarchate**; the popes lived in the Lateran Palace until the 14th century. When the pope moved to Avignon in 1305, the building fell into ruin and started to crumble away. When the papacy returned to Rome the old building was uninhabitable, so the papal palace was moved to the Vatican. The oldest obelisk in Rome, dating from the 15th century BC,

stands in the square. It was brought from Egypt to Rome by **Emperor Constantius II** in AD 357 and put in the middle of the Circus Maximus. After it was found broken into 3 pieces **Pope Sixtus V** brought the obelisk to its present site in 1587 and destroyed the old Palace of the Patriarchate.

Within the San Giovanni in Laterano Basilica and Palace Complex:

Basilica (Facade, 1736 **A. Galilei**) The first basilica was built by **Constantine**, above the barracks of his private guards. Through the ages, the building suffered from invading armies, earthquakes, and fires. **Borromini** completely redesigned the interior in 1646. Don't miss the bronze doors (from the Senate House), or the fragment of a **Giotto** fresco, or the glittering marble floor made of ancient scraps arranged in beautiful patterns like a mosaic. ♦ Daily 7AM-7PM

The Baptistry Built on the baths of the private house of **Fausta**, Constantine's second wife. The first Christian baptism in Rome was held here in these baths. The baptisms used to involve total immersion of the body, so the practice of using separate baths or at least separate buildings evolved. Constantine's first building was rebuilt during the reign of **Pope Sixtus III** (432-440). Eight porphyry columns surround the font—porphyry, the rarest marble, looks like dense red paint dotted with beige speckles. Marble reserves from the mine were exhausted in 300 BC. Don't miss the bronze music doors; they make a strange plaintive sound when they are moved. It is rumored that they come from the **Baths of Caracalla**. ♦ Daily 8AM-noon, 3PM-dusk

For a swim and a sandwich in the height of summer, visit the Hotel Villa (next to the gardens of Villa Pamphilli), the Hilton Hotel, or Hotel Aldrovandi.

The Cloisters (1230) Enter on the left aisle through a small doorway. These beautiful arcades were built by the **Cosmati** family. Each pillar seems to have a different shape, with contrasting mosaic patterns sparkling on their twisted stems and capitals. The harmony of gold, red, green, and white with a garden courtyard in the background make this a haven from the noisy bustle of the world outside. ♦ Daily 9AM-6PM

Scala Santa The only remaining part of the original palace with the private chapel of the popes—the *Sanctum Sanctorum*. It was built on the site of the house of **Empress Fausta**, probably by **Pope Sylvester** (314-335), after the Empress' death. Tradition requires Roman Catholics to go up these stairs on their knees. The pope's private chapel is full of lovely Byzantine mosaics. ♦ Daily 6AM-noon, 2:30-7PM. Piazza di San Giovanni in Laterano

9 Santa Pudenziana (AD 384, **Pope Siricius**) Once thought to have been a church built on top of **Senator Pudens' House**—whose daughter was baptized by **St. Peter** when he

stayed with the family. Later the building was discovered to be a 2nd-century Roman bath converted into a church in the late 4th century. It is possible that Pudens' house was here before the baths. Santa Pudenziana remains an old and beautiful church. **Pope Hadrian** (AD 772-795) did some restoration work, as did **Cardinal Caetani** in 1588. If the church is closed, ring at the door on the left. ♦ Via Urbana at the bottom of Piazza dell'Esquilino

Restaurants/Clubs: Red   **Hotels:** Blue
Shops/Parks: Green   **Sights/Culture:** Black

10 Santa Maria Maggiore One of Rome's 4 major basilicas located at the top of the Esquiline, one of the Seven Hills of Rome. Though the **Ferdinando Fuga** facade (1743-1750) is majestic, the real splendor lies within: a perfectly proportioned nave, equal in width and height, and wonderful 5th-century mosaics that are among the finest and oldest in all of Rome. The ceiling coffers are gilded with some of the first gold to arrive from Peru.

Originally built by **Sixtus III** (432-440), it was rebuilt in the 12th, 16th, 17th, and 18th centuries.

The mosaics are extraordinary, beginning with scenes from Genesis and Abraham on the left side toward the chancel and moving through scenes of Jacob, Moses, and Joshua. The **Sfora Chapel** on the left was probably based on designs by **Michelangelo**. ♦ Piazza di Santa Maria Maggiore

11 Baths of Diocletian (AD 298) There were 9026 baths in Rome in AD 540 according to the chronicles of **Cardinal Mai**, who visited the abandoned city after the Fall of the Roman Empire. Presumably this record includes the private ones as well as the public ones. He also noted *324 streets, 2 capitols—the Tarpeian and the Quirinal, 80 gilt statues of the gods* [only the Hercules remains], *66 ivory statues of the gods, 46,608 houses, 17,097 palaces, 13,052 fountains, 3785 statues of emperors and generals in bronze, 22 great equestrian statues of bronze* [only the Marcus Aurelius remains], *2 colossi (Marcus Aurelius and Trajan), 31 theaters, and 8 amphitheaters.*

The Romans liked bathing as much as contemporary Americans like showering. But the **rite of the bath** was much more complete in their day than ours. **Diocletian's Baths** were among the latest and largest—he probably felt he had to outdo **Caracalla**. Roman baths were not just places to wash but also to exercise and work up a sweat, with ball games, wrestling and athletics. There were also gardens and porticoes for older people to stroll about, and, of course, massages and saunas were also provided. Finally, for the mind and soul, there were libraries, sculpture gardens, and theaters.

The Baths of Diocletian were so vast that today the area includes **Museo delle Terme** with its gardens, the **Church of Santa Maria degli Angeli**, and the **Piazza della Repubblica**, with restaurants, edifices, and living quarters for functionaries.

Within the area of the Baths of Diocletian:

Museo delle Terme (National Museum of Rome) Called the finest collection of antique sculpture and mosaics in the world. The first 7 rooms are part of the frigidarium and are filled with superb sarcophagi. Two large mosaics are worth noting, one of Africa with Pigmies running about is quite amazingly true-to-life; the shapes of the bodies and the colors are right on. The mosaic of chariot races is very exciting, especially as it has a portrait of the horse **Itala**, famous throughout the country as fortunes were won and lost on him. The next huge area once housed the open-air swimming pool—a vast body of water that mirrored the niches with statues in them. Go to the bar, have coffee, and catch your breath; thus refreshed you will be able to continue. Next is the **Ludovisi** collection, so named because it was collected by the Ludovisi princes. Don't miss the Greek throne, or was it an altar? It dates from the 5th century BC and perhaps was **Aphrodite**'s chair from her temple of **Erice**—a mountain pinnacle of startling grandeur in western Sicily called *Magna Grecia* in those days. ◆ Tu-Sa 9AM-1:30PM; Su 9AM-12:30PM. Viale delle Terme. 460856

Santa Maria degli Angeli Church. (1561, **Michelangelo**) Converted from only half of the large frigidarium, or cold pool, which was 9000 square feet in size. As architect, Michelangelo respected the old building and made minimal changes. **Piranesi** made some etchings of what this looked like before the church was built: 100-foot-high ceilings, statues everywhere, and sunlight shining through the mica windows.

12 Sant'Agnese Fuori le Mura (St. Agnes Outside the Walls) (AD 623, **Pope Honorius I**) **Emperor Constantine**'s daughter **Princess Constantia** built the original church near the **Catacombs of St. Agnes**. This building no longer exists but Constantia's tomb still stands with its distinctive Roman-style mosaics (AD 350) on its vaulted corridor that depict putti crushing grapes to make wine. The church is built atop the catacombs where St. Agnes was buried and is one of the few churches that was not redesigned in the Renaissance or Baroque periods. Some mosaics are influenced by the Byzantine style. The original papal throne is still here. ◆ Via Nomentana

Near Sant'Agnese Fuori le Mura:
Il Consolato d'Abruzzo Wonderful sausages, salamis, and hot or cold cuts of meat. ◆ Closed Monday; Sunday PM. Piazza Elio Callisto 15. 8393649

13 Mr. Lin ★★$$ **Mr. Jerry Lin**, with his wife and family, is from Shanghai. The food, including dim sum and Peking duck, is from heaven. Off the beaten track but attractive and soigné. ◆ Closed Monday. Via Fogliano 38. 8380562

14 La Lampada—da Tonino ★★★★$$$ Temple of mushrooms. This charming place gets its fourth star for its devotion to the succulent toadstool. In winter, when they are in season, the pungent smell of mushrooms assails your nostrils as you walk in; and the sight of large porcini mushrooms nestling in a basket wakes up the most dormant appetite. **Tonino Fereale** and **Madame** make the best mushroom soup in town, but you should also try roasted porcini or fettucine—either with *funghi porcini* or with truffles (white or black) and cream. On your table is dark-green olive oil from Sarona. A good cantina of wine and homemade ricotta cheesecake round out your meal. Don't expect quick service; but we are partisans of Slow Food. ◆ Closed Sunday. Via Q. Sella 25. Reservations required. 4744323

15 L'Oriental ★★$ If you're stuck near the railway station and on the lookout for delicious *satays*, visit **Ah Cheng** and her family in this charming restaurant. Authentic Malaysian, and other Far Eastern cuisines. ◆ Closed Tuesday. Via Calatafimi 27. 4746820

16 Piedre del Sol ★★$$ Bright and clean, the newest restaurant in town is Mexican. This will make all those Californians feel they've found a home away from home. Honest Mexican food—but it could be hotter! ◆ Vicolo Rosini 6. Reservations recommended. 6873651

17 Nihonbashi ★★★$$$ The atmosphere is authentic and warm-hearted. The food is standard Japanese raw fish and rice, with variations—and strong green mustard. Tempura and sukiyaki are the other specialties. ◆ Closed Sunday. Via Torino 34. 4826970

18 Goffredo and Lino ★★★★$$ White cuffs billowing over the sleeves of his jacket, gold spoon and fork in his lapel, Goffredo choreographs the whole production. His own part—mixing the pasta with the *vongole voracie*, peeling the perfect orange standing at your table—is sublime show business. But this food ain't theater. It's the real thing. In a simple décor, with reasonable prices, he and Lino are the masters of honest cuisine. Goffredo tells us he knew the original Alfredo, who showed him the golden spoon and fork that **Douglas Fairbanks** awarded him many years ago. Our man's loyal clientele felt he deserved as much, and clubbed together to give him the same award. ◆ Closed Sunday. Via Panisperna 231. Reservations required. 4740620

19 Monti ★★★$$$ Temple of truffles during the winter. Superb eating all year-round with **Mario** and **Franca Camerucci**. The pasta specialties are tortellini, tortelli, and tortelloni (big, bigger, biggest). The Florentine T-bone steak pleases even the most sophisticated Tuscan marquess. ◆Closed Tuesday. Via San Vito 13A. 733285

Outside Rome:
Al Sabba delle Streghe ★★★$$ Forty-five-minutes drive from downtown—but worth it. Not far from the seashore south of Rome is the ancient city that was called *Lavinium* 2000 years ago. Now it is a tiny walled village with 2 streets; cowstalls below and this sumptuous 17th-century restaurant above. Light and airy, and delicious food. Fish is fresh daily. ◆ Closed Tuesday. Via Lavinia 1, Practica di Mare, Province of Rome. Reservations required. 9122055

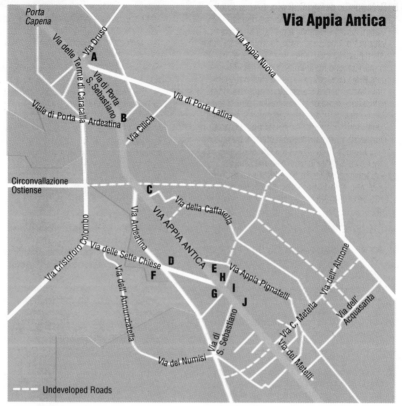

Porta Capena

Via Druso

Via delle Terme di Caracalla

Via di Porta S. Sebastiano

Viale di Porta Ardeatina

Via Cilicia

Via di Porta Latina

Via Appia Nuova

Circonvallazione Ostiense

Via della Caffarella

VIA APPIA ANTICA

Via Ardeatina

Via Cristoforo Colombo

Via delle Sette Chiese

Via dell' Annunziatella

Via Appia Pignatelli

Via dell' Almone

Via dell' Acquasanta

Via C. Metella

Via di S. Sebastiano

Via dei Numisi

Via dei Merelli

--- Undeveloped Roads

20 **Via Appia Antica** (313 BC, **Consul Appius Claudius Caecus**) The original road began right after Circus Maximus, following the present Viale delle Terme di Caracalla and Via di Porta San Sebastiano. But one feels that Via Appia starts after the **Baths of Caracalla**; at that point the topography ceases to be urban and becomes more countrified. Nowadays Via Appia Antica officially starts where the walls of Rome end. The road was wide enough for 5 Roman soldiers to march abreast. About 100 yards down Via Appia Antica are vestiges of tombs. On the right is the first milestone—a shiny marble shaft marking the distance from the original starting point of Via Appia, one Roman mile (roughly equivalent to our measure) back in town. Via Appia was the most important consular road running south from Rome and the best preserved. Once it was finished and reached **Brindisi**, on the Adriatic Sea, many of the previous coastal way stations around the foot of Italy fell into disrepair. For instance, **Paestum**, which in its heyday thrived on refurbishing the galleys as they passed by on their way to Rome's port of Ostia, disappeared for about 2000 years, covered by thick underbrush, but its temples have been restored to their original beauty. At certain points this road looks just as it did 1000 years ago. During the intervening period, which continued up until the 19th century, Via Appia was an unpleasant place due to the thievery by highwaymen of toll castles.

A **Orazio** ★$$ Located on a little road to the left of the junction of **Via di Porta San Sebastiano** and **Porta Latina**. Plunge on to the right and you will arrive in a pleasant room that opens onto an out-

door terrace. Antipasto trays stretch out enticingly, and on an early spring day you can find wild asparagus on the menu! The menu includes *alici sotto aceto* (whitebait marinated in vinegar), *bruschetta* (country bread toasted with garlic, sometimes spread with tomato or pâté), all meats on the charcoal fire, and a strange dessert called *affogato al whisky* (drowned in whisky). The food and service are excellent. It also welcomes guests who arrive after 2:30PM. ◆ Closed Tuesday. Viale Claudio Marcello. 777339, 7593401

B **Museum of the Walls and Walks of Rome** One can walk a short way along the top of the walls, just as the Roman legionnaires must have done during their duty. ◆ Tu-Th 9AM-1:30PM, 4-7PM; W-F, Sa 9AM-1:30PM; Su 9AM-1PM. In Porta San Sebastiano on Via di Porta San Sebastiano.

C **Domine, Quo Vadis Church** (1637) Built where St. Peter supposedly saw a vision of Christ as he was running away from Rome to safety. Startled, he asked, *Domine, quo vadis?* (Lord, where are you going?), and Christ replied, *I'm going to Rome to be crucified a second time.* Christ then disappeared. St. Peter was so ashamed that he turned back and was martyred.

Quo Vadis ★$$ Named after the nearby church, this restaurant has a fine view of the back lawn from the tables outside on the terrace. Roman fare of spaghetti with various sauces, a good salad and grilled veal chops, roast pork with fried potatoes, and ice cream for dessert. ◆ Closed Tuesday. Via Appia Antica 38. No credit cards. 5136795

D Catacombs of San Callisto The catacombs are through the gates just after the Domine, Quo Vadis Church, where Via Appia branches to the left and Via Ardeatina begins on the right. If you go up this little road to the catacombs, you will be immersed in gentle countryside. In the 3rd century, **Pope Zephyrinus** made **Callistus** responsible for the cemeteries on the Appian way. Prior to that time, there were no formal Christian cemeteries. Instead, Christians were buried at private family burial grounds. The catacombs are vast. During the terrorist kidnapping of **Prime Minister Aldo Moro** in 1978, one of the police theories was that he was hidden in part of the catacombs. ♦ Admission. M-Tu, Th-Su 8:30AM-noon, 2:30-6PM, May-Sep; M-Tu, Th-Su 8:30AM-noon, 2:30-5PM, Oct-Apr

E Liberti ★★$$ (Located on the left another 200 yards along Via Appia Antica if you have not branched off to the Catacombs.) In summer dine outdoors among the beautiful ruins known as the **Columbarium**. You might think this means dovecote, but in reality all the little so-called dove houses are niches for burial urns. This restaurant is called Liberti because it was the burial place of liberated slaves. (Great houses often had a columbarium for burying their household servants—sometimes 6000 souls; one inscription even recalled the beloved lapdog.) It's actually pleasant, not spooky, to dine at night protected by the centuries-old walls. The cuisine is Roman: salami, prosciutto, *bresaola* (cured beef), spaghetti with tomatoes, grilled meats, salad, and ice cream. ♦ Closed Tuesday. Via Appia Antica 87. 5132888

F Catacombs of Domitilla Vast underground galleries that were once the private burial grounds of **Domitilla**, niece of **Emperor Domitian** (AD 81-96) and a member of the rich **Flavian** family. Domitilla's husband, **Flavius Clemens**, was a martyred Christian; it was through him that the area became Christian—hence the catacombs. A guidebook written 100 years ago calls it nonsense to say that visiting the catacombs is dangerous or that they are so cold that one can catch the ague there; in reality the temperatures are mild and warm. ♦ M, W-Su 8:30AM-noon, 2:30-6PM, May-Sep; M, W-Su 8:30AM-noon, 2:30-5PM, Oct-Apr. Via delle Sette Chiese 282

G Catacombs and Church of San Sebastiano Inside the church, in a chapel on the left, is a smooth white-marble statue of **Saint Sebastian** full of arrow holes, sculpted by one of **Bernini**'s students (17th century). The catacombs—the ones first referred to by this name—are on various levels and were mostly constructed in the 3rd and 4th centuries. These burial places outside Rome's walls did not originate out of Roman discrimination against the Christians. In fact, there are Jewish catacombs not far from here at Via Appia Antica 119A, and the Via Appia is lined with tombs of non-Christian Romans. Both Christians and Jews buried the whole body, as opposed to the Roman practice of cremation and burial of the ashes in an urn. There was a law (for hygienic reasons) that required all Romans, including Christians (with certain exceptions, such as in the case of emperors), to bury their dead outside the city walls. The health hazards were manifold,

even though in Roman times there was running water in public lavatories and squadrons of workers who had specific cleaning tasks, including cleaning out cesspools, carting refuse, street sweeping, and food-market cleanings.

During periods of persecution, Christians had to hide and hold their cult services in the burial chambers. The pavement bearing the supposed imprint of Christ's feet when he chastised St. Peter—at the nearby Domine, Quo Vadis Church—is here. ♦ M-W, F-Su 8:30AM-noon, 2:30-6PM, May-Sep; M-W, F-Su 8:30AM-noon, 2:30-5PM. Via Appia Antica 110

H Cecilia Metella ★$$$ Right opposite the Church of San Sebastiano, up a little private road behind a fountain of spring water (Romans come here with cases of empty bottles and fill them with the free mineral water), is the best known restaurant of Via Appia. Here couples have wedding feasts on Saturday and Sunday, and Roman families come to fill up after family events: births, confirmations, marriages, deaths. There is a wood fire for barbecuing meats, a marvelous terrace for outdoor eating in the summer, and ample parking. ♦ Closed Monday. Via Appia Antica 125. 5136743, 5110213

I Hostaria L'Archeologia ★$$ This old farmhouse-turned-restaurant is a skip and a jump further on down Via Appia, on the same side of the street as the restaurant Cecilia Metella, but with its entrance and car park on the little side road Vicolo della Basilica. A hundred-plus-year-old wisteria vine makes shade in the courtyard for summer lunching, and a welcoming fire burns merrily inside during the winter. Antipasto, spaghetti, fettucine, and grilled meats are especially good. The *lombata di vitello* (veal chop on the bone, really more like a pale-pink steak) and a great chocolate cake are 2 dishes that stand out. Service is slow, so watch that wine consumption. ♦ Closed Monday. Via Appia Antica 139. No credit cards. 7880494

J Tomb of Romulus (AD 309) Built by **Maxentius** to honor his son, who died young. This tomb was immense, and the medieval house in the next field (after the Archeologia restaurant) stands right at the entrance to the tomb's core. The house and the round tomb behind it become an island in a lake during the rainy winter months. Maxentius also built a temple to honor his son on the Via Sacra.

J Circus Maxentius Located right beyond Romulus' tomb. Built for chariot racing, this enormous area (about one quarter-mile long) stretches away among the sloping green fields, with only the songbirds to interrupt the stillness where 18,000 spectators once shouted their encouragement to the charioteer they were betting on—in the hopes he would win the 7-lap race and they would go home rich. The **Obelisk of Diocletian**, now in the Piazza Navona, used to stand on the dividing island running down the center of the track. Notice that the overarching canopy above the bleachers was made of masonry lightened by the insertion of hollow pots. ♦ Admission fee valid for both Circus and tomb. Tu, Th 9AM-1:45PM, 4-7PM; W, F-Sa 9AM-1:45PM; Su 9AM-12:45PM. Via Appia Antica 153. 7801324

Day Trips

Hadrian's Villa and Tivoli

Wealthy Romans used to build their summer palaces in this area, just 23 miles east of Rome. Two of the best known are Hadrian's Villa (about 3.5 miles southwest of the town of Tivoli) and the **Villa d'Este** (in Tivoli proper), famous for its terraced gardens and fountains. Allow yourself a day to visit both, stopping at Hadrian's Villa first and Tivoli second.

Hadrian's Villa (AD 120, **Emperor Hadrian**) Hadrian built a giant pleasure dome below the chic area the Romans traveled to when the heat of the

summer became unbearable in Rome. As architect, poet, soldier, lover, and statesman, his travels around his empire inspired him to design this superb, enormous palace—his version of what he had seen abroad. The place never ceases to amaze. You will see separate dining rooms and private baths for both winter and summer, golden courtyards, and a private athletic track. Don't miss the **Hospitaria**, rooms for guests complete with their own lavatories and bathrooms, where all the floors are made of

black-and-white mosaics, each room with a different pattern. The grandeur of the place is staggering. Servants were hardly ever seen or heard as they had a network of underground passageways to keep them out of the way. A sunny, unhurried day would be ideal for visiting the pastoral setting of the greatest country palace of them all. ♦ Admission. Daily 9AM-1 hr before sunset. 0774/21249, 0774/530203

Adriano ★$$ This restaurant is just outside the gates of Hadrian's Villa. It serves decent food and you can choose from the different varieties of homemade pasta drying for your pleasure in the entrance to the vast kitchen. *Lombata di vitello* (Roman veal chop with fresh lemon) is very good. Green vegetables, a summer salad with *rughetta* (arugula), or *caprese* (tomatoes, mozzarella, and fresh basil leaves). Ice cream and fruit in season, all washed down with some modest local Castelli wine. White wine is the most appreciated in Rome and Latium, and small wineries (rather than those like Fontana Candida) are preferred. ♦ Closed Monday. Villa Adriano. 0774/529174

Restaurants/Clubs: Red   **Hotels:** Blue
Shops/Parks: Green   **Sights/Culture:** Black

Tivoli Local handicrafts: beaten copper and anything made of travertine marble. From here on the hills, the plain below looks like one piece of marble!

Villa d'Este (1550, **Pirro Ligorio**) The best time to see the palace and gardens is at night when the interplay between the water and lights is glorious. **Cardinal d'Este**, son of **Lucrezia Borgia** and the **Duke of Ferrara**, led a luxurious life and laid out one of the most beautiful gardens in the world tiered down the steep hillside, with literally hundreds of fountains of different sizes and shapes. One is called the *organ*—when the water passes through the organ tubes it emits strange musical sounds (rather like groaning). The palace is also impressive, with Mannerist frescoes, some painted by students of **Federigo Zuccari**. Four nearby aqueducts from this mountainous area provide Rome with most of her water supply. ♦ 9AM-1 hr before sunset. Gardens illuminated 9-11PM, Easter to Sep. 0774/21249

Temple of Sibilla Located in the ancient heart of Tivoli—whose origins are earlier than Rome's. In Augustus' time an old soothsayer predicted the birth of Christ—*someone greater than the Emperor*. ♦ Entrance through the restaurant Sibilla

Sibilla ★★★$$$ As you walk in the door of this touristy but definitely spectacular restaurant, **Maria** takes over. In summer, she'll seat you in the superb terraced garden, where 100-year-old wisteria vines give you shade from the harsh sun and where you have an incomparable closeup of the ancient and elegant **Temple of Sibilla**. Maria will bring you a carafe of delicious, slightly sparkly local wine. Antipasto can be *bruschetta* with *rughetta* and tomato, or prosciutto with marvelously ripe figs or melon in season. And have the *ovoline*, small buffalo-milk mozzarella balls. The difference between these and that bland imitation, the cow's-milk variety, is marked and these require a very sophisticated palate; you may notice a slight separation of the skin from the center section. Pasta dishes include ravioli of ricotta and 4 cheeses; also *bombolotti*, big macaroni usually served with green cauliflower. If, like maestro **Peter Duchin** during a recent visit, you're so enthusiastic that you want more, try the *pollo alla diavolo*, chicken squashed flat on the grill until crispy, then ice cream or cakes. ♦ Closed Tuesday. Via della Sibilla 50, Tivoli. 0774/20281

Il Ciocco ★★$$ For those who abjure anything touristy, circle around the spectacular ravine to the *other* restaurant, where the Italians go. Everything from a pizzeria to a piano bar, at reasonable prices. On different levels, with part actually inside a grotto, this place affords the perfect Piranesian view of Sibilla's Temple, glistening white of a summer's night. ♦ Closed Monday. Via Ponte Gregoriano 33, Tivoli. 0774/292482

Day Trips

Hadrian's Villa and Tivoli are:

45 minutes by car from Rome. Take Via Tibertina to just beyond Bagni di Tivoli. Turn right to Hadrian's Villa (signpost). After seeing Hadrian's Villa go up to Tivoli by following the signposts.

Buses leave from Via Gaeta near Piazzale dei Cinquecento (460124) to Tivoli. There are also tour buses to Tivoli.

Cerveteri Necropolis (8th-3rd century BC)

This whole cemetery town, which extended much farther than the visible area, served the ancient Etruscan city of **Caere**. Tomb-robbers have been kept busy here for centuries, discovering and plundering these magnificent, gigantic tomb-houses. Enormous conical houses, much like those of the living, stretch in every direction. They are built of local tufa stone—soft when excavated, it hardens in the air. Large earth hills were heaped atop these tombs, which are now covered in grass, making a landscape of strange hills and dales. You can visit most tombs. Although they are open, all the objects and furniture—useful articles the dead had with them, such as saucepans for cooking, eating vessels, candlesticks and oil lamps, food and ornaments, and precious objects—have either been robbed or moved to museums. The celebrated **Sarcophagus of the Married Couple**, now in Rome's **Villa Giulia Museum**, came from here. Ask to see the **Tomba dei Rilievi**, which is the finest tomb, but unfortunately is often closed. Located about one mile outside the town of Cerveteri. ◆ Daily 9AM-1 hr before sunset

Museo Nazionale Cerite

Housed in the refurbished old Castello Ruspoli, called La Rocca (for obvious reasons), near the town's central square. It has a wealth of artifacts from the necropolis nearby, presented clearly in glass cases. ◆ Daily 9AM-1 hr before sunset. Piazza Santa Maria. 9941354

L'Oasi—Da Pino $ All the standard Roman seafood. Pasta and risotto with shellfish. ◆ Closed Monday. Via Morelli 2 (toward the Via Aurelia) No credit cards. 9953482

Ladispoli A nearby town where various seafront establishments serve fish. The volcanic sand is black, and the beach has a desolate quality in winter. Spaghetti *alle vongole* (clams), *spiedino di mazzancolle* (prawns on a skewer), and *spigola* (sea bass) can be sampled in any of the restaurants.

Cerveteri is:

45 minutes by car from Rome. Take Via Aurelia until you pass Ladispoli. The next turn on the right will be for Cerveteri.

Buses leave from Via Lepanto Metro (386406).

Nemi

The lake of Nemi is a dark pool of water at the bottom of an extinct volcano. In ancient times it was called the *Specchio di Diana* (the Mirror of the Goddess Diana); in its thickly wooded hills a giant temple was built to that goddess. As recorded in the main chapters of *The Golden Bough*, the priests of Diana could

only be changed by violence. A priest-aspirant had to creep up, take the incumbent priest unawares, and kill him in order to accede to the position. The **Emperor Caligula** (AD 37-41), who kept 2 magnificent boats on this lake, proclaimed himself the god who would marry Diana. To act out his fantasy, the role of the goddess was assigned to local girls of great beauty, with whom Caligula's own rites on board these floating palaces were all too earthy. Engineers in **Mussolini**'s time, with his encouragement, ingeniously drained the lake to see if the Caligula story

was truth or fiction, and found to their amazement the 2 boats resting in the mud at the bottom. A museum was built by the lakeside to house them, and people could come here to admire Roman knowhow. But for all too short a time. At the end of World War II the Germans firebombed the little museum, and the boats burned up—at least that's one version; some say it was an inside job. Even today one feels the mysterious air, full of omens, while walking up the winding road through the footpath to the 12th-century town perched on top. There is a tower of the medieval **Ruspoli Castle**, which sometimes has art or flower shows; follow the castle walk down to a belvedere (beautiful view), where you can have an ice cream and enjoy the view. There is a smattering of restaurants and cafés in town. The best time to go is late May/early June, when the *Sagra delle Fragolini* (Festival of Wild Strawberries) is celebrated. This is a joyous affair of processions and brass bands when everyone eats enormous quantities of the local specialty—the tiny, delicious, woodsy wild strawberries. Part of the forbidding woodland down in the volcano's inner curve has been cleared for cultivation of this delicacy.

Museo delle Navi

This Museum of the Boats, as recounted above, was opened in **Mussolini**'s time to house **Caligula**'s 2 ancient barks, which the water and the mud had preserved for 2 millenia. The imperial yachts, over 210 feet long and 60 feet wide, burned during the night of 1 June 1944, under mysterious circumstances allegedly connected with the war. Recently reopened, the museum contains scale models of the boats, 1/5 the original size, as well as some of the classical artifacts discovered during various salvaging operations over the last 500 years. ◆ Admission. Daily 9AM-2PM. Via del Lago di Nemi. 9368140

Specchio di Diana ★$$ This restaurant in town is up a flight of stairs with a moderate view over the road to the lake. In summer you can dine outside on the terrace. Spaghetti *alle lepre* (hare sauce) and chicken with mushrooms, with fresh local salads, are good; and, of course, the sublime wild strawberries are served in a variety of ways—with white wine, cream, lemon juice, or simply on their own. ◆ Closed Wednesday. Via Vittorio Emanuele 13. No credit cards. 9368016

Capriccio sul Lago ★$$ Same sort of fare as up on the volcano lip, but with fresh eels (rather greasy) in summer and a more pastoral mood as you lunch almost at the lake's edge among the bulrushes. ◆ Closed Monday. Via del Lago di Nemi. No credit cards. 9368120

Castel Gandolfo

Located at the next volcano is this 18th-century town poised on the rim of a larger, extinct volcano, called **Lake Albano**. The Pope spends the hottest months of the summer here, and blesses the crowd in the tiny town square after Mass on Sunday around noon. He sometimes holds a general audience at 11AM on Wednesday in the large auditorium at the **Villa Cyba**. However, you must apply for tickets in advance to the Prefettura della Casa Vatican (Citta del Vaticano, 00120 Rome, phone 6982).

While building **Fiumicino Airport**, near Ostia Antica, workers found the remains of the oldest (1st century AD) and largest Jewish synagogue in the Western world.

Ristorante Bucci ★★$ This simple-but-honest family restaurant has a terrace overlooking the dark-emerald lake far below. Other jewels include home-made pastas, lake trout, and fruit tart. House wine from freshly picked grapes. ♦ Closed Friday. Via dei Zecchini 31. No credit cards. 9323334

Trattoria Pizzeria al Cacciatore ★$ Rustic environs with 6 tables on the public pavement overlooking the lake. The wine in carafes is the restaurant's own. Roman cooking with pizzas at night. Just off the main square toward the lake. ♦ Closed Tuesday. Via dei Zecchni 1

Nemi is:

45 minutes by car from Rome. Take the Via Appia Nuova past Ciampino Airport and turn left immediately toward Marino. Continue until you reach a large crossroad. Take the direction of Nemi (signpost). Do not go toward Marino or Castel Gandolfo. Skirt around Lake Albano, the large volcano rim (with Castel Gandolfo on the other side), and follow signs to Nemi. After a very woodsy road there will be a turn off to the right for Nemi.

Buses leave from Anagnina Metro (7222153).

Ostia Antica

Started BC, abandoned 5th century AD. If you really want to get a feel for how the ancient Romans lived, go to Ostia Antica. Here, a prosperous town—the major port of what was the most important city in the world—lies dormant, just as the Romans left it. The end wasn't a cataclysm like Pompei, covered by Vesuvius' lava in 2 days of agony; it was subtle, drifting away as the Empire declined and fell and Rome stopped being the hub of the universe. Then the malaria mosquito (literally *mal-aria*: bad air) spawned in the stagnant water that built up as the canals fell into disuse, and the port itself (now partially under the airport of **Fiumicino**—Leonardo da Vinci) silted up. Stroll down the **Decumanus Maximus** (Main Street) and get a feel for how every Roman town was rigorously laid out. A citizen of Rome couldn't get lost abroad, because all towns built by Romans had the same grid. The ancient town was vast. It included 2 major public baths, lavatories, many temples, a courthouse, taverns, fish-and-chips shops, apartment buildings (5 stories high), lovely private houses with gardens, barracks for the soldiers and firefighters, a large town square with mosaics depicting what each shop traded, and a theater where even today plays are performed in summer. There is a small museum with fine statuary and arbitrary opening hours. Don't miss the superb mosaics in the 2 baths. ♦ Tu-Su 9AM-6:30PM, summer; Tu-Sa 9AM-4:30PM, winter. 5650022

Il Monumento ★★$$ In the new village of Ostia Antica (built by the populous around the Middle Ages), tucked into the lea of the 15th-century walls of the medieval castle. Small, with a protected outside terrace for lunching from the early spring on, this restaurant specializes in grilled or broiled fish with a green sauce. Spaghetti starters or seafood salad are good, as is a generous slice of cake or tart for dessert. ♦ Closed Monday and 20 August-6 September. Piazza Umberto Primero 8. 5650021

Isola Sacra (Sacred Island) Where the cemetery is located. Worth a visit to see how the ancients were buried, and particularly to see how everybody got a tomb—but some were more equal than others.

Fiumicino This port city is known for having given the airport (formerly **Leonardo da Vinci Airport**) its name. But to some of us it means seafood, specifically fish restaurants, which are almost uniformly good, despite the fact that the fish sold here may well hail from the faraway Atlantic Ocean, airfreighted via Royal Air Maroc by Casablanca's seafood wholesalers. The shellfish you buy along the quai are probably fresh, but check the bigger fish to make sure their gills are purple, their eyes are lifelike, and their muscles stiff—the 3 signs of a recently caught specimen. Nearby, **Trajan's Port** has recently been closed to the public; this is a precisely hexagonal basin built in AD 103 by the emperor Trajan to provide a well-protected port to serve the growing needs of burgeoning Rome.

Il Pescatore ★★★★$$ First-class seafood and fish specialties. **Domenico Zafrani** will take care of your every need. After a few years' absence, he has returned to run this large and attractive restaurant that spreads into the garden courtyard in the summer. One of the best dishes is spaghetti in *cartoscia*, cooked in greaseproof paper and lightly touched with tomato sauce and perfumed with prawns, lobster tails, or whatever the fresh specialty of that day might be. ♦ Closed Thursday. Via Torre Clementina 154. 6440189

Miranda ★★$$ **Domenico Zafrani**'s other place. ♦ Closed Tuesday. Lungomare della Salute 39. 6440077

Bastianelli al Molo ★★$$$ Another fish chain with shellfish specialties and a view of the sea. A little like a factory but in a pretty, whitewashed Spanish-type building. ♦ Closed Monday. Via Torre Clementina 314. 6440358

Gina ★★$$$ Known for a giant table of seafood hors d'oeuvres. Sculptor **Beverly Pepper**'s favorite. ♦ Closed Wednesday and last half of August. Viale Traino 141 (across the canal) 6820422

Ostia Antica is:

45 minutes by car from Rome. Take the superhighway to Fiumicino Airport and then follow the signposts to Fiumicino and Ostia. On the flyover, do not go to the town of Fiumicino but continue to Ostia Antica. When you reach a turn about 4 kilometers down this road, do not go to the ugly resort of Ostia but toward Ostia Antica and Rome. Signposts are scarce but it's not that difficult to find. For 1700 years the sea has receded so the old port is now inland.

Metro to Magliana, then the local tram to Ostia Antica.

Ninfa

(A fiefdom of Rome since 320 BC.) The botanical garden of Ninfa is situated immediately below the town of **Norma**, which sits precariously on the enormous cliff behind, originally part of a giant volcano. The **River Ninfa** forms a large, crystal-clear pond where many varieties of fish live and breed. In ancient Roman times the fertile **Pontine Marshes** were drained and 23 cities dotted the plain. Three ancient consular roads, **Via Appia, Via Setina,** and **Via Corana,** all passed near Ninfa. Via Appia had hostelries every 7 or 8 miles with changes of horses and bed-and-board for the travelers available. Many sacred temples were built here, including one to the **Nereidi** (gods of the water) and one to the **Driadi** (gods of the woods). The ancient Roman author **Pliny** wrote of Ninfa having islands in the lakes where people played music and danced. But bad times followed. First the Barbarians raided frequently, followed by a time of consolidation under **Pope Zaccaria** (AD 700). Then came the Arab domination. Around 880 the Saracens invaded. Their technical know-how and engineering skills were greatly admired for centuries as they put them to good use here; it was thanks to the Arabs that water mills were installed in the whole region. But the Catholic church rejected them due to religious differences. In 1000 Ninfa was a beautiful city, home to soldiers, peasants, and artisans. The **Caetani** family members were the ruling princes. The town boasted over 10 churches, 2 hospitals, 4 monasteries, 5 principal gates of entry, 4 bridges across the river, and a double protective wall to repel invaders. Straddling the river were innumerable water mills, which crushed the grain into flour, olives into oil, grapes into wine. What went wrong? Why was it abandoned? The Roman drainage canals, no longer maintained during the Middle Ages, little by little silted up and large bodies of stagnant water formed on the rich plain where everything had grown in abundance. In 1159 **Pope Alexander III** was crowned in Ninfa because the Holy Roman emperor **Frederick Barbarossa** had usurped the Church's power in Rome. Barbarossa punished Ninfa and the surrounding area by a little destruction here and there. Ninfa changed hands many times; once **Pope Alexander VII** gave it to his daughter **Lucrezia Borgia,** but it was ultimately returned to the Caetani family. Its final destruction began with a war between 2 Caetani brothers, followed by attacks from jealous, neighboring towns at the end of the 14th century. Meanwhile, the stagnant waterways were providing an ideal environment for malarial mosquitoes to breed in. Fever and death followed. The town was completely abandoned—forever.

In 1765 a few repairs were done, but Ninfa remained a piteously poor region infested by malaria, and only in the winter could the water mills be used for grinding grain. The last male Caetani descendant, **Prince Gelassio Caetani,** started the long uphill struggle to save Ninfa. His son-in-law, the Honorable **Hubert Howard,** took up the work of planting the abandoned area with rare trees and flowers, buttressing the ruins, draining the marshes, cleaning the rivers. The

Day Trips

mosquito has moved on, with no more stagnant waters to live in. Thanks to Gelassio's British son-in-law, a paradise has been born again.

Botanical Garden Ninfa is proud of the number of different birds, fish, and animals that live here, and the **World Wildlife Fund** has declared this a sanctuary. To visit this beautiful botanical garden set in the ruins of the 14th-century town is an extraordinary experience. ◆ 1st Sa-Su of every month 9AM-sunset. 0773/34241

Sermoneta Known for its summer music festival.

Il Mulino ★★$$ Considered by food and travel writer **Frances Saunders** to have, along with **Il Laghetto** in the nearby La Selva Nature Park, the best cuisine between Rome and Naples. ◆ Sermoneta (Latina) 0773/30009

Borgo Grappa Thirty minutes by car from Ninfa, near the sea.

Trattoria Giggetto ★★$$$ The most famous restaurant near Ninfa is known for its *strozzapreti alla giggetto* (spaghetti that looks, as the name implies in Italian, like a cord for throttling priests), risotto with mussels, and chicken livers with onions. The local olive oil and wine are excellent, as is the mozzarella. The water buffalo whose milk is used to make this mozzarella are grazing nearby. Afterward, go for a swim at the beautiful white-sand beach nearby. ◆ Closed Monday PM and Tuesday. Via Mediana (opposite the Carabinieri station) Borgo Grappa (Latina) No credit cards. 0773/20007

Cori Fifteen minutes by car from Ninfa on a nearby hill.

Zampi ★$$ In this trattoria situated above the madding crowd you will find good family fare. Don't be surprised if you come across a wedding or anniversary banquet, either of which will give you a unique perspective on rural Italian life. Dishes include lasagna, *buccatini,* and **Ottavio Zampi's** specialty—fettucine with a ragout meat sauce. ◆ Closed Monday. Via Leopardi 17, Cori (Latina) 9679688

Ninfa is:

70 minutes by car from Rome. Take Via Appia to Cisterna di Latina. Continue on Via Appia until the next left, to Doganella. Over crossroads, continue to Ninfa. Or take Via Appia and turn off toward Velletri. Pass Cori. At Donagella turn left to Ninfa.

Buses leave from Eur-Fermi Metro stop (5920402) to Latina or from Subaugusta Metro stop to Cori. Then take a taxi to Ninfa.

Sperlonga

We recommend you drive here as it is not easy to reach by public transportation. You may also want to visit the bustling market town and seaport of **Terracina** (over one hour south of Rome). Standing on top of the high cliffs above Terracina, which is nestled on a spit of land between the promontory and the sea, is the mighty temple of **Jupiter Anxur.** From here you can see a magnificent panorama across the Fondi plains to Mount Circeo; even the island of Ischia is visible in good weather. This whole area is rich in lovely seacoast (take a swimsuit), good restaurants, salt- and sweet-water lakes, and ancient sites like the windswept temple guarding Terracina from the wrath of the gods. The attractive town of Sperlonga, a 20-minute drive from the temple, was a 12th-century enclave of houses, with a fortress on the cliff's edge facing the sea. The name is from *sperlunca* (cave).

Praetorium Palace This was the imperial villa of the **Emperor Tiberius** (AD 14-37). In 1954, archeologists discovered the palace and the adjacent cave. By 1957 they concluded that it was, beyond all doubt, Tiberius' country estate. The grotto was the famous (or infamous) one where the Emperor liked to dally, and at one point was almost killed by a landslide. Today, falling rock is still a peril. The excavations in the pool at the entrance to the cave produced many bits of marble statues that were pieced together and proved to be a *Laocoön* statue (see **National Archeological Museum** below). There were explosives hidden all around—remains from World War II—so uncovering this palace was a dangerous undertaking. The smaller, seawater swimming pool was also used by Tiberius as a reflecting pond for the many marble statues that were gracefully placed around the circumference. In ancient times, this region was full of beautiful country estates, so the Emperor's house was surrounded by houses of the patricians of his court. Legend has it that Tiberius liked both boys and girls. Supposedly, one of the pools was filled with crocodiles and the other with piranhas. If a youth or maiden was reluctant to succumb to the Emperor's advances, he or she was thrown into one of the pools to the general merriment of the assembled courtiers. (On the Isle of Capri, Tiberius tossed the recalcitrant ones over the cliff.) There were also fish-breeding pools with niches for hatching the eggs. Locks and passages regulated the flow of water. Some of the rooms are as close to the sea as the cave; it has been said that from here the master could cast his fish nets from his bed! In mythological times this stretch of coast was known for its seductive sirens and dangerous sea monsters. (For Ulysses' passage during his trip back from the wars, read **Homer**'s *Odyssey* .) The Romans built pleasure domes that incorporated walkways for their 2-wheeled carriages (like rickshaws) and human-carried litters, Greek *thinking pavilions*, shooting lodges, multiple dining rooms, libraries, gymnasiums, theaters, parks, vantage view points, and shady pergolas. Later, after the fall of the Roman Empire, peasants would crush and burn marble statues, reducing them to a sticky lime substance used for building. The beach is a pretty half-moon curve between the grotto and the promontory of Sperlonga, where families picnic and swim. In the town are antique stores and art shops, with a couple of restaurants and a pizzeria on the outskirts.

Museo Archeologico Nazionale di Sperlonga

(National Archeological Museum of Sperlonga) Filled with the statues and fragments found on the site of Tiberius' grotto. This museum was mainly built to house the large *Laocoön* sculpture (Room 2). It is often compared to the famous *Laocoön* in the Vatican museums, but experts differ as to which one is the finer work of art. ♦ Via Flacca. 0771/54028

Il Fortino Just beyond Tiberius' tunnel on the road south. A good fish restaurant on the side of the cliff with a beautiful view toward the sea. We recommend the prawns. ♦ Closed Wednesday. Via Flacca. 0771/54337

Sperlonga is:

90 minutes by car from Rome. Take Via Pontina toward Terracina. On the bypass, skirt around Terracina. Then take Via Flacca to Sperlonga.

Buses leave from Eur-Fermi Metro stop (5920402) to Terracina, Sperlonga, and Formia.

Trains leave from Stazione Termini to Fondi-Sperlonga.

For all destinations:

Bus information: **ACOTRAL**, Via Portonaccio 25. 57531, 57005

Train information: **Stazione Termini**, Piazza Cinquecento. 47751

Rome From the Sky

Elitrans will fly you over Rome in a helicopter or take you by private jet to that meeting in Milan. ♦ Rome Urbe Airport, Via Salaria 825. 8128271/3017/3754; telex 621603 Elicsa-1; fax 8110709

Other private plane companies:

Air Capitol ♦ Via Salaria. 81008952

Ali ♦ Ciampino General Aviation. 7240261/2/3/4/5

Mistral Air ♦ Via Mameli (pal 135) Ciampino. 7240614

Panair International Ciampino ♦ 7240533

Truth is Stranger than Fiction

The Italians Drink the Most Bizarre Aperitifs

Cynar—artichokes

Vov—eggnog (sweet)

Ramazzotti—ginseng and herbs (bitter)

Aperol—sweet

Rabarbaro—bitter

Punt-e-mes—bittersweet

Strega—saffron (sweet)

Mistra—aniseed

Fernet Branca—bitter herbs

Amaretto di Saronno—almonds (sweet)

Sambuca Molinari—elderberry (sweet)

Borsei San Marzano—herbs (sweet)

Mandarinetto Isola Bella—tangerines

The Coffee Rite

Un expresso can be imbibed in a variety of ways:

caffe (one inch)

caffe doppio (double)

capuccino (one-half espresso, one-half frothy milk, with a sprinkling of cocoa on top)

caffe macchiato—pronounced make-ee-ah-tow— (one drop of milk with your espresso)

caffe Hag (decafeinated espresso) In the old days they always served a glass of water with the coffee; ask for it, as it is much nicer that way.

You'll never be rushed if you sit at a table, and the price is only a bit more than at the bar.

E.U.R. (Universal Exhibition in Rome) is the satellite city designed under **Mussolini**'s instructions for the 1942 world cultural fair, which never took place because of the war. Though typically facist in its grandiose scale and inhuman conception, the parts of E.U.R. that were carried out according to the original design (some actually built in the 1950's) are handsome, solid, and pleasing.

Restaurants/Clubs: Red	Hotels: Blue
Shops/Parks: Green	**Sights/Culture:** Black

Timeline

	775 BC	Etruscan bride-and-groom sculpture created in terra cotta
Founding of Rome by Romulus and Remus	753 BC	
Temple of Jupiter Optimus Maximus built on Capitoline Hill	715 BC	King Numa Pompilius of Sabina—initiating 99 years of rule by Sabine kings
Mamertine Prison		First Temple of Vesta
Forum laid out	616 BC	King Tarquinius of Etruria—117 years of Etruscan rule
Cloaca Maxima constructed (giant drain under Forum)	509 BC	King Tarquinius Superbus (the Greatest) overthrown Republic of Rome declared

THE REPUBLIC (527-09 BC)

	484 BC	Temple of Castor and Pollux
Lex Lanuleia permits intermarriage between patricians and plebians	445 BC	
	431 BC	Temple of Apollo
Romans destroy major Etruscan city of Veli	396 BC	
	390 BC	Gauls sack Rome. Romans decide to consolidate their power
Servian Wall built around Rome	378 BC	
	312 BC	Appian Way, first aqueduct. (The arch, aqueduct, and physical gymnastics come from the Etruscans)
Romans capture Corsica	283 BC	
	270 BC	Rome fights Magna Grecia (Greater Greece) in the Battle of Taranto
Demarius, the first Roman silver coin, issued	268 BC	
	264 BC	First public gladiator combat in Rome
First Punic War (against Carthage in present-day Tunisia)	264-241 BC	
	220 BC	Flavian Way built from Rome to Rimini
Second Punic War	219-201 BC	

Timeline

	216 BC	Hannibal, the Carthaginian, crosses the Alps with elephants and almost wipes out Rome
Scipio defeats Hannibal near present-day Tunis	212 BC	

Macedonian Wars against Philip of Macedonia, Greece	197-148 BC	
	159 BC	First clepsydra (water-clock) in Rome
Third Punic War. Total destruction of Carthage; the Romans sow salt to prevent anything from growing again	149-146 BC	
	146 BC	Destruction of Corinth, Greece. Seven provinces of Roman Empire: Sicily, Sardinia, Corsica, 2 Spains, Gallia Transalpina, Africa, and Macedonia (includes present-day Britain and France) Asia Minor becomes eighth Roman province
Strict self-discipline of Romans begins to waver imperceptibly	133 BC	
Revolt of the Gladiators—70,000 led by Spartacus defeated and 6000 survivors crucified on the road between Rome and Capua	133-62 BC	The Social War—Italians want the same social rights as Romans. Lasts until 90 BC
	89-82 BC	First civil war between Populares and Optimates (aristocrats)
Arch of Titus	70 BC	
	68 BC	Pompey conquers Palestine
Julius Caesar comes to power—forms first Triumvirate with Crassus and Pompey	60 BC	
	59 BC	Curia—the Senate Building and Theater of Pompey constructed
Introduction of Julian calendar, 365 days per year	46 BC	
	44 BC	Caesar stabbed to death on his way to the Senate moments before he is to be proclaimed King of the Orient
Second Triumvirate—end of Republic	44-27 BC	Pyramid of Cestius built and Theater of Marcellus started
Laocoön, the marble statue, created	38 BC	
	31 BC	Egypt conquered; Cleopatra and Anthony commit suicide
	27 BC	First Pantheon built by Agrippa

BEGINNING OF THE EMPIRE (27 BC-AD 14)

		Octavius-Augustus becomes first emperor— reign referred to as Augustan Age. Roman culture flourishes—includes writers such as Virgil, Horace, Ovid, Livy
Mausoleum of Augustus	23 BC	

11 BC	Theater of Marcellus completed
9 BC	Altar of Heavenly Peace (Ara Pacis)
AD 1	Palatine stops being chic area to live and becomes location of the Palace, residence of the Emperor
14-37	Tiberius reigns
37-41	Caligula rules until assassinated
41-54	Claudius rules till poisoned by fourth wife
54-68	Nero (son of Cladius' fourth wife) is so hated that the people want to kill him; he asks his slave to help plunge sword into himself
64	Fire destroys much of Rome. Nero blames this on the Christians and uses it as an excuse for the first major persecution of Christians; St. Peter martyred
67	Martyrdom of St. Paul
70	Jews revolt against Roman rule. Jerusalem destroyed
69-79	Vespasian rules; era noted for order, prosperity, peace lasts 150 years
72	Vespasian starts Colosseum
79-81	Titus, son of Vespasian, rules; Beginning of Flavian dynasty
80	Flavian Amphitheater (Colosseum) completed
81-96	Domitian, Titus' younger brother, rules
83	Arch of Titus constructed by Domitian to commemorate Titus' conquest of Jerusalem
88-97	Pope Clement I
96-98	Nerva rules
98-117	Trajan—Roman Empire expands to its largest extent
113	Trajan's Forum inaugurated
117-138	Hadrian rules
117-138	Roman Forum expanded
125	Pantheon rebuilt
127	Castel Sant'Angelo (Hadrian's Tomb) erected
138-161	Antoninus Pius rules
161-180	Marcus Aurelius rules
164-180	Great plague throughout Roman Empire
180-192	Commodus rules
192-211	Septimius Severus rules—forbids conversion to Christianity
193	Marcus Aurelius column erected in Piazza Colonna
203	Arch of Septimius Severus erected to commemorate victories of Severus and his sons
211-217	Caracalla and his more popular brother, Geta, succeed their father. Caracalla murders Geta, then he is murdered
212-217	Baths of Caracalla built
218-222	Temple to the Sun built; Heliogabulus (Elagabalus) succeeds cousin Caracalla
222	Original Church of Santa Maria in Trastevere built to honor St. Calisto
225-235	Alexander Severus
235-268	Military anarchy (9 emperors as the Empire starts to fall apart) Invasions from north and east
250	Persecution of Christians increases
268-282	Illyrian emperors reign, including Aurelius (270-275), who hurriedly walls Rome and reunites the Empire
284-305	Empire divided into East (ruled by Galerius) and West (ruled by Diocletian) Rome is no longer the capital
306	Baths of Diocletian
306-337	Battle of Milvium—turning point for Christianity as Constantine becomes first Christian emperor after a dream in which he saw a cross while on the battlefield; Constantine I (The Great) Empire reunited, with capital in the East
313	Edict of Milan declares tolerance of Christianity
314	Arch of Constantine
330	Capital moves to Byzantium and renamed as Constantinople
334	First church of Sant'Agnese and her tomb, built by Constantine's daughter, Constantia
337-364	Eleven emperors in 27 years concurrently in Milvium, Ravenna, and Constantinople
352	Santa Maria in Trastevere Church (rebuilt 1148)
364-476	Western Empire: 28 emperors in 12 years. Theodosius rules both Eastern and Western empires
390	San Clemente Church

394	Theodosius I, pushed by Bishop of Milan, obliges Senate to order abolition of paganism
401-476	Series of successful invasions by the barbarians culminates in Fall of Roman Empire
403	Porta Pinciana constructed
411	Rome captured by Alaric, King of the Visigoths
438	Santa Maria Maggiore Church
440	Leo the Great becomes Pope
455	Rome sacked by Geseric, King of Vandals

FALL OF THE ROMAN EMPIRE (AD 476)

476	Fall of Western Empire. Rome conquered by Odocer, King of Heruli. More invasions follow
546	Rome sacked and abandoned
590	Gregory the Great becomes first pope to successfully intervene in politics. Western Empire dissolved—seat of the Empire moves to Constantinople; Ravenna becomes a more important city
756	Pope gets power over Rome as Papal States are established
800	Charlemagne proclaimed Emperor of Rome—crowned by Pope Leo III in St. Peter's
852	Walls built around Vatican by Pope Leo IV after Saracen raids
962	Holy Roman Empire founded by Otto I, a Saxon king, at the request of Pope John XII (955-964)
1084	Henry IV invades Rome, followed by Robert Guiscard from Normandy
1099	Santa Maria del Popolo Church
1142-1159	Pope Hadrian IV (English)—some say really Pope Joan—stoned to death while giving birth during papal procession to the Church of San Giovanni in Laterano
1309-1377	Popes in Avignon, France. Rome in state of anarchy; princely families and Cola di Rienzo vying for power
1334	Widespread plague epidemic begins in Constantinople, spreads throughout Europe via Crusaders
1378	The Great Schism: 2 popes, one in Avignon, one in Rome
1409	Third pope in Pisa
1417	Pope reinstated in Rome
1455	Palazzo Venezia begun
1471	Era of the popes. Capitoline Museum founded by Pope Sixtus IV
1475	Ponte Sisto named after Pope Sixtus IV
1481	San Pietro in Montorio Church
1483	Palazzo della Cancelleria
1489	Sant'Agostino built with travertine stolen from the Colosseum
1492-1503	Louis XII of France tries to interfere in Italian wars, first on one side then on the other. Alexander VI (Borgia) reigns. Son Cesare tries to conquer more land for papacy (or himself)
1494	Charles VIII of France tries to conquer Italy
1495	Trinità dei Monti Church founded by Charles VIII of France
1500	The Pietà created by Michelangelo
1502	Bramante completes the Tempietto
1506	Pope Julius II starts to rebuild St. Peter's Basilica with Bramante as architect
1508	Raphael—Stanze, Vatican. Michelangelo paints Sistine Chapel (until 1541)
1510	Palazzo dei Convertendi designed by Bramante
1511	Raphael starts painting his love, La Fornarina—continues until his death in 1520
1513-1522	Pope Leo X (Medici)
1514	Palazzo Farnese begun; completed by Michelangelo
1515	Statue of Moses by Michelangelo in San Pietro in Vincoli
1517-1520	Raphael—Villa Farnesina frescoes
1520	Luther publishes Great Reforming Theses, the basis of the Protestant Reformation
1522	Pope Hadrian VI (Dutch and later non-Italian pope)
1523-1534	Pope Clement VII (Medici)
1527	(5 May) Sack of Rome by Charles V, Holy Roman Emperor, Lutheran mercenaries
1534-50	Pope Paul III (Farnese)

Porta Santo Spirito, fortification of the Vatican designed by Sangallo	1538
Palazzo Spada—Guido Merisi de Caravaggio	1540
Council of Trent establishes Counter Reformation (Inquisition)	1545-1563
Pope Julius III commissions Vignola to design Villa Giulia	1551
Pope Pius IV (Medici)	1559-1566
San Giacomo alla Lungara Church built	1560
Vignola builds Church of the Gesù	1568
Pope Gregory XII (Boncompagni)	1572-1585
Chigi Palazzo	1582
Lateran Palace	1582
Pope Sixtus V begins urban development of Rome. Dome of St. Peter's completed under Pope Sixtus V	1585-1590
Quattro Fontane commissioned by Pope Sixtus V	1585-1590
Church of Santa Maria della Scala and Old Farmacia	1592-1605
Pope Clement VIII (Aldobrandini)	1592-1605
Fountain of La Barcaccia at the bottom of the Spanish Steps	1598
Pope Leo XI (Medici)	1605-1621
Fontana Paola	1612
Thirty Years War, for religious and territorial reasons	1618-1648
Pope Urbano VIII (Barberini) reigns during Baroque period in Rome	1623-1644
Pope Urbano VIII commissions Rome's top Baroque artists—Maderno, Bernini, and Borromini—to work on the Palazzo Barberini	1625
Pope Urban VIII commissions Bernini to design the Baldacchino in St. Peter's Basilica	1633
Sant'Ivo alla Sapienza Church (Borromini)	1648
Sant'Agnese in Agone Church, Piazza Navona (Borromini)	1655
Palazzo Colonna (Antonia del Grande) Galleria Colonna	1665
St. Peter's Square completed by Bernini	1667
Spanish Steps constructed	1721
Palazzo Corsini (facade by Ferdinando Fuga)	1736
Trevi Fountain	1762
Papal States cede Avignon and environs to France	1791
Napoleon and Pope Urbano VIII sign a treaty	1797
French troops occupy Rome, Pope Urbano VIII expelled, dies in France. Rome becomes a Republic	1798
New Pope Pius VII arrives in Rome	1800
Francis II abdicates marking the end of the Holy Roman Empire	1806
Rome occupied by French troops again; Pope imprisoned in Quirinal Palace	1808
France annexes Papal States	1809
Pius VII returns to Rome from exile in France	1814
The process of unifying Italy begins. Garibaldi, Mazzini, & Cavour lead Il Risorgimento movement. Italy becomes a kingdom; Victor Emmanuel of Piedmont becomes first king	1820-1861
Papal States conquered; Rome made capital of unified Italy	1870
Monument to Vittorio Emanuele by Guiseppe Saccone	1885-1911
Main Jewish synagogue built in Rome	1904
Mussolini seizes power	1926
Lateran Treaty signed. Separate Vatican State declared	1929
E.U.R. new quarter of Rome—the Square Colosseum	1940
World War II—Italy fights with Germany against Allies. Mussolin hanged as traitor	1940-1945
Republic of Italy established by popular vote	1946
European Common Market proclaimed in Rome	1957
Federico Fellini films La Dolce Vita	1959
Pier Luigi Nervi—Palazzo and Palazetto dello Sport built for the Olympic Games	1960
Second Vatican Council under Pope John XXIII initiates many reforms	1962
Karol Wojtyla, Polish cardinal, becomes Pope John Paul II, first non-Italian pope since 1523	1979
Restoration of Sistine Chapel begins, funded by the Nippon Television Network of Tokyo	1984
Pope John Paul II makes first papal visit to a Jewish synagogue	1986
World Soccer Championships	1990

Essentials

Back in the dim past, around 100 and something, **Anno Domini**, a Roman man of letters, wrote wearily about the advent of a new guidebook to Rome, saying that EVERYTHING had already been said about Rome that could possibly be said, and therefore, why yet another guide? Since that far-off time people haven't stopped writing about Rome. The earliest record we have after the Fall of Rome (AD 476) is of a pilgrim who, around AD 800, walked all the way to Rome from Britain. (The Wessex kings started that vogue.) A German wrote about his travels in the 14th century, and it hasn't stopped since. We have tried to learn from all the scholarly books written about Rome, and from some of the less scholarly as well.

Thanks for **Rome**ACCESS® should go especially to:

Gregorovius, *Rome in the Middle Ages* (1879)

Augustus Hare, *Walks in Rome* (1893)

S. Russell Forbes, *Rambles in Rome* (1899)

Samuel B. Plattner and **Thomas Ashby**, *A Topographical Dictionary of Ancient Rome* (1929)

Lord Rennell of Rodd, *Rome* (1932)

Georgina Masson, *The Companion Guide to Rome* (1965)

Anthony Blunt, *Guide to Baroque Rome* (1982)

When In Rome...

The secret of success in Rome is to relax. Romans urge *pazienza* (take it easy). And they respond to a smile with the same. They greet each other, in shops for instance, with *Buon giorno*; after 2PM this becomes *Buona sera*. When they leave they say *Arrivederla*, more polite, when you don't know someone, than *Arrivederci*. They use *Ciao* with close friends and children. Italians shake hands when meeting or leaving, and relatives and friends (even 2 men) kiss each other on both cheeks when greeting.

Italians are an impatient lot and queuing (standing in line) goes against their grain. Expect this and stand your ground. The typical queue at a Roman bank window looks more like an amoeba reproducing under a microscope than like its German equivalent.

Safety

Keep your handbag on the building side, slung across your body, preferably under your arm, especially when walking down the old cobblestone streets without pavements. As in other big cities, the motorbike brigades are experts at revving past a hapless woman, yanking her bag as they go. (If possible, ask a male companion to walk on the road side for extra protection.) Don't put your wallet in your back pocket. Use common sense and you will outwit the bag, camera, and wallet snatchers. And please, don't leave any goodies visible in the car you've rented.

The Italian government requires cars to carry a warning triangle to place in the road in case of breakdown. If you need to rent a triangle, pay a visit to the ACI (Italian Automobile Club).

Latin Lovers

Squeezing and pinching on crowded buses are referred to as *mano morta* (dead hand—but where it shouldn't be) and *mano lesta* (molesting hand). Use a sharp elbow jab or a good heel kick to get rid of unwelcome attention. Ignore the man in the street who tries to pick you up. If you can't shake him, say what the Roman women say: *Crepa!* —which roughly translates to *go and die!* Unfortunately, this annoyance is a national male pastime.

Hours

General Shopping:

M-F 9:30AM-1:30PM, 4:30-7:30PM, Sa 9AM-1PM, June-mid Sep; M 3:30-7:30PM, Tu-Sa 9:30AM-1:30PM, 3:30-7PM, mid Sep-May. Some large stores have been practicing *No-Stop*, meaning they don't close for lunch/siesta.

In practice, stores won't commit themselves as to their future opening hours. So we have not always included hours when shops are open, but have included phone numbers. Call ahead.

Food Stores: M-F 8AM-2:30PM, 5-8PM, Sa 8AM-1:30PM, June-mid Sep; M-W, F-Sa 9AM-2PM, 4:30-7:30PM, Th 8AM-1:30PM, mid Sep-May.

Banking: M-F 8:30AM-1:30PM, 2:45-3:45PM.

A convenient central bank (the manager is **Sophia Loren**'s brother): **Banca Nazionale del Lavoro**, Via Veneto 11. Open for money changing M-Sa 8:30AM-6PM. (This bank's main office, at Via Veneto 119, handles all other transactions and is open M-F 8:30AM-1:30PM, 2:45-3:45PM.)

American Express ♦ M-F 9AM-5:30PM; Sa 9AM-12:30PM. Piazza di Spagna 38. 6788874

Money changer in the great hall of **Termini Station**. ♦ Daily 7AM-1PM, 2-9PM.

Street Numbering

Don't be discouraged if the street numbers seem topsy-turvy. They are! Some streets have even numbers on one side and odd on the other, the way we do; on other streets, the numbers go consecutively right down one side of the street and up the other. And sometimes the numbers don't start at the beginning of the street, but somewhere at random in the middle of the street.

Buses, Trams, and the Metro

A *B.I.G.* ticket, covering all public surface transport and subways for the whole day at approximately 2800 lire, is on sale at the **ATAC** (tram and bus authority) office in front of the **Termini Railroad Station**, Piazza Cinquecento (46954444). For single rides on the tram or bus you are supposed to buy your 200-lire ticket ahead of time at a bar, tobacco store, or newspaper kiosk that displays the ATAC sign. But don't be surprised if you're the only person who slots a ticket into the mashing machine in the rear of the bus or tram. Many Romans, particularly the young, will think you naive if you feel obligated to ay for your ride. But there are ATAC inspectors, and e know people who have been threatened with arst for failing to present a ticket; they escaped by leading, with a heavy accent, *No capish Italiano*. Let our conscience be your guide. In any case, you on't get through the subway turnstiles without the 00-lire ticket obtained conveniently from one of the oin-vending machines prominently placed in all me-o stations.

riving

n the film *Ben Hur*, the wheels of the chariots that ace around Circus Maximus are outfitted with lades. Driving around Rome today can be just as air-raising an experience. So, don't drive unless you ave nerves of steel. And the patience of Job. One-ay signs are merely pretty pictures; cars zoom own streets the opposite way unless there's a po-ceman to stop them, which is highly unlikely. The rections of Rome's one-way streets change fre-uently and without notice (or logic)—which is why ur maps do not show which way traffic goes. Some-mes the tiniest alleys are 2-way, whereas adjacent road avenues are one-way—without apparent rea-on. Large portions of central Rome are closed to ehicles without special permission. These "pedes-ian island" rules produce mammoth gridlock else-here. Roman drivers usually carry a newspaper or a ook. Again, the rules change frequently; new areas re suddenly closed and others opened. Also, at nchtime the cops magically disappear, leaving you go anywhere you wish—though not always. mile!

as Stations

eginning of Viale Trastevere (near Ponte Garibaldi) n the right side. Lungotevere at the end of Via della ungara (near the tunnel and Ponte Amedeo Savoia 'Aosta).

or diesel fuel:

ungotevere a Ripa near Via Ripense, after Ponte alatino.

iazza Porte Portese, next to Ponte Sublicio.

PERTO means open, but not during lunch or after PM.

loped and Bike Rental

coot-along Motor scooters. ♦ Via Cavour 302. 780206

lotonoleggio Scooters and bicycles. ♦ Via della urificazione 66. 465485

n good weather, bicycles can be rented on the street here you see a large gathering of yellow 2-wheel-rs. They move, like gypsies, but can usually be und near tourist spots such as **Piazza di Spagna** nd **Piazza del Popolo**. Or phone **Bicinoleggio elefonico**, 6543394.

axis

 is better to telephone for a cab as there are few ruising cabs and few stands. Call 3875, 4994, 3570, 8177.

 you find a cruising cab, be sure it is a yellow cab ith a meter rather than a wise guy who accosts you t the airport or train station (where cabs are in short upply). If you fall for the con artist, you will end up

in a hassle. There are different tariffs, but rides to the airport have a particularly hefty surcharge. At night, there is also a surcharge. Baggage is charged per piece.

All-Night Newsstands

Antica Edicola Gigli, on Via Vittorio Veneto opposite the Excelsior Hotel, has everything—including **Rome**ACCESS®.

Other stands at **Piazza Ungheria, Viale dei Parioli**, and **Piazza Colonna**.

Seven English Language Book Stores (ask for **Rome**ACCESS®)

Ancora Bookshop ♦ Via della Conciliazione 63. 6568820

Anglo-American ♦ Via della Vite 57. 6795222

Economy Book and Video Center ♦ Via Torino 136. 4746877

Food For Thought ♦ FAO Headquarters. Room B-056. 57973127

Lion Bookshop ♦ Via del Babuino 181. 3605837

Open Door Bookshop ♦ Via della Lugaretta 25. 5896478

The Bookshelf ♦ Via Due Macelli 23. 6784096

Doctors

For information concerning a doctor or dentist, ask your hotel concierge or contact the consular section of your embassy (46742207, 46742405 (US), 4755551, 4755441 (UK).

English is spoken at the private **Salvator Mundi Clinic**, Via delle Mura Gianicolensi 66, 586041. The clinic has excellent doctors, impeccable rooms, efficient outpatient service, and experienced nuns who are registered nurses, but there is no emergency room.

In an **emergency** go to a hospital that has a **Pronto Soccorso** service, such as **Policlinico**, Viale Policlinico, 4997; **Policlinico Gemelli**, Largo A. Gemelli 8, 33051; or **Fattebenefratelli** (that means *do good, brothers*), Isola Tiberina, 58731.

Pharmacies

Internazionale Via Barberini 49. 462996

Spinedi Via Arenula 73. 6543278

The pharmacy at **Termini Station** is open daily 7AM-11:30PM. Most pharmacies close 1-4PM. For the location of a pharmacy open after shopping hours, call 1921.

Mail

If you want to have mail sent to you in Rome, but you don't know where you will be staying, use the address of **American Express**, Piazza di Spagna 38, Roma 00186, Italia (phone 67641, M-F 9AM-

5:30PM; Sa 9AM-12:30PM)—or the central post office, **Ferma Posta Palazzo delle Poste**, Piazza San Silvestre, Roma 00186, Italia (phone 160, M-F 8:30AM-9PM; Sa 8AM-noon).

At the **San Silvestro Post Office** all postal operations are available, including cables, telex, fax. Local post offices throughout Rome, including **Termini Railroad Station** (4745640), are open M-F 8:30AM-1:45PM; Sa 8:30-11:45AM. Stamps are sold at every tobacco shop, easily identified by the **T** outside.

Walking

Wear comfortable walking shoes and be especially careful on the old cobblestone streets. Women should not wear stiletto heels.

Lavatories

A few years ago Rome had public lavatories for men and women. Now only men are accommodated with a few desultory open-air places along the Tiber embankment, the traditional *vespasians*. Women have to either walk confidently past the concierge in the nearest hotel or go to a bar and "buy" bathroom privileges for the price of a coffee.

Seeing is Believing

Try to bring a pair of binoculars with you to places with domes and high ceilings, such as the Sistine Chapel, in order to fully appreciate the detailed architectural work or frescoes.

Universities and Schools Where Classes Are Taught in English

John Cabot International College ♦ Via Massaua 6. 8395519, 8312105

Overseas School of Rome ♦ Via Cassia 811. 3664841

Other Places to Stay

Residences (apartment hotels by the week or month):

Barberini Residence ♦ Via Quattro Fontane 171. 4817617

Palazzo al Velabro ♦ Via del Velabro 16. 6792758

Residence in Trastevere ♦ Vicolo Moroni 35/36. 582768

Residence Ripetta ♦ Via di Ripetta 231. 672141

Ripa Residence ♦ Via Orti di Trastevere 1. 58611

Religious Houses:

Centro Diffusiene Spiritualità ♦ Via dei Riari 43. 6540122

Instituto Suore Obiate Apostiniane ♦ Via Garibaldi 27. 738623

Boarding for Students and Youth:

International Youth Hostel For hostel-card holders, only. ♦ Viale delle Olimpiadi 61. 3964709, 3960009

Salvation Army Youth Center ♦ Via degli Apuli 41. 490558

Ravesco Institute ♦ Via di St. Pietro 37. 632768

YWCA For women, only. ♦ Via C. Balbo 4. 460460

Essentials

For Elders:

Adorers of the Holy Sacrament ♦ Via Trionfale 7071. 343061

Pensions:

Sabrina ♦ Via Lombardia 30. 4741627

Sicilia ♦ Via Sicilia 24. 4823712, 4821913

Trinità dei Monti ♦ Via Sistina 91. 6797206

Using the Telephone

There are 3 kinds of coin phones in Rome, all of which allow you to dial direct anywhere in the world. The small green ones take only a special Italian phone slug, called a *gettone* (pronounced *jet-own-ee*). The larger, silver-colored phones and the small red ones give you a choice of using a *gettone*, a 200-lire piece, or two 100-lire coins.

Ten thousand-lire cards, which fit into those metal boxes adjacent to the coin phones in many public places such as airports, are sold at SIP (phone company) offices. The card loses value each time you use it, until, finally, the machine eats it up—and you must buy another. Don't forget to clip off the top corner along the dotted line the first time you use it.

Instructions for coin phones:

1. Take *gettones* or coins out of your pocket.

2. Lift up the receiver; if by any chance it is working, you will hear a dial tone.

3. Put in the coin(s).

4. Dial your number.

5. Answer when spoken to.

6. If you are dialing long distance put in all the coins you think you will need for the entire conversation. When you hang up, press the coin-return button—it's red and halfway down the machine. The unused coin(s) will be returned to you. (Watch the Italians press this button after each call; sometimes they get a few extra coins. You, too, can try for the jackpot.)

The phone company has several phone centers where long distance and international calls are easy to make. They can be found at **Fiumicino Airport** (8AM-8:45PM), **Termini Railroad Station** (7AM-midnight), and **Piazza San Silvestro** (8:30AM-8PM).

Rome Phone Numbers In Rome, consistency is considered the hobgoblin of little minds. Phone numbers can have 4,5,6,7—and even 8—digits. They can also change, with minimum notice, from having few numbers to having many. So, do not be surprised if each of your Roman contacts gives you a phone number with a different number of digits.

Interruptions Unlimited When the phone number you've been dialing nonstop is still busy, you can cut through the conversation by dialing 197, then the number you want. A recorded voice interrupts the talkers, telling them someone is trying to reach them. Hold on, and with luck the other party will hang up so your call can go through.

Restaurant Tips
Ask for your food unsalted in cheap restaurants—they tend to oversalt.
Most restaurants don't require reservations unless there are more than 4 people in your party.

Restaurants/Clubs: Red   **Hotels:** Blue
Shops/Parks: Green   **Sights/Culture:** Black

Useful Numbers

Emergencies

AA 6780320

American Lawyer:
Alegi and Associates 4820147

Emergency Assistance:
(police/fire/ambulance) 113

Emergency Room (*Pronto Soccorso*):
Ospedale Policlinico, Viale del Policlinico 492341

English-Speaking Doctors:
(M-F 7:30AM-noon, 5-7PM;
Sa 7:30AM-noon) 3588385

Fire 115,44444

Hospital with English-Speaking Staff:
Salvadori Mundi,
Via delle Mura Gianicolensi 66 586041

Local Police (Carabinieri) 112

Poison Treatment Center 490663

Police Headquarters (Questura) 4686

Red Cross Ambulance 5100

Tourist First Aid Service 462371

24-hour Dental Service:
Instituto George Eastman,
Viale Regina Margherita 287B 4453228

24-hour Pharmacy Location 1921

Transportation

Airport Limousine 6798207, 2320

Car Rental:
Avis 436961
Budget 461905
Hertz 51711
National/Europcar 6888029

Fiumicino, Leonardo da Vinci Airport 60121

Pet Pensions 6868764,4751325

Road Breakdown Service 116, 4212

Road Report 194

Taxi 3875, 3570, 4994, 88177

Train Information Stazione Termini
(daily 7AM-1:30PM) 4775

Train Reservations 110

Telephone Information

Direct Dial US .... 001-Area Code-Number

Long Distance Operator:
National 10
Europe and North Africa 15
Overseas 170

Rome Directory Information 12

To USA via AT&T operator
for calling card or collect calls 1721011

To USA via MCI operator 1721022

To USA via CCCS charged
to a major credit card 167874001

Visitor Information

Berlitz Language Schools 8313785
312343
6542501

Current Time 161

Golf Clubs:
Acqua Santa 783407
Olgiata 3789141

Horoscope 195

Morning Wakeup Service 114

News Briefs 190

Nobili Language Tutoring 4743806

Postal Information 180, 160

Rome Provincial Tourist Information
Via Parigi 11 461851

US Embassy 46741

US Embassy Health Unit 46742150, 46742151

Weather Report 1911

Daily Specials

Monday

through Saturday. Campo dei Fiori The most beautiful fruit-and-vegetable market in Rome is in an incomparable setting of medieval houses. ♦ 7AM-1PM. Piazza Campo dei Fiori

through Saturday. Market of Prints and Old Books Small market of stalls with prints, maps, original art works, old books, and some silver. Bargains can be found. ♦ 7AM-1PM. Piazza Borghese

Tuesday

Flower Market Beautiful profusion of flowers. In Italy, superstition warns that even numbers of flowers bring bad luck so only buy odd numbers of flowers (3,5,7, or 9). Don't give chrysanthemums as they are only for funerals. ♦ 10AM-2PM. Via Trionfale at the intersection with Via Paolo Scarpi, due north of Vatican City

Wednesday

Mass and Blessing The open-air Mass is a spectacle to see, even if you're not Catholic. All of St. Peter's Square is filled with pilgrims from all over the world, and their excitement is heightened when the pope addresses them in their own language. When it rains the Mass is held indoors in the nearby Pier Luigi Nervi Hall, an ugly, vast auditorium to the left of the Colonnade. The event rivals a big Hollywood production. ♦ 10:30AM-noon

Essentials

Villa Medici Visit the gardens. ♦ 9-11AM

Palazzo Farnese A quick visit is possible if you get permission first by submitting your passport. ♦ 3:45PM

Saturday

San Giovani Flea Market Just outside the walls of Rome there is a very small section with scruffy antiques, and a very large section with clothes, towels, suitcases, furs, and leather coats and jackets. Cut-rate prices and bargains can still be found. ♦ M-F 7AM-1PM; Sa noon-dusk

Sunday

Porta Portese Flea Market. ♦ 7AM-1PM

Piazza San Pietro If he is in Rome, the pope comes to his window, high up in the building to your right as you face St. Peter's, to bless the crowd in the square below. ♦ Noon

Monthly Specials

January

Sales in chic shops of clothes, shoes, etc.

1 New Year's Day (Holiday)

6 Epiphany (Holiday); End of the Toy Fair in Piazza Navona.

February

Carnival (Mardi Gras) Children of all ages get dressed up and parade for days up and down the streets, especially Via Cola di Rienzo. Private parties.

March

16 Only day of the year when you can visit the Chapel of Palazzo Massimo alle Colonne. See the Corso Vittorio Emanuele walk.

19 St. Joseph (Holiday)

April

Spring Festival. Spanish Steps covered with azaleas.

21 Rome's birthday. Roman candles all the way up the stairs and on the roof tops of the Capitoline (Piazza del Campidoglio). Absolutely beautiful.

25 National Holiday

May

Antiques Fair in Via dei Coronati; Sagra of cherries in nearby Farfa and Fara Sabina; Rose show on the Aventine Hill gardens.

Sagra of wild strawberries in Nemi; Via del Orso Antiques Fair.

1 May Day

1-10 International Horse Show at Piazza Sienna in the Villa Borghese gardens.

June

Via Giulia Music Festival. In the courtyards of this street's beautiful palazzos.

Festival of Art, Via Margutta.

23-24 Feast of St. John—in San Giovanni district—dancing in the streets and a feast of suckling pig.

Essentials

July

Roma Estate (Summer Fair of Rome) Outdoor classical music concerts on the Capitoline; film festival; opera in the baths of Caracalla; outdoor theater (ancient Roman at Ostia Antica); folklore.

Festival of Italian products along the quays of the Tiber river between Ponte Margherita and Ponte Sant'Angelo. A simple restaurant, bar, and open-air dancing as well.

Sales in chic shops of summer clothes, shoes, etc.

Last 2 weeks in July Festival Noantri (Trastevere). Street stalls along Lungotevere and Viale Trastevere, with fireworks display to close the fair.

14 Bastille Day. Horses in Piazza Farnese. Ball for the privileged in the French Embassy.

August

City is fairly empty and a lot of places are closed.

Roma Estate Summer Fair continues.

15 Ferragosta (Assumption) Holiday.

September

Chestnut Sagra in nearby Rocca di Pappa.

Second fair on the quays of the river (10 days).

October

Chestnut Festival continues.

Second Via del'Orso Antique Fair.

Sagra of grapes in nearby Marino.

Second Antique Fair on Via del Coronari.

Second Via Margutta Art Fair.

November

1 All Saints' Day

December

Natale Oggi. Fair of Italian and foreign gifts, goods, foods, at Fiera di Roma, near E.U.R. section.

Piazza Navona filled with Christmas stalls, like in former centuries, selling toys, decorations, creche figurines. Also food and shooting galleries.

8 Feast of the Immaculate Conception. Pope meets with mayor of Rome in Piazza di Spagna and holds a service at the Column of the Virgin.

24 Giant midnight Mass at St. Peter's. Glorious.

25 Christmas Day

26 Holiday

Climate

January-March Average daytime temperatures 40-50 degrees F. Lots of rain, but the temperature rarely drops below freezing. Late Jan and early Feb are the most likely months for a few snowflakes. There may be 4 to 5 days of sun at a time. Cold at night.

April-June Average daytime temperatures 52-75 degrees F. Spring weather, sun and showers. By the middle of May, temperatures are at the top of this bracket. June temperatures can easily go higher, and the nights are cloudless.

July-September Average daytime temperatures 80-95 degrees F. Lots of hot sun, especially in July. Dramatic thunderstorms with drums and cymbals in August. In late September storms can last 3 days, with

ertical curtains of water, which then give way to 2
eeks of clear skies and sunshine.

ctober-December Average daytime temperatures
5-70 degrees F. October can be as hot as Septem-
er, 70 degrees F, but with slightly more rain. No-
ember and December have mild days, enabling you
o lunch outside in the sun. Bring warm sweaters and
oats, too (inside it can be cold as the large palaces
ften have no heating).

ightlife

legant, rich, infinitely refined, with 2000 years of
nowing HOW to do it, palazzi groaning with price-
ss works of art—Rome is the Maximum. If you
ant the best, why not

ent a castle for a great party?

Castello Orsini Odescalchi Beautiful medieval castle
on a lake 20 miles from Rome for your wedding reception or birthday! ♦ Bracciano. 6792153, 9024003

Casina Valadier The charming "folly" of the Borghese family in their garden, now a restaurant on the
ground floor (see page 62). The top floor has a terrace and lovely view, and can be rented for private
parties. ♦ Closed Monday. On the Pincio Hill.
6796368

Rent a Limousine?

Malta V. ♦ Via Garenta 16. 3378935

COOP U.A.R.A. ♦ Via Parispeina 261. 6798207,
6792320

Rent an antique Rolls-Royce?

Auto Antiche Ghisù ♦ Via Filippo Meda 183.
4511367

Pasta

lasagne

tripolini

fettuccini

malfaldine

penne

elbow maccheroni

conchiglie

occhi di lupo

farfalle

occhi di pernice

ravioli

ziti

ruote

spaghetti

gnocchi

Index

Pyramid of Cajo Cestio

N

O

P

Porta Maggiore

Porta Tiburtina

Index

Rome Restaurant Index

Only restaurants with star ratings are listed below. All restaurants are listed alphabetically in the main index.

Rome Hotel Index

Rome BESTS Index

Tempio d'Ercole a Tivoli

Language Hints

Italian, unlike French, is very phonetic. All letters are always pronounced the same way (h is always silent.) Certain pronunciations, however, often confuse English speakers. Here are some hints:

Italian spelling	sounds like English
ce, ci	chay, chee
che, chi	kay, key
ge, gi	jay, gee
gl	ly
ghe, ghi	gay, ghee
sce, sci	shay, she
sche, schi	skay, ski

after *dopo*
always *sempre*
arrival *arrivo*
bad *male*
bathroom *toiletta, gabinetto*
before *prima*
check *assegno*
closed *chiuso*
congratulations *congratulazioni*
danger *pericolo*
departure *partenza*
difficult *difficile*
discount *sconto*
easy *facile*
empty *vuoto*
enough *basta*
exchange *cambio*
excuse me *mi scusi*
far *lontano*
fast *veloce*
full (up) *pieno*
good *buono, bene*
here *qui*
large *grande*
later *più tardi*
left *sinistra*
less *meno*
maybe *forse*
more *più*
near *vicino*
never *mai*
no *no*
now *addesso*
okay *d'accordo, va bene*
open *aperto*
payment *pagamento*
please *prego, per favore*
postcards *cartoline*
right *destra*
sales *saldi*
slow *lento*
small *piccolo*
stamps *francobolli*
stop *fermata, stop*
straight *dritto*
thank you, so much *grazie, mille*
today *oggi*
tomorrow *domani*
too much *troppo*
when? *quando?*
where is? *dov'è?*
why? *perché?*
yes *si*

Numbers, time

1,2,3 *uno, due, tre*
4,5,6 *quattro, cinque, sei*
7,8,9,10 *sette, otto, nove, dieci*
half an hour *mezz'ora*
one hour *un'ora*
one minute *un minuto*
quarter of an hour *un quarto d'ora*

Useful Phrases

Can you repeat that? *Può ripeterlo?*
Do you speak English? *Parla Inglese?*
Fuck Off! *Vaffanculo!*
Get out! *Fuori!*
Happy Birthday! *Buon Compleanno!*
how much, how much does it cost? *quanto? quanto costa?*
I don't understand *Non capisco*
I hate you *Ti detesto*
I have a credit card *Ho una carta di credito*
I love you *Ti amo*
I understand *Lo capisco*
I'm crazy about you *Mi piaci un sacco*
It is very kind of you *E molto gentile da parta sua*
let's go *andiamo*
of course! *naturalmente! certo!*
that's better *questo è meglio*
that's worse *questo è peggio*
what a pity! *che peccato!*
Where is the nearest bank, please? *Prego, dov'è la banca più vicina?*
Who are you? *Chi è lei?*
You speak very quickly *Lei parla velocemente*

At the restaurant

The menu, please *La lista, prego*
anchovy *alici*
apple *mela*
apricot *albicocca*
bass *spigola*
beans *fagioli*
beer *birra*
bread *pane*
bread sticks *grissini*
cheese *formaggio*
clams *vongole*
dessert *dolce*
eggs *uova*
figs *fichi*
fish *pesce*
fork *forchetta*
fruit *frutta*
garlic *aglio*
garlic bread (sometimes with tomatoes or pâté) *bruschetta*
glass *bicchiere*
grapes *uve*
green beans *fagiolini*
ham, cured, cooked *prosciutto, crudo, cotto*
knife *coltello*
lamb *agnello*
lemon *limone*
meat *carne*
melon *melone*
mineral water *acqua minerale;* carbonated *gassata;* still *naturale*
mushrooms *funghi*
napkin *tovagliolo*
orange *arancia*
peach *pesca*
pear *pera*
pepper *pepe*
plate *piatto*
pork *carne di maiale*
prawns *scampi*
rare, well-done *poccocotto, bencotto*
raspberries *lamponi*
red, white, rose *rosso, bianco, rosa*
salad *insalata*
salt *sale*
shrimps *gamberetti*
spaghetti *pasta*
spinach *spinaci*
spoon *cucchiaio*
steak *bistecca;* T-bone *fiorentino*
strawberry *fragola*
tomatoes *pomodori*
trout *trotta*
veal *vitello*
vegetables *verdura*
wild strawberries *fragolini*
wine *vino*
the bill, please *il conto, per favore*

Index

Distinctive features of **ACCESS**® Travel Guides

- Organized by neighborhood, the way natives know a city and visitors experience it.

- Color-coded entries distinguish restaurants, hotels, shops, parks, architecture and places of interest.

- Generous use of maps with points of interest identified.

- Easy to use and a pleasure to read.

- Each city's flavor is conveyed by descriptions of its history, by lists of the personal favorites of people who know and love the city, by trivia and lavish illustrations of important buildings and places of interest.

- Perfect preparation for a visit, enjoyment of a city or recollection of a trip.

BARCELONAACCESS®
An up-to-the-minute guide to Spain's avant-garde city, home of the 1992 Summer Olympic Games.
144 pages, $16.95

BOSTONACCESS®
A guide to the many charms of America's Revolutionary capital, from historic landmarks to where to shop, stay and dine.
208 pages, $16.95

CHICAGOACCESS®
The key to inimitable Chicago style, from architecture to deep-dish pizza.
192 pages, $16.95

DCACCESS®
A comprehensive guide to the nation's capital with abundant descriptions of the beautiful and historic places that encircle it.
216 pages, $12.95

FLORENCE/VENICE/MILAN
ACCESS®
A grand tour through Northern Italy's three major cities, in one comprehensive guide.
240 pages, $16.95

HAWAIIACCESS®
Organized island by island...where to stay...what to see...what to do.
192 pages, $14.95

LAACCESS®
The city's characteristic urban sprawl and profusion of personalities rendered accessible.
224 pages, $16.95

LONDONACCESS®
The first winner from abroad of the London Tourist Board's Guidebook of the Year Award!
216 pages, $16.95

NYCACCESS®
For natives and visitors...the ultimate guide to the city famous for everything except subtlety and understatement.
312 pages, $16.95

PARISACCESS®
For the first-time and the veteran visitor, a guide that opens doors to the city's magic and nuances.
216 pages, $16.95

ROMEACCESS®
Award-winning guidebook, featuring favorite promenades of the Eternal City.
176 pages, $16.95

SAN FRANCISCOACCESS®
Our best-selling guide to the much-loved city...includes daytrips around the Bay Area.
208 pages, $16.95

To order these **ACCESS**®Guides, please see the other side of this page.

ACCESS® GUIDES

Order by phone, toll-free: 1-800-**ACCESS**-4 or 1-800-345-8112

Name _____ Phone _____

Address _____

City _____ State _____ Zip _____

Please send me the following **ACCESS**®Guides:

☐ **BARCELONA**ACCESS®, $16.95
Available Fall 1991 BA92

☐ **BOSTON**ACCESS®, $16.95
BO91

☐ **CHICAGO**ACCESS®, $16.95
CH91

☐ **DC**ACCESS®, $12.95
DCØ288

☐ **FLORENCE/VENICE/ MILAN**ACCESS®, $16.95
FVM91

☐ **HAWAII**ACCESS®, $14.95
HIØ288

☐ **LA**ACCESS®, $16.95
LA91

☐ **LONDON**ACCESS®, $16.95
LN91

☐ **NYC**ACCESS®, $16.95
NY91

☐ **PARIS**ACCESS®, $16.95
PR91

☐ **ROME**ACCESS®, $16.95
RM91

☐ **SAN FRANCISCO** ACCESS®, $16.95
SF91

Total for **ACCESS**®Guides:	$
For PA delivery please include sales tax:	
Add $4.00 for first book S&H, $1.00 per additional book:	
Total payment:	$

☐ Check or Money Order enclosed. Please make payable to **ACCESS**®PRESS

☐ Charge my credit card ☐ American Express ☐ Visa ☐ Mastercard

Card no. _____ Exp. date _____

Signature _____
WI91

☐ Please add my name to your mailing list for news of other **ACCESS**Guides.

Send orders to:

ACCESS®PRESS
P.O. Box 664
Holmes, PA 19043-9964

Send correspondence to:

ACCESS®PRESS
10 East 53rd. Street
New York, NY 10022

Praise for **ACCESS**® Guides

Finally, books that look at cities the way tourists do—block by block...**ACCESS**® may be the best series for the chronically lost. **USA Today**

It combines the best of the practical directories with the superior artwork of the hardcover coffee-table books at an affordable price. **New York Times**

Beautiful to behold, yet practical as a hammer and screwdriver.
Travel & Leisure Magazine

Each book is a piece of graphic ingenuity. Maps & diagrams lead its readers around the places where they go. The result for newcomer or native, is a pleasure to use and, for that matter, to peruse from the speculative comforts of home. The **ACCESS**® Guides are visual treats first and foremost. **Publisher's Weekly**